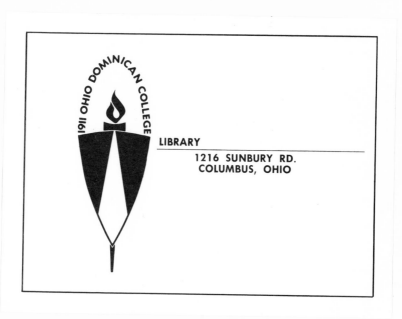

Mr. Dooley's Chicago

MR. DOOLEY'S CHICAGO

by
Barbara C. Schaaf

ANCHOR PRESS/DOUBLEDAY
Garden City, New York
1977

I am very grateful for the assistance of Evelyn Nelson in the selection of the photographs for this book.

Library of Congress Cataloging in Publication Data

Schaaf, Barbara C
  Mr. Dooley's Chicago.

  Bibliography
  Includes index.
    1. Dunne, Finley Peter, 1867–1936–Criticism and interpretation.
2. Chicago in literature. 3. Chicago–Anecdotes, facetiae, satire, etc. I. Title.
PS3507.U6755Z88   818'.5'207

ISBN: 0-385-02023-6
Library of Congress Catalog Card Number 76-23793

To William and Mary Schaaf, my father and mother,
for all those times when, like Mr. Hennessy,
they "suffered and were silent."

Contents

Introduction

There's a man that's known to all, a man of great renown,
A man whose name is on the lips of everyone in town;
You read about him every day, you've heard his name no doubt,
And if he even sneezes they will get an extra out.

Oh Misther Dooley, Misther Dooley,
The greatest man the country ever knew,
So diplomatic and democratic,
Is Misther Dooley, ooley, ooley, oo,
                    —From a song popular at the turn of the century

Martin J. Dooley was the quintessential Chicagoan. He had come from someplace else to settle in the raw, new metropolis on the shore of the great lake. He brought with him little more than his native wit and his native hustle, along with a sense of Celtic gloom that while things might be hopeless, they were never serious.

Although he was sometimes a little late in paying his liquor license fees for his saloon on Archey Road, he had, through hard work, established himself as a prosperous, respected member of the Irish-American community of Bridgeport in Chicago. By nature he was not so much disillusioned as lacking in illusions, so that what might have been a harsh cynicism in another man was merely a warm skepticism in him. He loved to ridicule the smug attitudes of his times; he saw behind the jingoistic use of words like "social welfare," "manifest destiny," and "democracy." Through his friends and foils, McKenna, Hennessy, Father Kelly, Hogan, and Molly Donahue, he was able to reflect just about every nuance of life in the roistering, restless city that was Chicago. Here was the perfect, the ultimate Chicagoan, possibly his city's most famous son—yet he never existed. He was a product of the imagination of Finley Peter Dunne, a Chicago journalist.

It was fortunate for American literature that conditions in Chicago in the 1890s were conducive to Dooley's creation, for he could only have come from the atmosphere of that city at that time. Chicagoans were confident of their place in the cosmos. They had survived a great fire and several panics, strikes and storms. They were undaunted by adversity and paid homage to nobody. Thus, the climate was ripe for someone who would tell them the truth about themselves and what was going on in their city, even one who hid behind a bar and a brogue.

Mr. Dooley's readers responded not only to his topicality, but also to his high spirits, enormous vitality, resiliency, and lack of regard for established institutions. At a time when every newspaper—and there were many of them in Chicago then—ran at least one humor column, it was Mr. Dooley who struck a responsive chord with the public and immediately became a local sensation. He said something that needed to be said. There is no other way to account for his popularity.

Finley Peter Dunne, Mr. Dooley's creator, was a member of two minority groups against which there was considerable discrimination. First, he was Irish. However, while he took pride in his Celtic heritage, he was not a professional Irishman, nor did he write as a hyphenated American. Dunne used dialect merely as a device to get around possible editorial censorship.

Second, by birth and upbringing he was a Roman Catholic. According to his son, when asked if he was a Roman Catholic, Dunne replied, "No, I'm a Chicago Catholic." Although in his adult life he kept an amiable distance from the

Church, the Dooley columns were filled with parish doings and the wisdom of the mythical priest Father Kelly. Yet Dunne did not present the Catholic viewpoint. He was impressed and sometimes amused by the workings of the Church as both a social and political institution, but it exerted no control over him.

He made two trips to Italy and wrote back to his sister in Chicago, "I don't understand how anyone can be a Protestant after a visit to Rome." But even St. Peter's could not keep Dunne solemn for long. He enjoyed telling about one trip when he had an audience with the pope. As he was waiting for it to begin, one of the lesser clerics approached him, saying, "You're Dunne from Chicago, aren't you? How's young Carter Harrison making out as mayor, anyhow?"

On another trip to Rome, Dunne had a private audience with the pope. It went so well that when the Holy Father had to leave for another appointment, he asked Dunne to remain so they could continue their conversation, to which request Dunne naturally agreed. Now Peter Dunne had a terrible cigarette habit and could not go for long without one. Smoking was not permitted in the papal audience chamber, so while he was waiting, Dunne decided to slip downstairs to the cloakroom for a few quick puffs. The attendant, misunderstanding Dunne's purpose, kept trying to press his hat and coat on him and rush him out the door. Dunne had no Italian and was unable to explain that he was merely enjoying a brief intermission. Exasperated at his inability to communicate with the functionary, he cast his memory back to all those hours spent before the altar at St. Patrick's Church, and it struck him that they did share a common language. With a soothing smile and appropriate gestures, he assured the man, *"Requiescat in pace. Resurgam!"*

Although Father Kelly, the mythical pastor of St. Bridget's Church in Bridgeport, was the hero of many columns,

Dunne had a curiously ambivalent attitude toward priests.
It is recorded by Elmer Ellis, his biographer, that when
Dunne was a child of about ten, a visitor noticed his quick
mind and suggested he be aimed at the priesthood, but
Dunne's father rejected this idea, saying there would be no
"made" priests in his family. What influence this had on
Dunne no one knows, but later he was to comment to one of
his own sons that while all the priests he had known were
worthy men, "the less one had to do with them the better."

Nonetheless, for some reason—perhaps it was atavistic—
Dunne never totally relinquished his Catholicism. His wife,
Margaret Abbott, was descended from an old Boston family
and was brought up in a time and at a place where marrying
an Irishman just was not "done." The Dunnes were married
in the Catholic Church, and their four children were bap-
tized in it and observed its fast days. Peter Dunne acceded
to his wife's wish that their sons be sent to Harvard but
balked at letting them prepare at Groton (a seminary for
young Englishmen born in America, Mr. Dooley called it)
because they would have had to give at least lip service to
the Episcopal Church. Instead, the Dunnes compromised on
Middlesex, apparently because, as Philip Dunne described
it, its chapel was vaguely nonsectarian.

Dunne's dim view of men of the cloth was not confined to
his own religion. In his memoirs he relates how close the Republican James G. Blaine came to beating the Democrat
Grover Cleveland for the presidency in 1884 with the help
of Irish-American voters. Some experts believe that an in-
temperate remark by Dr. Samuel Burchard, a Protestant
minister and Blaine supporter, calling the Democrats the
party of "rum, romanism, and rebellion" cost Blaine the
Irish vote and the election. At any rate, Dunne believed it
to be so, and his comment was, "Is there, in all the history
of human folly, a greater fool than a clergyman in politics?"

Mr. Dooley and Mr. Dunne had suffered more than just
fools in politics. Commenting on his experience in Chicago

journalism, one of Dunne's colleagues, Brand Whitlock, said that "the moral atmosphere of politics was a joke among the newspapermen, who had little respect for the men who filled the positions of power and responsibility; the wonder was, indeed, after such an association that they had any respect left for anything in the world."

Mr. Dooley recognized the political corruption that was probably the salient feature of the city at the time, and while he attacked it and its practitioners vigorously, he understood the circumstances that spawned them. Because of Dunne's own involvement with the local reform element, some regard him as a forerunner of the muckrakers. However, he was far more than a simple exposer of sordid scandals. Instead, he was the urban inheritor of the tradition of a long line of cracker-barrel philosophers who had become an American institution. In addition, while Mr. Dooley had low regard for history—saying, "But Hennessy, the past always looks better than it was. It's only pleasant because it isn't here"—the old philosopher had a sharp eye for trends and details that made him an excellent historian of his time.

Dunne, who bore witness to all of the evil and corruption that lay in Chicago's streets, never lost his belief in the essential sweetness of human nature. That is what made the difference between Dunne and another contemporary, San Francisco journalist Ambrose Bierce. As William Dean Howells commented on Dunne, "To have one's heart in the right place is much; it is, in fact, rather indispensable: but to have one's head in the right place, also, adds immeasurably to the other advantage."

In the Chicago days of the Dooley columns, political satire was not always the basis for an essay. Dunne had spent his formative years out in the streets, listening to how people lived and learning much about human misery. Some of his most affecting efforts were about some local tragedy, yet he was able to communicate the attitude that there was always a good reason for going forward, and these columns became a source of solace to Chicagoans who found them a confirmation of what they felt but could not articulate.

However, as Elmer Ellis notes, the pathetic and tragic pieces had almost totally ceased when national syndication started about the time of the Spanish-American War (1898), and they vanished completely when Dunne left Chicago in 1900.

In 1899, during his first flush of international success, Dunne took a trip to England, stopping off in New York en route. While he had long been a social and political figure in Chicago, he was treated as a matter of fact there, but in New York he was a celebrity, and he enjoyed it. During the stopover he accepted an invitation proffered by some fellow journalists to a dinner in his honor. They were aware of his reputation for having a ready wit and planned to challenge it. The lead-off man was Richard Harding Davis, who started out by saying, "Mr. Dunne, your appearance surprises most of us, because from your writings we assumed we would see a tough old chap with red galloway whiskers, and smoking a clay pipe." Nothing daunted, Dunne responded, "Expectations are often deceptive, Mr. Davis. Now I thought I would find you wearing a silk shirtwaist with lace sleeves." And that was the end of that.

Dunne was, of course, a man of great wit and charm, and these qualities together with the popularity of the Dooley columns gave him an entree anywhere. He returned to Chicago journalism for only a brief time after his sortie abroad, but found he had fallen victim to the attractions that New York has always had for writers everywhere in the United States. He made his move there in 1900.

All at once he was welcomed by Presidents and Princes, and this reception no doubt made it difficult to toss as many bricks as he had in the days when Archey Road was just a streetcar ride rather than half a continent away. He found great satisfaction in leading the life of a well-to-do gentleman and gradually settled into a kind of Henry Jamesian existence. He once met James through the good offices of Edith Wharton, who remembered the encounter thus:

> . . . I perceived as I watched them after dinner, that Peter Dunne was floundering helplessly in the heavy seas of James' parentheses; and the next time we met, after speaking of his delight in having at last seen James, he added mournfully: "What a pity it takes him so long to say anything! Everything he said was so splendid—but I felt like telling him all the time: 'Just 'pit it right up into Popper's hand.'"

Dunne's sources were the people in the streets. When he cut himself off from them, he began to suffer pangs in his productivity. The problem first became acute in England and was to dog him the rest of his writing career. Writing had never come easily to him and the situation was complicated by the fact that he tended to accept more assignments than he could possibly complete. He commented on his difficulty in writing late in his life, when he was suffering from a terminal illness and his son was trying to persuade him to write his memoirs. "You want me to work to take my mind off my troubles," he said. "With me, it's always been the other way around. I've invented my troubles to take my mind off my work." After his departure from Chicago and the sources of his inspiration, his Dooley writings showed a steady decline, in number if not in quality, over a period of about fifteen years into what was tantamount to journalistic paralysis. Although the Dooley pieces were always in demand, they appeared only sporadically, and Dunne eventually ceased writing them altogether.

But when he left Chicago, Dunne left behind him a special legacy—over seven years' worth of humor, satire, and pathos that not only spoke to Chicagoans at all levels, but also made some of them think. And that is all that Dunne ever really hoped for. He did not share with the Progressives

that notion that social education would reform the human
race—or even that it needed reforming. As he said once
through Mr. Dooley, "Th' future might bring a great manny
changes in ladies' hats an' th' means iv transportation, but
not much in annything else."

Chicago in the 1890s was a city on the brink of its greatness.
In less than twenty years it would be celebrated by Carl
Sandburg as the dynamic city of the big shoulders. But in
1890 the glory of Chicago was its rebirth from the ashes of
the cataclysmic fire of 1871. The details of the great disaster
were familiar to every man, woman, and child: two thousand acres reduced to rubble, ninety thousand people homeless, hundreds dead, nearly $200 million in damage; this evi-
dence of the impermanence of man's handiwork was at the
back of everyone's mind. Instead of dwelling on the great
calamity that had befallen them, Chicagoans reacted to an
atmosphere that was turbulent, seething, and restless with
an unquenchable spirit that became the city's foremost and
best characteristic. Cut off from their past in a single stroke,
Chicagoans turned their attention to the future. In the absence of the old rules to guide them, they made their own.

The manifestation of this spirit made Chicago a city of su-
perlatives. In the nineteen years that had gone by since the
fire, the city had exploded to cover 181 square miles, more
than any other metropolis in the United States. Its population more than tripled in that time until it was second only
to New York. Yearly trade skyrocketed to about $1,600 mil-
lion, once again second only to New York. Chicago was the
greatest railroad center in the United States, and more ships
docked at Chicago piers than at any other port in the country. Major industries included the manufacture of iron and
steel products (the largest rolling mills in the world), meat
and meat by-products (the busiest stockyards in the country), railway cars, leather goods, textiles, chemicals, agricultural tools, beer and liquor.

The Chicago spirit was equal to any problem. For instance, waste products from the Chicago River were befouling Lake Michigan and the city's supply of drinking water. The solution was a typical piece of Chicago audacity—they simply reversed the flow of the river, saving the Lake and sending the pollution in the opposite direction, down to St. Louis.

But it would be a mistake to think of the Chicago spirit as being restricted only to commerce; its presence could be felt in the city's architecture, in its recreational facilities and its educational institutions. For example, Chicago was the birthplace of the skyscraper. Unsatisfied with the limitations placed on the height of buildings by old methods, William Jenney developed the structural steel frame. His creation made possible the construction to lofty heights of such buildings as the Monadnock, the Board of Trade, the Auditorium, and the Rookery, which offered vistas unparalleled elsewhere. From such a perch the historian J. C. Ridpath overlooked the city and declared that it was his opinion that, "Even from the dome of St. Peter's the landscape is by no means so fine, so extended, so full of life and progress."

On the Midway, the new University of Chicago was building. The city boasted three comprehensive libraries. A new home was being constructed for the Art Institute, which possessed a growing number of important and valuable collections. The Chicago Symphony Orchestra had been organized, and many theaters and opera houses catered to a wide range of tastes.

Near the downtown district elegant ladies and fastidious gentlemen could be seen driving their horse-drawn carriages down Lake Shore Drive and through the lovely Lake Front Park, the beginning of a system of almost two thousand acres of parks scattered throughout the city and connected by a series of broad, leafy esplanades. Out on the South Side in Jackson Park rose the fabulous White City, site of the

World's Columbian Exposition which opened in 1893 and attracted hundreds of thousands of visitors.

However, as G. W. Steevens, a visiting English journalist, observed:

. . . there is another side to Chicago. There is the back side to her 15 hundred million dollars of trade, her 17 thousand vessels and her network of 90 thousand miles of rail. Away from the towering offices, lying off from the smiling parks, is a vast wilderness of shabby houses —a larger and more desolate Whitechapel that can hardly have a parallel for sordid dreariness in the whole world.

According to Steevens, "everybody is fighting to be rich, is then straining to be refined, and nobody can attend to making the city fit to live in." In 1893 another English visitor, W. T. Stead, a journalist and editor, published *If Christ Came to Chicago,* which landed like a bombshell in the midst of the local establishment. Stead, a sharp-eyed social critic as well as a journalist, found that, "The corporations have grabbed or stolen everything." Big business snuggled up to big politics and not even the city streets were safe. "The citizens have not even a miserable revenue from the franchises which give the corporations their power," he went on. "They have barely a right of way on their own streets." He deplored the political machine, but admitted that the Democratic Party fulfilled a necessary function, almost replacing the Church as a social service institution, although this was based "upon bribery, intimidation, bulldozing of every kind, knifing, shooting and the whole swimming in whiskey."

Alcoholism was not the only vice rampant on the city streets. Prostitution and gambling flourished, and the rate of violent crime was high. In addition, there was considerable industrial strife, especially after the depression of 1893 brought unemployment to the masses.

But for all of this, Chicago had a special quality. The American humorist George Ade called Chicago a mining town five stories high. Theodore Dreiser said it made him "crazy with life." Rudyard Kipling, who hated the city, credited it with a "grotesque ferocity." So hectic was the pace of life that, when asked who should be named patron saint for the hustling city, one wag suggested St. Vitus. In short, Chicago was a boom town—with all of the excesses that implies.

Nowhere was this spirit of boom more apparent than in the profession of journalism. In 1890 fully 68 per cent of Chicago's population were immigrants, and of the remaining 32 per cent many were the children of immigrants or came from other parts of the country to take advantage of the greater opportunities the city offered. These people looked to the newspaper as the bearer of gossip and education. As a result, the popularity of the style of personal journalism that had evolved since the Civil War was especially great in Chicago, where people missed the homely communications network they had left behind in their small towns, or where others from abroad wanted to learn the English language and American ways.

A reporter who could develop a colorful, interesting style could win a promotion and even fame. Newspapers were exuberant, high-spirited, and opinionated to a degree that makes today's papers pale in comparison. While no effort was made to keep editorializing to the editorial page, the editorials themselves were predictable since the management of all the newspapers was conservative. Adherence to the publisher's editorial policy was mandatory in all departments of the newspaper. Since most of the reporters in Chicago had liberal leanings, this led to a basic conflict in philosophy. In some cases, it led to finding a different outlet for both energy and attitudes. The result was that such talented

men as George Ade wrote humor; Theodore Dreiser wrote
fiction; Eugene Field wrote poetry; Brand Whitlock became
a politician; and Finley Peter Dunne wrote political satire.

Peter Dunne Senior immigrated from Ireland to New
Brunswick, Canada, before moving to the United States
when he was just six years old. Brought up on the East
Coast, Dunne became a carpenter and pursued this craft as
he moved west to make Chicago his home. A sober, indus-
trious man, Dunne achieved some status in the West Side
Irish section of Chicago as an owner of real estate and a
staunch member of the Democratic Party. Although he had
left the old country at an early age, he was a member in
good standing of a number of Irish associations. His wife,
Ellen Finley Dunne, also was brought to the United States
from Ireland as a child. She represented a gentle contrast to
her husband, being young, blithe, and merry, and she in-
stilled in their children the love of English and Irish literature that was so important to her. Together the Dunnes
created an atmosphere that was stable and solid, characterized by a love of learning, an awareness of the day-to-day
political world around them, and a sense of continuity from
their Irish forebears. It was into this household that Finley
Peter Dunne was born on July 10, 1867.

Peter was a precocious infant who talked early and
delighted his family with his gift for mimicry. Even as a
child he was a keen observer of his time and surroundings,
and there were certainly plenty of things going on around
him. The West Side was the center of the Irish settlement in
Chicago, and from his exposure to the rich life of the community he gained a solid knowledge of the Irish-American
make-up. In addition, his home was located at Adams and
DesPlaines streets, close to the city's business district and to
City Hall, so that he received a grounding in the everyday
aspects of urban life.

Peter sailed through the elementary grades and entered

high school to pursue a curriculum that would prepare him for college. Although he demonstrated his facility with words on the debating team and the school newspaper, his educational record was not remarkable. The invalidism of his mother and her early death from tuberculosis influenced his adolescence. When he lost her, Peter lost his greatest champion. He finished last in his class at West Division High, and his father decreed that rather than attending college, Peter would have to go to work.

> Th' newspapers ar-re a gr-reat blessin'. I don't know what I'd do without thim. If it wasn't f'r thim I'd have no society fit to assocyate with—on'y people like ye'er-silf an' Hogan. But th' pa-apers opens up life to me an' gives me a speakin' acquaintance with th' whole wur-ruld . . . I know more about th' Imp'ror iv Chiny thin me father knew about th' people in th' next parish.

Whether by accident or design, in June 1884, Peter took his first job in a menial capacity on a newspaper, the Chicago *Telegram*. He readily demonstrated that he was street-smart and knew his way around town, with the result that he was quickly named police reporter. After only a short time in that job, he was offered a general assignment position on a larger paper, the *News*.

He had a brief fling as a sports reporter with the *News*, but when the *Times*, a lively, Democratic-oriented paper controlled by James J. West, contacted him about joining it as a political writer, he accepted immediately. He covered both national presidential conventions of 1888 and was assigned as a political editorial writer as well. He so impressed West that he was named city editor that year—at the tender age of twenty-one.

At only twenty-two, while city editor of the *Times*, Dunne scored a coup of which any reporter could be proud. He was a strong friend of John Devoy, the national leader of the

Clan-na-Gael, an Irish organization formed in the United States to help the Irish back home. Initially, the Clan was involved in purely Irish matters, but gradually it became a vehicle for Irish-American politics as well.

In Chicago the local Clan branch was headed by Alexander Sullivan. He was something of an anomaly, an Irish Republican, and he claimed to have been promised the cabinet post of Attorney General by James G. Blaine in 1884.

Under Sullivan's control, Clan money was being diverted from its object, which, according to Dunne, was to arm "agents of the Clan with weapons to destroy Windsor Castle, Buckingham Palace, the Houses of Parliament, and the Bank of England . . ." Instead, the money was being employed by Sullivan in his speculations at the Chicago Board of Trade. Once his activities were discovered by his opposition within the Clan, Sullivan promised to put the cash back —which promise was good enough for most of the Clan members, but not for Dr. John Patrick Cronin, a physician hitherto noted mainly for his fine tenor voice. Cronin mounted a one-man campaign against Sullivan which was striking for its lack of impact.

But then, one day, Dr. Cronin went missing. Someone had called for him in a carriage drawn by a distinctive white horse, saying he was needed at the ice house of one O'Sullivan, with whom he had an agreement to treat his employees. When the doctor did not return, his landlord went to the police, where the case was given to a detective named Daniel Coughlin. No one took much notice of the disappearance until John Devoy arrived back in town after quitting his job on the New York *Herald*. Devoy went straight to Dunne and told him of the Clan situation, which miraculously had escaped the notice of the press, and declared that he was sure Cronin was dead.

Suddenly Dunne was besieged by men who drifted into his office for diverse reasons, but who always ended with a tip about Cronin—that he had been spotted in Canada, that he had fled after performing an abortion, that he was a British spy on his way to London, and so on.

Determined to get to the bottom of this puzzling situation, Dunne went to his friend Bill Pinkerton, head of the detective agency, who in turn contacted a good friend of his who was the chief of the Canadian police. The chief wired back that there was no sign that Cronin had ever entered Canada. Pinkerton told Dunne that he shared Devoy's conviction that Cronin had been murdered, and Dunne tried to interest him further in the case, but Pinkerton replied, "You newspaper fellows all think you are better detectives than we are. Go find the murderer. I'll not help you. I don't care what you Irishmen do to each other. I'm Scotch."

When Dunne printed his news from Canada, the tipsters stopped coming round, and Dan Coughlin began a flurry of activity on the case. After a period of concerted effort, he announced to the press that he had turned up no proof that Cronin had been murdered.

The very next day a city work crew checking out the sewers found the badly beaten body of Dr. Cronin. Coughlin swore he would not rest till the murderers were found.

The discovery fed Dunne's obsession with getting to the bottom of the matter. He followed every lead—and there were many—but one day at lunch he got the one he had been waiting for. He bumped into Pat Ryan, a former detective who had kept his lines of information open. He told Dunne that Coughlin had tried on at least one occasion to hire two men to beat Cronin up.

From that time on, Dunne made sure that Coughlin's every move was watched, and he began to gather evidence against the policeman. The case was broken when a disreputable character named Joe Dunlop approached Dunne. When the *Times* was purchased by J. J. West from the widow of Wilbur Storey, one of the terms of the transaction was the continued employment of Dunlop. No one knew why; according to Dunne, Dunlop never did anything but

"look disgusting." He possessed some rather shady contacts,
though, and one night when Dunne and his crew were sty-
mied by their inability to find the livery stable where the
white horse had been hired, Dunlop gave them the tip they
needed. The man who hired the horse and buggy was Dan
Coughlin.

Dunne rushed to West's office with the news, and West
gave the thrilling order to stop the presses. As soon as he
had scored his beat, Dunne went to the mayor and the chief
of police with the evidence. Once Coughlin was arrested,
Dunne put out an extra edition, telling Chicago that the
murderer of Dr. Cronin was the detective in charge of the
case.

Coughlin was convicted and sentenced to life imprisonment, together with his two fellow conspirators. The sentence was later reversed and he was retried. This time he
was found not guilty. He went to work for Alexander Sullivan, whose complicity was suspected by some but never
proven, but he quickly found himself in trouble again. He
left Chicago one step ahead of the law and ended his life as
a drifter.

A struggle among the *Times*'s directors in 1889 removed
Dunne's patron as publisher of the paper, and Dunne was
forced to leave the *Times* too. Although depressed by the
untimely end of this venture, he quickly was taken on by the
Tribune, but in a lesser capacity. As a result of his most recent experience, he realized that it was the publishers who
had the upper hand in journalism and he resolved to advance to that level in order to wield influence.

In 1890 he became editor of the *Sunday Tribune*, and that
same year moved on once again, this time joining the *Herald*, which was noted for the number of bright young men
on its staff. However, he became increasingly dissatisfied
with general assignment reporting, and in 1892 he welcomed a transfer to the *Herald*'s sister publication, the *Evening Post*.

When Dunne assumed editorial charge of the *Post*, he believed that he would find success by writing literate and rational editorials that would move men's minds. His greatest success, however, was come from quite a different direction and as the result of a rather casual decision to write a weekly humor column for a new Sunday edition.

During the period from 1884, when he got his first job on a paper, to 1892, when he started writing dialect columns, Dunne covered just about everything: prize fights, murders, books, politics, the social scene—as well as writing editorials. His experience acted on Dunne as a catalytic force, enabling him to collect and distill the multitudinous flavors of Chicago life. Also, he came to know just about everyone in Chicago journalism, which in the 1890s was most impressive: Brand Whitlock, Wallace Rice, Opie Read, Theodore Dreiser, Frederick Upham Adams, Eugene Field, George Ade, Will Payne, and John McCutcheon were just a few of his colleagues.

Dunne was both well-known and well-liked. He was one of the leading members of the Whitechapel Club, a society named for Jack the Ripper's section of London, and formed by local newspapermen to foster conviviality and frank talk. It gave its members a feeling of fraternity and a forum for the liberal opinions they were largely unable to express in print. The club met amid a collection of ghoulish appointments in the back room of a bar on Calhoun Place off La Salle Street between Washington and Madison. It was also known as "Newsboys Alley" because it was close by the offices of the major newspapers.

Many years later George Ade put down his recollections of Dunne and the Whitechapel Club. When Ade met Peter Dunne in 1890, he impressed Ade as being "informed, wise, vested with authority, superior, cynical and controversial." All this at the ripe old age of twenty-three!

Ade felt that the reputation of the Whitechapel Club for being "a collection of harum scarum irresponsibles," non-

conformists, Bohemians, and heavy, steady drinkers was not
entirely deserved as it provided a critical forum for young
intellectuals who were attempting to determine their places
during a period of cultural turmoil and whose jobs in the
conservative establishment did not afford them an outlet to
express themselves. However, people now tend to remember
them for the scrapes they got into. On one occasion, they
challenged members of a similar group from Philadelphia,
the Clover Club to a duel of wits, bested them, and then
stood back in amusement when the local police raided the
Whitechapel Club (by prearrangement, of course). The
guests thought it was the real thing, and were treated to a
harrowing jaunt around town in a paddy wagon before
being deposited back at their hotel.

In an excess of high spirits one year, club members decided to run their own candidate for mayor. The funds that
they raised to prosecute the campaign later turned up in the
club treasury—about $1,000. Frederick Upham (Grizzly)
Adams, their nominee, received the full treatment in the
press from his fellow club members, but his candidacy,
which was run on a platform of "no gas, no water, no police," only brought him approximately one thousand votes.

On another occasion, club members obtained the body of
the last member of the Suicide Club of Dallas, which they
cremated on the Indiana sand dunes outside Chicago, to the
accompaniment of zither music and other complicated obse-
quies.

Yet the club served a serious purpose too, for it encouraged its members to develop their abilities and it served
as a forum for criticism. There is no doubt that the support
of his colleagues was important to the development of Finley Peter Dunne's native wit.

It was during his membership in the Whitechapel Club
that Dunne developed two loves—one of liquor and the
other of club life. Dunne, while not an alcoholic, was a pro-

digious drinker. At one dinner held in Southampton, Long
Island, around 1928, he received the following salute:

> So drink a toast
> To our brave host
> And also to good Peter Dunne
> Our man of fun
> Who drinks a tun
> Without a bun
> The man beloved by everyone

According to his son Philip, the need for alcohol was not
pathological with him; he just enjoyed it. Philip Dunne re-
calls that once his father met Louis Stoddard, an old friend,
on a Manhattan street. Stoddard approached him saying,
"Hello, Peter, drinking anything?" "Anything," was Dunne's
immediate response. And on this subject, Mr. Hennessy and
Mr. Dooley had the following exchange:

> "Ye ra-aly do think dhrink is a nicissry evil?" said Mr.
> Hennessy.
> "Well," said Mr. Dooley, "if it's an evil to a man, it's
> not nicissry, an' if it's nicissry, it's an evil."

Especially after he settled in New York, Peter Dunne enjoyed repairing to one of the clubs to which he belonged to
share a glass or two (or more) with some of his like-minded
friends. It is reported by his biographer that one day as he
was coming into the Links Club, he spied one of the elderly
retainers who had slipped and fallen on the floor. Dunne admonished him, "You'll have to be careful, old man, or you'll
be mistaken for one of the members." The point is that almost without exception, the members of such exclusive New
York gentlemen's clubs as the Knickerbocker, the Century,
and the Links, were extraordinarily heavy drinkers—
especially considering that they were by and large the

leaders of business, finance, and society. No stigma was at-
tached to such a habit among such people.

In view of his clever and sometimes irreverent editorials,
when it was decided that the *Post* would publish a new Sunday edition it was only natural that Dunne be asked to turn
in a satirical essay. The new avenue for self-expression and
the extra $10 per column convinced him to make an at-
tempt, and thus on December 4, 1892, his first Irish dialect
essay appeared. When the Sunday edition proved unprofitable and was discontinued in August 1893, Colonel
McNeery's success dictated the continuation of the column,
usually (but not always) in the Saturday edition of the
daily.

It was not until October 7, 1893, that Mr. Dooley made
his first public appearance. Until then, the main character in
the early columns was a bartender named Colonel McNeery,
proprietor of a downtown saloon. McNeery quickly acquired
a following, so that when the person upon whom the character was based complained that the articles held him up to
ridicule, no consideration was given to stopping them. However, Colonel McNeery was dispatched home to Ireland,
and Dunne moved his location to Bridgeport in the Irish
part of the South Side, inventing a new protagonist, Martin
J. Dooley.

While both talked with an Irish brogue and were saloonkeepers, there was a considerable difference between
McNeery and Dooley. McNeery was more urbane, less pro-
vincial, than Dooley. McNeery's clientele consisted mainly
of journalists and the local literary crowd, while over at
Dooley's place you were most likely to meet men who carried the hod or shoveled slag at the rolling mills. Out in
Bridgeport lived the shanty Irish—the people Dunne had
come to know so well in his early years, and whom he described as "knowing but innocent; moral, but giving no
heed at all to patented political moralities." Once he was
writing from Archey Road (Chicago's Archer Avenue),

Dunne began to alternate his satirical pieces with columns that described the actual tragedies that befell his common folk. Dunne's biographer, Elmer Ellis, relates that Dunne once told a friend that he "wanted to make the world see itself through a picture of the simple life of the Irish immigrant in Chicago—'simple like th' air or th' deep blue sea.'"

Mr. Dooley was an instant local success and there was much speculation as to who provided the inspiration for the popular saloonkeeper. For a time even the identity of the author was not known, since Dunne did not sign the columns. It was likely that Mr. Dooley himself was a composite of a number of Irishmen Dunne had known over the years rather than being any single living person.

The Dooley columns were, in the main, devoted to the satirical treatment of local personages and events. Dunne particularly enjoyed directing his thrusts at political figures and the corruption that surrounded them, so that Dooley became an auxiliary to his editorials in the *Post*'s clean-up campaign. Dunne was close to the reformers and gave them the benefit of his advice as well as his wit. Mr. Dooley became one of the most valuable tools they had in their efforts.

Both the *Post* and the *Herald* were owned by John R. Walsh, a local banker, but the *Herald* was published by James W. Scott, a popular liberal Democrat. In 1895 Scott was able to purchase control of the *Post* and the *Herald* and to merge the latter with the *Times*, the other Democratic morning paper. Dunne looked forward to developing the *Times-Herald* into a great newspaper. But in only two weeks Scott was dead of apoplexy at forty-six, and his majority in the two papers was purchased by Herman Kohlsaat, an ardent Republican and follower of William McKinley. Some time in late 1895 or early 1896, Dunne was transferred to the *Times-Herald*, although the Dooley columns continued to run in the *Post* until 1898. With a switch in editorial policy of both papers from independent to Republican, the Dooley pieces became increasingly important to Dunne as an outlet for the expression of his liberal and reform beliefs.

In 1896 he was assigned to cover both national presidential conventions, and Mr. Dooley devoted a good deal of space to the contest as well. Originally writing primarily about local affairs, through Dooley Dunne attacked all the humbug, sham, and corruption of city life in both humorous and tragic columns. As he broadened his horizons, taking a deeper interest in the national political scene, Mr. Dooley began to appeal to an audience outside Chicago, and gradually his columns were picked up by a number of out-of-town newspapers. Local figures dreaded the barbed wit of Mr. Dooley, as did national leaders, as Dunne cast his net ever wider for material. It was with the Spanish-American War of 1898 that Dunne achieved international fame and that made Mr. Dooley a national institution from that year until 1912, when it was said that Martin J. Dooley was better known than the Vice President of the United States.

Dunne remembered Dooley's rise to national prominence during the Spanish-American War as "amazing." He believed it came about because of the nature of this particular conflict: that beneath the hysteria, the American people were uncomfortable about it and knew it was not a worthy exercise. "It is humiliating to recall the spasm of craven fear that spread across the nation," Dunne said, "when a lying report was circulated that Dewey had been beaten at Manila Bay. Then came Ed Harden's flash from Hong Kong . . . telling of the complete annihilation of the Spanish fleet . . . the public gave full rein to the comic relief and laughed at . . . the absurd heroics of the 'opera bouffe war.' " Neither Mr. Dunne nor Mr. Dooley could tolerate the spectacle of a society deluding itself as to its motives. Dooley's gibes were welcome because they "helped to puncture and deflate some of the humbug and sham and cowardice and false pretense."

The column which started the chain reaction and made Dunne's fortune had to do with Admiral George Dewey's attack on the Spanish fleet lying off Manila. The jingos had stirred the emotions of the American public to a fever pitch. Everyone knew Dewey had sailed into Manila harbor in Spain's Philippine Islands, but because a cable (under Dewey's orders) had been cut, there was no news of the battle. In the absence of any hard news, speculation ran wild. As he was to do so often, Mr. Dooley stepped into the breach.

"Well," said Mr. Hennessy, in tones of chastened joy. "Dewey didn't do a thing to thim. I hope th' poor lad ain't cooped up there in Minneapolis."

"Niver fear," said Mr. Dooley, calmly. "Cousin George is all right."

"Cousin George?" Mr. Hennessy exclaimed.

"Sure," said Mr. Dooley. "Dewey or Dooley, 'tis all th' same. We dhrop a letter here an' there, except th' haitches—we niver drop thim—but we're th' same breed iv fightin' men. Georgy has th' thraits iv th' fam'ly. Me uncle Mike, that was a handy man, was tol' wanst he'd be sint to hell f'r his manny sins, an' he desarved it; f'r, lavin' out th' wan sin iv runnin' away fr'm annywan, he was booked f'r ivrything fr'm murdher to missin' mass. 'Well,' he says, 'anny place I can get into,' he says, 'I can get out iv,' he says. 'Ye bet on that,' he says.

"So it is with Cousin George. He knew th' way in, an' it's th' same way out. He didn't go in be th' fam'ly inthrance, sneakin' along with th' can undher his coat. He left Ding Dong, or whativer 'tis ye call it, an' says he, 'Thank Gawd,' he says, 'I'm where no man can give me his idees iv how to run a quiltin' party, an' call it war,' he says. An' so he sint a man down in a divin' shute, an' cut th' cables, so's Mack cudden't chat with him . . .

"Well, sir, in twenty-eight minyits be th' clock Dewey he had all th' Spanish boats sunk, an' that there harbor lookin' like a Spanish stew. Thin he run down th' bay, an' handed a few warm wans into th' town. He set it on fire, an' thin wint ashore to warm his poor hands an' feet. It chills th' blood not to have annythin' to do f'r an hour or more."

"Thin why don't he write something?" Mr. Hennessy demanded.

"Write?" echoed Mr. Dooley. "Write? Why shud he write? D'ye think Cousin George ain't got nawthin' to do but to set down with a fountain pen, an' write: 'Dear Mack, At 8 o'clock I begun a peaceful blockade iv this town. Ye can see th' pieces ivrywhere. I hope ye're injyin' th' same great blessin'. So no more at prisint. Fr'm ye'ers thruly, George Dooley.' He ain't that kind. 'Tis a nice day, an' he's there smokin' a good tin-cint seegar, an' throwin' dice f'r th' dhrinks. He don't care whether we know what he's done or not. I'll bet ye, whin we come to find out about him, we'll hear he's ilicted himself king iv th' F'lipine Islands. Dooley th' Wanst. He'll be settin' up there undher a pa'mthree with naygurs fannin' him an' a dhrop iv licker in th' hollow iv his arm, an' hootchy-kootchy girls dancin' befure him, an' ivry tin or twinty minyits some wan bringin' a prisoner in. 'Who's this?' says King Dooley. 'A spanish gin'ral,' says th' copper. 'Give him a typewriter an' set him to wurruk,' says th' king. 'On with th' dance,' he says. An' afther a while, whin he gits tired iv th' game, he'll write home an' say he's got th' islands; an' he'll turn thim over to th' gover'mint an' go back to his ship, an' Mark Hanna'll organize th' F'lipine Islands Jute an' Cider Comp'ny, an' th' rivolutchinists'll wish they hadn't. That's what'll happen. Mark me wurrud."

Another column was to become at least as popular, if not more so, than the Dewey article. Increasingly, Mr. Dooley was commenting on matters of national interest. He was especially fierce in his pursuit of the expansionists, not just the British, but American imperialists as well.

So it was the last straw when, in 1899, Dunne picked up a volume authored by Theodore Roosevelt about his war experiences with American forces in Cuba called *The Rough Riders*. Dunne himself said he was "especially peevish" that day, and he saw T.R.'s rather self-centered account of his adventures as perfect material for Mr. Dooley. The result was "A Book Review":

"Well, sir," said Mr. Dooley. "I jus' got hold iv a book, Hinnissy, that suits me up to th' handle, a gran' book, th' grandest iver seen. Ye know I'm not much throubled be lithrachoor, havin' manny worries iv me own, but I'm not prejudiced again' books. I am not. Whin a rale good book comes along I'm as quick as anny wan to say it isn't so bad, an' this here book is fine. I tell ye 'tis fine."

"What is it?" Mr. Hennessy asked languidly.

"'Tis 'Th' Biography iv a Hero be Wan who Knows.' 'Tis 'Th' Darin' Exploits iv a Brave Man be an Actual Eye Witness.' 'Tis 'Th' Account iv th' Desthruction iv Spanish Power in th' Ant Hills,' as it fell fr'm th' lips iv Tiddy Rosenfelt an' was took down be his own hands. Ye see 'twas this way, Hinnissy, as I r-read th' book. Whin Tiddy was blowed up in th' harbor iv Havana he instantly con-cluded they must be war. He debated th' question long an' earnestly an' fin'lly passed a jint resolution declarin' war. So far so good. But there was no wan to carry it on. What shud he do? I will lave th' janial author tell th' story in his own wurruds . . .

"'I felt I was incompetent fr to command a rig'mint raised be another,' he says. 'I detarmined to raise wan iv me own,' he says. 'I selected fr'm me acquaintances in th' West,' he says, 'men that had thravelled with me acrost th' desert an' th' storm-wreathed mountain,' he

says, 'sharin' me burdens an' at times confrontin' perils
almost as gr-reat as anny that beset me path,' he
says. . . . 'On th' thransport goin' to Cubia,' he says, 'I
wud stand beside wan iv these r-rough men threatin'
him as a akel, which he was in ivrything but birth, education, rank an' courage, an' together we wud look up
at th' admirable stars iv that tolerable southern sky an'
quote th' bible fr'm Walt Whitman,' he says. . . .

"'We had no sooner landed in Cubia than it become
nicessry f'r me to take command iv th' ar-rmy which I
did at wanst. A number iv days was spint be me in
reconnoitring, attinded on'y be me brave an' fluent
body guard, Richard Harding Davis . . . This showed
me 'tud be impossible f'r to carry th' war to a successful
conclusion unless I was free so I sint th' ar-rmy home
an' attackted San Joon hill. Ar-rmed on'y with a small
thirty-two which I used in th' West to shoot th' fleet
prairie dog, I climbed that precipitous ascent in th' face
iv th' most gallin' fire I iver knew or heerd iv. But I had
a few r-rounds iv gall mesilf an' what cared I. I dashed
madly on cheerin' as I wint . . .

"'They has been some discussion as to who was th'
first man to r-reach th' summit iv San Joon hill. I will
not attempt to dispute th' merits iv th' manny gallant
sojers, statesmen, corryspondints an' kinetoscope men
who claim th' distinction. They ar-re all brave men an'
if they wish to wear my laurels they may. I have so
manny annyhow that it keeps me broke havin' thim
blocked an' irned. But I will say f'r th' binifit iv Posterity
that I was th' on'y man I see. An' I had a tillyscope.'"

. . . said Mr. Hennessy, "I think Tiddy Rosenfelt is
all r-right an' if he wants to blow his hor-rn lave him do
it."

"Thrue f'r ye," said Mr. Dooley, "an' if his valliant
deeds didn't get into this book 'twud be a long time
befure they appeared in [General] Shafter's histhry iv

th' war. No man that bears a gredge again' himsilf 'll iver be governor iv a state. An' if Tiddy done it all he ought to say so an' relieve th' suspinse. But if I was him I'd call th' book 'Alone in Cubia.'"

Roosevelt took all the guffaws with a good grace, however, and wrote Dunne, inviting him to visit the Roosevelts on his next trip East. Dunne did not take him up on that offer till a good deal later, and they became fast friends. In the meantime, however, Dunne bumped into the Roosevelts on a train. Mrs. Roosevelt mischievously urged her husband to tell Dunne of an encounter he had had.

"Well, I oughtn't to," said the colonel. "But I will. At a reception I was introduced to a very pretty young lady. She said, 'Oh, Governor, I've read everything you ever wrote.' 'Really! What book did you like best?' 'Why that one, you know, *Alone in Cuba.*'"

Meanwhile, in 1898, taking notice of the potential monetary rewards of reprinting Dooley columns, Dunne heeded the advice of friends and decided to publish a collection of old columns, entitled *Mr. Dooley in Peace and War.* It met with instant public and critical acclaim and remained on the best-seller list until 1899, when a second Dooley volume, *Mr. Dooley in the Hearts of His Countrymen,* was issued.

In the midst of all this furore stood Finley Peter Dunne, once a mere reporter and now an international celebrity. He still plied his trade, working from 1898 as managing editor of the Chicago *Journal.* While his head was not turned by the adulation that was now his, in the first blush of his extraordinary success he agreed to commitments he would be physically unable to meet. There was the Dooley series, of course, to be reprinted by *Harper's* as well as by a newspaper syndicate; a new series featuring Molly Donahue for the *Ladies' Home Journal;* yet another series, on Chicago,

for the *Saturday Evening Post;* and finally a work of fiction.

When he was offered a trip abroad to settle reprint rights with British publishers it is small wonder that he immediately accepted this chance to get away. He left Chicago in May 1899, stopping to be feted by fellow journalists in New York. It must have been a heady experience to have the likes of Richard Harding Davis at his feet. He was made no less welcome in London, and his arrival back in the United States in September was a matter of note.

Dunne returned to Chicago and the *Journal* only briefly, however. Once again, in 1900, he was assigned to cover the national presidential conventions, and it was at the Republican gathering in Philadelphia that he achieved the second and last news beat of his journalistic career. President McKinley was renominated automatically; the only question was who would be the nominee for Vice President. A political boss from New York insisted that Teddy Roosevelt, then governor of the state, be given the nod, despite the fact that McKinley disliked him. When queried as to why he was pushing so hard, the boss replied, "Well, I want to get rid of the ———. I don't want him raising hell in my state any longer. I want to bury him!"

Roosevelt was not quick to accept and kept his new suitors waiting. During the period of his supposed indecision he sent for Dunne for advice about an article he wanted to write. Dunne was not enthusiastic about heeding the summons; a lameduck governor was not an important figure to a big-city political reporter. On giving it further consideration, he decided to keep the appointment in the hope that Roosevelt would let slip whether or not he would accept the vice presidential nomination. Finding Roosevelt in a chatty mood, Dunne decided on a frontal attack and put the question to him straightaway. Roosevelt smiled and said, "I don't desire the office, but there has been such an apparently unanimous demand from all parts of the country for my services that I feel I have to accept. Now about that

article, I wish to say . . ." At that point, it looked as if T.R. were warming up for a full-scale oration, so Dunne fled, leaving the future President in mid-sentence, and beat his competition to the telegraph office by a scant five minutes.

Suddenly, Dooley-mania swept the country like a fever. Dooley was the subject of a popular song in a hit show, a march, and innumerable poems and letters to the editor. A row in the Texas legislature was quieted by a reading of "On His Cousin George," about Admiral Dewey's lack of communications during his engagement in Manila Bay. This same piece was read by the American ambassador to Great Britain before a receptive English audience. Treasury Secretary Lyman J. Gage entertained President McKinley and the rest of the Cabinet with his readings from Mr. Dooley, done in an Irish brogue. Dunne was paid $1,000 and up for Dooley columns, an unheard of price at that time, and his books sold at the staggering rate of ten thousand per month. Presidents and cabinet members were devoted fans, and being taken up by Martin J. Dooley was a matter of some pride—if one could survive the thrust of his wit.

No wan iver writes to an iditor to say, "That was a fine article ye had in ye'er vallyable journal on th' decline iv Greek Art since th' Time iv Moses." No sir, whin an indignant subscriber takes his pen in hand at all it is to say: "Sir, me attintion has been called to a lyin' article in ye'er scurr'lous sheet called 'Is Pro-hibition a Failure?' This is to tell you that I will hinceforth niver call f'r ye'er dasthardly handbill at th' readin' room again. Print this if ye dare in ye'er mendacious organ iv th' Jesuits. Ye'ers very respectfully, Vox Populy an' tin thousand others.

In the late fall of 1900 Finley Peter Dunne, like so many other graduates of the Chicago school of journalism, had moved to New York. Because of his dissatisfaction with the

script for the Dooley play, he decided to drop that project. He returned to Chicago to spend Christmas with his family, arriving with a severe case of typhoid fever. A long recuperation was followed by another trip abroad, although he managed to continue the Dooley columns. In 1902, he accepted an editorial assignment with *Collier's* magazine in addition to his other commitments. Next, he welcomed a challenge offered by William C. Whitney to edit the New York *Morning Telegraph*, up to that time a theatrical and sporting sheet, and turn it into a great newspaper and a force of influence. He thought he had realized his Chicago dream. His hopes for this venture were dashed, however, when Whitney died in 1904. The *Telegraph* went to his son, and Harry Whitney bought Dunne out.

Between 1900 and 1906 Dunne published four volumes of the collected Dooley essays: *Mr. Dooley's Philosophy, Mr. Dooley's Opinions, Observations by Mr. Dooley,* and *Dissertations by Mr. Dooley,* all of which were well accepted. The Dooley columns were syndicated, but from time to time there were gaps in their production, and the next collection, *Mr. Dooley Says,* did not appear until 1910. Dunne also missed journalism and subsequently he worked on a number of magazines, including *McClure's, American Magazine,* and *Metropolitan,* as well as *Collier's.*

He welcomed the opportunity to produce, in addition to editorials for *American Magazine,* a page entitled "In the Interpreters House," a round-table discussion by a cast of characters about current events, and he continued to do this until 1915. He also tried his hand at writing a series of nondialect essays called "From the Bleachers" during a brief period in 1911 for *Metropolitan.*

Shortly after his move to the East, Dunne made some changes in his personal life too. He married Margaret Abbott, a young woman of charm and cultivation whom he had known in Chicago, fathered three sons and a daughter, and settled back to enjoy a life of pleasant and close friendships with people from all walks of American life.

Dunne continued to write Dooley columns fitfully until 1915, publishing one more collection, *Mr. Dooley on Making a Will and Other Necessary Evils*, in 1919. But there was nothing "opera bouffe" about World War I, and although the public clamor for Dooley increased during the troubled years 1914 to 1918, Dunne succumbed to a general malaise and discontinued Dooley, saying that insanity and racial murder were not fit subjects for humor. Instead, he rejoined *Collier's* as an editor in 1915, and later, as his contribution to the war effort, handled publicity for the New York War Savings Stamp Program. Except for a brief period after the war when he needed the money, Dunne never wrote through the old philosopher again.

Dunne's "serious" writings never achieved the readership or acclaim that Dooley did; like so many other writers, Dunne became a prisoner of his most successful and earliest creation. There is no indication that this engendered any bitterness or resentment on his part, however. Unlike so many of the writers who got their start in Chicago on the newspapers of the 1890s and whose writings reflected the pessimism, disillusionment, and bitterness of the urban milieu, Dunne was not driven to extreme positions by his experiences. Perhaps it was his Irish Catholic background which helped him to develop a philosophy whereby he saw the world as quarrelsome, corrupt, and heartbreakingly sad, yet where the individual had innate worth and dignity.

Dunne had many friends from diverse backgrounds whom he enjoyed seeing regularly. Some were prominent businessmen and financiers, like William C. Whitney and his sons Harry and Payne. He did not forget his friends from the Chicago days; he kept track of them and wrote to them, though he did not often return to that city. He never lost his interest in politics and placed a high value on his friendship with Theodore Roosevelt. Roosevelt returned the compliment warmly, but perhaps a little carefully; one never knew when Mr. Dooley might strike again.

Peter Dunne was not above telling a little story on himself, and one of his most delightful tales concerned the twenty-sixth President. Apparently Dunne had a terrible memory for names. One night at a dinner party he found himself seated next to a lady whom he recognized immediately but whose name, despite his most desperate efforts, eluded him. He saw his chance to make some progress when she said, "Oh, I saw my brother last week and he sent you fond regards." Seeking a further clue, Dunne responded, "Oh, yes, your brother. Tell me, what's he doing these days?" "He's still President of the United States," she replied. She was, of course, T.R.'s sister.

Dunne was comfortable in the reform era, but he did not consider himself a card-carrying reformer, although he was quick to expose the evils he saw around him and Mr. Dooley could wield a devastating weapon in reform-type battles. At the same time, Dunne took the muckrakers to task when he felt they were getting too puffed up and preoccupied with sensationalism (which must have made for interesting days at the office, for he worked on several magazines with the leading lights of the muckrake pack) and favorite targets (while close personal friends) included Ida M. Tarbell and Norman Hapgood (Idarem and Slapgood to Dooley). Dunne was skeptical, irreverent, and had no illusions, but the fun-loving Irishman was never far from the surface.

Dunne did not have much use for Woodrow Wilson, the 1912 Democratic candidate for President. Philip Dunne suggests that he disagreed with him over war "preparedness," but it may also have been due to the fact that the Bull Moose campaign of 1912 against Wilson was Teddy Roosevelt's last hurrah. After the war he liked Warren G. Harding and played a brief, uncharacteristic role in the Republican presidential campaign of 1920 on Harding's behalf. During the campaign he had the dubious distinction of introducing Harry M. Daugherty, Harding's campaign manager, future Attorney General and major fund-raiser, to oil man Harry Sinclair and thus played some role in setting into motion the chain of events that was to lead to the Teapot Dome scandal. In 1928, when Sinclair went on trial for fraud as a result of his "loan" of $100,000 to Interior Secretary Albert B. Fall in return for the right to exploit the U. S. Navy's oil reserves, Peter Dunne took the stand as a character witness in Sinclair's behalf. Although Sinclair was acquitted of the criminal charges, the U. S. Supreme Court acted on a civil suit to annul the oil leases on the grounds of "fraud," "conspiracy," and "collusion."

Dunne returned to the party of his father and Mr. Dooley, though, and in 1928 he supported Governor Al Smith of New York in his unsuccessful bid for President. During Prohibition, Mr. Dooley had to turn his tavern into a soft-drink parlor, but his patrons could still get a glass of the old "shtuff" there. According to Mr. Hennessy, under the Eighteenth Amendment, "There ain't as much dhrunkenness as there was. I know that." "No," said Mr. Dooley, "but what there is is a much more finished product." Dunne agreed with President Franklin Roosevelt on more than just Repeal and liked to chaff his staunch Republican friends about their horror over the new President, whom they felt to be a dangerous fellow.

Dunne numbered among his friends the major journalists of his time, and enjoyed people from the theater as well. Ethel Barrymore was a witness at his wedding and godmother to his son Philip, for example. The Dunnes were close friends of the artist Charles Dana Gibson and his beautiful wife, Irene, whose sister was to become Lady Astor. One of the relationships Dunne prized most highly was with Mark Twain. The two great humorists had an easy, mutually respectful attitude toward each other. Dunne was later to recall a chance encounter he had with Twain shortly after his move to New York:

One bright spring afternoon I met him at the crowded corner of Fifth Avenue and 42nd Street. As

usual we stopped to exchange our customary banter
about the ignorance of youth and the impotence of age.
Thousands and thousands of men, women and children
passed us and every mother's son and daughter turned
his head to look at the picturesque figure. Some of them
stopped and listened. At one time there must have been
fifteen or twenty typical New York rufuses gawking at
him. Mark loved it. His face was aflame. His eyes
shone. He talked better and louder than I had ever
heard him. Finally I said, "Let's get out of here and go
over to the Century and have a drink."

"I'm not a member of the Century. What's the matter
with staying here?"

"But aren't you embarrassed standing here in these
crowds talking to a celebrity?" I said.

He answered like a man coming out of a trance. His
eyes were wide open and staring. He stammered, "Wh-
wh-why, do you think these people are looking at you?
Why, you conceited fellow, they're looking at me!"

Then the fact dawned on him that youth had at last
rebelled. His face broke into a great grin. "Oh, come on
over to the Century and have a drink."

"But you just said you weren't a member."

"I'm not. That makes my hospitality all the more remarkable. What could be finer than to entertain a
friend at a club where you're not a member?"

"But I'm a member."

"I knew that or I wouldn't have invited you to have a
drink."

In 1935 Dunne discovered he was suffering from cancer of
the throat. His son Philip, warned of the bad news, flew
cross-country from Los Angeles, where he was a successful
screenwriter, expecting to find a tragic figure, a dying man.
Instead, he found his father the genial host of a jolly gathering in his hotel suite. In the knowledge that death was prob-

ably near, he informed Philip that he hoped to have the last word for the last time. He wanted a very simple funeral, and he was worried that a friend, Frank Garvan, one of the leading laymen of the American Catholic Church, would sway his family toward holding an elaborate ceremony. As he told Philip, "Frank is the grandest fellow that ever lived, but he's by nature a body-snatcher, as dangerous in his way as Burke and Hare. It's a matter of religious principle with him. He's saved his own soul and now he feels a call to save mine as well . . . He promised me he'd respect my wishes and then I'm positive he went straight to the archbishop who hears his confession and received absolution for a bare-faced lie. So it's up to you [to stop him] . . . The only place a man can't hide is at his own funeral. Every scoundrel and bore he's spent his life avoiding is privileged to step up, view the carcase and tell the world what a dear friend he has lost in good old what's his name. If that ever happens to me, I'll find the strength to jump up and punch him in the nose."

But Finley Peter died suddenly in 1936, before his family could reach him from the West Coast. By the time they got to New York, Garvan had snatched the body, as predicted by the deceased, and scheduled a requiem mass at St. Patrick's Cathedral, which was crowded with both the bores Dunne feared, but with his cherished friends as well.

And the last word was delivered not by Dunne himself, but by one of his dear friends. The family's knowledge of Catholic ritual was sketchy at best, so, being in doubt as to what to do, they remained standing throughout the lengthy service, causing the rest of the mourners to do the same. On the way out, his aged legs creaking from the strain, Judge Morgan O'Brien observed, "Well, Peter spent more time in church today than he did in all the years of his life."

All of Finley Peter Dunne's works received critical praise, and, of course, Dooley was a huge popular success and many of his observations can easily be quoted about current day situations. Some have questioned the authenticity of the

Irish dialect in the Dooley pieces, but Dunne never claimed
that he was writing "pure" Roscommon talk. Indeed, his
own rendering of the dialect changed as he went from column to column, and even sometimes within the same column (although some of the discrepancies may be due to the
whimsy of the typesetters, whose job was not an easy one).
In speaking of some contemporary authors who wrote pho-
tographic dialogue, Dunne observed, "They are wonderful.
But they don't make anything up." No one could ever ac-
cuse him of that. His technique is rated as superb. He aimed
for purity of language in his nondialect writings and he was
scathing in his denunciation of sloppy grammar and literary
vulgarities. He was an exceptionally well read man, especially in the classics, who in addition to great learning possessed tremendous personal charm and wit.

"I'm goin' away," said Mr. Dooley.

"What?" exclaimed Mr. Hennessy.

"I've got a right to quit ye, Hinnissy, though ye'er a
good man an' so 'm I, be th' same token. F'r years an'
years I've been standin' behind this counter tellin' ye
thruths ye'd hear nowhere else—not in th' good book or
in th' Lives iv th' Saints. Why did I do it? Th' Lord on'y
knows. But whin I get talkin' I can't stop anny more
thin if I'd started to run down th' span iv th' r-red
bridge. Some iv th' things I've said was wrong, an' some
was right, an' most iv thim was foolish, but this much I
know, I've thried to give it out strait. An' what's it come
to? What's all th' histhry an' pothry an' philosophy I've
give ye an' th' Archey road f'r all these years come to?
Nawthin'. Th' la-ads I abused ar-re makin' money so
fast it threatens to smother thim. Th' wans I stud up f'r
is some in jail an' some out iv wurruk. I've bore with
iverything. I've stud Yerkuss, an' Bill Lorimer and Bath
House Jawn an' th' Relief and Aid Society, an'
Schwartzmeister cuttin' th' price iv pints. I've seen all

kinds of onjestice done an' all kinds iv goodness punished. I seen civil service an' I stud that. Man an' boy, I've lived here f'r thirty-forty year an' paid me taxes an' disthributed liquor that didn't have a fight or a headache in a bar'l iv it, but whin they ask me to live in a state run be a counthry sausage I've got to quit. I've got to quit. I've got to go. A man that knowed Stephen A. Douglas an' wanst thried to break up a meetin' where Ab'ram Lincoln was has no place in th' state iv Illinye."

"Good-by," said Mr. Hennessy. "Ye'll think betther iv it.

"Mebbe," said Mr. Dooley. "'Tis har-rd f'r me to lave off talkin'. Good-by."

Alas, Mr. Dooley has had to lave off talkin'. But still the Dooley columns are a joy to read today, as well as being pertinent—not because Dunne anticipated the happenings of our time, but because he was such an excellent critic of the events of his own.

I

Before Dooley

The impetus for Finley Peter Dunne to write an Irish dialect column came from two directions. First, in 1892 the Chicago *Evening Post* decided to enlarge its scope—and, it was hoped, its circulation—by publishing a Sunday edition and required more feature articles to fill up the space. Second, they offered Dunne $10 for each column. Although it seems a small fee by modern standards, the extra money was important to him, for he had begun to enjoy the convivial but costly evenings out with his colleagues which were a prelude to the club atmosphere he came to value so much in later life.

The *Post* was an independent paper in terms of politics, and Dunne had considerable latitude in his editorial page writings. Further, he enjoyed rapport with Cornelius McAuliff, the managing editor. Both men came from similar Irish Catholic backgrounds and were for and against the same things. However liberal they were and however independent the *Post* was in terms of partisan politics, the philosophy of the paper was basically conservative, in keeping with that of its owner, John R. Walsh. The dialect column offered Dunne an opportunity to get away with far more liberal comment—particularly when it came to municipal reform—than he could in his wise and witty editorials.

The dialect columns were unsigned, although many believed they were Dunne's work. The fact that he was indeed the author was revealed in an interview published by the *Post* in June 1895. In this article he described how the dialect columns began.

"In fact, it came about this way: I was on *The Sunday Post* and hadn't enough to do to keep me going, so one day I wrote an Irish sketch merely by way of giving a rational excuse for my existence on the staff. It was an interview with an old Irishman, and I tried to write just as he had talked, using but little dialect. The Sunday editor liked it, and asked me to write something else in the same strain. After a few weeks I did so, and I've kept it up. . . . It wasn't anything I sat down and thought out—it was only a little work that I did as I went along, and people have been foolish enough to think it good! That's all!"

Then, after a thoughtful pause: "No, not all either. There was 'ten per' which Dooley brought in. He is a good pot boiler."

2

In this first dialect column, an anonymous Irishman with a curious brogue visits the saloon owned by John Powers, alias Johnny de Pow, Nineteenth Ward alderman, to relate an apocryphal tale of a visit between Frank Lawler, a Chicago congressman and big-time political boss, and the newly elected President, Grover Cleveland.

Powers took no offense at the sobriquet of "Prince of Boodlers" which was applied to him; in fact, he rather enjoyed it. It was, after all, a distinction to be at the top of one's trade, for this was a time when the Civic Federation, a Chicago watchdog association, observed that sixty-eight of the aldermen for thirty-four wards were on the take. Johnny Powers teamed up with Chicago traction magnate Charles T. Yerkes, who was not always able to keep one step ahead of the law, and became Yerkes' mouthpiece on the City Council. The council had a practice of selling franchises to the city streets to streetcar or elevated companies or to the various utility firms. Powers had developed a finely honed method whereby he could sell a street more than once; for example, the surface level would go to a streetcar line, the air rights to an elevated line, and the underground to the gas company.

There was a mayoral election in Chicago in early 1893 and Powers was quick to ally himself with a Democrat and former mayor, Carter H. Harrison, Sr., and soon worked himself into the position, if not the title, of campaign manager. With Harrison's re-election, Powers was even more firmly entrenched as the man who pulled the strings in council meetings. Even before Harrison's term began, Powers moved ahead with a mass of new ordinances. For example, he became the gushing proponent of the Hygeia Mineral Springs Company, which promised to pump to Chicago fresh spring water from Waukesha, Wisconsin, during the 1893 World's Fair. In the course of the council debate on the matter, Powers enthused, "If this ordinance passes, we'll all be drinking spring water right in our own homes . . . The people of Chicago demand the ordinance. I want Waukesha water in my house, and so will you!" To which another alderman queried, "How many men supporting the ordinance ever drink water? What one of these aldermen ever drinks water?" It was a good question, but it went unanswered. With Powers' deft handling, the ordinance passed the council. Soon a similar bill passed the Wisconsin legislature in Madison, despite the opposition of the citizens of Waukesha, who threw a picket line around the state capitol building, its members singing "Throw Out the Pipe Line," to the tune of the hymn, "Throw Out the Lifeline." However, water-drinking aldermen, if indeed there were any, had to be content with their old source of supply, because the governor of Wisconsin and the outgoing mayor of Chicago both vetoed their respective bills on the Waukesha project.

The Irish in Chicago felt they had demonstrated their good faith and good works at the polls in behalf of Grover Cleveland, and they were chagrined when he cheated them of the spoils of victory after his election in 1892. Frank Lawler was not appointed postmaster of Chicago; instead that plum went to another Chicagoan, Washington Hesing, member of a German-American family prominent in local politics and publisher of the largest German-language newspaper in the state. The appointment of one of the hated "Hun" was a particularly bitter pill for the Irish to swallow.

When he began writing dialect essays, Dunne did not take the work seriously, much less anticipate that his fame was to come from such activity. A few days after the following column appeared, he wrote, "There is no doubt that the dialect story is a very bad thing and abundantly deserves every uncomplimentary remark that anybody may find time to make about it . . . That is our honest opinion of the dialect story. Of course it might be different if we had ever heard of anybody who had succeeded in reading one." Fortunately for Dunne and American humor, hundreds of thousands of people were to succeed in reading his dialect stories, which began with the following brief sketch.

CHICAGO *SUNDAY POST*, December 4, 1892

FRANK'S VISIT TO GROVER

AUTHENTIC STORY OF EX-CONGRESSMAN LAWLER'S
RECENT EASTERN TRIP

Frank Lawler is a candidate for postmaster, as everybody knows. Nearly everybody in Chicago hopes he will get it, and the Nineteenth Ward to a man is sure he has it already since he went to New York and saw Mr. Cleveland. Exaggerated reports of this trip have been

floating about the ward for a week and they were all expressed by a little man who sat at a table in Alderman
Little Jawnny Powers' place the other night.

"Gimme a loight, Jawnny," said the little man. "Hov
ye hur-rd about Lawluhr? Na-aw! He's been down to
see Grover. What th' 'ill! He's as good as Grover anny
day. He wint there loike a man an' knockit at th' dure.
Whin th' hoired gurl come he sez: 'Miss, me compli-
mints, Mr. Lawluhr wants to see th' Prisidunt.' 'He
won't see ye,' sez th' hoired gurl. 'He's afther turnin'
away Gorman 'n Crokhur 'n Shahan 'n th' rist an' he
won't see no man,' she sez. 'Ta-ak up me ca-a-r-rd,' sez
Lawluhr, 'an' Oi'll wait by the duhr till ye do come
down.' 'Ahl right,' sez th' gurl, 'but ye'll be trun out ahl
the same,' sez she. Well, Lawluhr shtands be the duhr
an' thin he hears ould Grover upstairs bawlin' out:
'Lawluhr, iv Chicaggy,' he sez. 'Tell him to hist himself
inty th' settin'-room,' he sez. 'Oi'll be down,' he sez, 'as
soon's Oi putt on me shkates,' sez he, for th' poor man
was walkin' around wud th' babby in his shtockin' feet.
Whin he comes down he grabs Lawluhr be the coat,
and sez: 'Well, Frank me bucko, an' how ar-re ye?' 'Ahl
roight,' sez Lawluhr, 'an' how's thricks wud you?' 'Ah,
Oi'm in mortial sorrow,' sez big Steve. 'Me haar-rts gray
wud th' push that's afther me fur awffus,' he sez. 'It's
ondacint. But whur've ye been so long?' he sez. 'I see be
th' *Irish World* two days ago that you were in town,' he
sez. 'That's roight,' sez Lawluhr. 'But some of me
friends . . .' 'Say no more,' sez Grover. 'Buck up,' he
sez. 'Ar-re ye down here fur th' post-awfuss?' 'Oi am,'
sez Lawluhr. 'Ye've got it, ahlready,' sez Grover. 'An'
now how's me ould frind, little Jawnny Powers?' Oh,
'tis thrue, Jawnny, 's God's me judge, he asked for
you. Na-aw, but he's rid about ye in th' paper. An' he
sez: 'How's Tommy.' 'A-aw, Tommy's married 'n settled
down,' sez Lawluhr. Just thin in comes Frankie an' she

was dyloighted tuh see Lawluhr. 'An' where've ye ben, ye dear man,' sez she. 'How's th' kid?' sez Lawluhr. 'As big an' ugly as his dad,' sez Mrs. C. 'Hav' ye seen Misther Whitney?' 'Begor, I haven't,' sez Lawluhr. 'Is he here?' 'He is,' sez she, an' she calls Whitney downstairs. Will, Jawnny, they set there 'n chewed the rug for near an hour. Foin'ily Lawluhr, he sez: 'Oi think Oi'll put on me rollers an' duck,' he sez. 'Wait a minute,' sez Mrs. Cleveland. 'Can't ye shtay over Sunday an' go to the Vanderbilt's surprise party?' 'Na-aw,' sez Frank. 'Oi must get baack to me constit,' he sez. 'Let me tell ye, thin,' sez she. 'Ye can hav' annythin' ye wan' from the ould man,' sez she, 'for he thinks the wurrld of ye,' she sez. An' whin Lawluhr wint out Grover an' Bill Whitney wint would 'im an' they mopped in a few shills of beer an' Lawluhr bate thim playin' pool by pocketin' th' fifteen balls from th' bust, an' the last thing Grover sez, he sez: 'Raymimber me koindly to little Jawnny Powers.' Oi'll taak me oath he said it. Oi wuddent loi, Jawnny. A bit from th' cooler, Jawn."

3

The next edition of the *Sunday Post* saw the introduction of a new mouthpiece for Dunne's wit, Colonel McNeery, proprietor of a saloon on Dearborn Street near Chicago's newspaper row.

Dunne freely admitted that he patterned Colonel McNeery after a friend of his, James McGarry, who also owned a saloon on Dearborn Street which was popular with the newspaper crowd. This is how Dunne remembered it in *Mr. Dooley at His Best*:

In Dearborn Street near the *Chicago Tribune* office Mr. James McGarry kept an excellent public house.

McGarry, born in the County Roscommon, had lived long in Chicago and both by reason of his natural qualities and his position as presiding officer of what he called "the best club in town, not exclusive minje but refined," had an acquaintance amounting to intimacy with nearly everybody worth knowing in politics, on the bench, at the bar, in trade, on the stage or in journalism. I have no hesitation in saying that most of the local copy for the *Tribune* and much for the *Herald* and *News* was written in McGarry's back room. He was a stout, rosy-faced, blue-eyed man of sententious personage who was not alone the friend and host of the most brilliant newspaper writers of that period but their counselor and banker as well.

Mr. McKenna, who was soon to become McNeery's foil, considered that McGarry was "a man who liked to tend bar." McGarry was a big man—over six feet tall and more than 250 pounds—and he had the wit and charm to keep pace with the most talented of his clientele. McGarry considered his establishment to be a classy one, without a need for chairs, or gimmicks like the free lunch; in McGarry's words, it was a "drinking place for gentlemen, not a restaurant."

CHICAGO *SUNDAY POST*, December 11, 1892

HE LEAVES HIS MONEY BEHIND

COLONEL MC NEERY RUMINATES ON THE
LESSON OF JAY GOULD'S LIFE

"I see me friend Jay Gould is dead," said Colonel McNeery, turning from his regular noonday survey of the procession of fair ones on Dearborn Street. "Vanderbilt is dead. Mike Casey is dead. They're all dead and gone, poor men, and none of them took his money with him. Jay Gould had no fun in life. My friend there, little

Johnny McKenna, would have more fun at a dance at
Brighton Park, ten times over, for McKenna could get
up the next morning and eat a side of bacon, cabbage
and boiled potatoes, put on his cambric shirt and come
down town as fresh as e'er a man you know, while
Gould, sure, th' poor little wisp of a man, if he ate one
egg for breakfast he'd be doubled up with sorrow in his
stomach. Besides, McKenna never had fear of mortal
man nailing him with a bomb. The worst he ever got was
some friend of McElligott's soaking him with a brick,
and divil a bit they care for that in Bridgeport. It's a
mere diversion, but Gould, the unhappy divvil, the minute he poked his whiskers out of his office some crazy
arnychist was liable to crack away at him with a gaspipe
bomb full of dynamite or some strong-arm man toss him
into a coal hole. Now he's dead, and what of it? He has
a fine box and a mausolyum and manny's the boy I've
seen as contented and gay in one of Gavin's old wood
crates as if he was laid out in a rosewood casket, with a
satin pillow under his head, and making no more kick to
be dumped into a hole in Calvary than he was out on a
shelf in a vault like a jar of pickles. It's little difference
it makes to a man when he's dead. He didn't take anything with him barring a new suit of clothes. He had to
leave all the coin behind. I see he left his son George
only $5,000,000 for the three years' work. It's a burnin'
shame. Faith, I hope the lad will be able to get through
the winter though it's little enough with hard coal at $8
a ton and Boyle contemplatin' a lift in the price of steak.
And an actress for a wife, at that. Them actresses is
spenders. I wonder if the boy will ever think of his father
or will he think of the money all the time. Aha! it'll be
little pleasure he'll take from pondering on the old man
if what Shakespeare says is true that it will be easier for
a camel to go through the eye of one of them little cambric needles than for a rich man to enter the kingdom of
heaven."

4

City leaders worked hard to secure the World's Columbian Exposition for Chicago and succeeded in convincing Congress that it should have the right to hold the fair celebrating the four hundredth anniversary of Columbus' discovery of America. Chicagoans hoped that the beauty and grace of the exposition would remove the commonly held impression of their city as a rough-and-ready town where anything and everything went. As one Chicagoan observed during the negotiations over the fair, they didn't have culture in his city yet, but that when they got some, Chicagoans would make it hum.

In 1891 a group of architects who were to work on the fair gathered on the barren stretch of land that was to be the fair site. Although it was impossible to have the grounds ready for the actual celebration year of 1892, it was announced to those men by Daniel Burnham, the noted architect and later the author of the plan that was to preserve Chicago's lake front, that the fair would open its doors in 1893.

During the two years between 1891 and 1893 it seemed as if the whole city concentrated on the fair and what it would mean to Chicago. Typically, Chicagoans responded enthusiastically to the tremendous challenge presented by completing the fairgrounds in so short a period of time.

Daniel Burnham was a go-getter. First, he convinced the building and grounds committee that running a contest for choosing the architects was a poor idea; instead, a group of architects from across the nation were appointed by the committee at Burnham's urging. Although local firms were well represented and despite the already established reputation of the modern school of Chicago architecture, the over-all design theme of the fair followed the classical tradition associated with the East. The best representative of the Chicago school was the Adler-Sullivan Transportation Building.

Burnham also invited a group of noted American sculptors to create the statuary and fountains that were to grace the fairgrounds. Among them were Augustus Saint-Gaudens and Chicago's own Lorado Taft.

Another coup was scored when a member of the fair board secured the services of Frederick Law Olmsted, the famous landscape architect, to transform the sandy wastes of Jackson Park into a beautiful garden. Unwilling at first to take on the seemingly impossible chore, Olmsted was offered $15 million and a free hand. Who could resist such an offer? Certainly not Olmsted.

Wanting to be sure everything down to the last detail was perfect, Burnham saw to it that one artist be appointed director of color. After considerable scrapping and a change of personnel, it was discovered that co-ordination of the various color schemes had been let go till the last minute. When it became obvious that a workable scheme could not be developed, it was decided by the director of color that the theme of the fair should be an absence of color. They whitewashed each building with a squirt gun, and the fair became known as the "White City."

Colonel McNeery had mixed emotions about the fair, although he allowed himself to be coaxed into visiting it. In this tale of his visit to the midway he reveals a certain prudery which one would not have expected from so worldly (in his own estimation) a person.

CHICAGO *SUNDAY POST*, June 4, 1893

M'NEERY AT THE FAIR

O'CONNOR TOOK HIM, UNWILLING,
TO THE FRENCH ART SECTION

HE WAS COVERED WITH SHAME BUT FLED
AND FOUND RELIEF IN THE IRISH VILLAGE

"THE NUDE IN ART"

"Paintin'," said Colonel McNeery, "paintin' has no cha-
arms for me, Jawnny, and when O'Connor tuk me over
to the a-art palace at th' wurruld's fair I kicked, I did.
'Let's go to the Irish village,' I says. 'Never,' says he.
'An' why?' says I. 'Because, faith,' says he, 'they'd be
keepin' us there as exhibits,' he says. 'Not of Irish industries,' says I, 'for divil a lick of wurrk ye've done sence
ye pulled the red ticket out of ye'er hat in Batthery
Park.'[1] 'Ah,' he says, 'come in and see the pectures,' he
says, 'an' improve ye'er crazy old mind.' I don't like
O'Connor's way of ta-alkin' to me, Jawnny; I don't indeed, an' he'll find it out th' next time he opens his head
to me in that parnicious manner; but he's the only man
I knew on the growns an' he's acquainted with all th'
coppers an' he can find th' only place in Midway where
they sell beer for five a throw an' so I says: 'Lead on,' I
says, like Shakespeare; 'lead on, O'Connor, an' dam'd be
he who first cries hold, enough.'

"I told ye some time ago, Jawnny, me lad, never to
go near th' Midway, but I take that back. I'm sorry I
spoke, for th' Midway is like th' life iv th' good man in
the christian duty compared wid that art gallery. I pass

[1] McNeery is probably referring to the ticket issued to those more
fortunate immigrants who either had money to move on to the interior of the U.S. or who had the promise of a job or relatives waiting
for them there.

over th' Swedish pictures, although I moight admit to ye that I was surprised to find a Swede that cud paint a picture, for all th' good I ever knew thim for was to make janitors an' knock blazes out iv Danny O'Brien an' Philly Furlong in th' Twenty-third Wa-ard on primary day. An' I also pass over th' Dutch pictures in order to tell ye about the French section. Now, Jawnny, ye know I'm no methodist. Ye know that well, for haven't I been takin' th' *Police Gazett* since th' first issue of it? I have, I have. But if I didn't have to put me hand over me eyes whin I tuk th' first sight of thim pictures may I never shtir foot from this bar."

"What ailed the pictures?" asked McKenna.

"What ailed thim, is it? Nothin', Jawnny; nothin' save an' except that there wasn't a pair of pants or a petticoat in the room. Ne'er a one. Every man and woman that had his picture took for that gallery was as bare as th' front of me hand."

" 'Take down ye'er hands,' says O'Connor. 'Would ye be makin' a fool of us before all these people?'

" 'I'll not luk at thim naked women,' I says.

" 'Ah,' sez he, sarcastic. 'Ye've made a mistake,' he says. 'It's th' merchant tailors' buildin' ye ought to be in,' he says.

" 'Is it thin?' says I. 'Is it, O'Connor? Well, let me tell ye one thing, Misther O'Connor, an' that ain't two things, an' that is that this here is no place ayether for th' young or th' ould. An' I knew ye're folks in th' ould counthry, Misther O'Connor, an' ye'er respected grandfather—a man 's good, barrin' a combative nature, as iver breathed th' breath o' life'—I says, 'wud r-rise from th' grave an' fetch ye a clout in the job if he'd seen ye standin' here wid ye're eye out on ye're cheek starin' at thim bould divils iv Frinch women. It wasn't Paree or Boolonje that ye come from, but from th' dacint, or-dherly, christyan County Waterford, where people wear

their pants in public,' I says, 'an' where th' divvle that
painted such pictures as thim wud be read from th'
altar. Ye've tuk me in here, O'Connor, an', by gar, I'll
take ye out.' 'Let go me arrum,' he says. 'I'll let go
nawthin',' I says. 'Ye're disgracin' me, ye foolish ould
fool,' he says, looking around at th' doods and th' on-
blushin' women that was pikin' at th' pictures through
specs on the ends of shtrings. 'Ye're disgracin' me,' I
says. 'Come on,' and I drags him resistin' through th'
dure.

"I had him down to th' Irish village after that an' I
showed him around among th' butthermakers an' th'
lacemakers an' where they do have th' map of Ireland
on top of Blarney Castle. That is th' real Irish village,
for bechune you an' me, Jawnny, I think th' other one
from Donegal is a sort of bunk, I do, an' I niver liked
Donegal anny how. It was a man from Donegal that hit
my fa-ather with a scythe.

"'Isn't this better?' I says.

"O'Connor said nothin'.

"'Isn't this better than thim dizzy pictures?'

"'Well,' he says, 'this is good; but, Mac, there was no
ants on th' pictures nayther.'

"So," concluded Colonel McNeery, "this ends O'Connor with me. He's no morals an' I shake him from now
on."

5

In the first McNeery column the colonel referred to his good
friend little Johnny McKenna of Brighton Park, and from
then on McKenna was on hand to serve as the straight man
for McNeery and later for Dooley. Unlike McGarry/
McNeery, Dunne made no attempt to throw a cloak
about McKenna's identity; he was a real person and there is

every evidence that he loved the recognition the columns brought to him. John McKenna was something of an anomaly—an Irish Republican from the Irish Democratic bastion on the South Side. As a reward for his constancy in making the usually futile gesture each Election Day, he was given a number of political jobs, capping his career in public service as chief inspector of private employment agencies for the state of Illinois. He kept in touch with Dunne throughout his life and eventually, in 1918, wrote a book of his own, entitled *Stories by the Original Jawn McKenna from Archy Road of the Sun Worshipers Club of McKinley Park*.

There were many aspects of the World's Fair, enough to hold the attention of a broad audience. One of the attractions for those who were interested in culture as well as pure entertainment was a literary congress. It was meant to be a dignified convention, with scholarly papers presented for the edification of all.

To the dismay of some and the delight of others, the authors' meeting turned into an intellectual brawl, Chicago style. At a session on "Aspects of Modern Fiction," an argument which had hitherto been prosecuted in the pages of scholarly journals erupted into open war, forcing participants to choose up sides. In one corner were the proponents of realism in fiction who felt there was a "distinctive American literature" emanating from the West. In the opposite corner were defenders of the old, established, genteel tradition which was the legacy of Europe through the East.

Eugene Field was a western writer who was under the sway of the eastern romantic tradition. In one of the several Chicago *Daily News*' articles which covered the dispute, he wrote:

The chances are that to the end of our earthly career we shall keep on regretting that we were not present at that session of the Congress of Authors when Mr. Ham-

lin Garland and Mrs. Mary Hartwell Catherwood had
their famous intellectual wrestling match. Garland is
one of the apostles of realism. Mrs. Catherwood has
chosen the better part; she loves the fanciful in fiction;
she believes, with us, in fairy godmothers and valorous
knights and beautiful princesses who have fallen victims to wicked old witches.

Mr. Garland's heroes sweat and do not wear socks;
his heroines eat cold huckleberry pie and are so un-
feminine as to call a cow "he."

Mrs. Catherwood's heroes—and they are the heroes
we like—are aggressive, courtly, dashing, picturesque
fellows, and her heroines are timid, staunch, beautiful
women, and they, too, are our kind of people. Mr. Garland's *in hoc signo* is a dungfork or a butterpaddle; Mrs.
Catherwood's is a lance or an embroidery needle. Give
us the lance and its companions every time.

And the controversy raged on.

6

CHICAGO *SUNDAY POST*, July 16, 1893

AMONG THE "POTES"

COLONEL MC NEERY WAS DOWN AT THE
LITHRY CONGRESS LAST WEEK

'TWAS A SAD DISAPPOINTMENT

THEY TALKED OF WAGES AND STRIKES AND MR. BONNEY
WAS THE ONLY WIDE AWAKE POET PRESENT

"Say," asked Mr. McKenna, who had been reading the
paper. "What the divvle is folk-lore?"

"Di'lect pothry," replied Colonel McNeery promptly.
"If you was to put ye'er conversations in pothry, Jawn,

thim 'd be folk-lore an' ye'd be a folk-lorist. Ye have th'
hell's own di'lect, Jawn. Ye niver come fr'm Roscommon
in all ye'er born days. Ye'er farther down thin that.
Folk-lore's di'lect pothry, an' ghost stories an' talks iv
th' pookies[2] that made so much throuble with th' blue-
berries iv a halloween. They're folk-lore too. D'ye mind
the ya-arn O'Connor used to tell about his Uncle Aloysius that had th' rasslin match with th' ghost iv Red
Hugh O'Neill[3] near Clontarf?"

"I mind it well," said Mr. McKenna.

"Where th' ghost accused O'Connor's uncle iv pickin'
up th' mit he thrun away an' demanded him to give it
back because th' poor ghost couldn't cut his meat with
only wan dook," the colonel said. "Well, that's a folk-
lore."

"Faith, it may be," said Mr. McKenna, "but it always
looked like a whaling big lie to me."

"McKenna," replied the colonel, sententiously, "ye'er
a gom.[4] Ye know naw more about lithratoor than ye
know about th' catechism an' ye'er as innocint as iv that
as the unbaptized haythen. If ye cud've been down to

[2] pookies—in Irish folklore, supernatural creatures which assume the
shape of either horses or dogs and are usually black in color. Their
activity is generally restricted to breathing on ripe berries, rendering
them inedible.

[3] Red Hugh O'Neill—member of the O'Neill family, hereditary kings
of Ireland, later known as holders of the earldom of Tyrone. Together
with another Ulster man, Hugh O'Donnell of Tyrconnel, he fought
off the armies of Queen Elizabeth I for nine years. During this time
the two Hughs exported their brand of guerrilla warfare throughout
Ireland, and it has persisted to this day. In 1607, after the pacification
of Ireland, O'Neill was pardoned, but he found life in his captive homeland unbearable. He rounded up ninety-eight of his fellow chieftains
—the pride of Northern Ireland—and set sail for the Continent and
exile. By this action, they left Northern Ireland wide open for what
was called the "Plantation of Ireland," wherein the Irish who remained were forced off their lands and were supplanted by Scottish
Presbyterians and English Protestants. Thus, the seeds for the current
problem in Ulster were sown over three hundred years ago.

[4] gom—fool.

the lithry congress with me ye'd larned that truth in
a-art ain't got no more place than a pool check in a
temp'rance collection. There was a rooster there be the
names iv Charles Dudley Warner[5] that gave us that
song, an' faith, I'm thinkin' he's right. 'Th' wan aim,'
says Charles, 'in a-art,' he says, 'is th' beautiful. Naw
slang,' he says, 'or low people,' he says, 'but beautiful
conversation like them we larn'd in "Hickey's Christian
Dooty" under the hedge.' Ah-ha, he's th' boy f'r my
money, is Char-les. What th' 'ell do I care f'r low life an'
common people whin I picks up me fambly shtory
paper at night. Th' likes iv you an' th' likes iv me,
McKenna, wants princes and dooks an' kings an' pot-
tentates an' all th' world full iv flowers an' sunshine an'
music f'r our readin'. Did ye niver read 'Thadjus iv
Warsaw' Jawn? Iv coorse not. Faith, I might 've known
better than I've asked ye. Well, sir, there's my idale iv a
good smashin' book. There's nobody in there lower than
th' big casino. I'm not sure, but fr'm what I heard tell
I'm thinkin' me friend Charles Dudley wrote that there
book.

"I've been a hot sport this week. I taken in all th'
fash'nable shindigs—th' world's fair, th' prize fight an'
th' lithry congress. I've an inthrist in lithratoor an' me
frind Tiddy comes in an' he says, says he, 'Mack,' he
says, 'lam over with me to th' A-art Institutoot,' he says,
'an' see th' big guys in lithrachoor,' he says. 'All right,'
says I. 'I'll go ye,' I says. So we ups an' goes to th' A-art
Institutoot an' takes a seat with th' lads that has no cre-
dentials for to go on th' sta-age. I asks Tiddy about th'
guys above. 'What's that?' I says, pointin' out a gazabo

[5] Charles Dudley Warner—Warner (1829–1900) was a New England author, particularly of travel books. He collaborated with Mark
Twain on a novel, *The Gilded Age*. His style is best described as
pedestrian, and his favorite topic was the attainment of success without
any accompanying social values.

with long hair. 'That's Gilder,'[6] he says. 'He's a great pote.' 'Glory be to Gawd,' I says, 'is that so? What did he write?' 'Dam'd if I know,' says Tiddy. 'I niver know'd what he wrote, but he's a great pote.' 'An' who's th' duck next to him,' I says. 'That,' he says, 'is Charles Dudley Warner, th' famous novelist.' 'Dear, oh dear,' I says. 'An' what novel do th' poor man write?' 'He niver wrote no novels,' says Tiddy. 'He's an iditor,' he says. 'By gar,' I says, surprised. 'There's that cheeky Oogene Field[7] up there be th' sta-age,' I says. 'It bates th' divvle what nerve them rayporthers have,' I says. 'Gowan,' says he. 'He ain't no rayporther,' he says. 'He's a lithry guy,' he says. 'An' he writes pothry,' he says. 'Now hould ye'er head,' he says. 'They're off.'

"With that th' intertainment begins, an' faith, Jawnny, I niver see a poorer show in all th' days iv me life. Naw music, naw dancin', not even no pothry-makin', oney just a lot iv guys readin' papers in speakin' voices like a man readin' a tax list. Divvle a word about pothry. It was like a meetin' iv th' Bricklayers Union, it was, so it was, with all th' talk about how it takes th' poor potes an' grindin' thim down in th' ground. I says to Tiddy, I says, 'Musha, it's a little old Bill Shakespeare iver cared f'r th' coin,' I says. 'An' he cud write pothry

---

[6] Richard Watson Gilder—Gilder (1844–1909), quondam poet and editor of *Century Magazine,* a moderate reformer, as compared to his contemporaries of the muckrake pack.

[7] Dunne had met Eugene Field (1850–95) when both were on the staff of the Chicago *Daily News.* Dunne was just starting out and had great admiration for Field, whose column "Sharps and Flats" was well established, as was his reputation as a poet. Field had his own unique sense of humor. Once, when asked by the English novelist Mrs. Humphry Ward if he did not find that the social atmosphere in Chicago was too crude to furnish him with intellectual companionship, Field replied, "Really, Mrs. Ward, I do not consider myself competent to give an opinion on the matter. Please bear in mind that up to the time Barnum captured me and took me to Chicago to be civilized I had always lived in a tree in the wilds of Missouri."

like a wild man,' I says. 'Thrue f'r ye,' says Tiddy, who's
as close to Shakespeare as I am to this ice box, Jawn.

"Well, sir, be this an' be that, it turned out that there
were oney wan pote in th' whole house. An' in th' name
iv heaven who d'ye think it was? Bonney? Yis, yis, Divil
th' liss. That's him. Th' little lawyer. Th' little guy with
th' bunch iv whiskers. Oh dear, oh dear. Well, sir, if th'
pope iv Rome, Gawd f'rgive me f'r sayin' it, was to
come up that bar at this blissid moment an' ask f'r gin
an' bitthers, I'd be more taken aback. I niver knowed
Bonney was a pote; I thought he was more respectable.
But he read a pome, an' tho pothry ain't my long suit
savin' an' exciptin' Donnelly an' Cooper or Brinnin on
the Moor, or little Mickey Scanlan's pome, 'Th' Jacket
Green'—ye know it, Jawn; 'Arrah, whin down th' glin
rode Sarsfield's min an' they wear their jackets green'—
pothry's not a leg hould f'r me, but by gar I like Bon-
neys pothry. Listen.

" 'Th' splendid city built at Jackson Pa-ark,' he says
" 'To house,' he says, 'th' gathered treasure iv th'
world!

" 'Must pass away, but reproduced in books,' he says
" 'Th' wondhrous forms in beauty an' iv use'
" 'Which there,' he says, 'exotic amazements an'
delight'
" 'Shall put on immorality too (begar, that's wrong)
immortality and take,' says he
" 'Their lasting place in human hist'ry,' says Bonney.
" 'Well,' I says to Tiddy, 'that's a dam'd fine article iv
pothry,' I says. 'It sounds almost like prose,' I says. 'It is
prose,' says Tiddy. 'Then,' says I, 'divvil a bit the worse
it is for that,' says I. So we ups and goes to the prize
fight.

"Well," said the colonel thoughtfully, "Bonney is a
good pote, but there do be no lilies on Solly Smith either."

7

It is impossible to know why Colonel McNeery could be as flippant as he was about the very serious panic of 1893; perhaps he was a precursor of the University of Chicago school of economic thought. It is more likely, though, that he was able to joke about it because the full severity of the depression did not hit Chicago until the following year, partly because of the jobs and activity generated by the World's Columbian Exposition.

The first intimation of the coming disaster occurred in 1890, when the failure of Baring Brothers, a prominent London banking firm, forced foreigners holding American stocks and bonds to liquidate them and curtailed the availability of foreign investment capital in the United States. Gold prices in the world market began falling dramatically in 1891, while prices and income remained at approximately the same level. Because of mounting pressure from silver supporters in the United States and the possibility of victory by the free silver forces, there was growing uncertainty both at home and abroad that the country would remain on the gold standard, so that confidence in the dollar as a stable currency fluctuated sharply.

By 1892 the United States Treasury surplus (the excess of revenues over expenditures) had all but disappeared, and gold reserves were shrinking at an alarming pace. In a last ditch effort to postpone disaster, at least until after he left office, in January 1893 President Benjamin Harrison and his Secretary of the Treasury, Charles Foster, persuaded some New York banks to swap $6 million in gold for paper. When Grover Cleveland was inaugurated two months later, he found himself left with a gold reserve of only $100,982,410. The panic began in earnest in April, when United States gold reserves fell below the rock-bottom, essential minimum of $100 million, causing people to lose confidence in the safety (and, some felt, the wisdom) of the gold standard. This happened at least in part because of the considerable outflow needed to pay for a steadily increasing level of imports. Also, the Sherman Silver Purchase Act of 1890 required the federal government to acquire twice as much silver per month as was previously the case and to issue Treasury notes, which while based on silver, had to be redeemed in gold.

Although these were the immediate causes and results, there is some evidence that the hard times had their beginning much earlier, in the 1880s. The agricultural areas of the West and South were in serious trouble following several years of drought and crop failures: there was a steady lessening of investment capital from the East and of purchasing power. This meant that businesses which based their success on dealing in the farm markets went into a steady decline. It was during the eighties that the nation saw the rise of the great trusts, of the continent-crossing railroads, and the rapid growth of major cities. All of these factors helped dry up the nation's investment resources.

By October 1893 eight thousand businesses, with liabilities of $285 million, had gone under. Even such railroad giants as the Union Pacific, the Northern Pacific, and the Erie went into receivership—a total of 156 railroad companies alone. Over four hundred banks, primarily in the South and out West, failed too.

So, while the diversity of industry held the panic at bay for a while, hard times were just around the corner for Chicago. By December 1893 thousands of men were without jobs; while Chicago was rapidly becoming a feast for the eyes (if you were careful where you looked), with the White City, the new public library and the Art Institute, shop girls went hungry. Because they had no place else to go, the unemployed took to sleeping on the floors and in the stairwells of City Hall; it got so bad that if you had offi-

cial business to transact, it was virtually impossible to walk
down the aisles without treading on your homeless fellow
citizens. While prices and rents remained at their prepanic
levels, wages plummeted and many could find no work at
all.

CHICAGO *SUNDAY POST*, August 6, 1893

HARD TIMES THESE

COLONEL MC NEERY SEES MANY SIGNS
OF A MONETARY STRINGENCY

LACE ON MANY MEN'S TROUSERS
EVEN THAYDOOR THOMAS HAS TO SUCCUMB

THE POPULAR CONCERT AND THE IMPOLITE LADY

"No," said Colonel McNeery to the poet, "I can lind
ye no money. Th' financial stringency have become so
ser'ous a matther that I'm thinkin' iv rayjoocin' th'
amount iv cheese in th' bowl an' liquidatin' all out-
shtandin' tea. I am that. Did ye niver see annything as
singlar as this here panic? A few months ago iverybody
had th' rowly-bowlys.[8] There did be long green
shtickin' out iv vest pockets an' men 'd drink nawthin'
but champagny an' ate nawthin but cold turkey. Now
look at it. The same men does be lammin' up th' sthreet
with lace curtains on th' buttoms of their pa-ants an' th'
sheriff afther thim with a writ. I see a man yisterday
settin' over in Mr. Coalsack's atin' wheat ca-akes an'
coffee come along that last winter chewed up be th'
Richaloo[9] off chiny plates an' picked his teeth after th'
meal with a silver fork.

"An' what's it all about? What's it all about? Well,
sir, a panic's a hard thing for to understand. Now

[8] rowly-bowlys—money; sometimes used to mean graft.
[9] Richaloo—the Richelieu Hotel, an elegant watering place in downtown Chicago.

there's just as much money as ever there was, an' more, too, with th' governmint turnin' it out ivery day, not to speak iv thim Indiana preachers that can make a gold dollar out iv a piece iv lid pipe an' a pane iv windyglass. There's plinty iv coin and plinty iv ways of spindin' it. But somebody says: 'Dear, oh dear,' he says. 'Th' country's on th' brink iv roon.' The man next to him on th' ca-ar says: 'By gar! maybe th' boy's right,' an' off he goes an' soaks his dough away in th' bureau drawer along with his marridge license. Thin what's th' raysult? A panic. An' nobody gets anny th' best iv it but th' burglars that breaks in an steals.

"I heerd th' other day that me old friend Jawn Cuddy[10] was on th' r-run. They've been callin' him Coodyhie since he got th' money, but I'll bet it will be Cuddy now he's broke. 'Well,' I says, 'I'll go down to th' boord iv thrade an' see him go broke,' I says. An' with that I up to th' boord and sits in th' gallery an' puts me feet on th' railin'. The crazy lads was dancin' around on th' flure an' shakin' their fists under each others' noses like as if 'twas a wist town convention. I don't hear nothin' about Cuddy, I says. Thin a man that looked like a Jew man be his name an' talked like wan too, for he had th' divil's own accint, turns to me an' yells 'Boots,' and ivery man on th' flure stops fightin' an' points to me an' says 'Boots,' an' though I was wearing paytent lither ties I ups an' laves thim. An' I hear no more about Cuddy till a man come into th' place an' says, 'Cuddy's gawn.'

"Well, sir, ye cud've hit me with a feather. I thought th' Ba-ank iv England was no safer. But it plazed me to see th' way he wint, Tiddy. No pikin' out, now mind ye, but a bold play in pyrytechnics like th'

[10] Jawn Cuddy—John Cudahy was a member of the family of Michael Cudahy (1841–1910), an Irishman who founded a large meat-packing establishment which suffered during the depression.

last an' biggest wan in th' blissid Fourth iv July. A thrue
Irishman that Cuddy. He failed like hell an' all. I was
minded iv a shtory be th' failure. 'Twas about a mort
man that wint up a ladder with his hod twenty stories.
An' whin he got to th' top be reason iv an extra can he'd
taken at noon, he slipped his hould an' fill. Now, a
Dutchman would've hollered murther, but th' brave
mort man, he cried out: 'Oh, Mike!' 'What is it,
Terence?' says the bricklayer up above, peerin' over th'
wall. 'Here goes f'r a ha– iv a boomp, annyhow,' says th'
brave mort man. So be Cuddy. There was as much
diff'rence baytune his failure an' other failures as there
is baytune a man fallin' off the Auditorum an' off a
cable car. Just as much, faith.

"Even Thaydor Thomas[11] be affected by th' shtrin-
gency. I thought f'r a while there was no man under
Crozes cud touch Thaydoor. It lucked as if William
Vanderbilt 'd be around askin' Thaydoor for a handout.
Five thousand f'r music an' five thousand f'r instru-
ments an' five thousand for the use of his librey, when
anny kid can get a ticket at th' public librey for
nawthin', an' read *Thaddeus of Warsaw* an' *Th' Children iv th' Abbey;* then to say, nawthin' iv a bit iv
dough here an' there fr'm minin' a lot iv dough fr'm

[11] Thaydor Thomas—The conductor Theodore Thomas (1835–
1905) had been trying to introduce Chicago to classical music for a
number of years. In fact, on the day of the great Chicago Fire,
Thomas, together with his trainload of musicians were on the way to
play at Crosby's Opera House that evening. The train was turned
back at Twenty-second Street because of the intense heat. After many
visits to the city, he moved to Chicago to form a symphony in 1890.
When friends tried to dissuade him from moving to so uncultured a
metropolis, he replied, "I would go to hell if they would give me a
permanent orchestra." No one thought the analogy inept. His first
concerts were not successful, being too sophisticated for local tastes.
He then resorted to staging popular concerts, at the same time sneaking in a full symphony or a less-known composer. Despite Colonel
McNeery's reaction, Thomas' staging of Wagner proved surprisingly
successful with the public.

men that makes harps an' piannies. Why, the man was makin' more money than if he had a die an' stamp for to do business with. An' what for? I see out be th' door in th' hall where his band plays th' other day, an' it says: 'Pop'lar concert.' 'Well,' says I, 'that gets me,' I says, an' in I goes. What do they pla-ay? Well, sir, Tiddy, I was so far from knowin' what they was playin' I cuddent even read the names to th' pieces. There was three or four Dutchman beltin' away at drums, an' three or four sawin' away at th' fiddles, an' a guy with black whiskers blowin' a horn and none of thim payin' any heed to th' others, but ivry man f'r himself an' th' conductor havin' no more influence on thim than a referee in a football game. I turns to th' lady nixt to me an' says: 'What are they playin',' I says. 'Gotterdammerung,' says she, a fine looking lady, too, with specs. 'Well,' says I. 'Ye was badly brought up to say it,' I says. 'Ye was badly brought up to say it,' I says, 'but ye'er right,' and I goes."

8

The column that follows is virtually the only one where Dunne came to the defense of President Grover Cleveland. The irony of the situation is that the rumors were true, and Cleveland did in fact have cancer. It was many years, however, before the true story came out.

Cleveland hoped to restore public confidence in U.S. currency, which had suffered badly as a result of the depression and panic of 1893. He believed that the way to do this was to repeal the Sherman Silver Purchase Act, which required the Treasury to buy silver at market price, pay for it by issuing new notes, and store it as bullion. As a result, he decided to call a special session of Congress to repeal the Act. At the same time, he discovered that he had a cancerous growth on the roof of his mouth that also affected the bone and soft palate. An immediate operation was mandatory, but Cleveland was fearful that public knowledge of his illness would lead to a run on gold, particularly since his Vice President, Adlai E. Stevenson, was a silver man. To assure utmost secrecy, it was given out that the President was going on a yachting trip, and the operation was performed on the boat of a friend while it sailed up the East River off New York City. Despite all these efforts, there were widespread rumors that he was seriously, and even mortally, ill. It took the wholehearted lying of those who were in on the secret and the President's appearance on shore five days after the operation to quiet things down. Cleveland endured incredible pain in his attempts to carry on in a normal fashion by meeting regularly with congressional leaders and making public appearances. He eventually made a good recovery, but his friends felt he was never quite the same man after it.

CHICAGO *EVENING POST*, September 2, 1893

LEAVE GROVER ALONE

COLONEL MC NEERY SAYS THE PRESIDENT SHOULDN'T BE BOTHERED SUPPOSE HE HAS TOOTHACHE

THE NEWSPAPERS MAKE OUR STATESMEN PAY TOO HEAVY A PENALTY FOR FAME, SAYS THE COLONEL

"Fame to be a gr-reat thing," said Colonel McNeery, after he had put the paper away in a drawer where he could get it again when trade became slack. "If it wasn't f'r fame there'd be manny a rayporther that's dancin' around nowadays with his little pincil an' his wad iv paaper ma-akin' notes that'd be out be Jackson Park runnin' a push chair an' it'd be better f'r thim an' better for the world, too, if they were all in that implyment 'stid iv ma-akin' life a burden f'r taxpayers with shaky nerves.

"Now, suppose you or me, Jawn, had a toothache—

which Gawd forbid—would there be annything in th' pa-
apers about it? Would we pick up th' *Fried Press* or th'
A-arbeiter Zeitung in th' mornin' an' r-read: 'Special
despatch. Jawn McKenna's face gives him gr-reat pain.
'Tis feared he will have to have it pulled.' Faith, no. Ye
might have a jaw on ye as big as a toy balloon an' ne'er
a rayporther 'd luk twict at ye. But there's Big Steve, I
calls him, not to be disrayspectful, on'y to show that
we're on good terms—here's Big Steve, poor man, day-
vilops lumpy jaw an' calls in th' dintist an' has a tooth
pulled an' th' papers comes out an' prints th' divil's own
annydotes about it an' interviews th' dintist man, an'
before we have th' ind iv it 'twill be his head or his a-arm
or his leg that was pulled, tho, from all accounts, 'twud
be a strong man that cud do that last—a dam strong man.

"Why can't they lave th' poor man alone? Here he is
sittin' down at the breakfast table atin' his dish of codfish balls, and his gums do be sore annyhow, an' he pick
up a pa-aper. 'Grover Cleveland have cancer,' says th'
pa-aper. 'Th' 'ell he has,' says Grover. 'An' who tol' ye?'
'Th' truth has been kept from th' prisidint but 'tis a fact
larned be ye'er cawr'spondent that while undher th' influence iv ga-as a large two-be-four cancer was ray-
moved fr'm his head,' says th' pa-aper. Thin he throws it
down an' puts his fut on it an' goes into his breakfast.
Well, sir, afther a while th' jaw iv him do begin to ache
an' he thinks iv what he read in th' pa-aper an' he says,
says he: 'Maybe that dam'd story was right an' I do have
cancer.' An' th' more he thinks about it, th' more he believes he's got cancer that's atin' th' head off him an' he
can't fish no more, an' he can't sleep, an' he wants to lick
th' kid whin it cries, an' finally, says he, bein' a dahrin'
man, he says: 'If I'm gawn to die,' he says, 'I'll die in th'
harness,' he says, an' back he goes to Washington an'
finds Frankie Lawler sittin' on th' front porch with a pe-
tition in his mitt an' says Grover: 'It niver rains but it
pours,' says he.

"Now for what do they cross th' good man? Because a
toothache is a sinsation? No, faith. 'Tis fame does it all.
If he was livin' in Buffalo today atin' mutton golosh an'
dhrinkin' th' pilsner out iv a standpipe in a Garman
saloon it's thim that'd take no more notice iv his toothache thin if 'twas O'Connor's head there that was
swelled. Dam'd th' bit. They're caterin' to th' public,
says ye? Well, maybe they are. But what th' divil wud th'
public know about it if th' pa-apers didn't print it. You
pick up a paper nowadays and it says: 'Congressman
Simpson have no socks on his feet'; 'Congressman Du-
borow have discarded woolen underwear an' now wears
suits in pale yellow silk'; ''Tis said on good authority
that Congressman McGann is extremely fond iv wather-
millon.' What th' 'ell good is that? Can't a man lave off
his suspenders without having a rayporther lift up his
coattails f'r to see how he maintains his pants? Sure, a
man ought to have some rights av'n if he is a congressman, an' it don't make no difference to you or to me,
Jawn, whether he wipes his nose on th' tail iv his coat or
on a lace handkerchief, so long as he votes right on th'
silver question an' gets his constitooents jobs in th' post
office an' th' custom house an' on th' bridges, an' does his
duty by th' counthry."

"I see," said Mr. McKenna, "that th' *Eagle* has a picture of you and some anecdotes of your life."

"Ye don't tell me," said the colonel. "I must get it. It's
some iv Donovan's work. I've known Hawry for twenty
years, an' he's a fine lad an' a good friend iv mine."

9

The McNeery articles were so well received that they were
used in the advertisements for the *Sunday Post*. When that
paper proved unprofitable, the columns were continued in
the Saturday edition of the *Evening Post*. One reader who

did not enjoy them was Colonel James McGarry, who felt
that they were an insult to him. In *Mr. Dooley at His Best*,
published in 1938, Dunne recalled:

I was going on well and enjoying myself until one afternoon when I happened in at Jim McGarry's. My
friend scarcely spoke to me. I tried various topics of
conversation. He would have none of them. Suddenly
he shook his finger under my nose.

"You can't put printer's ink on me with impunity," he
cried.

"But Jim, What have I done?"

"I'll see ye'er boss, young man. I'll see Jawn R.
(Walsh, the owner of the *Post*)," he said and turned
away.

He also visited McAuliff, the managing editor. With
tears running down his cheeks, he said, "Now, Mack,
mind ye now, here I am r-runnin' me little dacint business an' heedin' no wan an' this here pa-aper comes out
iv a Saturdah night, an', by dad, I don't dare to go
home. Me fam'ly won't let me in, an' I've had to sleep
downtown ivry Saturdah since ye began to write me
up."

Sure enough, the next day I had a visit from John R.
Walsh, the banker who owned the *Chicago Herald* and
the *Evening Post*. I knew him well and liked him, even
if he was a pirate overpunished through President
Taft's malignant hatred of him. Walsh said he had a
favor to ask of me. I knew at once what it was.

"Jim McGarry has been to see you," I said.

"That's it," said my Boss. "You know the old fellow is
broken up over those McNeery articles. His friends are
laughing at him. Can't you change the name?"

So Colonel McNeery was sent back to Ireland in September 1893, and the stage was set for the arrival of Mr.
Dooley.

CHICAGO *EVENING POST*, September 30, 1893

COL. M'NEERY'S AWAY

HE WENT TO IRELAND AND LEFT
MR. MCKENNA DISCONSOLATE

THE BIG POLICEMAN CHEERS HIM

OFFICER ROWAN DISCOURSES ON IRISH DAY,
THE WEATHER AND VARIOUS OTHER TOPICS

"Jawnny," said Officer Stephen Rowan, as Mr. McKenna strolled up to where the big policeman was standing under the icewater statue of Columbus. "Ye look all broke up. What ails ye, man alive?"

"Nothing," said Mr. McKenna. "Except I'm lonesome now that Colonel McNeery has gone away."

"Sure, 'tis reason enough," said Mr. Rowan, "that ye'd be down in th' mouth, f'r close companions ye've been for these long years. Will he come back, he will? No? Thin 'tis you that'll miss him, for a fine big man he was, though I niver liked a hair in his head from th' moment I set eyes on him. He was a most sarcastic man, that there McNeery, an' no love had he f'r anny but thim that come from th' same dirty little parish with him. 'Tis not so with me, Jawn. I'm a thorough naytionalist, I am that, an' ne'er a man come fr'm Connock but I'd take him by th' hand, barrin' thim Mayo horsethiefs that Micky Garrity had corraled over be th' twenty-third ward. 'Tis not the likes iv me that'd be speakin' to th' likes iv thim if Ireland was never free.

"So th' old boy has gone back to th' dart. Well, musha, I wish him luck, an' between th' doods on th' corners an' th' weight of this here stick iv timber, manny a time I've been dhriven to wish I was home again where I come from, with a mud wall at me back an' a roof iv rushes over th' head iv me an' a great pot-

ful iv petaties boilin' in th' turf fire, an' maybe to make
the whole thing good, th' tinent next dure bein' thrun
out f'r not payin' rint. Not that our fam'ly had lived
much on petaties, Jawn. Don't think that f'r a minyit,
me la-ad. I had an uncle that died iv overeatin' reed
burruds,[12] I had, so I had. But this sportin' life over here
is killin' me be inches, with its lobsters ally Newburg
an' th' rist iv th' conthraptions. I'd give the eye out iv
me head to be back with McNeery, cross an old cow as
he was. By gar, he'll be th' 'ell's own man, won't he
though. Th' car men 'll take off their hats to him and th'
little gossoons 'll chase him down th' sthreet beggin' f'r
dough, an' th' parish priest 'll invite him to dinner, an'
maybe, by gar, he'll go to parlyment. Ye may take me
f'r a sixty-day man, if I wudden't give me life to see
McNeery makin' a speech to th' ol' queen. 'Twould be
no tin to wan he wudden't begin with, 'Mind ye now,'
an' conclude with, 'An' what's yours?' Thim was always
long favorites iv McNeery.

"But why didn't th' man stay home f'r Irish Day?[13]
Sure, barrin' th' shortness iv it, I'd as soon be at th' fair
tomorrow as I wud home. Ivrybody'll be there. Th' lord
mayor, with th' chain around his neck, proud man he is
iv th' chain. I ain't seen th' like iv it since Colonel
Cleary got away. Th' lord mayor 'll be there, an' that
quare lukin' man they calls a Irish tory he fetched over
with him, an' th' ex-mimber fr'm Tipperary, an' Gawd
knows who all else includin' Patsy Brannigan an'
Jawnny Shea. An' Finerty.[14] Aha, Finerty'll be there, no

[12] reed burruds—turkeys.
[13] Irish Day—at the World's Columbian Exposition.
[14] Finerty—Long John Finerty (1846–1908) was a Galway man of
colorful habits. After immigrating to the U.S. from Ireland, where he
did his best to make the English uncomfortable, he came to Chicago
and served as city editor of the Chicago *Republican*. He also went on
several expeditions against the Sioux and Northern Cheyenne in the
1870s and 1880s as a war correspondent, and he deserves to be re-

less, an' mark me well, McKenna, if there do be anything iv the British Blue lift whin Jawn Finerty gets
thru 'twill not be enough to be worth sendin' home. I'm
goin' down there if I have a leg to stand on an' join in
th' exercises. Th' Irishman that'll stay away is what th'
pome says that Honora Doolan recites, d'ye mind.
'Cowards and dastards clear th' way, knaves an' traitors
faugh a ballagh.[15] We'll all be there sittin' in peace an'
concord, an' if iver a man says ill iv Charles Stewart
Parnell[16] I'll poke him in th' eye if I die f'r it. No Dutch

---

membered for his accounts of these missions if for nothing else. Finerty served in the United States Congress where he was a thorough-
going and unabashed Irish nationalist. When queried as to whether
anything important had transpired on a particular day in the House
of Representatives, he replied, "No, nothing but damned American
business today."

[15] Faugh a ballagh—Gaelic for "clear the way" or "make a passage."

[16] Charles Stewart Parnell (1846–91) was perhaps the greatest
Irish leader of the nineteenth century. From a Protestant landowner
family, he was also the grandson of an American commodore who
fought the British in 1812. He was elected to Parliament in 1875 and
quickly became a champion of the Land League and chairman of the
Irish Parliamentary Party. Irish farmers were desperate over the
"rack rent" system and sometimes organized into secret societies to
murder landlords who evicted tenants and any farmers who succeeded
to the land. Parnell showed them a better way to handle such men.
He said, "Shun him on the roadside when you meet him; shun him
in the shop; shun him in the fair green and in the market place and
even in the place of worship . . . as if he were a leper of old." The
new method was first employed in 1880 against a Captain Charles
Boycott in County Mayo and was so effective that a new word came
into the language. As a result of these and other Parnell-directed activities, Parliament passed a land act ameliorating some of the worst
practices. British political realities and Parnell's brilliant leadership
brought home rule for Ireland ever closer to reality. Parnell visited
America to raise support and money and even addressed a joint session of Congress. He was a handsome, charismatic man, a tremendous
favorite with the American Irish. Then suddenly, in 1889, tragedy
struck. Parnell was named corespondent in a divorce suit brought by
Willie O'Shea, a former Irish M.P. The suit was undefended; it became common knowledge that Parnell had been living with O'Shea's
wife, Katharine, for some years (apparently with O'Shea's acquies-
cence). The divorce was granted in 1890 and Parnell married the

need apply tomorrow. Did ye see about th' Dutchman
over in Gilbert's office circulatin' a pettyshun agin
closin th' office f'r Irish Day. Well, sir, th' audacity iv
thim furners does bate th' divvle.

"Well, I hope ye'll have a good day," said Mr.
McKenna.

"Thru the goodness of Gawd we will, we will," said
the policeman confidently.

"How do you know all that?"

"Whisper," said Mr. Rowan, leaning over his friend,
"it rained on the diputies day."

Which shows how little reliance can be placed on
omens.

---

lady, but the storm crashed down upon him. His party and the Catholic hierarchy denounced him. Only the staunchest of the revolution-
aries in Ireland and America (including Long John Finerty in
Chicago) remained loyal to him. Beaten in three by-elections and
worn out with the struggle, he died less than a year later. According
to William Butler Yeats, "The modern literature of Ireland and indeed
all that stir of thought which prepared for the Anglo-Irish war began
when Parnell fell from power in 1891. A disillusioned and embittered
Ireland turned from parliamentary politics; an event was conceived,
and a race began, to be troubled by that event's long gestation."

II

Introducing Martin J. Dooley and Life on Archey Road

Leaving downtown Dearborn Street and McGarry's bar behind him, Dunne made several forays out into Bridgeport with John McKenna and decided to locate the saloon of one Martin J. Dooley on Archey Road (Chicago's Archer Avenue). Bridgeport was a more likely location for Dunne's protagonist than the more sophisticated Loop; although not as totally Irish as it had been, the Celts remained, in Dooley's words, the master race in the Sixth Ward. The change of location and character gave Dunne more room in which to maneuver; the people there ranged from so-called shanty Irish to the lace-curtain variety. (Fred Allen once defined lace-curtain Irish as "people who have fruit in the house when no one is sick.") If there was a specific person upon whom Dunne modeled Dooley, Dunne never admitted it, and it is far more likely that Dooley was a composite of a number of Irishmen Dunne had known since childhood.

In a newspaper interview in 1895, confirming to Chicago readers that he was the author of the Dooley columns, as many had suspected, Peter Dunne admitted that he wrote the Dooley essays with love. Although his creature was often depicted in cartoons as a sort of stage Irishman, Dunne maintained that he had drawn his inspiration from the real Irish Americans, the greenhorns of Bridgeport. He described them as philosophic, gentle, kindly, shrewd, and witty. He applauded their involvement in the issues of the day, despite their tendency to stay in their own tight little neighborhood, their support for the Church, their devotion to their families, and their loyalty to the Democratic Party. "This is the type . . . I endeavor to photograph. I do not need to embellish him or paint him other than he is. The Irishman has ever suffered from caricature."

What do we know about Dooley himself? He was balding, and what hair he had was reddish. He was of sturdy build, somewhat given to "embinpint." He was perennially sixty-five and had been in the saloon business at least ten years when the columns began. He had come over steerage from Ireland in his youth (indeed, there is a record of a Martin Dooley who stowed away on a ship at Ballyshannon, huddling in a provision locker; as a result, he had to have both legs amputated when the ship reached Boston). Our Martin Dooley was a Roscommon man who got his start in this country working on various railroads, and when he found that was not to his liking he turned to driving drays in Chicago. At one time he had a brilliant career as a precinct captain in the local Democratic machine, but he gave it all up when he opened his saloon.

2

Archey Road stretches back for many miles from the heart of an ugly city to the cabbage gardens that gave the maker of the Chicago seal his opportunity to call the city *"urbs in horto."* Somewhere between the two—that is to say, forninst th' gashouse and beyant Healey's slough and not far from the polis station—lives Martin J. Dooley, doctor of philosophy.

There was a time when Archey Road was purely Irish. But the Huns, turned back from the Adriatic and the stockyards and overrunning Archey Road, have nearly exhausted the original population—not driven them out as they drove out less vigorous races, with thick clubs and short spears, but edged them out with the more biting weapons of modern civilization—overworked and undereaten them into more languid surroundings remote from the tanks of the gashouse and the blast furnaces of the rolling mill.

But Mr. Dooley remains, and enough remain with him to save Archey Road. In this community you can hear all the various accents of Ireland, from the awkward brogue of the "far-downer" to the mild and aisy Elizabethan English of the southern Irishman, and all the exquisite variations to be heard between Armagh and Bantry Bay, with the difference that would naturally arise from substituting cinders and sulphuretted hydrogen for peat smoke and soft misty air. Here also you can see the wakes and christenings, the marriages and funerals, and the other fetes of the ol' counthry somewhat modified and darkened by American usage. The banshee has been heard many times in Archey Road. On the eve of All Saints' Day it is well known that here alone the pookies play thricks in cabbage gardens. In 1893 it was reported that Malachi Dempsey was called "by the other people" and disappeared west of the tracks and never came back.

A simple people. "Simple, says ye!" remarked Mr. Dooley. "Simple like th' air or th' deep sea. Not complicated like a watch that stops whin th' shoot iv clothes ye got it with wears out. Whin Father Butler wr-rote a book he niver finished, he said simplicity was not wearin' all ye had on ye'er shirt-front, like a tin-horn gambler with his di'mon stud. An' 'tis so."

The barbarians around them are moderately but firmly governed, encouraged to passionate votings for the ruling race, but restrained from the immoral pursuit of office.

The most generous, thoughtful, honest, and chaste people in the world are these friends of Mr. Dooley—knowing and innocent; moral, but giving no heed at all to patented political moralities.

Among them lives and prospers the traveler, archaeologist, historian, social observer, saloonkeeper, economist, and philosopher, who has not been out of the ward for twenty-five years "but twict." He reads the newspapers with solemn care, heartily hates them, and accepts all they print for the sake of drowning Hennessy's rising protests against his logic. From the cool heights of life on Archey Road, uninterrupted by the jarring noises of crickets and cows, he observes the passing show and meditates thereon. His impressions are transferred to the desensitized plate of Mr. Hennessy's mind, where they can do no harm.

"There's no betther place to see what's goin' on thin the Ar-rchey Road," says Mr. Dooley. "Whin th' ilicthric cars is hummin' down th' sthreet an' th' blast goin' sthrong at th' mills, th' noise is that gr-reat ye can't think."—Finley Peter Dunne in his own introduction to *Mr. Dooley in Peace and in War.*

And so Mr. Dooley makes his debut.

CHICAGO *EVENING POST*, October 7, 1893

UP IN ARCHEY ROAD
JOHN MC KENNA VISITS HIS OLD FRIEND MARTIN DOOLEY
NEWS OF BRIDGEPORT SOCIETY
THE MISADVENTURES OF MLLE. GROGAN AND M. RILEY
A GERMAN BAND AND ITS IRISH TUNES

Business was dull in the liquor-shop of Mr. Martin Dooley in Archey road last Wednesday night and Mr. Dooley was sitting back in the rear of the shop holding a newspaper at arm's length before him and reading the sporting news. In came Mr. John McKenna. Mr. McKenna has been exceedingly restless since Colonel McNeery went home to Ireland and on his way out to Brighton Park for consolation he bethought himself of

Martin Dooley. The lights were shining in the little tavern and the window decorations—green festoons, a single sheet poster of a Parnell[1] meeting in McCormick's Hall, and a pyramid of bottles filled with Medford rum and flies—evoked such cheery recollections of earlier years that Mr. McKenna hopped off the car and entered briskly.

"Good evening, Martin," he said.

"Hellow, Jawnny," replied Mr. Dooley, as if they had parted only the evening before. "How's thricks? I don't mind, Jawnny, if I do. 'Tis duller here than a ray-publican primary in the fourth wa-ard, th' night. Sure, ye're like a ray iv sunlight, ye are that. There's been no company in these pa-arts since Dominick Riley's big gossoon[2] was took up be th' polis. . . . What was he tuk up fur, says ye? Faith, I'll never tell ye. Th' polis had a gredge again him, like as not. I belave they do say he kilt a Chiney man, an' I'll not put it beyant him, f'r he is a wild lad no less, an' wan that'd carry th' joke to anny len'th.

"Dint know where ye've been all these days, man alive. I ain't seen ye, Jawn dear, since ye led th' gr-rand march in Finucane's Hall this tin years past. D'ye mind th' Grogan girls? Aha, amusha, I see ye do, ye cute man. An' well ye might. Th' oldest wan—Birdie she called hersel' in thim days though she was christened Bridget, an' I knowed it dam well, f'r I was at th' christenin', an' got this here scar on me nut f'rm an unruly Clare man that Jawnny Shea brung over with him—th' oldest one danced with ye, an' five years afterward her husband found in her pocket book a ca-ard sayin' 'Vote f'r Jawn McKinna' an' he was f'r suin' f'r a divorce, by gar, he

---

[1] Charles Stewart Parnell, who died in 1891, made several trips to the United States, including visits to Chicago, during the 1880s, so the poster would have to be at least five years old.

[2] gossoon—a corruption of the French garçon, meaning "boy."

was. She said ye give her a lot iv thim for to take home
to th' old man an' she on'y kept th' wan. An' ye haven't
seen her fr'm that day to this! Oh dear, oh dear! How
soon forgot we are! It's little ye think iv Bridgeport
whin ye'er gallopin' aroun' to wakes an' christenin's
with Potther Pammer and Hobart What th' 'ell's his
name Taylor.[8]

"I thought f'r to see ye at Irish Day. I dunnaw how I
missed ye. Did ye iver see th' like iv it? Rain, rain, rain
and dhrip, dhrip, dhrip. They used to be a sayin' at
home whin it was a clear day: 'It's a fine day, plaze
Gawd,' an' whin it rained cats an' dogs an' pokers: 'It's
a fine day f'r th' counthry.' An' mind ye, Jawn, I won't
deny it might be said last Sathedah with no ha-arm
done. Ye cuddent have got three hundhred thousan'
Irishmen together on a fine day without thim breakin'
loose. Th' rain kipt thim fr'm gettin' enthusiastic an'
by gar, f'r th' first time in th' histhry iv th' wurruld they
got thim in peace an' harmony. They was united in de-
nouncin' th' diputy f'r weather an' th' gazaboy that
pulled down th' flag. If they knowed it before they did
that, Orangey's 'd be orderin' lemonades in th' place
where Orangeys go through th' mercy of Gawd."

"I suppose you spent th' day in th' Irish village," suggested Mr. McKenna.

"Well, Jawn, to tell ye no lie," said Mr. Dooley, "an'
don't whisper it to Finerty if you meet him at th' nex'
sore-ree, but I didn't. I got mesilf fixed in a chair at th'
Dutch village, an' by gar, ne'er a fut I stirred fr'm it th'
livelong day. 'Twas most comfortin' an' th' band
played ivry Irish tune from 'Rambler fr'm Clare' to
'Connock's Man's Dhream,' on'y mind ye, with a slight
accint. There was wan lad that played th' ol' song,

[8] Potther Pammer and Hobart . . . Taylor—Potter Palmer and
Henry Hobart Taylor were leading Chicago businessmen and civic
lights.

'A-ha Limerick is Beautiful' an' a sweet ol' song it is, to be sure. Gawd forgive me f'r sayin' so, that hates a 'butthermilk.'[4] He played it without an accint, an' whin he come down, thinkin' he might be wan iv us, says I: 'Cunas thantu,'[5] I says. Well, sir, what d'ye think he replies? What d'ye think th' bpoor bosthoon replies? He says: 'Wee gates.'[6] Wee gates, he says, Jawn, or may I never stir fr'm th' spot. Well, sir, I laughed in his face. I did, I did.

"An' a-are ye gown, Jawn dear? How about thim two bowls? That's right. Twinty-five to you, Jawn. Good night an' th' Lord be between ye an' har-rm."

3

In this article Dooley bemoans the common fate of all barkeeps—having to listen to other people and render opinions and advice. It is difficult to believe that he does not really enjoy it, except perhaps once in a while when a highly emotional issue, such as the Cronin-Coughlin case, hits Archey Road and he is reluctant to take sides for fear of offending half of his clientele.

In fact, as explained at length in the Introduction, the solution of the Cronin murder case in 1889 was one of Finley Peter Dunne's greatest beats when he was working as a reporter. The Clan-na-Gael, an Irish nationalist secret society organized in 1869 after the failure of the Fenian invasion of Canada in 1866, unfortunately came to be manipulated by politicians for reasons of their own. John Devoy of New

[4] butthermilk—a derogatory term applied against men from Limerick. They were supposed to have the same characteristics as buttermilk—dull, wishy-washy, and tasteless.

[5] Cunas thantu—Gaelic for "How are you?".

[6] Wee gates—Dooley's rendering of the German *"Wie geht's?"* for the same question.

York was one of the original leaders, and he got into a wrangle with Alexander Sullivan of Chicago, who was responsible for the Clan's finances and whose handling of funds was questionable. The Clan leadership managed to keep this out of the newspapers but it left two warring factions—those supporting Sullivan and those who supported Devoy. In Chicago Sullivan was opposed by John Patrick Cronin, a doctor and a friend of Devoy. The struggle for control of the Clan continued until one day Cronin was summoned to make a house call. He never returned from it. Initially, no one paid much attention to the doctor's disappearance, accepting other explanations for his absence. When Cronin's body was found, public interest rose.

Dunne was covering the case and became so involved that breaking it became almost an obsession with him. He knew all of the principals and was well connected in Irish nationalist circles, as well as with the police department and some members of the Chicago underworld. Acting on a series of tips, he discovered that the policeman handling the investigation, Daniel Coughlin, had been in on the slaying. The mayor and chief of police were apprised of the situation, and Coughlin was arrested along with three other men and charged with the crime. One was acquitted; Coughlin and the other two were sentenced to life in prison. All of this happened in 1889.

The verdict discussed here was Coughlin's acquittal after a retrial had been ordered by a higher court. Upon release, Coughlin went to work in Alexander Sullivan's firm until his actions on the job became suspect and he had to flee the city and eventually the country. He was last heard from in the Orient.

CHICAGO *EVENING POST*, March 10, 1894

MR. DOOLEY'S TRIALS
THE PHILOSOPHER HAS TO FURNISH TOO MANY OPINIONS
GIVES NEWS TO EVERYBODY
HE DODGED VERY WELL ON THE VERDICT BUT WAS
FINALLY SNARED BY HIS FRIEND, JAWN

"Jawn," said Mr. Dooley when Mr. McKenna came in.

"What is it?" said his friend.

"F'r th' first time since I've knowed ye, an' I've knowed ye since ye was a little freckle-face kid that thrun stones at me whin I was dhrivin' dhray, I'm glad to see ye. F'r I've been seetin' here since noon today, by gar, sindin' me sowl to th' divvle be lyin', me that swore off lyin' durin' Lint."

"What have you been lying about?" asked Mr. McKenna.

"Well, sir, ivry man in th' A-archey road has his own opinions on matthers in gen'ral an' I have me own. Now, if a man keeps a grocery shop or r-runs a bakery no wan cares a dam about his opinion. He goes along with sellin' choo choo an' doughnuts an' sare a bit does he need to moind whither Gladstun have a game eye or Bisma-arck have made frinds with th' Geezer. No wan asks him what he things iv annything. But th' minyit a man opens a little licker shtore, be dad, his opinion is as valible as if he was th' dhriver iv a shtreetcar. By gar, Jawn, I've been supplyin' opinions to th' r-road f'r tin years. I have that. On'y last week th' man that runs that there bum little bank down be Finucane's he come in here an' says he: 'Well,' he says, 'what d'ye think iv that

schame iv issuin' certificates again th' saynorage,[7] he
says. 'I think,' says I, not knowin' anny more about
what th' idiot was dhrivin' at thin you, Jawn, 'I think,' I
says, "tis all r-right.' ''Tis not,' says he. 'Why d'ye say
it's all right?' 'Because,' says I to make good, 'he was
beat at th' prim'ries,' says I. 'An' thim Dutch always
makes a roar,' I says. 'Well,' he says. 'Ye'er a nice man
to be a citizen iv this counthry,' says he. 'Ye ought to
go back to Ireland,' he says. An' by gar, Jawnny, I—I almost had a fight.

"Well, sir, whin this here verdict was brought in ivry
wan in th' r-road asked me opinion iv it. Schneider, th'
low Dutchman what keeps down below, he come in an'
he says, says he, in his German brogue, he says, 'Well,
Mr. Dooley, what ye t'ink iv dis here Coughlin peez-
ness,' he says. 'Well,' says I, 'Bisma-arck' (I always calls
him Bisma-arck), 'Bisma-arck,' I says, 'I'm ashamed iv
me race,' I says. ''Tis a low outrage,' I says. ''Tis time
some wan stopped this here business,' says I. 'F'r,' I
says, 'if 'twas wan iv ye'er people he'd be hung,' I says.
He bought a dhrink or two an' wint away.

"Pretty soon I hears a r-roar an' in bounds Maloney,
th' new sanyer guardjeen iv th' Wolfe Tone Timp'rance
an' Beniv'lent sodality.[8] 'Huroo,' he says. 'Huroo,' says I.

[7] saynorage—seigniorage, the difference between the face value of
a coin and the actual cost of the metal contained therein plus the cost
of minting the coin.

[8] Wolfe Tone Timp'rance an' Beniv'lent sodality—Theobald Wolfe
Tone (1763–98) was the son of the Dublin coachmaker. Heavily influenced by the French Revolution and the American War for Independence, he organized the Society of United Irishmen, whose purpose
was to abolish religious distinctions and unite all Irishmen against the
"unjust influence" of Britain. He was able to make a broad appeal because at this time (1791) the Protestant nonconformists were feeling
the heavy hand of England as well as the Roman Catholics, who
had suffered for a longer period of time. Tone emigrated to America
in 1795 and then went to France, where he was able to secure financial support as well as troops to join with his membership of 150,000
to overthrow British rule in Ireland. Faced with bad weather, the

'Who's ilicted?' 'He's acquitted,' says he. 'Huroo, huroo,' says I. 'Huroo,' I says. ''Tis a vindication iv us again th' dips,' says I. ''Tis that,' says he. An' he bought an' wint away. Well, sir, he'd got no further than th' bridge whin in comes Hogan that's wan iv th' other side. 'Give us a dhrink,' he says. 'What d'ye think iv it?' ''Tis a nice clear day,' I says, duckin'. 'I mane th' verdict,' he says, lukin' at me hard. 'What verdict?' says I. 'Haven't ye hear-rd?' he says, brightenin' up. 'They've acquitted him.' 'Acquitted him,' says I. 'Glory be to Gawd,' I says. 'How cud they do it?' says I. ''Tis a disgrace,' I says, an' he bought another wan an' wint away.

"Well, Jawn, I was shtandin' at th' ind iv th' bar talkin' with th' doctor fr'm over to th' drugstore an' discussin' matters an' tellin' him that though I was supposed th' jury was honest I cuddent understand how they cud acquit whin Maloney come in an' sagged again th' cheese box. He'd been there no more than a minyit whin in come Hogan an' sagged again th' mirror. 'Dooley,' says Hogan. 'Give all th' gintlemin in th' house a dhrink,' he says. 'Maloney,' he says, 'can have a ba-ar iv soap.' 'Dooley,' says Maloney. 'I believe in threatin' th' unimployed right,' he says. 'Give Hogan a dhrink.' An' with that they clinched. Bedad, they'd'v massacreed each other if it wasn't f'r me puttin' th' feet into Hogan an' callin' for a German polisman."

French fleet, with Wolfe Tone aboard one ship, turned away from Bantry Bay and returned home. In 1797 the Society in Ireland tired of waiting for outside help, but their planned insurrection was doomed before it began. Someone betrayed the plans and the leaders were taken into custody. While priests in Wexford led a valiant peasant force into battle, they had no understanding of tactics and, more important, were armed only with pikes. By the time French reinforcements arrived months later, accompanied by Wolfe Tone, there was no longer any resistance movement for them to join and surrender was the only viable alternative. While in prison under a sentence of hanging for his revolutionary activities, Wolfe Tone slit his own throat.

"Oho," said Mr. McKenna, "of course you went for Hogan. You're a Clan all right."

"What's that?" demanded Mr. Dooley, starting up.

"You're in camp ninety-six,"[9] said Mr. McKenna, backing toward the door.

"I'll have ye to know," roared Mr. Dooley, rushing out and shaking his fist, "that ye'er a liar. I was in it long before they was a ninety-six."

Then he paused and let his hand drop. "Jawn," said he, "ye'er a British spy."

4

One of the things which made Dunne's pre-New York columns so special was his attention to the homely details of daily life on Archey Road. The citizens of Bridgeport engaged in a rich social and community life. They were a hard working lot; with the exception of local entrepreneurs like Mr. Dooley, the men mostly worked at laboring jobs in the immediate vicinity. Bridgeport was surrounded by industry —the stockyards were nearby, the steel mills were just to the south; the South Branch of the Chicago River and the Illinois & Michigan Canal ran by, and a McCormick Harvesting Machine plant was not far away down the "black road" (Blue Island Avenue). Many local Irishmen went into the construction trades, carrying the hods and laying the bricks.

Although there were tenements and one-room shanties in the area, many of these thrifty citizens owned their own homes, in which they exhibited a fierce pride. They were little more than cottages with their tiny, carefully cultivated vegetable gardens and the goat tethered in the backyard to provide milk for the children and to act as a primitive garbage disposal.

[9] camp ninety-six—The Clan-na-Gael was subdivided into camps. Camp ninety-six was Dr. Cronin's camp.

After putting in a hard day's physical labor, the men could repair to their club—a saloon like Mr. Dooley's. Or often there were meetings of Irish fraternal organizations like the Ancient Order of Hibernians at Finucane's Hall on Halsted Street. Another outlet for these natural extroverts was the Democratic Party. To be a precinct captain was a mark of distinction and a proof of leadership qualities; attendance at party meetings was *de rigueur;* and Election Day was a social occasion.

But the most important and frequent activities revolved around the family: christenings, communions, graduations, weddings, and wakes. In his early days Mr. Dooley delighted in chronicling such events. A little marital one-upsmanship and the process by which children were provided with upwardly mobile names supplied suitable grist for his mill.

CHICAGO *EVENING POST*, November 11, 1894

MRS. HOGAN'S NAMES
HOW THEY FELL UPON THE HAPPY HOGAN FAMILY

CHRISTENING IN ARCHEY ROAD
MR. HOGAN'S FUTILE ATTEMPTS TO PERPETUATE HIS FAMILY HISTORY AT THE BAPTISMAL FONT

Mr. Dooley yawned. "You look tired," said Mr. McKenna.

"I am that," said Mr. Dooley. "I was at Hogan's christenin' las' night an' 'twas 11 o'clock befure me an' Kelly come down th' road singin', 'Iv a-hall th' towns in I-er-land, Kil-a-kinny f'r me-e-e.'"

"Have Hogan another?"

"He have; th' tinth. An' 'twas near to breakin' up th' family. Ye know th' time we seen Hogan comin' out iv th' sicond story window in his shir-rtsleeves. That was whin he said they was no such a saint in th' catalogue

as Aloysius. He wanted f'r to na-ame th' kid befure this
wan Michael. 'Twas named Aloysius an' th' family calls
it Toodles, I belave. Be hivins, Hogan have growed
gray-haired an' bald thryin' f'r to inthrodjooce th' name
iv Michael or Bridget in th' family. Michael was his father's name an' Bridget was his mother's, an' good
names they ar-re; none better. Th' first wan was a boy
an afther Mrs. Hogan had th' polis in 'twas called
Sarsfield.[10] Th' second was a girl an' 'twas called Lucy,
d'ye mind? Lucy? Yes, by dad, Lucy Hogan. Thin they
was Honoria an' Veronica an' Arthur an' Charles Stewart Parnell, bor-rn durin' th' land lague,[11] an' Paul an'
Madge an' William Joyce Hogan, an' th' ol' ma-an all
this time tryin' f'r to edge in Michael or Bridget.

"Well, Hogan does be gettin' on in years now an'
whin th' last come an' th' good woman was strhong
enough f'r to walk around, says he, 'Whin ar-re ye goin'
to christen little Mike?' he says. 'Little who?' says she.
'Little Mike,' he says. 'Little Mike Hogan,' he says, 'th'

[10] Sarsfield—Patrick Sarsfield (d. 1693) and his 11,000 Limerick
men agreed in 1691 to a treaty with the British, which the British
promptly failed to keep. As a result, Sarsfield and his men left Ireland
forever, to become known as the "Wild Geese." In the next fifty
years, in France, over half a million Irishmen joined them, and these
Irishmen figured prominently in every major battle fought against
the English.

[11] land lague—The Irish Land League was formed in 1879 by
Charles Stewart Parnell and Michael Davitt (1846–1906) to break the
hold of the landlords. It was similar to a trade union; its members offered reduced rents to their landlords. If the landlord did not accept
the reduced rate, then all tenants withheld their rents. If the landlord's response was to evict the tenants, the next resort was the boycott, named, as we have seen, for Captain Charles Boycott, the first
man to whom it was applied as the result of widespread organization.
The boycott meant that no one would have anything to do with the
guilty landlord. No one would work for him, serve him, or even bury
his dead. The boycott was most effective, and as a result a land act
was passed by the British Parliament, giving the power to establish
rents to the courts rather than to the landlords and giving the tenant
security in his holding so long as he met the court-established rent.

kid.' 'Ther'll be no little Mikes around this house,' says she, 'unless they walk over me dead body,' she says. Jawn, she's County May-o[12] to th' backbone. 'D'ye think I'm goin' to sind th' child out into th' wurruld,' she says, 'with a name,' she says, 'that'll keep him from anny employmint,' she says, 'but goin' on th' polis force,' she says. 'Mike is a good name,' say Hogan. ''Twas me fa-ather's,' he says, 'an' he was as good as anny.' 'Don't tell me about ye'er father,' says she. 'Didn't I know him,' she says, 'carryin' around a piece iv ol' chalk,' she says, 'atin' wan ind iv it f'r heartburn an' usin' th' other ind iv it to chalk up for-rty-fives scores on th' table,' she says. 'I had a cousin a priest,' says Hogan. 'Match that if ye dahr.' 'Ye had wan a lamplighter,' says she. 'Me mother's brother kep' a cow,' he says. 'Not afther th' polis found it out,' says Mrs. Hogan. ''Twas me aunt Ayleonaras.' That thrun Hogan, but he come back sthrong: 'Ye'll be namin' no more children iv mine out iv dime novels,' he says. 'An' ye'll name no more iv mine out iv th' payroll iv th' bridge depar-rtmint,' says she. Thin Hogan wakened. 'What ar-re ye goin' to call it?' he says. 'Augustus,' says she. An' be hivins 'twas Augustus th' priest gave it. Th' poor, poor child!"

5

There is an old Irish proverb: "If you want praise, die; if you want blame, marry." To this day Ireland has a high percentage of bachelors and spinsters. Thus, the reluctant men of Bridgeport were merely following the long-established tradition of their race.

[12] May-o men—There was a good deal of rivalry between the counties of Ireland, and to Dooley, a Roscommon man, those who hailed from County Mayo were the worst. Mayo men were also among the poorest in Ireland, since the county had absorbed many of the Catholics who fled from Ulster during the periods of religious oppression.

It is also said that Irish men believe that "God, in creat-
ing the desire for woman in man, has been guilty of a lapse
of taste." As God's representative in Bridgeport, it was only
natural that Father Kelly should try to make up for this attitude and to shorten the courtship period. Father Kelly, pastor of St. Bridget's Church, played a continuing role in the
Dooley columns. During this time St. Bridget's parishioners
were participating in a unique ecclesiastical experiment in
participatory democracy, wherein they chose their pastor by
election. Thus, there was the implication that their priest,
even a fictional one, enjoyed the confidence of his little community. Father Kelly was the neighborhood humanitarian,
seeing to the spiritual and corporal requirements not only of
his own parishioners, but of the rest of the community as
well. His was not a wealthy flock, and in order to meet their
needs Father Kelly often had to deprive himself; Mr. Dooley
once said the good man had acquired a taste for caviar in
college which he had been satisfying with oatmeal stirabout
for years.

When Mr. Dooley's vision failed, as it sometimes did, for
he had his own set of prejudices, Father Kelly provided the
necessary breadth and scope. He was a well-educated man
and not just on religious matters, for his interest in and
knowledge of cultural things was evident. He provided the
perfect antithesis to Mr. Dooley's anti-intellectualism. Mr.
Dooley was an expert on life, not on letters. On one occasion
he told Father Kelly, "There is more life on a Saturdah night
in th' Ar-rchey Road thin in all th' books fr'm Shakespeare to
th' ray-port iv th' drainage trustees."

Father Kelly was himself a wise and kindly philosopher,
and by the example Dunne had him set, he was the conscience of Dooley's Bridgeport.

CHICAGO *EVENING POST*, December 8, 1894

"Ye wasn't up to Honoriah Nolan's widdin', was ye? No, nayether was I. I'm gettin' beyant thim doin's, but I sint thim a kag, tied in blue ribbons. If iver a girl deserved to have a nice home an' do her own washin' 'tis little Honoriah. Not that I ricommind marridge, Jawn. A man who has his sup iv tay an' his tin cint ceegar alone be himsilf is th' thrue philosopher, be hivins. But young min who spind their money on dhrink an' hor-rse races ought to marry. If they have to waste half their wages they might as well be wastin' thim on their wives. They might that.

"But they do tell me 'twas th' divvle's own time they had thryin' fr to bring Danny Duggan to th' scratch. Fr an impetchoos an' darin' people th' Irish is th' mos' cowardly whin it comes to methrimony that iver I heerd tell iv. Ye see pitchers iv other min kneelin' down fr to ask a girl to cook their meals fr betther or fr worse, as Shakespeare says, an' I mind wanst goin' into th' Widow Meyer's fr a tub iv beer an' findin' big Neumeister down on his knees before th' widow. What did I do? What would anny man do? I give him th' toe iv me boot an' th' widow marrid an iceman. Ye wouldn't get no Irishman to kneel. Why whin I asked—oho, nivver mind. I was tellin' ye about Honoriah. He'd been coortin' her steady fr two years, an' I knowed it. I've see thim coming along th' sthreet together ridin' in th' ca-ar together, skylarkin' fr'm th' ball together, her

laughin' an' walkin' proud an' happy an' with her pretty
head up in th' air, an' him slobberin' along lookin' f'r
fight. Ye can always tell whin wan iv us is in love with
th' woman we're with. We look so dam disagreeable.
'Tis thrue. Why full a year back Danny was that stuck
he'd hardly speak to her.

"Well, that was all right f'r Danny, but it didn't do f'r
th' girl. She minded well some stories she'd hear-rd iv
th' bashfulness iv th' Archey road lads. There was Dolan's daughter, who was coorted be Hannigan, th'
fireman, f'r fifteen years, an' would be coorted now if
she hadn't shamed him by sindin' him a wig f'r his bald
head las' Christmas. Thin there was Dacey, th' plumber,
who'd niver 'v marrid if he hadn't got into th' wrong
buildin' whin he wint to take out a license f'r his dog,
an' got a marridge license instid. Honoriah was no
belaver in death-bed marridges, an' she an' her mother
come together over th' thing an' decided on what Father Kelly calls a coop—be which he manes they cooped
Duggan, I suppose.

"He come in wan night to play a game iv forty-fives
with th' fam'ly an' after th' game they set around an'
talked an' smoked. Thin ol' man Nolan pulled off his
shoes an' said he thought he'd go to bed. He'd been
readin' th' pa-aper upside down, an' it made him sleepy.
Pretty soon Mrs. Nolan said she'd have to turn in. Duggan began to get frightened, an' just thin in come Father Kelly, th' saints bless th' good man's head.

"Bether thin he niver come to earth to lift the
weight fr'm thim that's weary an' heavy laden—an' a
powerful preacher. 'Oho,' says he. 'What's this?' he says.
'Am I breakin' in,' he says, 'on ye young people?' 'Not at
all,' says Honoriah. 'Ye'er welcome,' she says. 'Set
down,' she says. 'Move over, Danny,' says th' soggarth.[13]

[13] soggarth—priest.

'No! move down,' he says. 'I'll set on th' ind iv th' sofy,' he says. An' down he set. Well sir, I dinnaw what happened fr'm that on, Jawn, an' Nolan got a crick in his neck fr'm thryin' to hear, but 'tis me firm belief that Father Kelly—Gawd be good to him—proposed himself f'r Danny to Honoriah Nolan, f'r Cassidy, who wint by at th' time, 'll take his solemn oath that he seen th' good man down on his knees befure her. He was goin' on to call a polisman. Annyhow, all that Nolan knew was whin th' soggarth come to th' fut iv th' stairs with a tear in th' tail iv his eye, though his lips was laughin', an' calls out: 'Come down. Come down there, ye nigligent parents,' he says. 'I want to show ye something.' An' whin th' ol' man come down there was Duggan lookin' as if he was goin' to kill a Chineyman, an' th' dear little colleen thrimblin' an' cryin', but holdin' on to him like a pair iv ice tongs. 'Pax vobiscum,' says th' priest. 'Pax vobiscum.' An' thin Danny Duggan knelt down f'r th' first time. I see him goin' home in Father Kelly's horse an' buggy as happy as th' day is long. I niver see a more contented man. He wanted to get out an' whale me because I said: 'Good avnin'.' Th' weddin' was a gr-reat success an' they say Duggan showed fr'm th' sta-art that he'll be a good husband!"

"What did he do?" asked Mr. McKenna.

"He walked out to th' back a ya-ard ahead iv her," said Mr. Dooley.

6

Drunkenness among men, women and even children was a public scandal in Chicago of the 1890s. Beer was a special favorite, and according to *Mixed Drinks: The Saloonkeepers Journal,* per capita consumption in the city—even including

children—was forty-nine gallons per year in 1890. Thirsty
Chicagoans and their visitors consumed almost 3 million
barrels of malt drinks during the World's Fair year of 1893.
Thus, brewing was a profitable business and numerous companies entered the field, so that Chicago was sixth in production across the country. Despite the best efforts of these
breweries, they still could not meet the local need, so Chicago's lusty topers turned to Milwaukee for more supplies.

The local branch of the Woman's Christian Temperance
Union had been founded in suburban Evanston by Frances
Willard in 1874, and its members joined with the churches
and women's groups to combat what they believed was the
greatest menace to a healthy American home life. Although
lobbyists for these groups succeeded in obtaining passage
of state legislation establishing considerable licensing fees
and the teaching of the dangers of drink through physiology
classes in the public schools, they were unsuccessful with
other demands, such as Sunday closing.

As Mr. Dooley himself was to remark in a later column,
"th' frinds iv vice is too sthrong in this wurruld iv sin f'r th'
frinds iv varchue. Th' good man, th' crusader, on'y wurruks
at th' crusade wanst in five years, an' on'y whin he has time
to spare fr'm his other jooties . . . But th' defense iv vice is a
business with th' other la-ad an' he nails away at it week
days an' Sundahs, holy days an' fish days, mornin', noon an'
night."

Saloonkeepers, distillers, and brewers fought back hard,
and the reformers resorted to such tactics as kneel-ins in saloons. These efforts were doomed to failure.

Alcoholism was a particular concern to the Catholic
Church in the neighborhoods. Many pastors organized Father Matthew Societies in their parishes. Father Matthew
was a fiery Franciscan who traveled the length and breadth
of Ireland preaching a philosophy of temperance rather than
abstinence. It was an uphill battle, for drink has long been referred to as the "Irish problem." It was difficult for these

hardworking men to deny themselves the sociability of the saloon and the feeling of release from almost unceasing toil that drink could bring. Father Kelly recognized this when he said (recounted in Mr. Dooley's idiom) alcohol "has its place, but its place is not in a man's head. It ought to be his reward iv action, not th' cause iv it. Its f'r th' ind iv th' day, not th' beginnin'."

CHICAGO *EVENING POST*, February 23, 1895

DOOLEY'S LAST YARN

THE PARLOR SALOON AND ITS MOST UNHAPPY FATE

AN EXPERIMENT THAT FAILED

SOME ONE PUT UP A CRUEL JOB ON THE TAVERN WITH RESULTS PAINFUL TO NARRATE

"Over in St. Simeon's," said Mr. Dooley, "they're goin' to pettyshun th' archbishop f'r a new parish priest."

"What's the trouble?" asked Mr. McKenna.

"Throuble enough," said Mr. Dooley. "They had a timp-rance rayform movement last week an' near iv'ry man in th' parish took th' plidge. Hogan was over Choosdah an' he told me all th' dhrink he'd sold f'r two nights was a can iv butthermilk an' two bottles iv brown pop. But ye cudden't keep th' lads away fr'm th' saloons. They was around late an' early playin' dhry forty-fives f'r th' ciga-ars an' lookin' gloomy at th' ba-ar. Little Father Cassidy, a good man but as nervous as a hin, seen this, an' says he to himsilf: 'What'll I do?' he says. 'They'll not stay away fr'm th' saloons,' he says. 'The first thing I know they'll be dhrinkin' thin weiss beer with a dhrop iv kimmel into it,' he says, 'thin just wan tub iv lager,' he says, 'an' before Pathrick's Day th' prisidint iv th' Fa-ather Machoo's 'll be wallopin' th' sicritee with a chair leg an' there'll be a scandal in the

parish,' he says. 'I must do something,' he says to himself. So what does he do but starts a parlor saloon with
a bar in it an' a free lunch an' a cash register fr to make
it homelike.

"There was no sthrong dhrink to be had in it, d'ye
mind. Nawthin' but hot coffee an' milk an' cocoa an'
gruel an' thim things. But it looked like a saloon an' it
done a great business whin it opened. All th' Father
Machoo society come over in a body to give it a boost
an' dhrink thimsilves into chollery morbus with could
limonade. Harrigan, th' thrisurer, was laid up with a
game leg, but not to be last to help along th' movement
he r-rushed th' can over fr a pint iv beef tay. They say
it'd'v done ye'er heart good to see th' little soggarth's
eyes whin th' min at th' ba-ar lined up an' knocked
glasses. 'Here's to ye,' says they. 'Dhrink hearty,' says he,
an' th' noise they made pushin' down th' dhrink ye cud
hear on th' sidewalk. Thin some wan ordhered a second
round iv cocoa an' they got away an' shook hor-rses.
Ivry wan took limonade. Whin they'd got through
they shook back an' th' dhrinks was on th' house an'
they took sarsprilla pop. At th' tinth round they was
pale, but still dhrinkin' ice crame sody, but at th' elev-
inth little Dorsey, th' milkman, set down be th' stove
with his hand on his stummick. Harrity, th' lad from th'
wather office, said he had to meet a man an' wint over
to th' dhrug store on th' corner. Father Cassidy was still
game. 'Let's have a song,' he says. 'Give us "Cruiskeen
Lawn,"' he says to Doherty. Doherty thried fr to sing,
but whin he lifted his glass an' see what was in it his
voice died in his thrawt.

"At that moment in comes Dinny Bradley, a villain
he is, an' loaded to th' ga-ards. 'Good avnin,' says he to
th' barkeep. 'Good avnin,' says th' barkeep. 'Give me a
dhrop iv th' same thing,' says Dinny. 'We serve on'y
timprance dhrinks,' says th' barkeep. 'Thin give me a

beef-tay fizz,' says Bradley. 'We havn't anny,' says th' barkeep. 'What kind iv a laundhry is this?' says he. 'Can ye make me a cocoa cocktail?' says Dinny. 'No,' says th' barkeep. Bradley looked around him an' says he, 'I'll go down tomorrow,' he says, 'an' have ye'er license took away,' he says. An' he wint out.

"Now whither he had annything to do with what happened aftherward, I dinnaw, but annyhow he was seen talkin' with Hogan. Th' favor-ite dhrink in this parlor saloon was what they called 'maltopoorto,' because it was made iv malt an' tasted like beer an' was beer, on'y ye cud 've dhrunk a ton iv it without beatin' ye'er wife. Well, Jawn, so much iv it was dhrunk th' first mornin' that toward nightfall they had to sind f'r another kag. An' that kag was a ringer. It was a ringer, Jawn. Twinty minyits afther it was tapped th' line at th' ba-ar was gettin' gay. Clancy, th' horseshoer, that'd niver dhrunk a dhrop in his life, was tellin' iv'ry wan that he was goin' to r-run f'r alderman in th' spring. Little Mike Casey had his ar-rms around Dorgan's neck an' was thrying to convince him he was th' best frind he iver had, an' Sullivan th' cobbler was singin', 'Th' pretty girl milkin' th cow.' Whin th' good man come back th' prisidint iv th' Sons iv St. Joseph had th' recordin' sicri-tee iv th' Married Min's Sodality on th' flure. He r-rushed up to th' ba-ar an' put his nose in wan iv th' glasses. 'Th' Lord help us,' he says, 'it's beer.'

"That night th' bartinder runs away with th' cash drawer an' th' parlor saloon was closed, but th' parish is up in ar-rms again th' poor, good man. I seen Hogan last night an' he told me he had hired an extry bartinder."

7

For several decades the city of Chicago had a running
battle with the business interests, represented by the Illinois
Central Railroad, in its efforts to secure the lake front for the
people. Operating under a grant of land from the Illinois
legislature, the railroad wanted to use the land for commercial purposes. In 1888 the ICRR lost its claim to the land
east of the railroad tracks. It took several years, however,
before the decision of the lower court was confirmed by the
Supreme Court of the United States. In the interim, the
ICRR tried to push its claim to the lake frontage from Randolph Street south by literally putting a fence around the
Lake.

When it came, the Supreme Court's decision was vitally
important in stopping the encroachment of rapacious corporations on public lands, as well as to the physical layout of
Chicago. It allocated to the state one thousand acres of land
that was then under water. The expected scope of the decision was indicated by the statement that this was an area "as
large as that embraced by all the merchandise docks along
the Thames at London . . . larger than that included in the
famous docks and basins at Liverpool . . . twice that of the
port of Marseilles and near equal to the pier area along the
water front of the city of New York."

The Court went on to make the point that in view of the
lake traffic, with the number of arrivals and departures
equal to those of New York and Boston together, it would
not be "conceivable" that the legislature could have relegated control over this natural resource to a private company. The city of Chicago was the further beneficiary of this
decision, which granted it ownership of the downtown lake
front valued at $80 million at that time.

In the episode of the Mulligan's baby, Mr. Dooley took a

thoroughly modern position, putting himself squarely behind the conservationists and those who were responsible for saving Chicago's lake front for recreational purposes. While not surprising today because of the heightened interest in ecology, it was a most enlightened attitude for the time—although rapidly growing attention was being paid to landmark preservation and park building—and for the place, for anything that would promote business growth was thought to be of top priority in Chicago.

CHICAGO *EVENING POST*, August 10, 1895

"Jawn," said Mr. Dooley, "I had Hinnissy in with me las' night. He's a smart ol' buck, wanst in a while. He tol' me he's goin' to get up a new caddychism. It'll go like this: 'Who made ye?' 'Th' Illinye Cinthral made me.' 'An' why did it make ye?' 'That I might know it, love it, an' serve it all me days.' Be hivins, 'twould be a good thing. They's naw use teachin' th' childher what ain't thrue. What's th' good iv tellin' thim that th' Lord made th' wurruld whin they'll grow up an' find it in th' possission iv th' Illinye Cinthral.

"Th' ma-an that does be at th' head iv th' r-road is a man be th' name iv Fish.[14] I don't know what Fish he is, but he's no sucker.[15] He was a jood down in th' City iv New York an' th' Frindly Sons iv Saint Pathrick or th' Ivy Leaf Plisure Club or some other organ-ization give a party an' this here Fish he wanted f'r to be th' whole thing in it—wanted f'r to take th' tickets an' have th' ba-ar privilege an' lade th' gr-and ma-arch, 'd'ye mind.

[14] Fish—Stuyvesant Fish (1851–1923), who was imported from New York to be chief executive officer of the ICRR during the time the railroad was at odds with the city.

[15] I don't know what Fish he is, but he's no sucker—a play on words; the official fish of Illinois is the sucker fish, which explains why Illinois is sometimes known as the "sucker state."

'Naw,' says they. 'Naw. Ye can't be th' whole thing.' 'Thin,' says th' man Fish, 'I quit ye.' An' he come out here to run th' Illinye Cinthral.

"Well, he's runnin' it. He's runnin' th' Illinye Cinthral, an' he's runnin' th' earth, an' he's got an irne fince around th' lake, an' if he has his way he'll be puttin' th' stars in a cage an' chargin' ye two bits f'r a look at thim—show ye'er ticket to th' ma-an at th' gate.

"Jawn, I don't care no more f'r Lake Michigan than th' likes iv you cares f'r th' tin commandments. They're all right but ye don't use thim. In tin years I've set me eyes on it but twict, an' I on'y see it now as it comes out iv that there faucet. Whin I want what Hinnissy calls eequathic spoorts I goes over here to th' r-red bridge an' takes a ride with Brinnan. But there's thim that uses it an' they say 'tis good f'r babies.

"Ye mind th' Mulligans—thim that lives over beyant Casey's—th' little quite man with th' r-red whiskers. He wurruks hard, but all he's been able to lay up is throuble an' childher. He has tin iv thim old an' young, an' th' last to come is sick an' feverish. I seen th' good woman rockin' it wan day on th' stoop, an' says I, 'How's th' kid?' 'Poorly, thank ye,' says she. 'He seems throubled be th' heat. 'Tis mortal hot,' she says. 'Why don't ye take him where 'tis cool?' I says. 'I'm goin' to tomorrah, praise Gawd,' she says. 'I'm goin to take thim down an' give him a r-ride around on th' steamboat. Th' doctor tells me th' lake air 'll make him right,' she says. ''Tis ixpinsive,' she says. 'Five cints on th' ca-ars wan way an' five cints th' other, an' tin cints on th' boat, but 'tis betther than to have th' poor chick sufferin' an' I'm goin' to do it.'

"Ye see, she'd been brought up on th' ol' caddychism an' thought Gawd ownded th' wurruld, an' she'd niver heerd tell iv th' man Fish. So I see her goin' off downtown with th' baby in her arms, shieldin' its face fr'm th' blazin' sun bright an' early. How she found her way acrost th' city I dinnaw. F'r mesilf, I'd as lave attimpt to cross hell as State sthreet. I was r-run over be a grip-ca-ar th' last time I was there. But annyhow, she got acrost to where she cud see th' blue wather iv th' la-ake an' th' crib that Tom Gahan built. 'Twas there she found who ownded th' wurruld. She wint along th' irne fince lookin' f'r a gate an' they was no gate. Thin she wint into th' little deepo an' says she: 'I want to go over to thim boats,' she says. 'Tin cints,' says th' man. 'But,' says she, 'I've on'y th' fifteen left,' she says, 'an' th' boat costs tin cints,' she says. 'Lave me in,' she says. 'I can't help it,' says th' man. ' 'Tis me ordhers,' he says. Ye see, th' man Fish had tol' thim not to let annywan to go to his lake, th' wan he made, d'ye mind, on th' sicond day. An' there she stood, peerin' through th' irne fince an' lookin' out at th' lake—at th' Illinye Cinthral's lake—an' glory be, I suppose she didn't undherstand it, but no more does she understand why it is f'r some to live off th' fat iv th' land an' f'r her on'y to bear childher an' see thim die or go to th' bad.

"She comes home afther a while whin th' baby got cross again. I seen her that night. 'Did ye like th' lake?' I says. 'I didn't go,' she says. 'F'r why?' says I. 'Th' Illinye Cinthral wudden't let me,' she says. 'I think it'd done th' baby good,' she says. 'He's onaisy tonight. Maria,' says she, 'will ye take Tiddy while I cuk ye'er father's supper?'

"So I think with Hinnissy they'll have to make a new caddychism, Jawn. I hope th' Illinye Cinthral 'll be kinder to Mulligan's baby in th' nix' wurruld than its been in this, f'r unless me eyes have gone back on me they'll be another sthring iv crape on Mulligan's dure tomorrah mornin'."

8

Despite the fact that they came from a rural and agricultural economy, the immigrant Irish settled in the cities in large numbers and came to view the rural areas and farmers with distrust.

Martin J. Dooley was relentlessly urban; he drew his comfort from the turbulent city and refused to be parted from it. As he himself said: "No wan iv our fam'ly iver lived in th' counthry. We live in th' city, where they burn gas an' have a polis foorce to get on to. We're no farmers, divvle th' bit. We belong to th' industhreel classes."

Chicago was a polluted place, and in Bridgeport the smell alone must have been overwhelming. To the south were the rolling mills, which burned coal or oil, and the rendering plants and stockyards. Other factories made fertilizer, or soap, or glue. All of these unclean places dumped effluent into the Chicago River and poured it into the air. Some days the miasma was so foul and the visibility so poor that the street lamps had to be lit at noon. Garbage pickups were casual—that is, when times in Bridgeport were good enough that people could afford the luxury of throwing anything away—and outside privies contributed to the stink.

In this column Dooley pays an almost lyrical tribute to his city, recognizing that despite the parlous state of the environment, it was the only place he could live and be comfortable.

CHICAGO *EVENING POST*, September 4, 1897

"Ye shud take a vacation," said Mr. Hennessy when the philosopher complained of a slight headache. "Ye ought to go away an' have a few weeks' fishin' or r-run down to Westbaden[16] an' be biled out, or indulge in some other form iv spoort."

"I shud not," retorted Mr. Dooley firmly. "I'm well enough off where I am. They'se no disease that afflicts th' American people akel to th' vacation habit. Ye take a big sthrong man that's lived in Chicago all his life, an' if he stays on here he'll niver know a day iv ill health. He goes out in th' mornin' an' dhrinks in th' impure an' healthy air, filled with mickrobes an' soot an' iron filin's, an' his chist expands. He ates onwholesome, rich an' appetizin' food. His muscles is kept firm be dodgin' cable cars an' express wagons. His mind is rooned an' made ca'm be readin' th' newspapers. His happy home is infested with sewer gas, an' if he survives he's th' sthrongest thing that iver was made. But ye take that man out iv his parnicious an' agreeable atmosphere an' sind him to th' counthry. He ates wholesome food that his stomach, bein' used to th' best Luetgert[17] society, rayfuses to intertain. His lungs cave in fr'm consumin' pure air that, like iverything pure, is too thin. He misses his daily sewer gas an' he finds cows' milk a poor substitute for docthered whisky an' beer with aloes in it. Th' man suffers. He does so. He rayturns to Chicago a shattered invalid an' it takes months iv livin' in onsanitary tinimints an' a steady dite iv cigaroots an' bakin' powdher biscuits to restore him to his proper condition iv robust bad health.

"Now, look at ol' Duggan. There was th' healthiest

[16] Westbaden—a watering place for Chicago Democrats in nearby Indiana. Republicans went to French Lick for the cure.

[17] Luetgert society—The 1897 trial of Adolph Louis Luetgert, a sausage manufacturer, for the murder of his wife was one of Chicago's more *outré* happenings. As Mr. Dooley summed it up, the case before the court was this: "A large German man is charged with puttin' his wife away into a breakfas'-dish, an' he says he didn't do it. Th' on'y question, thin, is, Did or did not Alphonse [*sic*] Lootgert stick Mrs. L. into a vat, an' rayjooce her to a quick lunch?"

man in th' wa-ard f'r his age. He was bor-rn an' raised
on th' banks iv th' slip where ye can hear th' wather
poppin' fr'm wan year's ind to another like a shelf iv cat-
sup bottles on a hot night. Th' air was so thick with poi-
sonous gases that a wagon loaded with scrap iron wud
float at an ilivation iv tin feet. He lived below th' grade
an' th' rain backed into his bedroom. He wurruked in a
white lead facthry at night an' had to cross twenty-five
railroad thracks an' an ilictric switch on his way to wurruk. He lived mos'ly on canned goods an' fried pork an'
drank his beer at an Irish saloon an' his whisky at a
German's. Not bein' a corpse befure he was twenty-five
it was a sure thing he'd be a joynt at fifty. An' so he
was. A sthronger man niver breathed. But some wan
put it in his head he ought to go off to the counthry f'r
his vacation, an' he wint dhrivin' a canal boat mule or
cuttin' hay. Whin he come back he was that weak a
child cud go to th' flure with him. 'Where have ye
been?' says I. 'On me vacation,' says he. 'Well,' I says,
'ye'er pretty near vacated,' I says. 'Yis,' he says, 'I'm
glad to get back,' he says. 'I need tinder care,' he says.
They nursed him back to life, but 'twas not till his
house'd been declared unfit f'r habitation be th' health
departmint an' he'd been ejicted afther a free fight be
his landlord an' r-run in wanst be th' polis an' over
twict be a mail wagon an' was back to wurruk breathin'
lead dust be th' quart that he raycovered his ol' sperrits.

"I niver lave town mesilf. I take a vacation be settin'
here at me front dure lookin' up at Gawd's an' th'
Illinye Steel Company's black-an'-blue sky. Th' ilictric
ca-ars go singin' by an' th' air is filled with th' melody iv
goats an' curdogs. Ivry breeze that blows fr'm th' south
brings th' welcome tidings that me frind Phil Armour is
still stickin' to th' glue business. I cannot see th' river,
but I know that it's rollin' grandly backward tord its
sewerce laden with lumber hookers an' ol' vigitables.

Occasin'lly I hear a tugboat cooin' to its mate an' now an' thin a pathrol wagon flits by on its errand iv love. At night th' tired but unhappy lab'rers rayturns fr'm their tile an' th' air is laden with th' sound iv fryin' liver an' th' cheery perfume iv bilin' cabbage. Whin I want more active amusemint I go in an' start a bung or angle with a fork fr a sardine. So whin me vacation is over I ray-turn rayfrished an' eager fr th' battle iv life. I don't have to get th' taste iv good butter out iv me mouth.

"They'se no use fr a Chicago man thryin' to take his vacation out iv town till they put up a summer hotel in th' crather iv Mount Vasuvyous. Ayether he ought niver to go away, or—"

"He ought niver to come back," suggested Mr. Hennessy.

"Ye'er r-right," said Mr. Dooley.

9

Some Chicagoans were self-conscious over their inability to claim a distinguished literary tradition. As one man wrote, "We don't have much use for poetry in Chicago, ex-cept in streetcar ads."

Many Chicagoans were unaware of the intellectual fer-ment taking place in their city in the 1890s. There were those men who were products of the Chicago school of jour-nalism, like Finley Peter Dunne and his fellow members of the Whitechapel Club. Some of these men also belonged to another, perhaps more polite, refined group called the Little Room. Rather than meeting in the back room of a saloon, the Little Room originally gathered in Lorado Taft's studio and then moved over to the Fine Arts Building. Among the regu-lars were publisher Melville Stone, poet Harriet Monroe, Hull House founder Jane Addams, pianist Fannie Zeisler, and novelist Henry Blake Fuller.

Despite this flourishing home-grown culture, Chicagoans still had an inferiority complex and found it hard to believe that anything of high intellectual quality could be generated locally. This attitude prompted one man to write in *The Dial*, a literary magazine published in Chicago;

I have heard a good deal lately about Chicago as a literary center and the building up of a Western literature. Now it seems to me that what is needed to make a Western literature is not so much Western writers as Western readers . . . Whenever shall there be, among our millions, a few thousands, who on seeing any Chicago book announced, cry "Hello! What's this? I must buy it and see," there will be a Western literature.

This attitude also made Chicago a popular stop on the literary lecture circuit. Local audiences were often on the receiving end of barbs and insults from such imported luminaries as Charles Dickens, Rudyard Kipling, and Oscar Wilde, as well as lesser lights. Some endured these performances with a will that bordered on masochism. Not Martin J. Dooley. He took an acid view of such attacks; indeed, he saw them for what they were—a sure way of getting more publicity for the visitor.

CHICAGO *JOURNAL*, January 7, 1899

MEDITATIONS OF MARTIN DOOLEY
ON THE FASHION OF LITERARY LION HUNTING

"Wan iv th' things that ye'd notice about Chicago, Hinnissy, if ye'd lived here as long as I have," said Mr. Dooley, "is th' sthrong way we've come along on lithrachoor. Whin I was a young man th' only lithry guy we had was Tim Scanlan,[18] that wrote 'Th' Jacket's

[18] Tim Scanlan—"Th' Jacket's Green" was attributed to a poet named Mike Scanlan in one of the early McNeery columns. According to

Green'—ye know th' song. It begins 'Whin I was a
maiden fair an' young'—Scanlan was an ol' bachelor an'
had no hair—an' Long John Wentworth,[19] that ownded
a newspaper an' inthrajooced th' first steam fire injine
iver seen in th' west. I mind whin a man be th' name iv
Char-les Dickens come here—he was a Sassenach—an'
thried f'r to separate us fr'm our good money an' they
was a ball that night iv th' Happy Sons iv th' Gloryous
West, an' th' la-ad talked to th' man that had his books
on sale an' th' janitor iv th hall. All th' other pathrons iv
lithrachoor wint to th' ball.

"'Tis diff'rent now. They're as manny authors in Ar-
rchey road as I've unpaid tabs in th' dhrawers. About
th' same number. Young Hogan is prisidint iv th' 'Sons
iv Saint Joseph an' O-Mara Khy-am sodality.' He tells
me that this here O'Mara is an alias f'r a lithry guy be
th' name iv Fitzgerald. I've knowed a few Fitzgeralds.
Wan iv thim used to r-run a hall down be Halsted
sthreet, an' they was another in th' wather office, but I
wudden't name Casey's cow after ayether iv thim, let
alone a sodality. An' instead of th' young ladies sewin'
society they've started th' 'Mrs. Humphrey Ward an'
Pleasure club,' an' Molly Donahue's th' head iv that.
What do they do? Well, 'tis this way. Whin anny man

McNeery, when Scanlan would "feel th' pomes comin' on him he'd go
to writin' letters about th' tahriff. An' sometimes th' fit'd get that bad
on him that he'd confuse pothry an' th' tahriff, an' I mind him well
writin' a letter to th' *Freeman's Journal* that shtarted like this: 'Arrah,
Kerry is a plisint place beyant all guile an' sin, an' th' jooty's 33 percent
on ahl imported tin.'"

[19] Long John Wentworth—John Wentworth (1815–88) deserved
his nickname, since he was 6 feet 6 inches tall and weighed 300
pounds. He originally came to the city to study law, but instead became editor and eventually publisher of the Chicago *Democrat*, the
first daily Democratic publication of the northwest area. He was twice
elected mayor of Chicago and attacked his duties vigorously and with
some distinction. In addition he served twelve years in the Congress
of the United States. He was easily one of the most colorful politicians
in early Chicago history.

writes so manny pieces f'r th' paper where he lives that
no wan'll have annything to do with him, they sind him
a letther askin' him to come out an' r-read th' pieces to
thim. Thin they give a ball f'r to pay th' ixpinses an'
sind th' proceeds to him. If he's a good man an' don't
dhrink, he comes out. They put him in th' finest r-room
at th' Transit house that two dollars can buy an' young
Hogan gets th' rayporther iv th' *Halsted Sthreet Gazoot*
f'r to intherview him. 'What d'ye think iv our World's
Fair city?' says th' rayporther. 'Rotten,' says th' lithry
guy. 'Have ye seen anny iv th' lithry projuce iv Chicago?' 'I niver eat annything canned.' 'What's ye'er
opinyon iv th' bible?' 'A vastly overrated wurruk. Th'
charackters is not dhrawed fr'm nature an' th' language
is coarse.' 'Ye have a poor opinyon iv Shakspere?' 'Th'
wurst in th' wurruld. Have ye a pitcher iv me? Well,
here's twinty. Go now, ye impydint outcast, an' see that
they're printed in ye'er scand'lous an' odjous newspaper, which I despise,' he says. 'Th' vileness iv th'
press iv America,' he says, 'is beyond annything I know,'
he says. 'Manny an' manny's th' time th' privacy iv me
r-room has been invaded be rayporthers, an' th' secrets
iv me ar-rt an' me life wrinched fr'm me, an' thin they
didn't print more thin half what I said,' he says. 'Go,' he
says, 'an' vent ye'er cur-rsed spite on me,' he says. 'Tell
thim ivrything about me,' he says. 'Tell thim I'm th' gr-
reatest living author; tell thim I'm th' mos' fas'nably
dhressed man,' he says. 'Tell thim women go mad over
me,' he says. 'Expose me naked to th' wurruld,' he says.
'Ye'll find a pitcher iv me there in a goold bathtub attinded be th' prince iv Wales,' he says. 'Alas,' he says,
'that a man iv my standin' shud be so threated,' he says.
An' he weeps an' gives th' rayporther an eight cint seegar an' a vollum iv his well known thranslation iv Butthrick's Pattherns fr'm th' original Greek.

"They had a Jew man out here th' other day, th' author iv a pome called 'Childher iv th' Get-to-hell-out-of-this,' I think Hogan called it. I niver give th' Jews much credit f'r bein' lithry, an', be hivins, they niver give me much credit f'r annything else. But this lad was a lithry guy all r-right. He talked in th' school hall undher th' auspices iv th' O'Mara Khy-ams, an', says he: 'I'll make an ipigram,' he says. 'This is th' wor-rst town, an' this audjeence th' wor-rst mob iv imported immigrants I iver see,' he says. He didn't put it that sthrong but it sounded that way. 'I'm surprised to see ye here tonight,' he says, 'f'r none iv ye look as if ye iver arned more thin thirty cints in th' laundhry,' he says, 'or had brains enough,' he says, 'to buy a ticket,' he says. 'As I said to an audjeence th other night, in me style that's been so much copied ivry where,' he says, 'th' sea iv upturned faces befure me makes me want to go out an' hang mesilf f'r fear I'd be dhrownded,' he says. 'I doubt if anny iv ye'll undherstand annything I say,' he says, 'but I'll go ahead an' r-read fr'm th' wurruk iv th' gr-reatest author that was iver foaled,' he says. 'That is,' he says, 'mesilf,' he says. 'Th' first selection,' he says, 'will be "Th' Pawn Shop That Me Gran'pa Left To Me,"' he says. 'A wurruk,' he says, 'that I have universally admired,' he says. An' I come away an' wint down to Finucane's Hall an' broke into th' dance iv th' Gluemakers' union, an' had a time that reminded me iv th' good old days iv Chicago, befure th' r-run iv books was larger thin th' r-run iv hogs."

"Why didn't ye poke him wan?" asked Mr. Hennessy.

"That ain't th' thrue lithry feelin'," said Mr. Dooley. "That was th' feelin' befure th' Ar-rt Institute was built, whin they used to give a gr-reat author th' time iv his life be takin' him out to me ol' frind Armour's an' lavin' him belt a steer over th' head with a sledge-hammer."

III

Mr. Dooley on Chicago Politics

Not since Nineveh had there been a city as corrupt as Chicago in the 1890s. With the possible exception of New York's Tammany Hall, no city had a more corrupt political system. Literally everything and virtually everybody was for sale. The political bosses openly dealt away pieces of the city for hard cash. The people they dealt with were not just the shady characters of the Chicago underworld, but also civic leaders and officers of the largest and most respected corporations and business institutions.

In Chicago, as well as in other large American cities, the bosses maintained their machine, or "push," by adopting a sort of Robin Hood approach. They did indeed steal from the rich, and most of them gave to the poor, but they all added an intermediate step—wherein they pocketed for their own use a goodly portion of what they stole. These men could say, along with George Washington Plunkitt of Tammany Hall, "I see my opportunities and I take them."

Back in the wards, the bosses maintained their power by getting men jobs in city hall, on the police force, or sometimes with the private companies which operated the utilities; they bailed them out of jail; they got food to the families who were hungry; they lent tone to social occasions by attending christenings, weddings, and wakes. As Plunkitt said, "What tells in holding your grip on your district is to go right down among the poor families and help them in the way they need help."

Politics in Chicago presented the Irish with an opportunity to rise rapidly on the ladders of finance and prestige. Since they tended to settle into neighborhoods in large groups, they could be organized and controlled by a political boss of their own background and thus become powerful as voting blocs.

Finley Peter Dunne was basically a Democrat of liberal stripe (though he had a brief flirtation with the Republican Party in his later years in New York). His opinion of politics as a career was not high; in a commentary he wrote for his son Philip, Dunne admonished against following such a course, saying:

> . . . you are a young man, you have Irish blood in you, you might try to get into politics, and I want to warn you of the melancholy effect of being bitten by the political tsetse fly. The other fly causes physical coma; the political insect puts to sleep a man's moral nature, his proper ambitions, his self-respect, his pride. No one can take a chance with it. One attack doesn't give immunity. The oldest and craftiest men in politics suffer as badly as the novices.

In both his editorial writing and in the Dooley columns, Dunne dealt out criticism on a nonpartisan basis. He had no hesitation in taking to task officeholders who were guilty of wrongdoing, as well as the so-called pillars of Chicago society who worked with them to gain their own private, and frequently nefarious, ends at the expense of the people. Both Dunne and Dooley maintained a lively interest in politics, as did the real-life residents of Archer Road.

Dunne described Dooley as a solid citizen who probably reached the pinnacle of his life when he was "mentioned" for his ward's aldermanic nomination because of his stellar performance as a precinct captain from 1873 to 1875. But a certain independence, a certain fastidiousness, kept Mr.

Dooley from following a political career, although he was to maintain a constant interest in those who did and to dispense political wisdom along with strong spirits. "Politics," he was fond of saying, "ain't bean bag. 'Tis a man's game; an' women, childher, an' pro-hybitionists 'd do well to keep out iv it." And, "As Shakespear says, 'Ol' men f'r th' council, young men f'r th' ward.'"

> Th' throuble with most iv us, Hinnissy, is we swallow pollytical idees befure they're ripe an' they don't agree with us.

In his later years it was one of Peter Dunne's favorite notions that as a very young man he had been a radical, almost a socialist, but that he had turned away from that ism. If this was true, he was able to keep it from showing through in his writings at the time. In the three selections which follow he deals in humorous terms with radical movements in Chicago in the 1890s.

These essays demonstrate the measure of Dunne's ability to cut through the rhetoric which surrounded anarchism, populism, and socialism to the basically fuzzy thinking which marked all three. They also demonstrate his personal courage because there were people in Chicago at the time who were genuinely frightened by the radicals, especially the anarchists and the socialists. His poking fun at anarchy was particularly brave in a city which had known widespread panic only eight years before after the Haymarket riot and the trial of the supposed anarchists; only a year before this column was written, Governor John Peter Altgeld sacrificed his political future by pardoning three of the alleged perpetrators of the bombing which started the riot.

Dunne was ahead of his time in perceiving populism as a basically agrarian movement of little relevance to the city dweller. He saw the socialists as poseurs who specialized mainly in ponderous prose.

Summing up his attitude toward all three, Dunne proclaimed, "Above all, I hate humbug, high and low."

CHICAGO *EVENING POST*, June 9, 1894

THE STORY OF A RED

MR. DOOLEY ONCE KNEW AN ANARCHIST
FROM COLOGNE STREET

A RAGING, TEARING DYNAMITAND

THE THINGS HE USED TO SAY TO THE LITTLE TAILOR
AND HIS INGLORIOUS LAST APPEARANCE

"I see be this pa-aper," said Mr. Dooley, "that anarchy's torch do be uplifted, an' what th' 'ell it means, I
dinnaw. But this here I knaw, Jawn, that all arnychists
is inimies iv governmint an' all iv thim ought to be
hung up be th' nick. What are they anny how but fur-
riners an' what r-right have they to be holdin' tor-rch-
light procissions in this land iv th' free an' home iv
th' brave? Did ye iver see an American or an Irishman
an arnychist? Naw, an' ye niver will. Whin an Irishman
thinks th' way iv thim la-ads he goes on th' polis force
an' draws his eighty-three-thirty-three f'r throwin' lodgin'-house bums into th' pathrol wagon. An' there ye
a-are.

"I niver knowed but th' wan arnychist, an' he was th'
divvle's own wan f'r slaughterin' th' rich. He was a Boolgahrian man that lived down be Cologne shtreet, acrost
th' river, but he come over to Bridgeport whin he did
have his skates upon him, f'r th' liftinant over there was
again arnychists, an' 'twas dam'd little our own Jawnny
Shea cared f'r thim so long as they didn't bother him.
Well, sir, this here man's name was Owsky or something iv that sort, but I always called him Casey be way
iv a joke. He had whiskers on him like thim on a co-

kynut, an' I heerd he swore an oath niver to get shaved
till he'd killed a man that wore a shtovepipe hat.

"Be that as it may, Jawn, he was a most ferocious
man. Manny's th' time I've heerd him lecture to little
Matt Doolan asleep like a log behind th' shtove. 'What
ar-re we comin' to?' he'd say. 'What ar-re we comin' to?'
D'ye mind, Jawn, that's th' way he always began. 'What
ar-re we comin' to?' he says. 'Th' poor do be gettin'
richer an' th' rich poorer,' says he. 'Th' govermint,' he
says, 'is in th' hands iv th' monnopolists,' he says, 'an'
they're crushin' th' life out iv th' proolotoorios.' A proolotoorio, Jawn, is th' same thing as a hobo. 'Look at th'
Willum Haitch Vanderbilts,' says he, 'an' th' Gools an'
th' Astors,' says he, 'an' thin look at us,' he says; groun'
down,' he says, 'till we cries f'r bread on th' sthreet,' he
says, 'an' they give us a stone,' he says. 'Dooley,' he says,
'fetch in a tub iv beer an' lave th' collar off,' he says.

"Doolan 'd wake up with a shtart an' applaud at that.
He was a little tailor-man that wurruked in a panthry
downtown, an' I seen him weep whin a dog was r-run
over be a dhray. Thin Casey'd call on Doolan f'r to
shtand his ground an' destroy th' polis—'th' onions iv th'
monnopolists,' he called thim'—an' Doolan'd say, 'Hear,
hear,' till I thrun thim both out.

"I thought me frind Casey'd be taken up f'r histin' a
polisman f'r sure, though to be fair with him, I niver
knowed him to do but wan arnychist thing, and that
was to make faces at Willum Joyce because he lived in
a two-story an' bay-window brick house. Doolan said
that was gawn too far, because Willum Joyce usually
had th' price. Wan day Casey disappeared an' I heerd
he was marrid. He niver showed up f'r a year an' whin
he come in I hardly know'd him. His whiskers had been
filed an' his hair cut an' he was dhressed up to kill. An',
oh! but he had a good wan on, Jawn, a good wan. He
wint into th' back room an' Doolan was asleep there.

He woke him up an' made a speech to him that was full
iv slaughter an' bloodshed. Pretty soon in come a little
woman with a shawl over her head—a little German
lady. Says she: 'Where's me hoosband,' in a German
brogue ye cud cut with an ax. 'I don't know ye'er husband, ma'am,' says I. 'What's his name?' She told me an'
I seen she was Casey's wife. 'He's in there,' I says. 'In
back,' I says. 'Talkin' to Doolan, th' proolotoorio.' I wint
back with her an' there was Casey whalin' away to
Doolan. 'Ar-re ye min or ar-re ye slaves,' he says to
Doolan. 'Julius,' says his wife, 'vat ye doin' here, ye
blackgaard,' she says. 'Coomin' ze, or be hivens I'll
break ye'er jaw,' she says. Well, sir, he turned white an'
come over as meek as a lamb. She grabbed him be th'
ar-rm an' led him off an' 'twas th' last I seen iv him.
Afther a while Doolan woke up an' says he: 'Where's
me frin'?' 'Gone,' says I. 'His wife come in an' hooked
him off.' 'Well,' says Doolan, ''tis on'y another victhry iv
th' rulin' classes,' he says."

2

The People's (Populist) Party was launched at a convention
in Omaha, Nebraska, in 1892. It boasted a platform demanding reforms of policies on land, transportation, and finance
that were revolutionary, to put it mildly. One plank called
for extensive expansion of the currency through either is-
suance of paper money or free coinage of silver or both, to
"not less than $50 per capita."

Another called for government ownership of the railroads
and the telephone and telegraph systems. Also favored were
the graduated income tax, shorter working days, postal savings banks, the so-called Australian (secret) ballot, direct
election of U.S. Senators by the people, the initiative, and

referendum. The People's Party candidate for President was
James B. Weaver of Iowa. Hoping to lay the groundwork for
the 1896 presidential election, Weaver traveled mainly in
the southern and western states, with fellow agrarian Mary
Elizabeth Lease of Kansas, an advocate of "raising less corn
and more hell." Surprising even himself, Weaver polled over
one million votes. After that, the Populists were hot.

Despite efforts to appeal to the urban worker by including
prolabor planks in their platforms, the Populists had a hard
time organizing cities like Chicago. Like Mr. Dooley, many
city people perceived the Populist Party as a movement to
alleviate agricultural distress. Chicago was seen then as now
as a political prize, and so it was decided that a major effort
at uniting the farmer and labor groups be attempted in Illinois. Toward this end, a conference was called in 1894, with
delegates chosen by the farmers, the American Federation
of Labor, the Knights of Labor, the Chicago Single Tax
Clubs, local socialists, and other radical groups. Although
much energy was exerted to maintain every appearance of
harmony, there was considerable behind-the-scenes animos-
ity that could not be blunted. Farmers harrumphed about
"sidewalk radicals," while labor was dubious about "capitalists in shirtsleeves."

It did not help the Populist cause in Chicago when William Jennings Bryan was heard to opine, "Burn down your
cities and leave our farms, and your cities will spring up
again as if by magic; but destroy our farms and the grass
will grow in the streets of every city in the country." Although Chicago had sprung up again from the ashes of the
great holocaust of 1871, Chicagoans believed their city to
be vital to the economic well-being of the nation and not
secondary to some cornfield. So it was slim pickings for the
Populists in Chicago, and especially in Bridgeport, where
the Irish had traded their historical suspicion of the city for
a bias in favor of it.

In the end, for the Populists, whatever fusion of these two forces there was came as the result of the free silver issue, and not from the effort to weld the philosophies of the two divergent groups.

CHICAGO *EVENING POST*, September 15, 1894

O'BROYN IN TH' FIELD

MR. DOOLEY TELLS ABOUT A LIVELY POLITICAL MEETING

POPULISM ON ARCHEY ROAD

THE CANDIDATE WHO REGRETTED AN OPPORTUNITY TO VINDICATE HIS PRINCIPLES

GORMAN'S NARROW ESCAPE

"Jawn," said Mr. Dooley, "ye sh'd 've been up th' r-road las' Win'sday night."

"What was going on?" asked Mr. McKenna.

"Why, Bill O'Broyn, th' populist candydate f'r senator, had a meetin' at Finucane's Hall. Billy's th' frind iv th' fa-armers, d'ye mind. He used to open up his liquor store at 4 in th' mornin' whin th' rist iv us was asleep f'r to entertain th' German min comin' down th' road fr'm Brighton with cabbages an' wan thing or another. So there was on'y lift f'r th' fa-armer to get even to r-run Bill O'Broyn f'r th' sinate.

"Well, sir, they was th' gr-reatest gatherin' in Finucane's Hall that'd been seen there since Malachy Hogan come over an' run th' boxin' match between Dorsey an' O'Leary. Ivry fa-armer I know was there. In th' front seats was Callaghan, th' fa-armer iv th' mud scow Laura Lee; Casey, fr'm th' rollin' mills; Hogan, th' plumber; Finnigan, th' tailor-man fr'm Halsted sthreet; Cassidy, th' bill posther, an' th' Lord knows who all else. Well, sir, O'Broyn was received with th' gr-reatest cheers. They was a quartet on th' sta-age, with Tom Muldoon's big la-ad Mike singin' bass, an' him with a nick on him

as long as a rope, an' they set up a song: 'Three cheers
for O'Broyn an' three for MacVeagh too; rally 'round th'
good ol' flag, th' rid, white an' blue.' 'Hol' on, there,'
says little Mulvihill, th' socialist. 'Stop there,' he says.
'MacVeagh is no populist,' says he. 'He's no populist.'
'Th' 'ell he ain't,' said th' Muldoon la-ad, breakin' in
through th' middle iv th' song. Th' rist iv th' quartet
stopped singin' an' th' tinor wint out an' got a brick.
'No,' says Mulvihill, 'ye'll have to stick in some wan
else,' he says. 'Who?' says Muldoon. 'Waite,' says th' arnychist Mulvihill. 'Oh what th' 'ell,' says Muldoon. 'He
don't rhyme,' he says. 'Go ahead, la-ads,' an' some wan
give Mulvihill a wallop with a chair an' he wint out—
through th' window.

"Thin Bill O'Broyn he come up an' begin f'r to
speak. He'd no sooner started thin Hugh O'Neill Cassidy, wan iv Willum Joyce's bist friends an' a man that
have written resolutions at Ogden's Grove that put a
crimp in Queen Victoria's hair, he ups an' sa-ays he: 'Go
wan, ye fa-armer,' he says. 'Go wan, ye fa-armer,' he sa-
ays to Bill O'Broyn. 'What's that,' says Bill. 'Who's a fa-
armer,' he says. 'Is there anny bosthoon fr'm th' County
Tipperary,' he says, 'with a slingshot in his pocket,' he
says, 'just come fr'm Brinnan's surprise pa-arty,' he says,
'an' a frind iv th' thraiter Bill Joyce,' he says; 'is there
anny informer be th' na-ame iv Cassidy,' he sa-ays,
'that'll call me a farmer?' 'I done it,' says Cassidy, who
was up to here, up to here, Jawn. An' thin they pegged
him out iv th' window an' O'Broyn wint on with th'
speech. He says: 'Boys,' he says, 'if I get into th' sinate
an',' he says, 'an' Gorman thries f'r to put th' comether
over me,' he says, 'I'll throw him down,' he says, 'an'
beat his head off.'

"'Hol' on there,' says Ignatius Dochney fr'm th' platform. 'Hol' on there,' he says. 'Ye'er not goin' to th'
United States sinate.'

"'Where am I goin', thin?' says O'Broyn.

"'Ye'er goin' to th' Springfield sinate with Joe Mahoney an' th' rist.'

"Well, Jawn, he turned pale. 'Be dad,' he says. 'Cassidy was right,' he says. 'Fr'm Tipperary, but he was
right,' he says. 'I'm a fa-armer,' he says, 'an' they've took
me in,' he says. 'Disperse peaceably to ye'er homes,' he
says. 'Th' hall is rinted be th' hour.'

"An' he wint out with th' quartet chasin' him. He'd
neglicted to pay f'r their warbles."

3

In Chicago there had long been confusion between commu-
nism, socialism, anarchism, and syndicalism, and the terms
were used almost interchangeably. The "foreign Commu-
nists" as the Chicago *Tribune* called members of the Socialist Labor Party did elect a city councilman or two from
time to time. However, even in the worst of times (which
were the best of times for the radical and labor movements)
membership was low, and this was especially true among
the Irish. Perhaps this was because the anarchists would
overthrow the political system just when the Irish were coming to power through it; perhaps because they attacked organized religion, and the Irish venerated their Church; and
perhaps because they were for the most part German-speaking immigrants, and the Irish were in hot economic competition with the "Hun." Also, while the local Irish thought
nothing of financing acts of terror in England through the
Clan-na-Gael, they were less ready to advocate bloody
deeds at home.

The radicals' biggest impact and setback were felt as a result of the Haymarket riot in 1886. The anarchists and socialists supported labor in its attempts to win an eight-hour
day. Chicago was the storm center in this drive. On May 3
August Spies, one of the anarchist leaders, was addressing a

meeting of the striking Lumber Shovers Union near the
McCormick works (now International Harvester) on the
"black road" (Blue Island Avenue). While he was speaking,
the shift at the works ended and scabs accompanied by
Pinkerton agents who had been hired to protect them were
attacked by striking workers. Spies rushed to the scene,
where several strikers had been killed and about twenty
wounded, and then rushed back to the meeting to rally the
audience to the side of their fellow workers, but to no avail.

That night he wrote a circular demanding "Revenge! Revenge! Workmen to Arms!" The next evening about 1,500
people gathered at Haymarket Square near the Loop. The
crowd was orderly and the speeches dull; in fact, Mayor
Carter Harrison found the whole thing so harmless he left,
calling in at the DesPlaines Street police station, telling the
officer in charge no action would be necessary. Nonetheless,
after the mayor left, the police mustered their emergency
forces and their captain ordered the gathering to disperse.
The speaker objected, saying the crowd was peaceable, but
he did stop and stepped down from the wagon that had
been used as a podium. At that moment someone threw a
bomb, killing one policeman and wounding many others. A
general melee broke out, and when the smoke and gunfire
cleared, one policeman was dead and six were fatally
wounded; one civilian was dead; and about seventy others
were injured. A number of spectators had been hurt but
were able to flee the scene.

Public fear and indignation demanded scapegoats. Despite every effort to do so, the bomb thrower was never located. Instead, eight anarchists stood trial, even though
there was no evidence they had anything to do with making
or tossing the bomb, on the theory that because they sometimes espoused violent means, they had influenced someone
to take that type of action. In other words, they were tried
in a trial fraught with irregularities and convicted because
of their political beliefs. Seven were sentenced to death;

four were hanged, one killed himself in jail, two death sentences were commuted to life imprisonment; and one was sentenced to a lesser term. In 1893 as has been noted above, Governor Altgeld pardoned the two serving life terms and the third prisoner; such was the public resentment of this action that Altgeld's political career never recovered after his term as governor expired in 1896.

The city erected a monument, a statue of a policeman, at the approximate site of the riot on Randolph Street, but over the years it has been toppled so many times that it was deemed prudent to move it to a location where it would be more welcome; it now stands inside the quadrangle of the new police academy.

CHICAGO *EVENING POST*, September 25, 1897

"If half th' men iv this counthry was as tough as they'd like to make thimsilves out it'd be no place f'r a white man to live in," said Mr. Dooley.

"What makes ye say that?" demanded Mr. Hennessy.

"I was r-readin' th' speeches iv thim la-ads at th' socialist meetin' th' other night. They was meejim sthrong. Wan mild an' amyable philosopher was in favor iv placin' a small bunch iv dinnymite undher ivry naytional bank in Chicago, as if th' naytional banks cud be busted be dinnymite afther two years' experyence with Dimon' Match an' Wist Chicago. Another pote was detarmined that th' workingmen iv Chicago shud ar-rm thimsilves with Winchester rifles an' thin stand on th' corner regardless iv th' game laws an' pump bullets into ivry passing capitalist. Still another la-ad swore that he welcomed blood, an' if nicissary to th' prisirvation iv our liberties wud swim in it. Now that sounds bad, an' if I didn't know th' la-ads I'd fear to go to bed iv nights. But I know thim. Wan iv thim—th' dinnymite

la-ad—is a barber an' has no more idee iv what dinnymite is than th' man in th' moon. Th' la-ad that wants
Winchesters lost his week's salary thryin' to knock th'
tables down at th' las' picnic iv th' County Dimocracy.
Th' la-ad that wanted to swim in blood has been thryin'
f'r to get a job in th' wather office.

"So they go, an' I'm not afraid. Th' American rivolu-
tionist is th' mos' peaceful man on earth. He's as law
abidin', as ca'm an' as good natured as anny livin' man.
Did ye iver hear iv wan iv thim torch an' bomb lads
swingin' a torch or peggin' a bomb? Not wan. Afther
they're through th' little song an' dance on Sundah afthernoon they go home an' play with th' babies. Thank
th' Lord we'er a windy people an' can let out our bad
sintimints be wurrud iv mouth."

4

The members of the City Council in the 1890s were so notorious for their malfeasance that they were known as the
"Gray Wolves." Despite the fact that the pay came to only
$3.00 per meeting, there always were plenty of men ready to
vie for membership. This prompted the Chicago *Inter-
Ocean* to observe:

Even if they met everyday, the law prevents them from
making more than $1100 a year. Why are so many men
eager to become aldermen?

The answer, of course, was that there was plenty to be made
under the table. Their prices ranged from next to nothing to
$25,000 (the largest amount of graft paid for one vote in
Chicago so far as is known), and pieces of Chicago real estate, especially the public streets, were traded away under
the franchise system.

The political set-up went this way. Every year one alderman was elected from each ward for a two-year term (thus
giving each ward two representatives to the council; there
were thirty-four wards). If he was a new man, the odds
were strong that he would quickly join his more practiced
and practical colleagues in the occupation of boodling. Men
of the cloth and newspaper editors inveighed against the aldermen and the rotten system, and periodically strong reform societies were organized. They met with varying degrees of public acceptance; because of the laissez-faire
attitude of most Chicagoans, only the most outrageous
abuses could overcome public apathy. Dunne once observed that "Chicago is always on the point of hanging some
one and quartering him in hot pitch and assuring that he has
lost the respect of all honorable men." This indignation did
not last long, and besides, the aldermen were good at covering their tracks. As Dooley remarked, "Rayformers, Hinnissy,
is in favor of suppressin' ivrything, but rale pollyticians believe in suppressin' nawthin' but th' evidence."

There was another factor that mitigated against swift ret-
ribution for malfeasance in office: recognition by many
voters that if placed in a similar position they would see
their opportunities—and take them, too. Recognizing this,
Dooley said, "I'm an honest man meself as men go . . . But
honest as I am . . . if I was aldherman I wudden't say, be
hivins, I think I'll stand firm, but—well, if somewan come to
me an' said 'Dooley, here's fifty thousan' dollars f'r ye'er vote
to betray th' sacred inthrests iv Chicago,' I'd go to Father
Kelly an' ask th' prayers iv th' congregation."

Finally, the Civic Federation was organized in 1894 as "a
voluntary association of citizens for the mutual counsel, support and combined action of all the forms and forces for
good," with Lyman J. Gage, a well-known and prosperous
banker, as its leader. Because of Gage's fine reputation, he
was able to enlist the support of other city leaders of both
parties, such as Marshall Field, Harlow Higinbotham,

Franklin MacVeagh, and Cyrus McCormick, Jr. Not restricted to businessmen, the Civic Federation attracted social scientists and clergymen such as Jane Addams, Graham
Taylor, and Emil G. Hirsch. Society's Bertha (Mrs. Potter)
Palmer acted as first vice president, and labor was represented by J. J. McGrath. From time to time the Civic Federation was successful in electing reform aldermen to the
council, but frequently their success did not "take" and they
were denied re-election. In Dooley's opinion, this happened
because, "A rayformer thinks he was ilicted because he was
a rayformer, whin th' thruth iv th' matter is he was ilicted because no wan knew him. You can always ilicit a man in this
counthry on that platform." Dooley also felt the group spent
too much time dithering, and he conveyed this by referring
to it as the "Civic Featheration" in his columns.

In 1896 another reform group, the Municipal Voters
League, was organized. However, the population took such
a dim view of reform that men literally ran and hid at the
prospect of being asked to head it up. Finally, George E.
Cole, a diminutive (five-feet-tall) printer, agreed to accept
the presidency, with the stipulation that while the League's
bills would always be paid, the men who paid them would
not attempt to control his actions. Energetic, dynamic and
fearless, Cole formed ward organizations throughout Chicago in competition with both major political parties, and
these organizations elected independent candidates in thirty
wards. The boodlers were still in control of the council, but
gradually, in subsequent elections, the League was able to
get enough of its own men into office so that there was a
greater degree of honesty in the council than Chicago had
ever known. Through his editorials and his Dooley columns
as well as his advice and counsel, Finley Peter Dunne became one of Cole's greatest assets.

CHICAGO *EVENING POST*, February 11, 1896

"I'm not out f'r th' nommynation anymore," said Mr. Dooley, as Mr. McKenna entered.

"For what nomination, in the name of the saints?" asked Mr. McKenna.

"F'r Aldherman," said Mr. Dooley, drawing himself up perceptibly.

"Were you running?" Mr. McKenna asked.

"Was I runnin', is it?" returned the philosopher. "Was I runnin'? Did you see Jawn Finerty's pa-aper? Was I runnin? Havin't ye heered that I was waited on be a comity iv th' Civic Featheration askin' me not to? Sure, I was th' most prominent candydate in th' field till me frind Stuckart[1] took me down to th' city hall.

"They was all there—th' la-ads. Th' little bald-headed man was in th' chair an' a big bald-headed man was down below r-readin' to th' aldhermin things some iv thim cudden't r-read without their glasses an' some cudden't r-read at all. The big bald-headed man was callin' off his piece whin up come me frind Buck McCarty. I knowed him well years ago whin he cud weigh a hog on th' hoof within a scruple an' niver ask f'r th' scale.

"'Mister Chairman,' says he, 'this here is a little ordinance I want to get through,' he says. ''Tis f'r th' binifit iv me constitooency,' he says, 'an' intinded f'r to relieve th' workin'min everywhere,' he says. 'It's an ordinance givin' th' Internaytional Mickrobe Company a right to lay pipes an' pump mi-crobes throughout th' city.'[2]

---

[1] Stuckart—a Chicago alderman and one of the leading boodlers of the day.

[2] The granting of an ordinance to the International Microbe Company is not as wildly unlikely as it seems. Chicago had seen many ordinances passed for the most curious ventures—the piping of com-

" 'I'm agin this ordinance,' says a big guy be th' name
iv Lammers. 'F'r why?' says another aldherman. 'Because,' says Lammers, 'me frind on th' extreme lift wanst
hooked an eye out iv me.' 'That's no valid objection,'
says another aldherman. 'A man that wudden't lose an
eye f'r th' binifit iv his counthrymin, whin they'se something in it, 'd desarve to have his final papers took away
fr'm him.' 'I want to say,' says another aldherman, 'that
th' ord'nance is all right. While,' he says, 'I feel that th'
cramped condition iv th' city threeasury is such,' he
says, 'that some income might be exthracted fr'm th'
company, still,' he says, 'I feel that it'd be a mistake,' he
says, 'to put new burdens on an industhry that'se
conthributed so much to th' prosperity iv this gr-reat an'
imperyal city,' he says. 'Look,' he says, 'at our audjio-
torums an' our a-art institoots an' our Columbus mony-
mints an' our other pinal institutions,' he says. 'Look at
our bridweel an' our insane asylum,' he says. 'I say th'
prosperity iv th' gr-reat an' imperyal an' rootytoot City
iv Chicago dipinds upon th' way we threat these corporations,' he says. 'Refuse,' he says, 'an ordinance in this
here matther,' he says, 'an' th' whole mi-crobe industhry
'll be destroyed in this city,' he says. 'These people 'll go
to New York an' get capitalists to back thim an' set up
mi-crobe foundhries an' roon th' thrade iv Chicago,' he
says.

" 'But,' says a squealy voiced man, 'what do we need

---

pressed air and spring water from Waukesha, Wisconsin, into every
home were two of the more outrageous propositions. Both failed of
passage—not because they were ridiculous and an obvious attempt at
graft, but because not enough aldermen had been cut in on the deal.
In cases where businessmen proved balky in handing over the green
and crinkly, a group of aldermen would get together and form a
dummy corporation which would be in direct competition with the
legitimate business. Then the aldermen would grant themselves the
ordinance desired by the business interests. This almost always had
the desired effect, and the businessmen were forced to purchase the
dummy corporation for a large sum.

iv mi-crobes?' 'He's a rayformer,' says me frind Stuckart. 'Well,' says I, 'he ought to have a good punch in th'
eye,' I says. 'What d'ye let th' likes iv him in f'r?' I says.
'Oh,' says he, 'he doesn't count,' he says. 'Th' la-ad is all
right,' he says. 'An' th' more he talks th' betther f'r us.'

"'I won't speak longer iv mi-crobes,' says th' rayformer, 'but I'd wish to ree-mark that whin King Jawn
signed th' magna charta he gave to each an' all iv us th'
right f'r to exercise our judgment was we see fit,' he
says. 'Now,' he says, 'I'll refer ye to th' writin's iv Saint
Thomas a Kimpis f'r to show that whin a man does his
jooty—' 'Misther Chairman,' says Jawnny Powers, 'I
move ye th' prevyous quistion.' 'All in favor iv th' motion,' says th' little bald-headed man. 'What motion?'
says wan iv th' aldhermin. 'Th' wan ye was staked to,'
says th' la-ad nixt to him. An' it wint through."

"And is that what made you quit?" asked Mr.
McKenna.

"Well," said Mr. Dooley, "I'm particular. If I was in
th' council I might turn out as a rayformer, an' I don't
want to take anny chances on that."

5

Corrupt though Johnny Powers, the "Prince of Boodlers,"
and his ilk were, still they remained in power because of the
services they provided which filled a public need that was
unmet by any social or civic agency. W. T. Stead, the British
editor and crusader for social reform, took the citizenry by
storm with his exposé, *If Christ Came to Chicago*, published
in 1893. In it he included a map showing the locations of the
gambling and sporting houses, named the names of the
grafters and the graftees, and laid the blame for a large
share of the corruption at the feet of some of the most respected city leaders, who openly participated in it. At the

same time he was leveling this criticism, he remarked, "here
even in this nethermost depth . . . there was the recognition
of human obligation, set in motion, no doubt, for party reasons, and from a desire to control votes rather than to save
souls. But whatever might be the motive, the result was un-
mistakable. Rough and rude though it might be, the Democratic Party organization . . . [is] setting in motion an
agency for molding into one the heterogeneous elements of
various races, nationalities and religions which are gathered
together in Chicago."

In one of his editorials in the *Journal*, Dunne advised the
reform element on what they must do to win the voters
away from Johnny Powers and his colleagues:

> If he is defeated it must be by the use of the weapons
> similar to his own, the candidate who beats him must
> be:
> "A friend of the poor.
> "One whom the people can trust to make reform a
> perceptible benefit.
> "One who won't make reform an affliction and a re-
> straint on personal liberty.
> "A candidate who can conform to these specifications
> may beat Powers. For anyone who can't, to try to beat
> him will be a waste of effort."

In addition to the editorial attacks, Dunne often went
after the aldermen in his Dooley columns, but in this article
he shows his understanding of—if not his sympathy for—the
predicament of those who rose to the top of the political
heap from dire poverty. Mr. Dooley also took advantage of
this opportunity to aim a few darts at the business interests
who talked reform but acted differently, putting temptation
in the way of the politicians.

CHICAGO *EVENING POST*, January 15, 1898

MR. DOOLEY ON POLITICS

Mr. Dooley and Mr. Hennessy had been discussing politics as a business and Mr. Dooley said:

"I'm not settin' up nights wishin' fr th' desthruchion iv Jawnny Powers an' th' likes iv him. I've knowed Jawnny fr manny years, iver since he come here fr'm Waterford, with a face on him fr all th' wurruld like th' flap iv a envelope, an' wint to wurruk in th' grocery store down be Jefferson an' Harrison sthreet. He was a smooth little lad an' bimeby he marrid th' lady what ownded th' store an' wint into politics.

"I don't believe they was anny reason in Jawnny Powers' eddication fr to think that he'd throw away money because iv his conscience throublin' him. Th' place he lived in was th' toughest on earth. They was hardly a house around that didn't shelter a man that was wable to go out anny night with half a brick or th' end iv a bullyard cue an' arn his daily bread. Acrost fr'm where he sold groceries was Law [Lowe] avnoo, a sthreet that no polisman iver enthered an' come out with a whole skin. Back iv him was Sebor sthreet [now Vernon Park Place], where th' Cashin twins used fr to burn th' pathrol boxes, an' a few blocks west 'twas a strange night whin ye cudden't hear Chick McMillan's big revolever roarin' like a batthry iv artillry.

"They raise no saints in that part iv th' nineteenth ward, an' they was nawthin' Jawnny Powers seen afther he got into th' council that'd make him think th' worse iv Alick Swan iv Law avnoo. He didn't meet so manny men that'd steal a ham an' thin shoot a polisman over it. But he met a lot that'd steal th' whole West Side iv Chicago an' thin fix a gr-rand jury to get away with it.

It must've been a shock to Jawnny Powers, thim first two years in th' council. Think iv this quite, innocent little groceryman that knew no thieves but thim that lurked along alleys with their hats pulled over their eyes, bein' inthrojooced to bigger thieves that stole in th' light iv day, that paraded their stovepipe hats an' goold watches an chains in Mitchigan avnoo. Did ye iver see an aldherman go by th' Chicago Club? He looks at it as if he ownded it.

"Whin Jawnny Powers wint into th' council I don't suppose he had anny idee what a gr-reat man he'd make iv himsilf. He thought iv most all th' wurruld except th' nineteenth as honest. He believed that th' laads that presided over th' munycipyal purity meetin's was on th' square, an' he hated th' ladin' mimbers iv churches an th' boys that gives money to home missions an' thrainin' schools because he thought they were inhumanly honest. It didn't take long fr to make him see diff'rent. Inside iv his first term he begun to undherstand that they was rale, flesh-an'-blood, bribe-givin' men. They was good fellers, th' same as Chick McMillan, an' betther to dale with because if things didn't go right they'd not be apt to come down an' shoot bullets through th' store. An' whin wanst he got their measure, he knew how to threat thim. He's quick to larn, Jawnny Powers is. None quicker. But I wuddent iv had his expeeryence fr twict his money. I'd rather set back here an' believe that whin a man dhresses dacint he's respectible an' whin he has money he won't steal."

"Somethin' ought to be done to rayform th' rayformers," suggested Mr. Hennessy.

"Thrue," said Mr. Dooley. "I'm thinkin' iv gettin up an organization to do th' wurruk. I'd attimpt to put a branch in ivry church an' charitable society in Chicago an' in ivry club. An' whin anny man that abuses Jawnny Powers an' Yerkuss while buyin' th' wan' an' guaran-

teein' th' bonds iv th' other 'd come up f'r Main Shepherd or Chief Angel I'd agitate again him. I wudden't
let him set by while Jawnny Powers was bein' done up
an' purtend he was in on th' play. I'd get afther him.

"Thin I'd put up a social colony like Hull House
down town near th' banks an' th' boord iv thrade an' th'
stock exchange. I'd have ladin' citizens come in an' larn
be contact with poor an' honest people th' advantage iv
a life they've on'y heard iv. I think th' Hull House idee
is right, but I'd apply it diff'rent. A man wurrkin' in a
bank all day thryin' to get money anny way he can,
how's he goin' to know anny diff'rent? What he needs is
to be cheered up, have th' pi-anny played to him be
nice lookin' girls and find out somethin' iv th' beauties
iv honest poverty be con-varsin' with poor an' honest
people."

"But where'd ye get th' la-ads to r-run it?" asked Mr.
Hennessy.

"That's easy," said Mr. Dooley. "If ye'll get th'
bankers I'll get th' others. I know thousands iv poor but
honest men that ar-re on'y waitin' f'r th' chanst to get
wan crack at a banker."

6

Dunne was assigned to cover the presidential campaign of
1896, and it was during this time that Mr. Hennessy came to
be a permanent fixture in Dooley's Archey Road establishment. In fact, he took the place of John McKenna, much to
the dismay of the latter, who had come to enjoy his fame.
McKenna was a Republican, a city hall job holder, and a
resident of Brighton Park, all of which placed him in a
somewhat different position than that of the average resident of Bridgeport. Besides, he was a real person, and that

limited the amount of kidding or abuse that could be meted
out to him. With Hennessy there were limitless possibilities.
He spoke with a familiar brogue, was a Democrat, an em-
ployee of the rolling mills, and a family man. What's more,
he had a distinct tendency to sit at Mr. Dooley's feet and to
defer to the philosopher.

The questions of parity and free silver were a major concern of that time. City dwellers took an interest in parity
that is bewildering to a member of today's urban society. It
is estimated that in one year members of Congress dispatched over six million pieces of franked mail on parity to
constituents in Chicago, and it was almost impossible to escape the frequent lectures and discussions of the issue which
occurred in the most unlikely places. The currency debate,
of course, played a primary role in the campaign of 1896. In
Illinois it had been a burning issue, especially since the pre-
vious year, when Governor John Altgeld had called a convention of Illinois Democrats which endorsed the free
coinage of silver at a ratio of sixteen to one. Although an
uninvited guest, William Jennings Bryan attended the convocation and lobbied in behalf of this resolution. Altgeld's
action worked to divide even further the already troubled
Democratic Party, with supporters of Cleveland lining up
behind gold and the regular Democrats.

It is obvious that Mr. Hennessy had studied the issue
carefully and that he was most anxious to display his knowledge. The demonetization of silver was known as the "crime
of '73."

CHICAGO *EVENING POST*, June 4, 1896

It was the first time that Mr. McKenna and Mr.
Hennessy had met, and Mr. Dooley was more or less
proud to introduce them.

"Jawn," he said, "shake han's with me frind Hinnissy.

Ye've often heard me speak iv him. Tim, ye want to know Jawn; ye mus' know his father."

"Pleased to meet ye," said Mr. Hennessy. "I know ye'er brother well. Ye luk like him."

"I'm a better looking man," said Mr. McKenna.

"Faith, an' 'tis you that says it," said Mr. Dooley. "Will ye have something? Dhrink up Hinnissy, an' have a fresh wan. Misther Hinnissy here, Jawn, was jus' tellin' me th' advantages iv th' free coinage iv silver. Misther McKenna is a gould bug, Tim."

"I am," said Mr. McKenna, "for a part of the road, but I'm in favor of most any coin that will go over the bar."

"Most anny coin will go," said Mr. Dooley significantly.

"Well, I dinnaw," said Mr. Hinnissy, crossing his legs and laying his glass down slowly on the mahogany. "I have it fixed in me mind that if ye rayjooce th' volume iv th' currency ye certainly place th' counthry wrongly, f'r th' instant ye do it ye have conthributed in some degree to th' leg-an'-arm holt that Wall sthreet has on th' farmers.'

"An' what th' 'ell have ye to do with th' farmers?" asked Mr. Dooley contemptuously. "Ye niver was nearer a farm in ye'er life thin Randolph sthreet market, bad seran to ye!"

"I'll throuble ye not to interrupt me," said Mr. Hinnissy. "As I was sayin' to ye, Misther McKenna, whin th' ol' basthoon come in, th' parity mus' be restored. 'Tis this way. If ye have anny wan standard iv value ye cinthralize th' wealth iv th' counthry, an' th' raysult is that th' rich grows richer an' th' poor grows more an' more on th' slat train. Now, before th' crime iv sivinty-three—"

"That wasn't th' year he was kilt," interrupted Mr. Dooley.

"Who d'ye mane was kilt?" Mr. Hennessy demanded.
"Cronin."

"Oh, bad cess to ye, what ar-re ye talkin' about?" Mr.
Hennessy cried, walking up and down the room with
his fists clenched. "Ye know nothing about this here
thing. Ye don't care f'r annything but r-ready money. I
was sayin', Misther McKenna, addhressin' ye as an in-
telligent young man, that th' parity havin' been rayjooced be th' crime in sivinty-three, th' country bein'
put thin upon a goold basis an' silver bein' thrun down,
so to speak, th' parity was lost an' th' counthry was put
on a goold basis. D'ye follow me? If ye do not I'll stop
an' explain." (Mr. Hennessy said this rather expect-
antly.)

"I follow you," said Mr. McKenna dubiously.

"Very well, thin," rejoined Mr. Hennessy, attempting
to conceal his disappointment. "Very well, thin. Now
ye have it. Where did I lave it?"

"Ye was at th' Boolgahrian athrocities," said Mr.
Dooley. "Ye were jus' speakin' iv th' Czar iv Rooshia."

"No, no," said Mr. McKenna. "You was saying something about the parity, but what I want to know is this.
What's the difference between a silver dollar today, a
silver dollar before the massacre of '73 and a silver dollar after Altgeld and John Coughlin get in their work?"

"All th' diff'rence in th' wurruld. Th' dollar ye have
there is now worth on'y 50 cints, with free cynage it'd
be worth $2."

"D'ye mean to say that this buck is worth only 50
cents?" demanded Mr. McKenna.

"I do," said Mr. Hennessy, with a fine effort.

"I'll give you 55 cents for all you have in your
pocket," said Mr. McKenna.

"I see," said Mr. Hennessy, "that I was deceived.
"Ye'er a frind iv Cleveland."

"Me? Not me," declared Mr. McKenna. "I have no

more use for him than a policeman has for an alarm
clock. I'm through with him."

"Ar-re ye?" cried Mr. Hennessy. "Ar-re ye, avick?
Thin I'll f'rgive ye ye'er financial heresies. Come have a
dhrink."

"Gintlemin," said Mr. Dooley. "I've been a dimocrat
all me life, but th' dhrinks is on th' house."

7

The mayoral election of 1897 was a particularly hard-
fought contest. It pitted Carter H. Harrison, Jr., whose father had served as mayor for five terms until he was slain in
October 1893 by a disgruntled job seeker, against John
Maynard Harlan, whose father was a United States Supreme
Court associate justice. Harrison was the nominee of the
regular Democrats, while Harlan represented the reform element.

Like his father, young Carter believed in a free and easy
approach to city government. With so many others, he felt
that business was Chicago and that anything that was good
for business interests automatically benefited the city. Further, he drew a good deal of support from those both in and
outside of the party who had a vested interest in vice and
thus in keeping Chicago wide open. Harrison had no objection to saloons running seven days a week, despite a massive
lobbying effort by the Woman's Christian Temperance
Union and church groups to close them down on Sunday, or
to the houses of prostitution and gambling dens which
flourished in the central city. This attitude he shared with
his father, who once replied to charges that political and social corruption were ruining the city that "the young city is
not only vigorous but she laves her beautiful limbs daily in
Lake Michigan and comes out clean and pure every
morning."

Young Harrison defeated Harlan and the token Republican candidate and went on in his father's footsteps to serve five terms as mayor. In his memoirs Harrison *fils* remembered the city councils with which he had had to work:

. . . a rare conglomeration of city fathers [that] ruled Chicago in the nineties, a great growing energetic community, whose citizens for years from lack of interest, supineness, from absolute stupidity had permitted the control of public affairs to be the exclusive appendage of a low-browed, dull-witted, base-minded gang of pluguglies with no outstanding characteristic beyond an unquenchable lust for money, with but a single virtue, and that not possessed by all, a certain physical courage which enabled each to dominate his individual barnyard.

Although as Mr. Dooley said on one occasion, "'Tis manny years since I took an active part in that agrable game [politics] beyond stickin' up th' lithygrafts iv both th' distinguished lithygrafters that was runnin' f'r office in me front window," periodically a latent desire to hold office broke out in him. At one time he contemplated running for alderman, but decided that that office was too common. Now he outlines the platform upon which he will run for mayor to an astonished Hennessy.

CHICAGO *EVENING POST*, March 27, 1897

"Where ar-re ye-er pitchers iv th' candydate?" asked Mr. Hennessy. At this season of the year the houses of call along the Archey road are rendered more or less beautiful by the lithographs of the candidates for office. The German proprietors hang up all the pictures that are sent to them with exact impartiality. The members of the ruling race generally made a severe choice and exclude all others. But Mr. Dooley had none at all.

"I didn't want to hang up wan iv Carther Haitch's," he said, "an' if I hung up wan iv Harlan's O'Brien'd murdher me. I didn't have anny iv me own so I concluded I'd lave th' thing alone."

"An' ar-re ye a candydate, ould fool?" demanded Mr. Hennessy, his face breaking into a broad grin.

"Am I a candydate?" replied Mr. Dooley. "Am I a candydate? Iv coorse I am. D'ye suppose that I'm to be denied the same privilege that's ixtinded to ivry citizen iv Chicago? An I goin' to stay at home hidin' me lights undher this bar whin a majority iv me fellow citizens is proposin' to emolyate thimsilves on th' althar iv our beloved city? Did ye iver know me to flinch in th' face iv fire or r-run fr'm th' jooties imposed upon me be th' constitution? Iv coorse I'm a candydate, an' like ivry other candydate, bedad, I'm going to win!

"I studdid th' question a long time befure I consinted to accipt th' unanimous demand fr'm mesilf to offer me name fr th' suffrages iv th' people. It meant fr me that I wud have to give up me practice at th' bar in exchange fr sivin thousan' dollars a year salary, an' ye know what that means to a man that's makin' eight hundherd. It means that I'd have to abandon th' felicities iv domestic life fr th' hurly-burly iv th' campaign an' desert me wife an' childher, which I have none to speak of, in th' inthrests iv th' common veal. But me counthry called me an' I cud not lay down. I'm a candydate an' I have me platform.

"I med it out iv me own head, an' 'tis wan that will appeal to th' business inthrests iv th' community. I don't mean th' business inthrests in Janooary, whin th' rayform banquets ar-re held, but th' business inthrests

in March, just befure th' iliction.[3] In th' first place I'm
f'r that gran' old man Yerkuss. I am aware bad things
are said about him be people that ride on his sthreet-
cars, but ye must admit that he's done manny things f'r
th' divilopmint iv this gr-reat an' growin' city. I believe
in encouragin' him, f'r he carries th' prosperity iv Chicago on his shoulders, an' 'tis betther to give him more
sthreets than to make him take thim away fr'm us with
an ax. If I am mayor I pledge mesilf to give Yerkuss
anything he wants—at rejooced rates.

"I believe in fair assissmints provided th' rale estate
boord an' th' capitalists don't have to pay thim. Th' min
that ar-re buildin' up this gr-reat an' growin' city iv ours
sh'd not be worrid be havin' to pay taxes. They have
throuble enough buildin' steam yachts.

"I am in favor iv th' enforcemint iv th' civil sarvice
rayform[4] afther I've put me own people in office. 'Tis
necessary f'r th' proper pre-sarvation iv th' spirit iv rayform in this gr-reat and growin' city iv ours that th' lad
on th' red bridge sh'd be thrun out an' some good man
put in his place. Thin if another man wants it we'll give
him an examination that'll take his hide off.

"I believe in clean sthreets always, provided no taxes
is paid f'r to clean them. Th' business inthrests iv this
gr-reat an' growin' city iv ours should not be rayquired

[3] Many of the men who were most prominent in reform circles and
at reform meetings actually dealt directly and profitably with the
boodlers and were involved in the franchise game. As Chicago's election day (April 1897) grew closer, they became less enthusiastic about
the reform movement.

[4] civil sarvice rayform—While the reform movement was at its
height in Chicago one of the most important demands was for a civil
service, and a civil service ordinance was passed during the administration of John Patrick Hopkins (1858–1918). However, it was easy to
get around, for it exempted certain categories of jobs and allowed for
temporary appointments of up to 60-days duration, renewable. The
result was that many people went into retirement after years of duty
as temporary patronage employees.

to bear a heavier burden thin they now bear. Instead iv
hirin' men an' puttin' sweepers to wurruk, I'll organize
prayer meetin's to pray f'r rain.

"Th' polis sh'd be de-voorced fr'm politics.

"Gamblin' is a gr-reat evil an' I wud rigidly rigulate
it to th' downtown sthreets, where it wud help th' business inthrests iv this gr-reat an' growin' city iv ours.

"I am in favor iv th' departmint stores.[5] I reconize
thim as a monsthrous evil, but they are a sign iv th' gr-
reat an' growin' cinthrilization iv thrade an' cannot be
stopped so long as they pay rint an' advertise.

"I denounce th' sale iv opyum as detrimental to th'
morals an' injooryous to th' complexions iv th' race, but
owin' to th' lar-rge number iv houses in this gr-reat an'
growin' city iv ours that ar-re occupied by opyum j'ints
I wud so rigulate th' thrade that it cude grow without
inflictin' injury on th' people.

"Fin'lly, I denounce as criminal, wasteful, extrava-
gant, damnable, scand'lous an' low th' prisint administhration an' all administhrations past an' to come
an' on this platform," said Mr. Dooley, "I appeal to ye,
Hinnissy, f'r ye'er suffrages."

"I've on'y wan undher th' Austhrelyan law,"[6] said
Mr. Hennessy, "an' that's pledged already."

"Very well," said Mr. Dooley, "go on thin an' vote f'r
J. Irving Pearce, if ye want to."

[5] The small businessmen opposed the department stores because
they took away their business, much as the supermarket today has
pre-empted the "ma-and-pa" grocery store. Hatred of the department
stores would have been particularly strong among the dry goods and
variety store owners in Bridgeport. The department stores also were
disliked because they occasionally made deals with the City Council
for the purchase of public streets, in much the same way as did the
utilities.

[6] Austhrelyan law—The Australian system of having the government rather than the political parties print and deliver ballots was
adopted in Chicago in 1891.

8

In an earlier time Charles Tyson Yerkes would have been a corsair, sailing with letters patent from a greedy monarch, with a price on his head in every country but his own. In Chicago in the nineties, he was a buccaneer of business, a type all too common in turn-of-the-century America. Yerkes got his start in Philadelphia, where he was a stockbroker. When that city could not sell some of its bonds at the set price, it turned to Yerkes for help. He did unload them at a value of $11 million, but in the course of driving the price up he had to buy $5 million's worth himself. It might have worked, but it was 1871, and the Chicago Fire caused great losses in the East. His loans were called, and he could not cover himself. He was convicted of misappropriation of funds, and although he was eventually pardoned, when he finally got out of jail he decided to go West.

Backed financially by a couple of disreputable Philadelphia millionaires and through a succession of sharp deals and judicious bribery, Yerkes gained control of the Chicago trolley system and gathered up several small gas utilities into the Peoples Gas Company. His prescription for success, he told associates, was "Buy old junk, fix it up a little, unload it on the other fellow." It worked. Yerkes lived lavishly in one splendid mansion in Chicago and another in New York City. He was notorious not only for his ruthless pursuit of the dollar, but also for his devotion to the ladies, taking them on singly or in groups. This latter behavior offended the sensibilities of the local business barons (most of whom were bandits themselves). Upon emerging from a business meeting with Yerkes, Marshall Field, who could drive a hard bargain himself, shook his head and said, "He is not safe."

Around 1895 Yerkes realized that his street railway franchises had only a few years left to run. Since he first came to Chicago and bought the City Council ("You can't get elected to the council unless Mr. Yerkes says so," said Johnny Powers), he had broadened his holdings to include ownership of the state legislature. So he decided to call in his due bills by having passed a series of "eternal monopoly" laws that would extend his rights for ninety-nine years. He reckoned without Governor Altgeld, however; Altgeld turned down Yerkes' $500,000 bribe and vetoed the bills. "I admire that man," said an incredulous Yerkes.

At the next session of the legislature in 1897 there was a new, not so honest governor. After careful application of the half-million dollars Altgeld had refused, the Allen Bill was passed, allowing cities to negotiate franchises for up to fifty years, and it was signed by Governor John R. Tanner. Public reaction was loud and angry.

Ordinarily, this would not have fazed Yerkes. But there was one catch to the bill—it had to be passed by the Chicago City Council. Once again, this should not be a great problem, since Yerkes had owned most of the aldermen off and on for years. The difference was that the bill, once passed by the council, had to be signed by the mayor. As already has been noted, Harrison had a reform opponent in the 1897 mayoral election. Harrison considered himself a social liberal; he could not believe that allowing saloons to open on Sunday, for example, could be dangerous, and he was willing to tolerate a certain amount of gambling and prostitution as inevitable. In his campaign, he seized upon Yerkes and the Allen Bill to help him perform a balancing act, attracting reform support without alienating regulars.

Harrison vowed to eat his hat if Yerkes could get the Allen Bill past his veto. Once he was elected, the newspapers backed the mayor. As the *Tribune* put it, "The press of Chicago has no favorable regard or respect for a fellow who uses Chicago as a milch cow, and takes the butter and eggs to New York." At one of the many mass meetings that

were held on the subject, Thomas Bryan, the highly respected director of the 1893 World's Fair, asked the crowd,
"If you were a jury, what would you do with Yerkes?"
"Hang him!" came the reply. The mayor campaigned
against the adoption of the bill by the council all over town,
sometimes carrying a noose with him, as did other members
of the audience.

CHICAGO *EVENING POST*, June 5, 1897

"I'm glad to know th' ligislachure is gettin' through
its wurruk an' th' mimbers ar-re returnin' to Chicago,"
said Mr. Dooley. "There's been a turrible scarcity iv
baartinders this spring. I wondher who has th' vera-
scope r-rights."

"I dinnaw," said Mr. Hennessy, "but if there are
anny, William J. O'Brien'll get his share."

"He will so," said Mr. Dooley. "An' he desarves it.
Anny man does that's gone through th' session. It
wasn't on'y that he had to associate with Yerkuss, which
is bad f'r his morals, an' with th' Civic Featheration,
which is bad f'r his manners, an' th' guv'nor, which is
bad f'r his mind, but if he hadn't been a sthrong ar-
rmed la-ad, used to puttin' up beer kags on his shoulder
and holdin' out aces an' performin' other athletic feats,
he'd have been physically demoralized be th' debates. I
seen little Plevnak th' other day. He's a Bohemian, an'
unused to fightin' at close range. His favorite weepon,
an' th' favorite weepon iv his race, is bad language an' a
pop bottle. He was up here durin' a recess at
Springfield. He said he come up to see th' prisidint iv
the' Pullman ca-ar company about some repairs he
wanted made in his store—a new beer pump an' a bil-
lyard table. I undherstand he compromised f'r a stove.
Annyhow, he was th' worst-lookin' thing I iver set eyes

on. His right ear was bandaged to keep it fr'm fallin' off
like an overripe pear, wan eye was black, his right hand
was covered with coort plasther an' his mouth was
bigger be half than it had anny right to be.

"'What ails ye, Stanislow?' says I. 'I just come fr'm
Springfield,' says he. 'What's th' matther with ye'er
eye?' says I. 'That's an amindment to th' racin' bill.' 'An'
ye'er mouth? What gintleman done that?' 'Th' anti-
Allen bill steerin' comity,' he says. 'They must be strong
men,' says I. 'They ar-re,' says he. 'Very able men. They
took this lug, too,' he says, puttin' his hand on his ear.
'Did ye do nawthin' ye'ersilf?' says I. 'I did so,' says he
with pride. 'I got these knuckles in th' debate on gas
con-solidation,' he says. An' he wint his way.

"But it's all over now, an' th' boys ar-re comin' back
to Chicago to spind part iv th' money th' good Mr.
Yerkuss give thim to pay th' surgeon's bills. I don't suppose Mr. Yerkuss'll come home. He'll stay to r-rest himsilf afther his arjous labors, an' see th' Lincoln monymint an' go out to th' fairgrounds an' mebbe dhrop in at
th' gov'nor's mansion. I wondher if he's iver seen th' inside iv that beautiful house. It ought to be full iv
gloryous mim'ries fr him. It has sheltered manny of his
predecessors as binifacters iv th' people. Ol' Dick Yates
set there whin he sint so manny thousan's iv poor la-ads
to th' south to defind th' nation's honor. Oglesby an'
Palmer[7] come later. In his lifetime Lincoln often wint
to that ol' house, long before people burned gas or put
their trust in gas stock. It shielded John A. Logan[8] an'
Stephen A. Douglas manny a night. Th' ghosts iv thim
heroes wud rejoice to see Mr. Yerkuss enter th' dure. He
is their worthy successor, th' man that stands fr naytional honor an' th' rights iv th' people. How Lincoln

[7] Yates . . . Oglesby . . . Palmer—all former governors of Illinois.
[8] Logan—John A. Logan (1826–86), who went from Civil War general, to U.S. congressman, to senator.

must grieve to think iv th' chance he missed. If he hadn't relied upon laws an' armies, but had seen that th' way to ensure peace an' honor an' prosperity is to wather stock an' buy state sinitors, he might not have died a mere Prisidint iv th' United States. He wud've lived to be prisidint iv a great, throbbin' gas trust or a sthreet railroad comp'ny, with three millions iv property an' twinty millions iv stocks an' bonds. That was where A. Lincoln was foolish. He died too early, but I doubt if he'd succeeded anny betther if he'd lived till to-day. There's something about his face that says he cudden't raison it out with himsilf that th' way to make th' people happy was to take ivrything away fr'm thim. Now, if ye want to see a rale refined statesman's face, get a pitcher iv Yerkuss.

"Iv coorse ivry gr-reat man has his inimies, an' there ar-re people who say he's no better than he cud wud of shud've been, but we iv th' Inter-Ocean staff, who know his thrue heart, keen brain an' manny private binifactions, know how he has been misriprisinted. Instead iv abusin' him th' people iv Chicago ought to raise a monymint to his mim'ry."

"That won't do," said Mr. Hennessy. "Ye can't raise a monymint to a man till he dies."

"Well," said Mr. Dooley, "who's holdin' him?"

9

The Yerkes debate raged on. Since the press was united against him, Yerkes bought the Chicago *Inter-Ocean* and turned it into his personal "house organ." Then he visited Mayor Harrison at home and tried to bribe him. But the young mayor was no dummy—after all, he had grown up with Chicago politics—and he had members of his family listen in on the encounter, which he then revealed to the public.

Not only were the press and the mayor lined up against Yerkes, but so was the Municipal Voters League, which had helped elect several councilmen (as many as twenty, some thought) who were not beholden to Yerkes. Further, the public mood had turned ugly indeed.

Finally, in December, the Allen Bill came to a vote in the council and Yerkes was beaten. Chicago had finished with him. He swiftly moved to liquidate his holdings before the stock market could react to his defeat. Part of his stocks and holdings went to Marshall Field and his colleagues, whose sensibilities were not too delicate to prevent them from cashing in on a good deal wherever they found it. Taking about $30 million with him, Yerkes removed himself to his New York mansion, to contemplate the paintings in his private gallery and to begin plans for the London Underground. He continued to live the very good life, and by the time he died in 1903 he was on his uppers—down to his last million.

But Chicago had not heard the last of Yerkes. In 1912 Theodore Dreiser published *The Financier*, whose protagonist, Frank Cowperwood, was modeled on Yerkes. It was followed by the further adventures of Cowperwood/Yerkes in *The Titan* (1914), and, posthumously, *The Stoic* (1947).

Meanwhile, back in Chicago, reform societies such as the Civic Federation and the Municipal Voters League saw municipal ownership of utilities as one way of halting the rampaging corruption engendered by the private holding of such facilities. Having taken a sharp look at the members of the City Council, however, Mr. Dooley was not so sure that there would be a net gain in such a change, in view of the character of the men involved.

CHICAGO *EVENING POST*, October 16, 1897

DOOLEY ON CITY OWNERSHIP

"What we need in this counthry," said Mr. Dooley, "is muny-cipyal ownership."

"Oh, aye," said Mr. Hennessy in a puzzled tone.

"What we need," said Mr. Dooley, "is muny-cipyal ownership."

"Sure," said Mr. Hennessy. "What is it?"

"Here's a paper about it," said Mr. Dooley. "I got it off a man that was in here that'd just been discha-arged be Yerkuss f'r stoppin' at a sthreet corner f'r passengers. He give it to me. He's in favor iv it.

"Ye see, 'tis this way. Th' city is goin' to own th' sthreet railroads an' th' gashouses an' th' ilicthric lightin' plants an' all. Th' city'll own thim an' r-run thim f'r th' binifit iv th' people an' a ma-an instead iv payin' a nickel f'r ridin' in th' sthreet ca-ar to a la-ad he niver see befure will thransfer th' coin fr'm wan pocket to another an' ring up wan fare f'r himself.

" 'Twill make things good in politics again. Since th' clan wint to pieces an' me Boolgahrian frind Misther Kraus come into his job, politics has been so quite an' simple in th' sixth wa-ard that anny German cud undherstand thim. But whin we have muny-cipyal ownership, 'twill be diff'rent. Willum J. O'Brien will be prisidint iv th' sthreet ca-ar company, if he don't ac-quire it be degrees be that time, an' me frind little Jawnny Powers'll r-run th' gashouses. They'll meet together th' night befure th' prim-ries. 'Is Casey with us?' says Powers. 'I'm afraid not,' says O'Brien. 'I heerd him call f'r McInerney to sing 'Gawd Save Ireland' at th' picnic.' 'I'll cut off his gas to-morrow, an' do ye see that he walks

downtown f'r th' rist iv his nachural life,' says Powers.
'How is Adofski, th' Polish man?'

"'He's thrue as steel,' says O'Brien. 'Him an' his tin
thousan' Polackers is with us to a man.' 'Give him a season pass an' I'll see that his meter is turned back a few
thousan' feet,' says Powers. 'He's a good man. Is his
brother wur-rukin'?' 'I spoke to Coughlin las' week f'r to
make him superintindint iv th' tilliphone comp'ny, but
he had a man f'r th' place—th' big fellow named Smith
that done up Sandy Walters.' 'That's just like Coughlin,'
says Powers. 'He's a perfec' hog. Didn't we lave him put
Jawnny Sterchie in as threasurer iv th' clearin'-house
las' year? Ye'd bether see Brennan an' ask him if he
can't make Adofski's brother his sicrity in th' ilicthric
light wurruks. He's a good man. He can't read or write.'
'I'll do it,' says O'Brien. 'Ar-re th' boys r-ready f'r tomorrow?' 'They ar-re,' says Powers. 'All r-ready. We'll have
five thousan' in th' war-rd an' wan thousan' to go over
in thrucks to th' twenty-ninth whin McInerney goes f'r
to vote th' imployees iv th' Town iv Lake lines. He's goin'
to stop th' ca-ars all day. Don't ye think we'd bether do
th' same?' 'No,' says O'Brien. 'If we don't have some
ca-ars r-runnin' how can we get th' boys fr'm wan
prim'ry to th' other?'

"'Willyum, ye'er a janius,' says Powers. 'But how
about th' gas wurruks?' 'Shut thim down,' says O'Brien.
'Our fellows can wurruk a dale bether in th' dark.' 'So
they can, so they can.' 'I'll go to th' saloon now an' declare an exthra dividend. We'll need ivery cint tomorrah. I hear McInerney is givin' gas away free f'r this
week.' 'Th' ma-an's foolish,' says O'Brien. 'Th' day afther th' prim'ry I'm goin' to ask ye to call a meetin' iv
th' directors to raise th' price to $5 a thousan'.' 'I'm
afraid we can't get a quorum,' says Powers. 'Manny iv
th' la-ads is out iv town. Spike Hinnissy is off with his
sthring iv horses an' th' big Swede has been exthradited

to New York f'r blowin' a safe. Thin Carlson is out
throwin' th' shells afther a circus, an' on'y you an' me an'
Brenner is left iv th' whole boord.' 'Well, thin, we'll
have to pump in a little air,' says O'Brien. 'We've got to
get square somehow.' 'The people'll kick,' says Powers.
'Iv coorse they will,' says O'Brien. 'They kick about
iverything. Oh, 'tis a thankless task to sarve th' public.
Tin iv th' best years iv me life have I spint in their in-
threats, an' I'm growin' tired. I've half a mind to take
what there's left in th' dhrawer an' lave this ongrateful
counthry.' An' thin they'll go away together.

"Oh, 'twill be a great thing f'r th' city whin it gets
goin'."

"It'll niver get goin'," said Mr. Hennessy.

"An' why not?" said Mr. Dooley.

"Because th' la-ads that has hold now have a grip ye
cudden't break with an ice pick."

"Perhaps ye'er right," said Mr. Dooley. "An' I don't
know but what I'd as soon have Powers an' O'Brien as
thim we do have. It's on'y a question iv who does th'
robbin'. Th' diff'rence is between pickin' pockets an'
usin' a lead pipe."

10

In October 1897 Mayor Carter Harrison, Jr., ventured forth
to New York City with the flower of Cook County democracy to give aid and advice to the Tammany candidate for
mayor, Robert A. Van Wyck. Van Wyck was locked into a
race for the first mayorship of Greater New York, with several opponents, including Seth Low, the reformer; Henry
George, the single tax man; and General Benjamin F. Tracy,
the Republican.

Known as the "kid mayor" (he was thirty-seven and had
just completed six months in office), Harrison and his troops

were welcomed to the nation's largest city with cheers and banquets. When asked by reporters about the reform opposition in his own election contest (John M. Harlan), Harrison replied,

> Yes, we had reform out there and we roasted it good and hard. The reformers were trying to make the city too good—too good superficially, I mean. Chicago is a cosmopolitan city. In some places the saloons are open day and night, and I think they should be in those districts.

The hotel into which the Chicagoans had been booked refused to accommodate them because of their reputation for brawling, but Boss Croker of Tammany Hall was able to find them lodgings. According to newspaper accounts,

> . . . they did look well . . . Their hats were sleek, and most of them were worn at the proper angle. Only a baker's dozen were obviously under the influence of wine . . . They held their umbrellas like rifles, and marched as straight as veterans . . . They are to be banqueted in Tammany Hall, and the allowance is understood to be two quarts per man.

Despite his long-standing reluctance to leave Bridgeport, Mr. Dooley was sufficiently intrepid to venture downtown to see them "get away." All in all, the Chicagoans received a reception in which Dooley and his friends could take pride.

Whether or not it was Carter H. and his boys who gave him the necessary "push," Van Wyck won the election.

CHICAGO *EVENING POST*, October 30, 1897

DOOLEY ON THE COUNTY "DEMS"

"Did ye see thim get away?" Mr. Dooley asked.

This seems a vague question, but so few events are important to the philosopher of Archey Road that Mr. Hennessy instantly interpreted "thim" to mean the County Democracy Marching Club, and responded: "I didn't, an' I'm sorry f'r it."

"'Twas a prodeejous spectacle," said Mr. Dooley. "'Tis manny a day since I've seen th' like, an' though me feet has been too long hooked to me legs to be much use but f'r table ornamints, an' I'm no hand at dodgin' beceecles an' illicthric ca-ars I wint downtown with young Duffy to see thim off. Down th' sthreet they come, with Cap James Hinnery Farrell marchin' ahead. A fine lukkin' man is Cap Farrell since he stopped dyin' his hair. It's snow white now, an' he luks as though he cud go into anny bank in town as its prisidint if he preferred to inter it that way. His hat was on his right ear, he wore a dimon that burned th' eyes iv a man tin ya-ards away an' he'd dhropped a chunk iv cole slaw as big as ye'er two fists on his coat. An' such a band! Glory be, I niver enjoyed such hivinly music in me whole life. Ye cuddent've heerd a cannon while th' hor-rns was at it.

"Behind th' band come th' thrue la-ads. First come th' mayor, in a high hat an' yellow shoes, r-right-foot-left-footing between little Jawnny Powers an' Joe Kipley an' Tom Gahan an' th' other heroes iv honesty, fidelity an' economy. Behind thim was th' push—that cud give th' German army all th' Gatlin' guns that iver was made an' bate thim to death if ye'd put thim into a liquor store where there was a pool table. They was me

frind th' Hon'rable Mike Kenna; an' me frind th'
Hon'rable Hinnery Carmody, that I knowed whin he
was th' best lumber shover that iver carried a pine
scantlin' into a lumber hooker on th' South Branch.
They was Chick Curran, who's a good la-ad, but care-
less in his manners; an' Jimmy Quinn, th' Hatter, that if
he'd been a mean man instead iv a marchant prince an'
comityman fr'm th' twenty-fourth cud've unroofed ivery
la-ad in th' procission as clane as though they'd been
sthruck by a cyclone. I heerd him say to Aldherman
Brennan: 'Be careful with that bonnet, Jawn, or I'll
replevy it.' An' thin they was Willum J. O'Brien!
Hinnissy, I felt so proud whin I seen him that me feelin's as a citizen iv th' sixth wa-ard overcome me an'
tears gathered in me eyes. He ain't tall like Hinnery
Carmody, nor embinepint like Robert Immitt Burke,
but ye'd have to take a surveyor's chain to measure him
acrost. They was four men in iv'ry other line. They was
on'y two in his, an' th' little man alongside him was half
th' time walkin' through th' crowd. His hat was hung on
his head as though he'd left it there to go into dinner
an' his chin made a hole in th' back iv th' la-ad in front
iv him. Oh, he was an affectin' sight.

"Did they get a fine rayciption? Did they? Well, I
shud say they did. Sure ivrybody knew thim. 'Twas
'How do, Mike,' 'How ar-re ye, Tommy?' 'Mam-ma,
look at dada, with th' funny hat on.' I waved me hand
at Willum J. O'Brien an' says I, 'Good mornin', sinitor.'
Iv coorse it wasn't etiket f'r him to answer back. But I
seen be th' look in th' tail iv his eye that he reconized
me."

"They made a big hit in New York," said Mr.
Hennessy.

"Iv coorse they did. They make a big hit annywhere
where there's annything to be hit. In th' first place,
Charter Haitch is a man that can turn a few language

an' Robert Immitt Burke is a man to plaze th' hearts iv
statesmen. They was min in that procission that cud
dale with anny part iv th' pop'lation iv New York, fr'm
a profissor iv political economy to a boy that hurls th'
broads. D'ye think Wall sthreet 'd not stop business to
turn out an' see th' Hon'rable Richard Gunning with
thim splendid whiskers? Cud Seth Low or anny other
jam jood rayfuse to meet Willum J. O'Brien? He'd kick
th' dure down. He wud so. An' think iv a meeting between Willum Waldorf Asthor an' me honest little frind
Mike Kenna. I can see thim now settin' off in a corner
iv th' hotel dhrinkin' a bottle iv wine, with their feet on
th' stove, discussin' th' proper way iv gettin' out th'
lodgin'-house vote. I don't suppose Bill's lodgers 'd
stand f'r a biled egg, but before next election he'll be
givin' a prairie chicken with ivry quart iv champaigne.
Thim la-ads will teach New York a thrick or two worth
knowin'."

"They'se on'y wan thing that throubles me," added
Mr. Dooley thoughtfully.

"What's that?" asked Mr. Hennessy.

"What'll Jimmy Quinn, th' hatter, do with th' hats
whin he gets thim back?"

IV

Mr. Dooley on the Sporting Life

Despite Mr. Dooley's jaundiced view toward athletics, at the end of the nineteenth century all Chicagoans were sports crazy—both as spectators and participants. Baseball, football, and bicycling were probably the most popular athletic pursuits of the general public. Baseball was an old favorite—the organization of the Chicago White Stockings (now the Cubs) predated the Great Fire of '71, and the team attracted large and enthusiastic audiences at home games. Not content with just watching, many amateur clubs were formed and played on local sand lots.

A local football team, the Chicago Football Club, was established in 1876, and the game was a favorite on college campuses. Gradually it too became a popular pastime of the amateur. But in the 1890s it was the bicycle that supplied the major form of athletic endeavor to the average person. There were organized races, but bicycling was a form of recreation which both sexes could engage in on individual basis. Besides providing healthy activity, bicycles broadened horizons by allowing riders to travel farther away from home than before.

Other recreational activities which cut across class lines included skating, sleighing, card playing, and billiards (although the last two, like football and baseball, were virtually off limits to women). Fishing was both a sport and a way of augmenting a family's food supply.

Horse racing had long enjoyed a large following. Wrestling and amateur boxing exhibitions, although frowned upon, were scheduled throughout the year. Prize fighting was outlawed, but aficionados could journey south across the Indiana line to watch such matches, as well as to see cockfighting and dog baiting, which were also against Illinois law.

Tennis, golf, and equestrian activities were mostly restricted to the well-to-do who could afford to join clubs established for the practice of these aristocratic sports. Despite the availability of the lake front, there were no established public beaches, and swimming was not a major sport. Boating was enjoyed by those who had enough money to own or rent some sort of craft.

During his earliest days as a journalist, Peter Dunne had been assigned to cover the Chicago White Stockings; at this time (1885–86) the team held the league championship. Dunne became the first reporter in Chicago to write a narrative account of each game (before this only the results were reported), and his efforts were rewarded by a public hungry for such detail. He used slang in his colorful accounts, and among other terms, he is credited with first having used "southpaw" to describe a left-handed player.

Dunne traveled with the team and shared a sense of comradeship with its members and its management. However, even while assigned to cover baseball, he did not restrict himself to writing about it alone; instead, he allowed unathletic local commentary to creep in.

As for himself, Dunne was not a sportsman. Although his family had been relatively prosperous, there was no emphasis on athletics in the type of urban atmosphere in which he was reared and no evidence that he had any aptitude for sports. His son Philip relates that the only time he saw his father with a tennis racket in his hand was to deliver an obligatory paddling on Philip's birthday and that he never bothered to learn to drive a car. Dunne was amused and somewhat puzzled by the back-to-nature movement in the

United States and never understood why so many would willingly give up the benefits of modern civilization for the splendid discomforts of the rustic life.

Through Mr. Dooley, Dunne reflected this attitude in numerous columns, including this excerpt from one of Mr. Dooley's essays on baseball:

> In me younger days 'twas not considhered rayspictable f'r to be an athlete. An athlete was always a man that was not sthrong enough f'r wurruk. Fractions dhruv him fr'm school an' th' vagrancy laws dhruv him to baseball. We used to go out to th' ball game to see him sweat an' to throw pop bottles at th' empire, but none iv his fam'ly was iver proud iv him except his younger brother. A good seat on th' bleachers, a bottle handy for a neefaryous decision at first base an' a bag iv cracker-jack was as far as I iver got tow'rd bein' a spoortin' character an' look at me now! I gredge th' power I waste in walkin' upstairs or puttin' on me specs.

Golf was the one sport which Dunne enjoyed, but in which he did not particularly excel. He became such a duffer that in his New York years he purchased a home at Southampton in order to be near a golf club he had helped to organize. Though golf was mainly a preoccupation of his later life, he did manage to get in a fast eighteen holes now and then when he lived in Chicago. Indeed, Elmer Ellis, Dunne's biographer, tells of the time Dunne played in a foursome with Marshall Field, one of Chicago's richest men but not a fast man with a buck. After Field had muffed a shot and complained about it, Dunne suggested that he put a dollar on the ball next time. When Field asked what that would do to improve his game, Dunne replied, "Well, all Chicago believes that you can make a dollar go farther than anyone in the world."

On the whole, Dunne's view toward athletics is summed

up in a Dooley one-liner aimed at the aggressively out-doorsy Theodore Roosevelt:

I'd like to tell me frind Tiddy that they'se a sthrenuse life an' a sthrenuseless life.

2

Bicycles had been around since the 1870s, but their con-struction—a front wheel which could be as much as six feet high, with a much smaller wheel behind, called an "or-dinary"—limited their use to a few intrepid souls who were willing to risk the injuries that could come from a sudden nasty spill. However, in the 1880s the "safety" bicycle, with two wheels of the same size connected by a metal tube, was invented in England. A short time later the pneumatic tire was developed, making the ride smoother. Finally, in 1894 the coaster brake was invented, and the bicycle, pretty much as we know it today, went on the market.

Bicycle madness was rampant throughout the world in the 1890s. One night at Windsor Castle Queen Victoria was entertained by a ballet performed on bicycle-back. Chica-goans were no different. For around $100 you could pick up a brand new model made on Chicago's West Side by the new Arnold Schwinn Company. Used models sold for con-siderably less and were in the reach of almost everybody. Once mounted on your "scorcher" you could take to the 2,000 miles of paved road in and around town or wheel down the new bicycle paths provided by the city.

As popular as cycling was, there were quite a number of people who shared Mr. Dooley's aversion to it. Bicycles were excluded from Lincoln Park by an ordinance passed in 1879, which declared them to be a threat to "the peace of mind and safety of body necessary to the pursuit of happi-ness." The hordes of bicyclers who turned out especially on holidays were a threat to those pedestrians who were not fleet of foot, and they also interfered with the normal horse-drawn traffic.

Bicycling was especially important to the women of Chicago, for it afforded them a cheap means of transportation that made it respectable (eventually) for them to wander about the city and environs. It also allowed a more casual manner of dress, for the usual cyclist attire consisted of a shirtwaist and bloomers. One of Mr. Dooley's most popular columns was called "The Divided Skirt" and dealt with the new freedoms bicycling had brought to a young woman neighbor on Archey Road. There were those who were scandalized by such goings on, and doctors solemnly warned of the dangers to the race of overdeveloped leg muscles and what damage "scorcher's flush" could do to a lady's complexion.

Wheelmen quickly organized themselves into clubs; in the mid-1890s Chicago boasted about five hundred such groups, including the country's oldest, the Chicago Cycling Club, started in 1879. Typically Chicagoan, the club members realized they could use their organization for more than just sporting or social activities—they could exert political pressure as well. For example, the Viking Cycling Club warned, "This club and its associates control 1,800 political votes and will support those candidates favorable to wheelmen and wheeling." Carter Harrison, Jr., conscious of the broad appeal of bicycling and of the fact that his opponent had been a well-known football player, kicked off his first campaign for mayor in 1897 by completing a century—a hundred-mile round trip between Chicago, Waukegan, and Libertyville—in just over nine hours. One campaign poster portrayed him atop his bike, with the legend, "Not the champion cyclist but the cyclist's champion." He won.

Because the bicycle fanatics often exceeded the 8-mph speed limit and rode several abreast instead of in single file, the Chicago Police Department found it necessary to estab-

lish an elite squad of mounted—on bicycles—officers to arrest
scofflaws. Bicycle races were tremendously popular; though
they began as amateur contests, they evolved into professional ventures where individuals were sponsored by the
various bicycle manufacturers. Throngs attended the annual
bicycle shows, which resembled the auto shows of today,
complete with pretty young women daringly dressed in
bloomers who hawked the manufacturers' wares.

CHICAGO *EVENING POST*, May 19, 1894

DOOLEY ON THE WHEEL
THAT IS, OF COURSE, CONVERSATIONALLY, NOT ACTUALLY
HE OBJECTS TO THE BYCYCLES
THE FATES OF THE ONLY ONE THAT EVER GOT
INTO BRIDGEPORT WHEN DENNEHY TRIED IT

"There's wan thing with all me faults I niver done,"
said Mr. Dooley.

"And what's that?" asked Mr. McKenna.

"I niver r-rode a bicycle," replied the philosopher.
"I've been a r-rough man in me days an' I seen th' wurruld an' got me skates upon me, an' whin I was a la-ad
manny's th' timtation I let come between me an' me
jooty, but so help me hivins, Jawn, I niver done nothin'
th' like iv that. An' I'll say this here f'r Bridgeport, that
takin' it all an' all fr'm th' slip to Brighton Park I niver
seen a bicycle here but th' wan, an' that was, praise be
to th' saints, over in Mathias Dennehy's wood shed this
blissid moment waitin' f'r Marcella Dennehy, who have
an ingaynyous mind, f'r to schame some way iv makin'
ayether a bustle or a coal scuttle out iv it.

"'Twas young Sarsfield Dennehy ownded it. He
come back fr'm Norther Da-ame College las' summer
with his head so full iv quare notions that his poor ol'
man, as simple a soul, Jawn, d'ye mind, as iver put a

pick on his showlder, was afraid to open his mouth f'r
fear he'd say something that'd affind th' dam jood. He
got Dennehy that there scared, d'ye mind, that he wore
his shoes afther supper an' had to r-roll th' growler f'r
a pint in a handbag. He'd larned to r-ride a bycycle—
th' la-ad had—an' all winter he's been tellin' me he was
gawn to get a wheel. 'Ye'd betther be gettin' a wheel
barrow,' I says. ''Tis more in th' line iv ye'er fam'ly,' I
says. They're not much, Jawn. Not a priest belongin' to
thim.

"Well, sir, last Monday avnin' th' fam'ly was settin'
out on th' front stoop, Mrs. Dennehy in her Sundah
shawl an' th' ol' man tortured in a coat an' th' brogans
he'd wore all day an' glarin' acrost th' sthreet at Matt
Dorney, who'd come out iv th' saloon like th' mane
divvle he is, wipin his lips f'r to tantalize Dennehy—
they was settin' there whin up driv an expriss wagon an'
th' driver hauls out a bicycle. 'Glory be to Gawd, who's
that f'r?' says Dennehy. ''Tis me new wheel,' says th'
la-ad. 'Ye'er not gawn to r-ride it,' says th' ol' man. 'I am
that,' says th' la-ad. 'I am that,' he says. An' up he gets
on it an' goes hell bent down th' road. Well, sir, there
was th' divvle's own excitement. Th' people all come to
th' windows f'r to see th' bicycle an' all th' little lads
goes lammin' after it an' cheerin'. Th' wimmen come
out wipin' th' dish wather off their hands on their
aprons an' th' young girls stood on' th' sidewalk an'
giggled. Ol' Desmond th' shoemaker that ain't been east
iv Halsted sthreet since some wan tol' him he was
dhrafted f'r th' war, seen th' bicycle comin' an' ducked
in his shop an' closed th' dure.

"Well, sir, the la-ad gaws up an' down th' road till th'
polis had to turn out f'r to kape th' sidewalk clear. In
the manetime, ol' Dennehy had ducked acrost to th'
Dutchman's a hoisted a tub 'r two an' whin he wint out
he was walkin' wide an' mutterin' to himsilf. Th' la-ad

was through his r-ride an' was standin' tellin' th' crowd
about th' bicycle. 'Ye can't ride it,' says Dorney to th' ol'
man. 'By dad,' says Dennehy, 'I cud,' he says, 'if I
wanted to.' 'I dahr ye to,' says Dorney. 'Ill take naw
dahr,' says Dennehy, 'from any Roscommon hor-rse
thief,' he says. Well, sir, he makes a runnin' jump at it,
an' by gar he goes dam well f'r about a r-rod till he
turns to give Dorney th' laugh, whin bang he goes
again a pathrol box an' falls like as if he was dhropped
from th' top iv th' shot tower.

"Thin, what d'ye think he does? Oh, 'twas th' Irish iv
him. He r-runs into th' cellar, an' comes out with th' ax
an' goes at th' bicycle like a man choppin' wood. They
had th' 'ell's own time with him, an' whin he got
through th' bicycle looked like a bur-rud cage that'd
been run over be a dhray. Th' next night I seen him settin' on th' stoop with his coat an' shoes off dhrinkin' his
beer out iv—what d'ye suppose? Out iv a sprinklin'
can."

3

Like most other sports around the turn of the century, football was an amateur game; there was no professional football as we know it now, and even the college game was a
simpler one. Its greatest following was found on the campuses of the East Coast colleges, although in 1894 the University of Chicago traveled to California to play Stanford in
the first intersectional contest. In 1896 the Western Inter-
collegiate Conference, which came to be known as the Big
Ten, was formed.

The game itself was played under informal conditions.
The first football stadium was yet to be built. And the
players looked different, too. For example, they did not wear
helmets; instead, they let their hair grow long because they

thought this would act as a cushion to the jostling they received on the field. The common team uniform consisted of padded moleskin trousers, a jersey, a laced jacket, shoes, and socks. It cost about $10 to outfit a player in the 1890s; contrast that with the $250 it takes to put one of the Chicago Bears on the field today.

The game looked different as well. Rough and tumble as football may be today, in the 1890s it could be brutal and often even lethal. While a gain of five yards constituted a first down, this was just as difficult to achieve as today's ten-yard requirement and was accomplished by much pushing, punching, gouging, and shoving on the ground. The game became so violent that public opinion was aroused. Eventually, in 1905, during a match between Swarthmore College and the University of Pennsylvania, the Pennsylvania team pursued one of the Swarthmore linesmen until he was beaten bloody. As the player staggered off the field, a photographer got his picture. It was widely reprinted and prompted President Theodore Roosevelt to warn that unless the sport policed itself he would issue an executive order prohibiting it. The next year, eighteen footballers were killed and over a hundred seriously injured—and this was at a time when the game was not widespread. Fed up, the President summoned delegates from Harvard, Yale, and Princeton (for the sport was still strongest in the East) for a conference. As a result, new rules were made prohibiting the most punishing practices, abolishing the use of "tramp" players, outlawing fighting, and opening the game up through the forward pass.

The Chicago Irish of Bridgeport took all contests—even sporting ones—very seriously. Football was imported to Archey Road by a young collegian home from Notre Dame University for the holidays, and in this selection a pick-up game almost caused a religious schism.

CHICAGO *EVENING POST*, December 1, 1894

AN ARCHEY ROAD GAME

AN INCIDENT OF THE FOOTBALL CRAZE IN BRIDGEPORT

MR. GROGAN LOST HIS TEMPER

HOW THE PICKAX WAS BROUGHT INTO PLAY IN A CONTEST
ON THE GRIDIRON FIELD

"I've got to close up early tonight," said Mr. Dooley. "I'm gawn down to th' polis station f'r to bail out Grogan. They sint f'r me cousin, Judge Dooley, th' lord chafe justice iv th' high court iv Halsted street, but he was takin' tay with Ha-arlow Inn Higginbotham an' Loyman Jay Gage an' Willum Joyce at th' Ritchaloo Hot-el, d'ye mind, an' he sint back wurrud that he was not to be disturbed till tin o'clock."

"What's the matter with Grogan?" asked Mr. McKenna. "Drunk again?"

"Faith, no; they have him put away in th' booby hatch f'r assault with intint to dhrive a pickax into Sarsfield Casey's back. Didn't ye hear-r th' throuble, Jawn? Dear, oh dear, th' whole r-road is talkin' about it. Ye see, 'twas this here way; Sarsfield Casey is captain iv th' football team iv th' St. Aloysius Society iv th' Church iv th' Immaculate Conciption, an' Grogan's boy, Hugh O'Neill Grogan, he's captain iv th' football team iv our church. 'Twas Casey invinted th' game in Archey r-road. He was th' main finger iv th' team iv Nothre Da-ame an' whin he come back his hair was that long ye cud lose a sthreet ca-ar in it. Befure he'd been back a week he had half th' laads iv Bridgeport playin' football or givin' what th' likes iv him calls a 'college yell.' Wan night big Shaughnessy, ye know th' wan I mane, th' bum iv that name, he come into me place par-lyzed an screamin' 'Rah, rah, rah, Pontiac.' 'What's atin' ye?' says

I. 'What ails ye, man alive?' I says. 'I'm givin' me college yell,' he says. 'I done five years in Pontiac,' he says.
'Whin I was a kid,' he says, 'f'r stealin' a ham,' he says.

"Well, sir, th' first we knowed there was a match
game between th' Immaculate Conciptions an' Fa-ather
Kelly's church wist iv th' bridge. Th' la-ads practiced on
th' prairies an' half th' ward's been limpin' about with
bandages over their eyes. Th' ol' people thought th' la-
ads 'd on'y been fightin' among thimsilves an' paid no
attintion to it an' ivry father iv thim tur-rned out to th'
game up be th' rollin' mills Thanksgivin' day. 'Tis a
prowtestant holiday, annyhow. I didn't go, Jawn, avick.
I seen wan game, Jawn, an' I give ye me wurrud whin I
feel th' desire to see football I goes out an' makes a call
on me nivview Malachi, who's chief sticker f'r Armour
an' wan iv his most thrusted imployaze. He is that.

"But Grogan wint. He ma-arched out ear-rly with
his long coat on his back an' his shtovepipe hat tipped
over on wan side iv his head, ma-arkin' time with his
feet whin he walked, a Clare man fr'm th' crown to th'
sole. He had a front seat an' he cheered like th' divvle,
they tell me. Well, th' game began, an' th' first thing
Grogan see was Casey reachin' over an' givin Hugh
O'Neill a poke in th' eye. 'Oh, ye thafe,' he says, 'lanin'
over th' ropes, 'I'll have th' law on ye,' he says. 'Smash
him, Hughy,' he says. 'Ain't ye going to smash him, ye
disgrace to ye'er family.' 'Set down,' says th' audjeence.
'Set down,' they says, 'ye'er interruptin' th' game.' At th'
moment there was a r-rush an' Hugh come r-runnin'
down th' field with th' ball under his ar-rm an' young
Casey runnin' afther him. 'Stand ye'er groun',' yells
Grogan. 'Stand yer groun',' he says. 'Ar-re ye to be th'
first iv th' Grogans to r-run,' he says, 'fr'm a r-red
headed May-o man?' he says. 'Oh, me, oh, my, what'll I
tell his poor mother?' Thin whin Casey grabbed his lad
be th' legs an' thrun him like a steer an' all th' rist iv th'

la-ads jumped on him, Grogan called 'Polis! Is there no polisman here will privint murder? Officer Hinnissy,' he says, 'if ye don't save me boy fr'm bein' kilt I'll have ye'er star.'

"Well, they hauled him back an' he wint away. Th' game continued an' just whin our church was whackin' th' divvle out iv th' Immaculates down th' field came Grogan with his whiskers flyin' in th' air an' a pickax in his hands. He made straight f'r Casey n' 'twud've been all th' la-ad's life was worth if he'd reached him. It took two polismen to hold him till th' hurry up wagon come."

"I don't suppose they'll prosecute," ventured Mr. McKenna.

"Naw," said Mr. Dooley. "But that ain't th' worst. Father Kelly is mad through. He says he'll excommunicate Grogan. He broke up th' game befure his la-ads could scoor again' th' Immaculates an' since thin Father Gallagher have put on such airs that no priest in th' diocese can talk to him."

4

The Irish, accustomed as they were to religious holidays, were confused as to how to deal with such secular celebrations as Thanksgiving. According to Mr. Dooley, some of the Catholic clergy viewed the third Thursday of November as a pagan feast, but not Bridgeport's Father Kelly, who said it was founded by the Puritans to give thanks for being preserved from the Indians and that the Irish should keep it to give thanks that they were preserved from the Puritans.

Further, the holiday football game was an American institution long before the advent of television. According to Mr. Dooley, on Thanksgiving Day, "In iv'ry city iv this fair land

The Criterion

This is the second of The Criterion's Series of
its own Original Illustrations of Famous Books: "MR. DOOLEY"

Mr. Dooley

"Which would you rather be, famous or rich?" asked Mr. Hennessy. "I'd like
to be famous," said Mr. Dooley, "an' have money enough to buy off all the'
threatenin' biographers." (Courtesy, Chicago Historical Society)

Finley Peter Dunne (1867–1936) was only in his twenties when he created Mr. Dooley, who became the wit and censor of his era and whose genius has stood the test of time. (Courtesy, Chicago Historical Society)

A broadside printed in 1900 portrayed Martin Dooley in heroic drapery (with Finley Peter Dunne holding the pointer). Mr. Dooley was better known to the American and British public than the Vice President of the United States —and better liked, too. (Courtesy, Chicago Historical Society)

Whitechapel Club members gathered amid macabre appointments acquired under questionable circumstances. From left, Finley Peter Dunne, editor and columnist; Dr. H. B. Williams; Charles C. Perkins, court clerk; Henry Farnsworth; Wallace D. Rice, lawyer and poet; Brand Whitlock, reporter, later mayor of Toledo, Ohio, and a diplomat; Dr. Percy L. Clarke; Edward Bernard; and Arthur Henry. The exclusive club, with never more than ninety members, flourished in the early 1890s. Wit and originality were highly prized; a hackneyed tale would cause Whitechapelers to rise and sing the "Chestnut Song." One verse went like this:

> In the day of Old Rameses, are you on?
> In the days of Old Rameses, are you on?
> In the days of old Rameses,
> That story had paresis,
> Are you on, are you on, are you on?

Dunne, one of the club's five "sharpshooters," later said the talk there was the best in the world. (Courtesy, Chicago *Tribune*)

Debonair, determined Theodore Thomas (1835–1905) founded the Chicago
Symphony Orchestra in 1890 and established the standard of excellence for
which it is still known today. In 1871 the train bearing him and his traveling
orchestra to an engagement at the Opera House was turned back at Twenty-
second Street because the raging Chicago fire had melted the tracks. During
the labor riots of 1877 he played a five-week season with militia stationed
around the hall. He once remarked, "I would go to hell if they would give me
a permanent orchestra," and when he left New York for Chicago in 1890 to
fulfill his dream, some friends thought that's just where he was headed.
(Courtesy, Chicago Historical Society)

Carter H. Harrison, Jr., like his father before him, served five terms as Chicago's mayor. Known as the "kid mayor," he was incorruptible despite the blandishments of such experienced tempters as Charlie T. Yerkes. He once said of himself, "Chicago is fortunate in having a mayor who keeps his hands in his own pockets." (Courtesy, Chicago Historical Society)

th' churches is open an' empty, th' fleet anise seed bag is pursooed over th' smilin' potato patch an' th' groans iv th' dyin' resounded fr'm many a futball field."

So it was only natural that Dooley, with his contempt for written history, should take the notion that the first Thanksgiving was celebrated in Plymouth with the first American football game.

CHICAGO *EVENING POST*, November 28, 1896

"Ye see," said Mr. Dooley, "when 'tis done be la-ads that wur-ruks at it an' has no other occupation it's football, an' whin it's done in fun an' be way iv joke it's disorderly conduct, assault an' batthery an' rite."

Mr. Dooley had been explaining the pious Thanksgiving exercise, and that was his conclusion. He went on: "Still, ye know, if it wasn't fr football they'd be no Thanksgivin' Day, an' if they wasn't a Thanksgivin' Day they'd be no chanst fr Big Steve to issue a pro-clamation fr'm Wash'nton. I niver wint much on thim proclamations annyhow. They come to this: 'Whereas I've had a good job at fifty thousan' dollars a year fr four years an' th' ilictions come my way an' I don't have to wurruk anny more as long as I live, therefore, those iv ye that have gone hungry an' need clothes fr th' childher an' got on th' short side iv politics three weeks ago, praise Gawd fr'm whom my blessins flow or I'll r-run ye in.' I wonther what Bryan's got to be thankful fr! Mebbe it is that afther th' ice wagon r-run over him it didn't back down on him.

"Be that as it may, I'd give th' eye out iv me head to see th' first Thanksgivin' on Plymouth rock. It was a cold an' frosty mornin', an', as Bill Nugent says iv it, th' ocean waves leaped high again th' stern an' rock-bound grandstand. Prom-ply at iliven o'clock th' two teams lined up. Cotton Mather,[1] th' demon halfback captain iv th' Lambs, won th' toss an' took th' ball. Th' first play was a r-run around th' end be Praisegod Simpson, but he was downed in his thracks be Preserved Fish, th' terrific fullback iv th' Arks. A revolving wedge was thin thried again th' center f'r a gain iv five yards. Following this up Jawn Eliot, th' frightful tackle, made a hole bechune Canned Salmon an' Elihu Bradberry f'r a gain iv three yards. On th' next play Cotton Mather fumbled an' th' ball wint to th' Arks. A series iv frightful center r-rushes followed an' slowly but surely th' ball was carrid down to'rd th' Lambs' goold. 'Tear 'em into ribbons,' roared Jawn Eliot, as th' Arks again an' again broke through th' defense. Cotton Mather urged his men to stand together, an' fin'lly they succeeded in holdin' their opponents. Then th' signal was given f'r a kick. Th' punt was accurate, but th' ball fell into Cotton Mather's hands. Honest ol' Cotton was there, all right. With th' inergy bor-rn iv despair he started down th' field, protected be th' superb tacklin' iv Bradbury Standish, Holy Smoke an' other saints. Th' gigantic Arks thried to stop him, but he hurled thim to wan side or th' other, breakin' collar bones an' ribs an' th' tin commandmints as he wint. Down th' field he tore like a steam ingine that he knew nothin' about, his long hair flyin' in th' air, his sweater in ribbons, th' mud rainin' fr'm his heels. At last there was on'y wan man bechune him an' th' pricious an' valyable goold. That was Preserved Fish, th' demonyac fullback. Th' hearts iv th' Ark rooters rose to their throats as th' two men come together. Wud Cotton be stopped be Preserved or wud he

[1] Cotton Mather (1663–1728), New England clergyman and author, wrote a book entitled *Memorable Providences*, which described cases of alleged witchcraft in Boston. A sort of how-to-do-it book, the volume got into the hands of some impressionable young women in Salem, Massachusetts, and resulted in the Salem witch trials.

make a sucker iv Fish?' was th' question ivry wan asked
himsilf. Th' darin' fullback blew at his man like a tiger
an' grabbin' him be his ankles threw him heavily forward. 'Down,' roared th' spectators. 'Not on ye'er West-
minster confession,' roared Cotton, as playfully kickin'
th' demonyac child iv iniquity in th' face he dashed on
an' scored a touchdown amid th' r-roars iv th' inthrested
spectators. Th' Lambs thin gathered in th' centher iv th'
field an' give their well-known cry: 'Ivry time we buck
th' line we go, we go,' to th' chune iv th' long meter
doxology.

"What ar-re ye givin' us?" asked Mr. Hennessy who
had listened to the fancy sketch with much bewilderment displayed on his face. "Thim puritans didn't
know anny more about football thin about—about pin
pool."

"Ye'er mistaken, Hinnissy," returned Mr. Dooley
calmly. "It's a puritan custom, as ye'd know if ye r-read
th' histhry iv th' people that you an' I an' Billy Lorimer
an' Ole Oleson is descinded fr'm. It's to honor th' la-ads
that founded th' counthry an' whose spirit r-runs it now
on Sundays an' holidays, that th' people cillybrate it
with th' pious customs iv their ancistors. If that there
young woman Priscilla what-d'ye-call-her wasn't out on
top iv th' tally-ho seein' her lover sustainin' compound
fractures, she was no thrue puritan ancestress iv mine,
an' I'll have to back to where I was befure th' Frinch
got licked be th' Proosians an' claim Jones of Ark on me
father's side.

"On'y we're not allowed fr to cillybrate th' day properly south iv th' river an' wist iv th' thracks. Downtown
it's football; out here it's th' Irish killin' each other.
Downtown th' spectators sees it fr a dollar a piece; out
here it costs th' spectators ne'er a cent, but th' players
has to pay tin dollars an' costs."

5

Knowing baseball as well as he did, Dunne had plenty to
say about it through Mr. Dooley:

"D'ye iver go to a base'ball game?" asked Mr. Hennessy.

"Not now," said Mr. Dooley. "I haven't got th' in-
tellick for it. Whin I was a young fellow nawthin'
plazed me betther thin to go out to th' ball grounds, get
a good cosy seat in th' sun, take off me collar an' coat
an' buy a bottle iv pop, not so much, mind ye, f'r th'
refrishment, because I niver was much on pop, as to
have something handy to reprove th' empire with whin
he give an eeronyous decision. Not only that, me boy,
but I was a fine amachure ballplayer mesilf. I was first
baseman iv th' Prairie Wolves whin we beat th' nine iv
Injine Company Five be a scoor iv four hundherd an'
eight to three hundherd an' twinty-five. It was very
close. Th' game started just afther low mass on a Sundah mornin' an' was called on account iv darkness at th'
end iv th' fourth inning."

CHICAGO *EVENING POST*, June 22, 1895

"I've just come over fr'm Hinnissy's," said Mr. Dooley. "He's laid up in bed, covered that thick with bandages a coalminer cudden't get down to him in a day
with a pick an' a dhrill."

"What ails him?" asked Mr. McKenna.

"Ah," said Mr. Dooley with unusual disgust, "th' ol'
fool's been makin' a goat iv himsilf impirin' a baseball

game. May th' good Lord give him sinse befure he dies, an' be quick about it, for he must be past sixty now.

"Las' week th' Wolfe Tones wrote a challenge an' stuck it in Finerty's paper that they cud bate anny base-ball club iv rivolutionists in th' sixth wa-ard fr tin dollars a game. The Willum J. O'Brien Lith'ry an' Dhramatic Marchin' Club heerd iv it an' they took it up an' last Sundah th' la-ads come together in Grogan's lot back iv th' dumps. Near iv'ry wan in th' road wint to see th' game an' Clancy, who wants to be aldherman, bought a kag iv beer an' put it on third base. Such a scrap come up about who ought to play third that th' captains had to order th' kag off th' field.

"But that isn't what I was goin' to tell ye. I was talkin' about Hinnissy, th' ol' gazaboy. Whin they'd tossed up pinnies to see which side 'd go to bat first, an' th' Sarsfields won they begun lookin' about fr an impire. 'Tis no aisy job, Jawn. I'd as lave be a German minority judge at a prim'ry as impire a game in th' dumps. An' so would anny wan else that had sinse. Hinnissy has none no more than Hogan's cow. Whin they offered him th' job he stuck his thumbs in his vist an' says he: 'Oh, well, if no one else will, I will la-ads.' He was proud iv it. He hadn't held an office but th' wan iv bridgetinder under Colvin since th' war. 'Is he a good man?' says th' captain iv th' Willum J. O'Briens. 'He was out in 'forty-eight,' says th' captain iv th' Sarsfields. 'He looks too old,' says th' captain iv th' O'Briens. 'What's that?' he says. 'Look here, young man,' he says, tippin' his plug hat back until it hung on wan ear. 'Look here,' he says, 'I lay ye tin dollars that I can outrun ye, outlep ye an' outbox-ye,' he says—him, th' deluded ol' freak that had me up all las' month rubbin' his jints with arnica fr inflammathry rhoomatism.

"Well, they put him in behind th' bat an' he wint over th' way he'd seen other impires do, with his hands

undher th' tails iv his coat. 'Wan sthreek,' says he.
'What's that?' says th' man at th' bat—it was big Norty
Clancy—turnin' round on him. 'Wan ball, I mane,'
says Hinnissy. 'What's that?' says Owen Roe O'Neill
McCarthy who was catchin' f'r th' O'Briens. An' thin
both nines comes up an' gathers around him. I think
that was what th' ol' munkey wanted, f'r he cocked his
hat an' made a speech to th' assimbled multitood. 'I
want to say,' says he, 'that I'm impire iv this game.' 'An'
while,' he says, 'I'm impire iv this game,' he says, 'I'll be
impire iv th' game,' he says. 'Go over to ye'er corners,'
he says, 'an' we'll start over again.'

"Well, they was nawthin' else to do, f'r Hinnissy was
so old that no wan'd lick him, an' if they wanted
younger men th' Clan-na-Gael cud not impire wan iv
thim games, I tell ye, Jawn, an' get out iv th' hospital in
time to tind ba-ar at th' picnic. So they wint on. Norty
Clancy made a swipe at th' ball an' knocked it over th'
fince. Well, Hinnissy owns th' house nixt to th' fince an'
th' minyit he heerd th' ball smashin' through a pane iv
glass he started acrost th' field after Clancy, who was
tearin' along to'rd first base. 'Come back, ye murdhrin'
young vilyan,' he says. 'Come back here, now, an' pay
f'r that pane iv glass,' he says, 'or I'll have th' law on ye,'
he says. An' away he wint afther Clancy.

"Well, be this time, th' captain iv th' O'Briens he'd
got hold iv Hinnissy an' some more iv thim helped him.
'Go in,' says they 'an' tind to ye'er business,' they says.
They pushed him down th' field an' stuck him on th'
home plate just in time to have th' ball thrun in an' hit
him on his vin'rable stomach. He give wan look like a
sick cat to where I was settin', an' thin he lay down on
th' ground an' said no more f'r a matther iv five minyits.
Thin we picked him up an' I heerd him mutter something. 'What's that?' says I. He pointed to his face.
'Aha,' says I. 'Ladies an' gintlemin,' I says, 'this here im-

pire, this three-year-old, this threemenjous athlete,' I says, 'friskin' around, has lost his teeth,' I says. 'Both sets,' I says.

"Well, we took him home an' though he wanted th' priest we give him lini-ment instead, an' he ought to be able to get out in a week. I wint over to see him tonight. ''Twas all right,' says he, 'but ye oughtn't to 've humilyated me befure th' crowd,' he says. 'Hinnissy,' says I, 'whin a rispected citizen an' head iv a fam'ly goes round makin' a pink munkey iv himself,' I says, ''tis th' jooty iv a thrue frind to tip him off,' I says. 'Besides,' I says, 'what'd 've happened if Norty Clancy 'd come back?' I says. 'Would ye sooner lose ye'er teeth inside or out?' I says.

"An' 'tis thrue Jawn. As Shakespeare says, 'Ol' min f'r th' council, young min f'r th' ward.'"

6

The America's Cup started out in 1851 as a nameless trophy to be awarded by Queen Victoria to the winner of a sailing race around the Isle of Wight, on the southern coast of England. British yachtsmen had extended an invitation to the New York Yacht Club to enter the race. In response, the New Yorkers dispatched the schooner *America*, which won a protested victory. For years the cup gathered dust at the New York Yacht Club until 1870, when a British challenge to recapture the trophy was accepted. After that the America's Cup races were mounted sporadically until 1937.

The Earl of Dunraven, who was the British challenger in 1893, was an interesting person to the residents of Bridgeport both because one of his principal residences was in Ireland and because he brought his two daughters along to crew for him, which was quite unusual. In 1895 Dunraven made his second attempt to bear the cup back to Britain.

Surprisingly, the races, which were held off New York City, had turned into a great crowd pleaser, attracting some 65,000 fans in 1895, more than the popular baseball or football games. Spectators were transported by over two hundred excursion and sightseeing boats which crisscrossed the path of the race in order to obtain the best view. Just as the race was to start, the *Yorktown*, a pleasure steamer, forced Dunraven's boat, the *Valkyrie II*, to flee the starting line. When both ships returned to the starting place, the *Valkyrie's* boom hit the top mast of the American *Defender* and kept going, although the *Defender* immediately ran up a protest flag. Despite Dunraven's complaint that the *Defender* had caused the foul, the sponsoring committee awarded the race to the *Defender*. The next day Dunraven lost the second race. He complained again, demanding that the race be moved elsewhere because of crowding and that an observer be placed on board participating boats because he believed the *Defender* had illegally loaded ballast the night before. The press and the regatta committee were indignant, terming Dunraven's claims "atrocious" and unsportsmanlike.

On the third day Dunraven quickly turned the *Valkyrie* away from the starting line, giving up the race. A couple of months later, when he was safely back in England, Dunraven released his report to the challenging club to the British press, charging fraud. The manager of the *Defender's* syndicate demanded a court of inquiry, which upon due reflection cleared the syndicate and the New York Yacht Club. In the meantime, the press stirred up public opinion across the United States, claiming the national honor had been insulted.

The turmoil made Mr. Dooley recall his own yachting days, when "all a man needed to race was a flat-bottomed boat, an umbrella and a long dhrink." With all the charges, countercharges, and threats of litigation, Dooley believed every yachtsman needed a lawyer as a crew member.

At first glance, it would seem that yachting was about as far removed as possible from the daily life of the average citizen of Bridgeport. But everything was grist for Mr. Dooley's mill, and the running of the America's Cup race reminded him of a contest with similar results between garbage scows on the sanitary canal some years before.

CHICAGO *EVENING POST*, September 14, 1895

"Jawn," said Mr. Dooley, "they say this man Lord Dunraven is dayscinded fr'm an Irish king an' on th' square. I dinnaw whether 'tis thrue or not. Cassidy comes fr'm Brian Boru an' no wan on th' r-road 'd thrust him fr a pint iv milk if iver he needed milk. But if it's so I have me own opinion iv Irish kings. They'll not do to dhraw to.

"He may 've been Irish wanst, but he's English now. Ye see, years ago a boat wint over fr'm here an' raced with English boats an' got th' prize. They calls it a cup, but it looks like a bottle. Well, thin, th' English they had to come over here with a boat fr to win th' cup back, an' divvle th' wan cud they win. They thried an' thried, but 'twas no use. Well, this here Dunraven he got hold iv a boat an' he wint out fr to thry fr it an' they thrun him up in th' air like all th' rist. It made him sore, an', says he, 'I'll hock me coronet,' he says, 'or I'll get a boat that'll do thim,' an' over he comes with th' Vakrythree. Thin a lot iv good fellows down be th' city iv New York—Steve Brodie an' Dr. Parkhurst an' Roosefelt an' O'Donovan Rossa, all good fellows mind ye—they put in an' wint up again this here Lord Dunraven with a scow they called th' Definder.

"Th' Definder won th' first round an' Lord Dunraven, oh, man alive, but he was sore; he pulled his coronet down over his eyes an' swore he'd win in th' sicond

round or die f'r it. He wint out on th' wathers an' whin
they was ready to start this is what he done: I got it
sthraight from th' pa-apers; he hauled it aft an' let
down th' jibboom. Thin he aised up on th' bowsprit an'
blew up th' baloon an' instead iv haulin' fast th' wind-
ward he stuck his taraboom into th' Definder's back-
stays. Th' iffict iv this was to knock 'ell out iv th' main
lift an' throw th' Definder upon her forward stack. Th'
main guy was badly hurted. I don't know which wan iv
th' lads it was, but it must've been a bad hurt.

"'Hol' on there,' says wan iv th' min on th' Definder,
'ye've fouled us.'

"'Divvle th' bit care I,' says Dunraven, cockin' his
coronet over his ear. An' he wint with th' Definder
chasin' him an' its hallyards full iv peaks an' jibs. Iv
coorse th' comity thrun him out an' he's gone away sore.
'Ye'er no spoortsmin,' he says. 'Why over in my
counthry 'tis th' way we start,' he says. 'If wan boat
doesn't foul another,' he says, "tis no start.'

"Th' same case come up on th' canal twinty years
ago. Mike O'Brien had th' scow 'Long John' an' Dorsey
ownded th' 'Juniata.' Th' mules was dhruv be their two
sons. Wan day Dorsey started out down th' canal, an'
O'Brien came afther him. 'I'll race ye f'r a dollar to th'
Sag,' says O'Brien. 'I'll go ye,' says Dorsey. Well, th' two
kids whaled away at th' mules an' Dorsey an' O'Brien
stood on their boats an' yelled at each other. O'Brien
had th' fastest mule. He was out iv th' most famous
mule on th' canal—Lady Annabel, ownded be a man be
th' name iv Clancy. Th' 'Long Jawn' closed down on th'
'Juniata,' an' O'Brien yells out: 'Give way there,' he
says. 'Give way nothin',' says Dorsey, th' wise man
that'd figured O'Brien couldn't pass him on account iv
th' ropes bein' in th' way. Thin he sang 'A wet sheet an'
a flowin' wind,' an' sings out O'Brien to his boy, 'I, I,
pappa,' says th' la-ad. 'I'm goin' to slack out,' says

O'Brien, an' he an' th' other mariners aboord shoved off an' wint around th' 'Juniata,' an' faith th' towline took Dorsey on th' whiskers an' carrid him th' whole linth iv th' yat. I'm tellin' ye th' thruth. 'Twas so. I'll say this f'r O'Brien, that he took no advantage iv Dorsey. He waited f'r him at Willow Springs, an' they spint an hour or two rollin' each other into th' canal.

"Dorsey wudden't pay an' th' matther was referred to a comity at my place. Hannigan was th' chairman, a thrue spoort. Whin we'd heerd th' ividince he says: 'Fr'm reports wee've had we are con-vinced that "Long Jawn" deliberately fouled Dorsey's whiskers in crossing its line outside iv "Juniata." Therefore, we decide that "Juniata" wins, f'r tis th' rule iv yattin',' he says, 'that,' he says, 'th' scow that starts first is th' first at th' Sag. Heave two,' an' they heaved at least tin.

"Did O'Brien go back to Ireland? I sh'd say not. He turned in an' won th' dollar fr'm Dorsey shakin' dice."

7

Golf was a relative latecomer to the United States, but it was adopted enthusiastically when it finally did arrive. The game goes back to ancient times in the British Isles, particularly in Scotland; Mary Queen of Scots was known to have had at least one set of clubs. As Mr. Dooley once declared, "With th' exciption maybe iv th' theery iv infant damnation, Scotland has given nawthin' more cheerful to th' wurruld thin th' game iv galuf." The first golf club in America was probably organized by a Scotsman, John Reid, outside Yonkers, New York, in 1888. Called the St. Andrew's Golf Club after the ancient course in Scotland, it consisted of six holes, and membership dues were $5.00 a year.

In Chicago golfers owe a debt of thanks to an Irishman

who helped promote interest in the game. J. Marshall Weir
was sent by the Irish exhibitors to assist in establishing the
Irish display at the World's Columbian Exposition in 1893.
He was an effective and popular representative for Ireland
during the fair, and when it was over he decided he liked
Chicago so much that he chose not to return home.

Casting about for some way to support himself, he finally
was able to obtain the distributorship for both Irish and
Scotch whiskies. This was not the lucrative deal it would appear, for only very small quantities of either were consumed
by Americans, who preferred the home-grown product to
imports. After giving the matter some thought, Weir seized
upon golf—a Scottish game, of course—as an aid in popu-
larizing his wares. In no time he persuaded some of his
many affluent friends to build the Belmont Golf Club.
Around the same time, the Chicago Golf Club was constructed in nearby Wheaton, Illinois; and in 1894 the Chicago Golf Club, together with the St. Andrew's Club, the
Brookline (Mass.) Country Club, the Shinnecock (L.I.)
Golf Club, and the Newport (R.I.) Golf Club got together
and formed the United States Golf Association, which became the governing body of the game.

Mr. Dooley had an opinion on everything, and he felt that
the game gained such rapid popularity across the country
because "Th' next pleasantest feelin' in th' wurruld to bein'
perfectly happy is bein' perfectly cross. That's why it's took
up be middle-aged gintlemen. They want a chanst to go into
a towering rage in th' open an' undher th' blue sky."

As for Scotch and Irish whiskies, well, they are at least as
popular as golf today.

CHICAGO *EVENING POST*, September 12, 1896

"An' what's this game iv golf like, I dinnaw?" said
Mr. Hennessy, lighting his pipe with much unnecessary

noise. "Ye'er a good deal iv a spoort, Jawnny; did ye iver thry it?"

"No," asaid Mr. McKenna, "I used to roll a hoop once upon a time but I'm out of condition now."

"It ain't like baseball," said Mr. Hennessy, "an' it ain't like shinny, an' it ain't like lawn tennis, an' it ain't like forty-fives, an' it ain't—"

"Like canvas-back duck or anny other game ye know," said Mr. Dooley.

"Thin what is it like?" said Mr. Hennessy. "I see be th' pa-aper that Hobart What-in-th'-name-iv-Gawd-d'ye-call him is wan iv th' best at it. Th' other day he made a scoor iv wan hundherd an' sixty-eight, but whether 'twas miles or stitches I cudden't make out fr'm th' raypoorts. Thim raypoorters has a slovenly style."

"'Tis little ye know," said Mr. Dooley. "Th' game iv golf is as old as th' hills. Me father had golf links all over his place, an' whin I was a kid 'twas wan iv th' principal spoorts iv me life, afther I'd dug th' turf for th' avenin', to go out an' putt—"

"Poot, ye mean," said Mr. Hennessy. "They'se no such wurrud in th' English language as putt. Belinda called me down ha-ard on it no more thin las' night."

"There ye go," said Mr. Dooley angrily, "there ye go! D'ye think this here game iv golf is a spellin' match? 'Tis like ye, Hinnissy, to be refereein' a twenty-round glove context be th' rule iv three. I tell ye I used to go out in th' avenin' an' putt me mashie like hell-an'-all, till I was knowed fr'm wan ind iv th' county to th' other as th' champeen putter. I putted two min fr'm Roscommon in wan day, an' they had to be took home on a dure.

"In America th' ga-ame is played more ginteel an' is more like cigaret smokin' though less onhealthy fr th' lungs. 'Tis a good game to play in a hammock whin ye'er all tired out fr'm social duties or shovelin' coke. Out-iv-dure golf is played be th' followin' rules. If ye bring ye'er wife f'r to see th' game an' she has her name in th' paper that counts ye wan. So th' furst thing ye do is to find th' raypoorter an' tell him ye'er there. Thin ye ordher a bottle iv brown pop an' have ye'er second fan ye with a towel. Afther this ye dhress, an' here ye've got to be dam particklar or ye'll be stuck f'r th' dhrinks. If ye'er necktie is not on sthraight that counts ye'er opponent wan. If both ye an ye'er opponent have ye'er neckties on crooked th' first man that sees it gets th' stakes. Thin ye ordher a carredge—"

"Order what?" demanded Mr. McKenna.

"A carredge."

"What for?"

"F'r to take ye 'round th' links. Ye have a little boy followin' ye carryin' ye'er clubs. Th' man that has th' smallest little boy it counts him two. If th' little boy has th' rickets it counts th' man in th' carredge three. Th' little boys is called caddies, but Clarence Heaney that tol' me all this—he belongs to th' Foorth Wa-ard Golf an' McKinley Club—said what th' little boys calls th' players 'd not be fit f'r to repeat.

"Well, whin ye dhrive up to th' tea grounds—"

"Th' what?" demanded Mr. Hennessy.

"Th' tea grounds, that's like th' homeplate iv baseball or ordherin' a piece iv chalk in a game iv spoil five. It's th' be-ginnin' iv iverything. Whin ye get to th' tea grounds ye step out an' have ye'er hat irned be th' caddie. Thin ye'er man that ye'er goin' aginst comes up an' he asks ye: 'Do ye know Potther Pammer?' Well, if ye don't know Potther Pammer it's all up with ye; ye lose two points. But ye come right back at him with an upper cut: 'Do ye live on th' Lake Shore dhrive?' If he doesn't ye have him in th' nine hole. Ye needn't play with him annymore. But if ye do play with him he has to spot three balls. If he's a good man an' shifty on his feet he'll counter be askin' ye where ye spind th' sum-

mer. Now ye can't tell him that ye spint th' summer
with wan hook on th' free lunch an' another on th'
tickertape, an' so ye go back three. That needn't dis-
courage ye at all, at all. Here's ye'er chance to mix up,
an' ye ask him if he was iver in Scotland. If he wasn't it
counts ye five. Thin ye tell him that ye had an aunt
wanst that heerd th' Jook iv Argyle talk in a phono-
graph, an' unless he comes back an' shoots it into ye
that he was wanst run over be th' Prince iv Wales ye
have him groggy. I don't know whether th' Jook iv Argyle or th' Prince iv Wales counts f'r most. They're like
th' right an' left bower iv thrumps. Th' best players is
called scratch-min."

"What's that f'r?" Mr. Hennessy asked.

"It's a Scotch game," said Mr. Dooley with a wave of
his hand. "I wonder how it come out today. Here's th'
pa-aper. Let me see. McKinley at Canton. Still there.
He niver cared to wandher fr'm his own fireside. Bryan
on th' hog train. Collar-button min f'r th' gool' standard.
Statues iv Heidleback, Ickleheimer an' Company to be
erected in Washington. Another Vanderbilt weddin'.
That sounds like golf but it aint. Newport society livin'
in Mrs. Potther Pammer's cellar. Green-goods men declare f'r honest money. Anson in fourth place some
more. Pianny tuners f'r McKinley. Li Hung Chang
smells a rat. Abner McKinley supports th' goold standard. Wait a minyit; here it is: 'Golf in gay attire.' Let
me see. H'm. 'Foozled his approach'—nasty thing.
'Topped th' ball.' 'Three up an' two to play.' Ah, here's
th' scoor! 'Among those prisint were Messrs an' Mesdames—"

"Hol' on!" cried Mr. Hennessy, grabbing the paper
out of his friend's hands. "That's thim that was there."

"Well," said Mr. Dooley decisively, "that's th' golf
scoor."

V

Mr. Dooley on the Immigrant Experience

Eighteen-forty-five was the crucial year for the Irish in terms of emigration. They had already survived famines in 1822, 1831, 1835, and 1837 and a cholera epidemic in 1830. But in 1845 the potato blight struck and brought with it what came to be known as the "Great Famine." The Irish countryman depended almost solely on this one crop for his sustenance and livelihood; the blight brought with it disaster.

The dependence on this one vegetable had two main causes. First, Ireland was unlike other Western countries in its laws governing the distribution of property. Under the old Irish brehon law, land was held communally by the family or tribe, but this system of land ownership was steadily eroded by later Norman and English invasions.

When Cromwell's troops completed the conquest of Ireland in 1653, it was decided that all rebels would lose their land, with property east of the Shannon going to Protestant settlers, and Irish who could prove they were not rebels would receive property west of the Shannon, which land tended to be rocky and poor for farming. What happened essentially is that Irish Catholics lost the right to own their land and became tenants at the mercy of English and Scottish landlords who were opposed to the local peasantry's developing large and integrated farms.

Second, because the tendency was toward small landholdings, the type of crop planted had to be of the low-cost/high-yield variety. The potato, imported from America, filled the bill.

When the blight came, it lasted for five years, until 1850. Over 1.5 million Irish—men, women, and children—died alongside their rotting potato patches. The lucky ones—two million of them—emigrated, mostly to the United States.

Although they were not the first Irish to land on American soil, the sheer number of them in such a short period of time was staggering, and it was impossible for the country to absorb them readily. Assimilation into the native population was also difficult because most of those who came were desperate both in their poverty, thus needing aid of all kinds immediately, and in their lack of training for the type of life they would have to live in the United States.

It was ironic that these Irish, who were country people, should become not only city dwellers, but that they should eventually draw their strength from and demonstrate their power in the type of settlement they had always shunned in their homeland. At the time of the census of 1890, which found an all-time high in the number of Irish-born living in the United States, only 2 per cent of them were engaged in farming. Yet in Ireland the cities had always been the center of power for the oppressors—founded first by the Danes, then occupied by the Normans and finally the English. In the New World it was to the cities that the Irish flocked for a new chance at life. The average Irish immigrant was poor and knew no trade other than grubbing for potatoes and cutting turf for fires. Neither of these provided an appropriate background for the type of farming done in America. Further, after all they had suffered from trying to wrest a life from the land, it was natural that the Irish should turn away from it. And the cities were in their infancy when the first groundswell of Irish arrived; they could grow with each other.

What the Irish had to offer in the main was sheer physical power. Initially they formed a cheap source of manual labor in the seacoast cities. As these towns began to fill up, the Irish followed the canals and railroad lines, building them as they went, to the new inland settlements, where the life was hard but afforded opportunities which were lacking in the Old Country and even in the East.

In Chicago, as elsewhere, the Irish worked on the boats and the railroad cars, as well as helping literally to build the city by carrying the hod or working as carpenters or masons. Chicago was a rough town, but these men and women came from rough areas, where lawlessness was common and even approved when it was directed at the English invader. They were adaptable.

The Irish possessed two characteristics which other ethnic groups did not and which were to help them in their new life. First, they spoke the English language; Gaelic had disappeared from all but the most rustic parts of Ireland because it was deemed necessary to learn English in order to do business. Secondly, they had learned the value of collective action in their uprisings and political struggles with the landlords. The advantage conferred by the first was obvious, the second, while not as readily apparent, was to give the Irish a say in the forging of the city and its government by their coming together as a political voting block.

When the Irish arrived in Chicago, they tended to gather together in the same neighborhoods and to transfer the social institutions of their village life to the new settlements. The family, the Church, and the saloon were the main institutions in Bridgeport, just as they had been back in Roscommon. The Irish organized at least half a hundred Irish-oriented societies, some of them national and fraternal, such as the Ancient Order of Hibernians, and some of them national and nationalist, as the Clan-na-Gael and the Fenian Brotherhood. Others were local in nature and centered around church activities. Their chauvinistic attitude was a comfort and a prop to the new Irish-American in a city whose atmosphere was rough and ready.

For life in Chicago in the 1890s was not easy for the average workingman. An English journalist, George Steevens, who visited Chicago during this time, while the glories left by the World's Fair were still on view, described the other side of Chicago, away from the business section and the fine homes—a place where "The evening's vacancy brings relief from toil, the morning's toil relief from vacancy." The streets were lined with dirty little huts, steadily rotting away. The sidewalks were made of disintegrating planks, rising and falling by as much as a couple of feet without warning. In rainy weather the roads were oceans of mud; in dry, they were gray ruts. The police were unable to maintain order, and in most neighborhoods it was not advisable for citizens to venture out after dark for fear of the robbers that roamed the poorly lighted streets. Many Chicagoans either accepted the situation or were too apathetic to complain. Steevens summed up the Chicago philosophy toward such urban misery as, "If you come to your death by misadventure among these pitfalls, all the consolation your friends will get from Chicago is to be told that you ought to have taken better care of yourself. You were unfit; you did not survive. There is no more to be said about it."

2

For the great Gaels of Ireland
Are the men that God made mad,
For all their wars are merry,
And all their songs are sad.
—G. K. Chesterton

To be Irish in nineteenth-century Ireland meant to live a hardscrabble existence. One's life had to literally be torn from the stony soil; illness and death were constant, and in the case of the latter, even a welcome, presence. There was tremendous overcrowding, but yet in the midst of hardship, there was always room for one more. Liberties were sharply curtailed by an alien government; this made them all the more precious. Perhaps because they had so little to save, the Irish were a conservative lot. Education was limited because the British had prohibited Catholic Irishmen from using educational facilities in 1695. Schoolmasters caught teaching in defiance of the law were deported to the West Indies or America, where they taught the soon-to-be-seditious colonists. What education there was had to be snatched away from the small number of Irish "hedge" schools. The stereotype of the Irishman with the gift of gab was the result of the low literacy rate—because so few could read and/or write, oratorical ability was highly prized, and the oral tradition was the only way of preserving and passing on the country's history.

To be Irish was to suffer almost constant defeat in battle. Rebel hopes came forth, only to meet a sad and crushing end. Heroes possessed of courage and daring frequently were killed in abortive uprisings too numerous to mention, or they went into exile, leaving behind them a peasantry that was leaderless and demoralized. Under these circumstances, it was natural that the family should become the most important unit and that taking care of one's own should be the most important virtue.

To be Irish was to realize that often the only person upon whom one could depend was oneself; yet this reality made comradeship the more highly prized in Ireland than elsewhere.

According to one of his sons, Peter Dunne "was proud of his Irish blood, but disliked being described as an Irishman. In his own view he was simply an American whose ancestors happened to be Irish."

Nonetheless, it was with affection that Dunne treated the picnic held every August 15 at Ogden's Grove, a popular picnic site, under the aegis of Long John Finerty and the United Irish Societies. In addition to being a social occasion, the gathering served to reinforce Irish-American nationalist sentiment. As the day and the drink wore on, the speeches became more violent—but as Dooley observed, the picnic generated much rhetoric and very little action.

CHICAGO *EVENING POST*, August 18, 1894

TO FREE OLD IRELAND

IT'S DONE WITH PICNICS NOW IN PLACE OF DYNAMITE BOMBS

DOOLEY OUT AT OGDEN'S GROVE

THE REVOLUTIONISTS ENGAGE IN UNCOMMONLY PEACEFUL METHODS OF AGITATION AND ARE HAPPY

"There's wan thing about th' Irish iv this town," said Mr. Dooley.

"Th police!" said Mr. McKenna.

"No," said the philosopher. "But they does give picnics that bates all. Be hivins if Ireland cud be freed be a picnic it ud not on'y be free today, but an impire, by gorra, with Tim Haley, th' Banthry vaggybond, ayvictin' Lord Lord Sahlsb'ry fr'm his houldin'. 'Twould that.

"Jawn, th' la-ads have got th' thrick iv freein' Ireland down to a sinsible basis. In th' ol' da-ays they wint over with dinnymite bombs in their pockets an' eyether got their rowlers on thim in Cork an' blew thimsilves up or was arristed in Queenstown f'r disord'ly conduct. 'Twas a divvle iv a resky job to be a pathriot in thim days, an' none but those th't had no wan dipindint on thim c'd afoord it. But what was th' use? Ireland wint on bein' th' sa-ame opprissed green oil it had always been, an' th' on'y difference th' rivolutions made was ye sa-aw new faces on th' bridges an' th' Wolfe Tones[1] passed another set iv risolutions.

"'Tis different now. Whin we wants to smash th' Sassenach an' restore th' land iv th' birth iv some iv us to

[1] See note 7, Chapter 2.

her thrue place among th' nations, we gives a picnic. 'Tis a damn sight aisier thin goin' over with a slug iv joynt powder an' blown up a polis station with no wan in it. It costs less an' whin 'tis done a man can lep aboord a Clybourn avnoo ca-ar an' come home to his fam'ly an' sleep it off.

"I wint out las' Choosdah an' I suppose I must've freed as manny as eight counties in Ireland. All th' la-ads was there. The first ma-an I saw was Dorgan, the sanyour guarjeen[2] in th' Wolfe Tone Littery Society. He's th' la-ad that have made th' Prince iv Wales thrimble in his moccasins. I he-erd him wanst ma-akin' a speech that near injooced me to take a bomb in me hand an' blow up Westminsther Cathadral. 'A-are ye,' he says, 'min or a-are ye,' he says, 'slaves?' he says. 'Will ye,' he says, 'set idly by,' he says, 'while th' Sassenach,' he says, 'has th' counthry iv Immitt[3] an' O'Connell,'[4] he

[2] Sanyour guarjeen—the top officer of each camp of the Clan-na-Gael was the senior guardian.

[3] Immet—Robert Emmet (1778–1803), imbued with the spirit of the Society of United Irishmen, sparked another abortive uprising in Ireland in 1803. After a short period of street fighting, Emmet escaped to the mountains around Dublin where sympathizers hid him for weeks. He was finally captured; his trial lasted thirteen hours and he was, predictably, sentenced to the scaffold. His final speech was a dramatic rallying cry to the Irish people, and was for years declaimed regularly at Irish gatherings. Of him, his friend, the poet Tom Moore, wrote:

> O, breathe not his name! let it sleep in the shade,
> Where cold and unhonored his relics are laid;
> Sad, silent, and dark be the tears that we shed,
> As the night-dew that falls on the grave o'er his head.
>
> But the night-dew that falls, though in silence it weeps,
> Shall brighten with verdure the grave where he sleeps;
> And the tear that we shed, though in secret it rolls,
> Shall long keep his memory green in our souls.

[4] Daniel O'Connell (1775–1847) became the foremost spokesman on behalf of Irish civil rights during the first part of the nineteenth century. O'Connell, a Catholic from Kerry, was a Gaelic-speaking

says, 'an' Jawn Im Smyth,'[5] he says, 'under his heel,' he
says. 'Arouse,' he says, 'slaves an' dispots,' he says.
'Clear th' wa-ay,' he says. 'Cowards an' thraitors,' he
says, 'Faugh a ballagh,' he says. He had th' beer privilege at th' picnic, Jawn.

"Hinnissy, th' plumber, who blew wan iv his fingers
off with a bomb intinded f'r some iv th' archytecture iv
Liverpool, was runnin' th' knock-th'-ba-aby-down-an'-
get-a-nice-seegar jint. F'r th' good iv th' cause I
knocked th' ba-aby down, Jawn, an' I on'y wish th'
Queen iv England 'r th' Prince iv Wales c'd be injooced
to smoke wan iv th' see-gars. Ye might as well go again
a roman candle. Th' wan I get was ma-ade iv baled hay
an' 'twas rumored about th' pa-ark that Hinnissy was
wur-rkin' off his surplus stock iv bombs on th' pathriots.
His cousin Darcey had th' shootin' gallrey privilege an'
he done a business th' like iv which was niver knowed
be puttin' up th' figure iv a Irish polisman f'r th' la-ads
to shoot at. 'Twas bad in th' ind though, f'r a gang iv
Tipprary la-ads come along behind th' tint an' began
thrown stones at th' copper. Wan stone hit a Limerick
man, an' th' cry 'Butthermilk' wint around, an' be hivins
if it hadn't been that Mike Brennan, th' wise la-ad, sint
none but German polismen to th' picnic there'd not
been a man lift to tell th' tale."

"What's all that got to do with freeing Ireland?"
asked Mr. McKenna.

---

lawyer of compelling personality and splendid rhetorical ability. He
came along during the period of Irish political doldrums which began just after the Irish Parliament had been dissolved by Pitt's Act of
Union. One result of his efforts was the Emancipation Act of 1829
which allowed Catholics to serve in the British Parliament and in other
public offices.

[5] Jawn Im Smyth—Mr. Dooley travels from the sublime to the ridiculous here; John M. Smyth was a local Irish-American businessman
—born aboard ship as his parents sailed from Ireland to the United
States—and Republican politician.

"Well, 'tis no worse off thin it was befure, annyhow,"
said Mr. Dooley.

3

The Irish mass migration to the United States in the 1830s
and 1840s coincided with a rising demand for physical
labor, particularly on the new transportation system that
was being built. Most of the canals had been completed between 1820 to 1830, but thousands and thousands of miles of
railroad track were laid between 1830 and 1880, and a great
deal of it was done by Irish laborers. In those prebulldozer
days, all the digging was done by pick and shovel.

Until he left home, the Irishman regarded himself first as
the member of a family, then of a clan, next of a parish, then
of a county, and finally, sometimes, of a country. Among
these groups back in Ireland there were fierce rivalries, jeal-
ousies, and even hatreds. This did not immediately change
in America. The loneliness, the harshness of life, the herding
together of natural enemies (especially on construction
sites, railroads, and canals, where the workers usually lived
in spartan camps), all gave rise to brawling and skirmishing
known as "faction fighting" by rival gangs of Irish countrymen. Contractors often aggravated the already explosive
situation by providing the men with free whiskey. The
theory was that this would make them work faster, but instead, of course, it made them fight harder. The militia had
to be called out from time to time to quell the worst disturbances, which often resulted in serious injury and sometimes
even in death.

Crowded as it was with people living cheek by jowl, immigrant life was most often a solitary sort of existence. Male
immigrants outnumbered females, in some years by eight or
nine or even ten to one. Married men usually left their wives
and children in the Old Country and then labored for years

to save enough money for passage to bring them over. Those who did have families in America settled them in shanties in places like Bridgeport, which in its early days was described as "both morally and physically . . . a cesspool, a stench in everybody's nostrils." Single men had a hard time finding Irish lasses, women of their own kind, to marry.

On his way to becoming a saloonkeeper, Mr. Dooley tried at least two of the occupations common to the Irish immigrant of his time.

CHICAGO *EVENING POST*, December 22, 1894

WHY DOOLEY QUIT
REMINISCENCES OF THE PHILOSOPHER'S EARLY LIFE HERE
FOUND THE "COUNTIES" STRONG
THE "SHANNYVOGLES" SCARRED HIS LEGS AND THE "BUTTHERMILKS" TRIED TO MAKE A COUPLING WITH HIM

"How come I to go into th' liquor business?" Mr. Dooley repeated. "How come I to go into th' liquor business? Jawn, I give ye me wurrud I done it to get even with me own people. There's on'y two ways f'r to bate th' Irish. Wan is gowan th' polis foorce, an' th' other is to give thim tay. I had an uncle that was highly thought of at Maynooth. I cuddent be a polisman.

"Whin I come over here 'twas me intention f'r to have a goold orchard. All I had to do was to plant a handful iv small change an' thin lay undher th' trees an' blow th' tin dollar notes off th' bra-anches. Afther I'd been here a month I become scared thinkin' that if I got to coughin' I might be dhrownded in money, so I dhruv a dhray an' was without fear. I niver had enough to eat. Th' hor-rse died on me an' I wint to wurruk in th' Northwistrun freighthouse. I did that. An' 'twas beginnin' there I seen what th' Irish was.

"Jawn, I'll tell ye thrue, I'm a Connickman. I'll not

deny it. But I was born near enough to th' County
Clare fr to have to take along an ax whin I'd knocked
th' hurlin'[6] ball over th' bounds. I'll say that much. But
I'll say beyant that, that though Connickmin is put
down fr stealin' horses an' cuttin' th' ligs off cattle
they're no wor-rse thin th' rist iv th' counthry is. Divvle
th' bit. They was in this here freighthouse a man be
th' na-ame iv Casey, an' he was fr'm th' County Kilkinny. White stockin's an' no money, d'ye mind. A
proud people th' Kilkinny people—too proud to fight,
may th' divvle mind them. 'Twas thim that poored
wather on th' locks iv their guns in '98 an' opened th'
wa-ay fr Cromwill, or whoever th' 'ell it was, I dinnaw.
Annyway, I found all th' lead dumped on me thruck an'
all th' feathers on th' Kilkinny la-ads. I sthruck. I
sthruck a ma-an be th' name iv Finley an' th' foreman
sthruck me with a hook an' I was in th' hospital fr wan
whole week.

"Thin I wint to wurruk fr th' Pittsboorg, Fort Wayne
an' Chicago Railroad Comp'ny, an' th' foreman was fr'm
th' County Limerick. Butthermilks, ivry man jack iv
thim down to th' switchmin. I always got along with th'
butthermilks till thin, but whin they thried to make a
couplin' iv me bechune two freightca-ars I wint an' got
me time. 'Twas more thin I could stand. I moved over
to th' Alton, d'ye mind. Here 'twas Dublin. Th' foreman
'd been a jackeen an' there was divvle a wan iv thim
that hadn't dhruv a cab an' didn't know th' raison
Lorrd Friderick[7] was croaked. I said wan day that th'

[6] hurlin'—hurling has been described as a combination of field
hockey and sudden death.

[7] Lorrd Friderick—Lord Frederick Cavendish (1836–82) was assassinated by a band of Irish fanatics called the Invincibles while walking
in Dublin's Phoenix Park in 1882. Lord Frederick had just been appointed Chief Secretary of Ireland, and his murder brought with it
harsh reprisals on the Irish people.

Shannon[8] was beautifuller thin th' Liffey an' they med
me ate coal.

"Th' last job I took was in th' Burlin'ton. Well, iv all
th' places. Ye may ta-alk iv May-o min, but th' Waterford la-ads 'd cut th' buttons fr'm their coats. I was surrounded be Shannyvogles an' Perkladdies, an' before
I'd been there a week I had scars on th' back iv me legs
fr'm th' points iv their thrucks. I wint to th' foreman, an'
says I: 'Thim min is again me,' I says.

"'Fr why should they be?' he says.

"'Because they does be Perkladdies,' says I, 'an' I'm
fr'm Connick.'

"'Come,' says he, 'an' we'll roll around.'

"So we rolled. I was up first, but he took tin dollars
fr'm me time, an' I wint into th' saloon business.

"I had th' plisure three years aftherward iv disfran-
chisin' him. Me an' Donohue held him on th' flure while
big Dochney fed him with raypooblican posthers."

4

In order to write this column and others like it, Dunne drew
upon his store of childhood memories of family friends and
their wistful tales of life in Ireland. This type of sentimental
evocation of days Dunne himself never knew demonstrates
his keen ear, his sense of history, and his sensitivity to the
pain of others.

For despite the fact that Mr. Dooley knew he was better
off in Bridgeport than he would have been had he stayed in
Roscommon, he could not help feeling a pang now and then
for the life he had left behind. After all, like most of the
Irish immigrants to America, Martin J. Dooley did not willingly leave his home; instead he was forced out. Most Irish-

[8] The Shannon River runs through the west of Ireland, while the
Liffey runs through Dublin.

men were not even fortunate enough to own their own small
plot of land; they were known as "cottiers" and rented small
plots, which they cultivated while they worked for others.
At the best of times they lived on the brink of disaster, for
their one- or two-acre farmlets would not provide enough
food for their large families and work was often hard to get.
Irish soil is not rich; one has only to scrape a little to find the
rocky subsurface. As a result, Irish farmers used a mattock
(or a hoe) rather than a plow, which would dig too deep.
Ireland is a rainy country, especially during the growing
season, and in most areas farmers who planted grain crops
would sit and watch as the seed they had planted molded in
the earth from the damp. Even where the Irish farmer was
successful in sowing, the rain often prevented harvesting
any crop that grew.

To make matters worse, in 1846 the British Parliament
abolished the Corn Laws, forbidding the importation of
cheap foreign grain and passed a new set of laws encourag-
ing free trade, making the growing of crops less profitable.
In Ireland the result was the mass eviction of the cottiers
and the turning of their pitiful lots into pasture land.

Between 1820 and 1880 almost 3.5 million Irish came to
the United States. At first, until about 1845, the departures
were largely by skilled tradesmen and the better-off farmers.
Then in 1845, the Great Potato Famine combined with the
desire of the landlords to consolidate their holdings and
gave rise to the great escape. Anglo-Irish authorities, anxious to get the starving peasants off the parish charity rolls,
were only too happy to pay their way to America. In the
decade 1840–50, two million came. Like Mr. Dooley, they
came with an ache in the heart, a tear in the eye, and a sad
song on the lips.

> I'm bidding farewell to the land of my birth
> To wander far over the sea.

I am parting from all I hold dear on earth.
Oh, it's breaking my poor heart will be.
—a song written by Joseph Murphy
and popularized in the 1890s by
the Irish-American singer William
Scanlan

CHICAGO *EVENING POST*, December 23, 1893

IN AN OLDER TIME

HOW CHRISTMAS WAS CELEBRATED IN IRELAND
YEARS AGO WHEN MR. DOOLEY WAS THERE

THE WANDERERS RETURNED, THERE WAS GIVING OF GIFTS
AND DRINKING OF TOASTS, BUT NO SANTA CLAUS

There was a turkey raffle on Halsted Street last night
and Mr. McKenna shook forty-four. He came into Mr.
Dooley's with the turkey under his arm and Mr. Dooley, who was mixing a Tom-and-Jerry dope on the end
of the bar, paused to inquire, "Where'd ye get th' reed
burrd, Jawnny?"

"I won it at Donnelly's raffle," said Mr. McKenna.

"Ye ought to 've kep' it in a warm place," said Mr.
Dooley. "It's shrinkin' so 'twill be a fishball befure ye
get home. It must be a canned turkey. I've seen th' likes
iv that in th' ol' counthry f'r ivrybody that cud get thim
wanted turkey f'r Chris'mas an' if they cuddent get a
big fat gobbler with mate enough on him to feed a rig-
mint iv Mayo min they took what they got, an' they got
wan iv thim little herrin' turkeys like th' burrd ye have
under ye'er ar-rm. Faith, it wasn't all iv thim cud get
that much, poor things. There was places in th' pa-art iv
Ireland ye'er people come fr'm, Jawn, with ye'er
di'mons an' ye'er gol'headed umbrellas, where a piece iv
bacon an' an exthra allowance iv pitaties was a feast f'r
th' kids. 'Twas in ye'er town, Jawn, that th' little girl,

whin she wanted to remimber something, says to th' ol'
man; 'Why,' she says, 'ye remimber 'twas th' day we
had mate,' says she. She remimbered it because 'twas
th' day they had mate, Jawn. 'Twas like Christmas an'
th' Foorth iv July an' Pathrick's day, whin they had
mate in ye'er part iv Ireland, Jawn. On other occasions
they had pitaties an' butthermilk, or, if their neighbors
wuz kind, oatmale stirabout. Poor things! Did I iver tell
ye about me Uncle Clarence that died iv overatin' reed
burrds?"

"You did," said Mr. McKenna surlily, for it was a
point upon which Mr. Dooley often jibed him.

"Annyhow," said Mr. Dooley, grinning, "poor or rich
alike, th' people iv Ireland never let th' Christmas pass
without cellybratin'. Ye'd know th' day was comin' frim
th' gr-reat coortin' that'd be goin' on ivrywhere. Advint
week was always gr-reat coortin' time fr th' la-ads.
They'd make love befure Christmas an' get married
aftherward if th' gir-rls 'd have thim an' they mostly
would. That's a way th' gir-rls have th' whole wur-ruld
over.

"Thin ivery man 'd wish fr a snowy Chris'mas. A
green Chris'mas makes a fat churchyard, says th' good
book, an' like as not there'd be snow on th' ground, at
laste in Maynooth where I come fr'm. An' about
Chris'mas eve th' lads an' lasses 'd go into th' hills an'
fetch down ivry to hang above th' hearth an' all th' kids
'd go light on th' stirabout so's they could tuck in more
on th' morrow. Chris'mas eve th' lads that 'd been away
'd come thrampin' in from Gawd knows where, big lads
far fr'm home in Cork an' Limerick an' th' City iv Dublin—come thrampin' home stick in hand to ate their
Chris'mas dinner with th' ol' folks. Dear, oh dear, how I
remimber it. 'Twas a long road that led up to our house
an' me mother'd put a lamp in th' windy so's th' la-ads
could see th' way. Manny's th' time I've heerd th' beat

iv th' stick on th' road an' th' tap on th' pane an' me
mother runnin' to th' dure an' screamin' Mike, 'r Tim, 'r
Robert Immitt an' cryin' on his shoulder. 'Twas, let me
see, four fours is sixteen, an' thirty makes forty-six—
'twas in th' Christmas iv fifty-sivin I last seen me
brother Mike, poor fellow, poor fellow.

"We was up early, ye may say that, th' nex' mornin'.
Some iv th' pious wans 'd go to th' midnight mass an'
thim we called 'voteens.' But th' kids had little thought
iv mass till they opened their Chris'mas boxes. Poor little Chris'mas boxes they was, like enough a bit iv a
dolly f'r th' little girls an' a Jack-in-the-box with
whiskers like Postmaster Hesing's an' a stick iv candy.
There's on'y wan thing ye have over here that we niver
had at home, an' that's Sandy Clause. Why is it, 'd'ye
suppose? I never knew that St. Patrick druv him out
with th' snakes, but I niver heerd iv him till I come to
this counthry.

"Thin afther th' Chris'mas boxes th' kids 'd go out in
th' road an' holler 'Chris'mas box' at ivry man they met
an' thin wud be off to mass where th' priest's niece sung
th' 'Destah Fidelis,' an' ivry man chipped in a shillin' or
two f'r th' good man. By gar, some iv thim soggarths
was bor-rn politicians, f'r they cud jolly a man f'r givin'
big an' roast him f'r givin' a little till ivry citizen in th'
parish was thryin' to bate his neighbor like as if 'twas at
a game iv give-away. Ye'd hear thim comin' home fr'm
th' church. 'Th' iday iv Mike Casey givin' tin shillin's
whin Badalia Casey burrid a pinch iv tay fr'm me on'y
las' week.' 'What a poor lot thim Dugans is. Before I'd
be read frim th' altar with six pince afther me name I'd
sell th' shoes off me feet. I heerd Tim Dugan got three
poun' tin f'r that litther iv boneens. Did ye notice he
wint to his jooty today. Faith, 'tis time. I was thinkin'
he was goin' to join th' Prowtestants.'

"An' so 'twud go. Thin they was dinner, a hell iv a

dinner, iv turkey, or goose with bacon an' thin a bottle iv th' ol' shtuff with limon an' hot wather, an' toasts was drunk to th' la-ads far away an' to thim in prison an' to another reunion an' late at night me mother 'd tuck us all in bed an' lade me father to his room with his jag upon him singin' 'Th' Wearin' iv th' Green' at th' top iv his voice. Thim ol' days!"

"Well, Martin, good night," said McKenna. "A merry Christmas before I see you again."

"Merry Christmas," said Mr. Dooley. If Mr. McKenna had returned five minutes later he would have found Mr. Dooley sitting on the edge of the bed in the back room wiping his eyes on the bar towel.

5

The Irish were luckier than some of the other peasant classes which immigrated to America, for they had a rich culture and a history of group action. Most important, they had their Catholic Church to which they were fiercely loyal. This loyalty made them seem strange to other Americans, despite the common language. In 1820 there were at most 500,000 Roman Catholics in the United States, and the Church was regarded as a French institution. By 1880 there were more than six million Catholics, and most of them were Irish.

In early Chicago for a number of years there was only one Catholic church, St. Mary's, a "French" church. With more and more Irish and German Catholics flooding into the city, churches tended to be separated into English-speaking and German-speaking parishes. In some neighborhoods, though, the language decision was not clear cut and sometimes there was strife. In one parish the debate waxed long and acrimonious. Finally, the parish priest, an Irishman with the wisdom of Solomon, elected to sing mass in Gaelic, which of course neither group could understand.

As the city grew, the various nationalities put their stamp on the Church, and none more so than the Hibernians. When the Irish claimed a neighborhood, one of their first moves was to erect a church, which they paid for out of their own meager earnings. This gave them a much more proprietary attitude than they had had toward the already existing churches back in Ireland. The Catholic church was the pride of each Chicago parish; indeed, even today in Chicago there are those who identify themselves not in terms of what neighborhood they live in, but what parish they hail from.

In addition to serving spiritual needs, the church was the primary social center for the family unit. Mr. Dooley's story of a church fair in a neighboring parish details a common event in the life on Archey Road.

CHICAGO *EVENING POST*, December 29, 1894

DOOLEY AT THE FAIR

THE PHILOSOPHER ATTENDS A SOCIAL EVENT AT ST. HONORIA'S

CASUALTY AT THE ICE CREAM TABLE

THE HOLLOW VICTORY OF MR. COSTIGAN, OF MAYO, "THE MOST POPULAR MAN IN THE PARISH"

"Jawn, d'ye know who's th' most pop'lar man in St. Honoria's parish?" asked Mr. Dooley.

"The little priest ought to be," said Mr. McKenna.

"Well, iv coorse, we ba-ar him. Th' most pop'lar man in th' parish is Cornelius J. Costigan. He bate th' aldherman an' Aloysius Regan. He did that.

"I like Fa-ather Hogan, though he an' Fa-ather Kelly does be at outs over th' Nicene council an' th' ma-an Hopkins put to wurruk on th' r-rid bridge. So whin he

come over with tickets f'r th' fair an' I seen he had a
game lig fr'm toddlin' around in th' snow makin' sick
calls I bought two an' wint over th' closin' night—'twas
las' Saturdah. 'Twas a g-grand affair. They had Roddy's
Hibernyun band playin' on th' cor-rner an' th' basemint
iv th' church was packed. In th' ba-ack they had a shootin' gall'ry where ye got five shots f'r tin cints. Hogan,
th' milkman, was shootin whin I wint in an' iverybody
was out iv th' gall'ry. He missed eight shots an' thin he
thrun two lumps iv coal at th' ta-arget an' made two
bull's eyes. He is a Tipp'rary man an' th' raison he's over
here is he hit a polisman with a rock at twinty ya-ards—
without sights.

"I'd no more thin inthered th' fair thin who should
come up but Malachi Dorsey's little girl, Dalia. 'Good
avnin',' she says. 'Won't ye take a chanst?' she says. 'On
what?' says I. 'On a foldin' bed,' says she. 'Faith, I will
not,' I says. 'I'll take no chances on no foldin' bed,' I
says. 'I was locked up in wan wanst,' I says. She lift me
alone afther that, but she must've tipped me off to th'
others, f'r whin I come away I stood to win a doll, a
rockin' chair, a picture iv th' pope done by Mary Ann
O'Donoghue, a deck iv ca-ards an' a tidy. I'm all right if
th' combination comes out ayether way fr'm th' rockin'
chair to th' doll 'r th' tidy. But I wuddent know what th'
divvle to do if I sh'd catch th' pope iv R-rome an' th'
ca-ards.

"Th' booths was something iligant. Mrs. Dorsey had
th' first wan where she sold mottoes an' babies' clothes.
Next to hers was th' ice crame layout, with th' Widdow
Lonergan in cha-arge. Some wan touted big Hinnissy
again it. He got wan mouthful iv it an' began to holler.
'F'r th' love iv hivin' won't some wan give me a cup iv
tay,' he says. 'Me insides is like a skatin' rink.' He wint
over an' shtud be th' fire with his coattails apart till th'
sexton put him out.

"Acrost th' hall was th' table f'r church articles, where ye cude get 'Keys iv Hevin' an' 'St. Thomas a Kempises' an' ros'ries. It done a poor business they tell me, an' Miss Dolan was that sore at th' eyesther shtew thrade done be Mrs. Cassidy next dure that she come near soakin' her with th' 'Life iv St. Rose iv Lima'. 'Twas tur-r-ble.

"But I wanted to tell ye about th' mos' pop'lar man. Iv coorse, ye know th' ga-ame. Ye've been again it. Well, they had th' stand in th' middle iv th' flure an' 'twas bossed be Donnigan, th' lawyer. Donnigan is president iv the Young Married Min's Sodality an' dhraws all th' thrade iv th' parish; he's gettin' rich. Th' names iv th' candydates was on th' blackboord—th' aldherman, Costigan an' Regan. Ye know Regan. Real estate man. Costigan has made enough conthractin' to be thinkin' iv movin' away, an' th' aldherman was bound to win.[9] Regan is fr'm Kildare, Costigan's a black hear-rted villain fr'm th' County Mayo an' th' aldherman come fr'm Wexford, though a dacint man. He married a towny iv mine. She was second cousin iv me wife's[10] second cousin, Judy Flynn.

"Th' votes dhropped in mighty fast till iliven o'clock an' thin they poored in. Poor Doheny come fr'm threatin' th' ba-and an' he wint up to vote. 'How much?' says he. 'Fifty cints,' says Donnigan. ''Tis not enough,' says Doheny. 'Niver liss thin a dollar.' He'd hear-rd, d'ye mind, that th' candydates was spindin' money f'r votes an' he'd made a conthract f'r to bring down a lodgin' house. He was that mad.

[9] Costigan would indeed be taking his chances on getting further business from his Bridgeport neighbors if he did in fact move away, for it was one of the unwritten laws that the successful members of the community should stay there and help along their less successful brethren.

[10] Mr. Dooley is having a little fun with Mr. McKenna; of course, he was never married.

"Each wan iv th' three had some wan to place his
money. Donnigan kept thim runnin' for more. O'Malley'd come r-rushin' up with a bunch iv bills an' roar
'Wan hundherd votes f'r Costigan!' In a minyit they'd
be two more rolls undher Donnigan's nose. 'Wan hundherd an' fifty f'r th' aldherman!' 'Wan hundherd an'
thirty-five f'r Regan!' Whin we seen odd numbers
comin' we knowed Regan was down. He begun borryin'
fr'm his frins an' thin he dhropped out intirely, lavin' th'
race to Costigan an' th' aldherman. He made an assignment th' nex' day. Whin th' polls closed th' Mayo man
had him beat be two votes an' half th' people lef' in disgust."

"For why?" asked Mr. McKenna.

"F'r why?" said Mr. Dooley scornfully. "Th' idee
that anny rayspict'ble parish sh'd allow a May-o man to
go around wearin' a diamond stud an' boastin' himself
th' mos' pop'lar man! I tell ye what, Jawn, 'tis goin' too
far. I'll not knock anny church, d'ye mind, but I'll say
this here an' now, that manny nice people was that
angry they wint to th' Frinch church, where they cuddent undherstand th' announcement, th' next day."

6

John McKenna had been born in the United States—"away
from home," as Mr. Dooley put it. Mr. Dooley himself came
over on one of what the Irish called "coffin ships," for so
many died on them during the voyage. The fare varied from
around $12.50 to $25.00—a vast sum in those days, and one
which usually represented the pooled resources of a family
or even a village. The idea was that the successful immigrant would send for the others as he made money in the
New World. After gathering up the passage money and
whatever personal effects that could be transported, these

people, many of whom had not been beyond their own villages, stepped off for their adventure into the unknown. They begged for food along the walk to the closest seaport, and some died along the way. When they got to the port, they might have to wait for weeks in overcrowded lodging houses near the docks for the next sailing.

Once aboard ship, the crossing to America could take anywhere from three to six weeks. Overcrowding was a commonplace, but the cramming of human beings into tiny spaces became so outrageous that the United States finally ruled that the ships could take on only two passengers per ton of ship size. Passengers in steerage brought along their own food and prepared it themselves; if they misjudged the amount needed or if the passage took longer than expected, they either had to purchase additional supplies from rapacious captains or go hungry. While a handful of the fortunate lived in relative comfort in the cabins, below deck the immigrants huddled on small cots in communal quarters. Sanitation was totally neglected and such dread diseases as smallpox, cholera, yellow fever, and influenza thinned the ranks during the voyage, while seasickness contributed to further misery. When weather permitted, they were allowed on deck for a few hours of fresh air and exercise. Most of their time, however, was spent in the foul miasma of the hold. It was said in Boston that one could always tell when a load of Irishmen had arrived because of the smell. The end of the voyage brought little relief from anxiety. Those with contagious diseases faced quarantine, and all dreaded the physical examination because failure to pass it would mean being turned back home.

Once they had landed, the naïve immigrants were at the mercy of confidence men who preyed on the greenhorn by offering to help him find work and lodging for a price and then making off with what meager grubstake the poor soul had brought with him. It was the fortunate immigrant who had relatives already over who came to meet him or who had provided him with a ticket to the interior. Possessed of very slender means, it was essential that the newly arrived Irish find work immediately. Fortunately, the circumstances of the industrial revolution and national expansion provided a burgeoning market for cheap, unskilled labor. Straw bosses and foremen met the boats to hire the raw recruits.

CHICAGO *EVENING POST*, February 16, 1895

DOOLEY IN THE STORM

HIS EXPERIENCE IN CROSSING THE BROAD ATLANTIC

ROSCOMMON MAN'S REVENGE
AND THE MAN FROM TIPPERARY WITH HIS LITTLE BABY

TRAGEDY MIXED WITH COMEDY

"Poor lads, poor lads," said Mr. Dooley, putting aside the newspaper and rubbing his glasses. "'Tis a ha-ard lot their's, thim that go down into th' say in ships, as Shakespare says. Ye niver see a storm on th' ocean? Iv coorse ye didn't. How cud ye, ye that was bor-rn away fr'm home? But I have, Jawn, may th' saints save me fr'm another.

"I come over in th' bowels iv a big, crazy balloon iv a propeller like wan iv thim that ye see hooked up to Dimpsey's dock, loaded with lumber an' slabs an' Swedes. We watched th' little ol' island fadin' away behind us, with th' sun shtrikin' th' white house tops iv Queenstown an' lightin' up th' chimblies iv Martin Hogan's liquor shtore. Not wan iv us but had lift near all we loved behind, an' sare a chanst that we'd iver spoon th' stirabout out iv th' pot above th' ol' peat fire again. Yis, by dad, there was wan—a lad fr'm th' County Roscommon. Divvle th' tear he shed. But whin we had pa-arted fr'm land he turns to me an' says: 'Well, we're on our way,' he says. 'We are that,' says I. 'No chanst f'r thim to turn around an' go back,' says he. 'Divvle th' fut,' says I. 'Thin,' he says, raisin' his voice, 'to 'ell with th' Prince iv Wales,' he says. 'To 'ell with him,' he says.

"An' that was th' last we see iv sky or sun f'r six days. That night come up th' divvle's own storm. Th' waves tore an' walloped th' ol' boat an' th' wind howledgean' ye could hear th' machin'ry snortin' beyant. Murther, but I was sick. Wan time th' ship'd be sittin' on its tail, another it'd be standin' on its head, thin rowlin' over cowlike on th' side, an ivry time it lurched me stommick lurched with it, an' I was tore an' rint an' racked till if death 'd come it'd found me willin'. An' th' Roscommon man, glory be, but he was disthressed. He set on th' flure with his hands on his belt an' his face as white as stone, an' rocked to an' fro. 'Aho,' he says; 'aho, but me insides has torn loose,' he says, 'an' are tumblin' around,' he says. 'Say a pather an' avy,' says I, I was that mad with th' big bosthoon f'r blatherin' on th' flure. 'Say a pather an' avy,' I says, 'f'r ye'er near to death's dure, avick.' 'Am I,' says he, raisin' up. 'Thin,' says he, 'to 'ell with th' whole rile fam'ly' he says. Oh, he was a ribil!

"Through th' storm there was a babby cryin'. 'Twas a little wan no more thin a year ol', an' 'twas ownded by a Tipp'rary man, who come fr'm near Clonmel, a poor, weak, scarey lookin' little divvle that lost his wife an' thin see th' bailiff walk off with th' cow, an' thin see him come back again with th' process servers. An' so he was comin' over with th' babby, an' bein' mother an' father to it. He'd rock it be th' hour on his knees an' talk dam nonsinse to it an' sing to it. 'A-ah, 'twas there I mit a maiden, down be th' tanya-ard side,' an' 'Th' Wicklow Mountaineer,' an' 'Th' Rambler fr'm Clare,' an' 'O'Donnell Aboo'—croonin' thim in th' little babby's ear an' payin' no attintion to th' poorin' thunder above his head. Day an' night, day an' night, poor soul. An' th' babby cryin' out its heart an' him setting there with his eyes as red as his hair an' makin' no kick. Poor soul.

"But wan day th' ship settled down steady an' our ragin' stummicks with it, an' th' Roscommon man shakes himsilf an' says: 'To 'ell with th' Prince iv Wales an' th' Dook iv Edinboroo,' an' goes out, an' near all th' steerage followed, f'r th' storm had done its worst an' had gone on to throuble those that come afther, an' may th' divvle go with it. Th' waves was r-runnin' low an' peaceful, an' thinks I: "Twill be a rest f'r that little Tipp'rary man,' thinks I, 'f'r th' babby have stopped cryin'.' He had been settin' on a stool but he come over to me. 'Th' storm,' says I, 'is over.' 'Yis,' says he, "tis over.' "Twas wild while it lasted,' says I. 'Ye may say so,' says he. 'Well, please Gawd,' says I, 'that it left none worse off than us.' 'It blew ill f'r some an' also f'r others,' says he. 'Th' babby's gone.'

"An' so it was, Jawn, f'r all his rockin' an' singin'. An' in th' avnin' they burrid it over th' side into th' say, an' th' little Tipp-rary man wint up an' see thim do it. He see thim do it."

7

I don't believe in too much foorce, but ye've always got to flavor th' porridge with it.

—Mr. Dooley

The nationalism of American Irishmen led to the founding of a number of organizations whose main goal was to set about the freeing of Ireland. On the way to achieving that goal, these societies filled a need for a rallying point in the Irish-American community, and thus served more than one purpose.

The Fenian Brotherhood was named for a brave group of early Irishmen called the Fianna, whose feats of derring-do make up a good portion of early Irish folklore. The Fenians were organized in the United States in 1858 and were also known as the Irish Republican, or Revolutionary, Brotherhood, depending which side of the Atlantic you were on. During the American Civil War, the Fenians fought on both sides, sometimes meeting between the lines under a flag of truce to discuss the Irish campaign, and they hoped eventually to use their military training in an invasion of Ireland; when Mr. Dooley said, "I niver in me life seen anything done without they was a gun play somewhere concerned in it," he was voicing the opinion of most Irish Americans, peace loving as they were in their adopted country, that Ireland would never be free without a show of arms.

Finances and disparate factions made such an invasion impossible, so the Fenians picked a less distant target—Canada. In 1866 they launched their first offensive from Buffalo, New York, and St. Albans, Vermont. Dooley's Uncle Mike, together with about 1,000 other Chicagoans, was with the Buffalo group. The Fenian troops were driven back by Canadian militiamen to American territory without fighting even one skirmish. American authorities took a lenient attitude towards them.

While the Fenians won no honors on the battlefield, their attempt was widely publicized. Further, their efforts were tolerated by both political parties in the United States because of the vote the Fenians could deliver. The final Fenian offensive crossed the Canadian border at St. Albans in 1870, only to again be driven back in ignominious defeat. By this time the Fenians had also lost control over the Irish-American voter, and President Ulysses Grant announced that the pseudogovernmental activities of the Fenian movement would no longer be tolerated. It was soon succeeded by the Clan-na-Gael.

CHICAGO *EVENING POST*, June 15, 1895

"I see be th' pa-apers," said Mr. Dooley, "that Cleveland have sint out a tip to the Cuban rivoluters, that if they keep on rivolutin' on th' primises he'll have thim all arristed an' sint to th' bridewill f'r disordley conduct. There's an ordinance again rivolutin' in this counthry, though nawthin' has been said about it befure. 'Tis like midnight closin'. Wan administration laves us keep open till we get tired, an' another makes us shut up tight an' on'y let in thim polismin we know well. So be Cleveland an' th' Cuban rivoluters.

"D'ye know, Jawn, 'twas this same Cleveland that definded th' Fenians whin they was took up f'r invadin' Canada. 'Twas so. He was not much in thim days—a kid iv a lawyer, like Doheny's youngest, with a lot iv hair an' a long cooat an' a hungry look. Whin th' Fenians came back fr'm Canada in a boat an' landed in th' City iv Buffalo, New York, they was all run in, an' sare a lawyer cud they get to defind thim till this here Cleveland come up, an' says he: 'I'll take th' job,' he says. 'I'll go in an' do th' bist I can f'r ye.' Me uncle Mike was along with thim, an' he looked Cleveland over, an' says he: 'Ye'll do th' bist ye can f'r us,' he says, 'will ye?' he says. 'Well,' he says, 'I'll take no chances,' he says. 'Sind f'r th' disk sergeant,' he says. 'I'm goin' to plead guilty an' turn informer,' he says. 'Tis lucky f'r Cleveland me uncle Mike died befure he r-run f'r Prisidint. He'd've had wan vote liss.

"I'll niver forget th' night me uncle Mike come back fr'm Canada. Ye know he was wan iv th' mos' dis'prate Fenians that iver lived, an' whin th' movement begun he had to thread on no wan's shadow befure he was off f'r th' battle. Ivry wan in town knew he was goin', an' he wint away with a thrunk full iv bottles an' all th' good wishes iv th' neighborhood, more be reason iv th' fact that he was a boistherous man whin he was th' worse fr wear, with a bad habit iv throwin' bricks through his neighbors' windows. We cud see him as th' thrain moved out, walkin' up an' down th' aisle askin' if there was anny Englishmin in th' ca-ar that'd like to go out on th' platform an' rowl off with him.

"Well, he got up into New York somewhere an' met a lot iv other dis'prate min like himself an' they wint across th' border singin' songs an' carryin' on, an' all th' militia iv New York was under ar-rms, fr it'd been just like thim to turn round an' do their fightin' in New York. 'Twas damn little me uncle Mike cared who he fought.

"But be hook or be crook, they got to where th' other Fenians was an' jined in th' army. They'd come fr'm far an' near, an' they were young an' old, poor lads some iv thim bint on sthrikin' th' blow that'd break th' back iv British tyr-anny an' some jus' crazed fr fightin'. They had big guns an' little guns an' soord canes an' pitch-forks an' scythes an' wan or two min had come over armed with baseball bats. They had more gin'rals than ye cud find in a raypublican Wist Town convintion an' iv'ry private was at laste a colonel. They made me uncle Mike a brigadier gin'rall. 'That'll do fr a time,' says he; 'but whin th' fun begins I'll pull Dorney off his horse an' be a major gin'ral,' he says. An' he'd've done it too, on'y they was no fightin'. They marched on an' th' British ran away fr'm thim, an' be hivins me uncle Mike cud niver get a shot at a ridcoat, though he searched high an' low fr wan. Thin a big rainstorm come an' they was no tints to protict thim, an' they set around shiv'rin' an' swearin'. Me uncle Mike was a bit iv a politician an' he organized a meetin' iv th' la-ads that had come over with him an' sint a comity to wait on th' major gin'ral.

'Dorney,' says me uncle Mike, f'r he was chairman iv th' comity. 'Dorney,' he says, 'me an' me associated warriors wants to know what th' 'ell,' he says. 'What d'ye mane?' says Dorney. 'Ye brought us up here,' says me uncle Mike, 'to fight th' British,' he says. 'If ye think,' he says, 'that we come over,' he says, 'to engage in a six days' go-as-you-please walkin' match,' he says, 'Ye'd better go an' have ye'er head looked into be a vethrinary surgeon,' he says. 'Have ye anny British around here? Have ye e'er a Sassenach concealed about ye'er clothes?' he says. 'We can't do annything if they won't stand f'r us,' says Dorney. 'Thin,' says me uncle Mike, 'I wash me hands iv th' whole invasion,' he says. 'I'll throuble ye f'r me voucher,' he says. 'I'm goin' back to a counthry where they'll grow min that'll stand up an' fight back,' he says, an' he an' his lads wint over to Buffalo an' was locked up f'r rivolutin.'

"Me uncle Mike come home on th' bumpers iv a freightcar, which is th' way most rivoluters come home ixcipt thim that comes home in th' baggagecar—in crates. 'Uncle Mike,' says I to him, 'what's war like annyhow?' 'Well,' says he, 'in some rispicts 'tis like missin' th' las' ca-ar,' he says, 'an' in other rispicts 'tis like gettin' gay in front iv a polis station,' he says. An', by dad, whin I come to think iv what they call wars nowadays, I believe me uncle Mike was right. 'Twas diff'rent whin I was a la-ad. They had wars in thim days that was wars."

8

Accustomed as they were to hardship back home, the Irish often found their new life hard to bear as well. There was the extreme crowding, of course. Many worked as casual labor, hired by the day. They were always conscious of a nagging fear about tomorrow; would they find work? It was difficult to observe the holidays and holy days that had added an extra ounce of joy in the Old Country because work went on regardless; a seven-day week was not uncommon. And when the factory or building site did close down for Christmas or Easter, it was still not the lighthearted occasion one could wish, for no work meant no pay. In Bridgeport many of the men worked at seasonal jobs in the meatpacking plants (which only operated in the winter) or on construction, so that there was a high level of periodic unemployment.

The Chicago workingman's wage ranged between $1.25 for an unskilled man to $3.00 for a journeyman carpenter per day. Although the cost of living was much lower than it is today, it was still very hard to support a family on the average $9.00 a week take-home pay that most men received. This $9.00 was remuneration for a six-day week, and the eight-hour day was still a dream. Thus, the slightest increase in the cost of the necessities of life could mean disaster for a family. The men worked hard and under dangerous conditions, and either burned themselves out early or died young, leaving behind a poor widow with many children to support.

There is no satisfactory explanation for it, but it is true that the Irish seemed to be content with providing the brawn rather than the brains that built Chicago. The new immigrants and their children did not move as rapidly up the occupational ladder as did other ethnic groups, notably the Germans, who arrived in large numbers at about the same time. In the census of 1890, 34 per cent of the Irish men were unskilled laborers, as opposed to 18 per cent of the Germans and 6 per cent of the native born. In addition to working in the plants, factories, and railroads, a high percentage of employed Irish were bartenders, policemen, and domestics. Only 4 per cent of all lawyers were Irish, 3 per cent of the bankers, 2 per cent of the doctors.

Further, the Chicago workingman was a helpless pawn in the hands of his employers. Over his head there always hung the fear of the black list, a common device used by employers to keep undesirables off anyone's payroll. Mr. Dooley does not explain why Matthew Hagan had been black-listed in the first place, but he was a railroad man, and the railroad workers in Chicago were early and eager proponents of unionization. It is likely that Hagan might have engaged in such activity.

CHICAGO *EVENING POST*, November 30, 1895

"Th' minyit Thanksgivin' Day's over," said Mr. Dooley, "'tis forgotten; lasteways, ye begin thinkin' iv th' next wan. They'se no day afther with us. Sure th' min that made it must've been Appea'o, f'r puttin' it on a Thursdah. To fall fr'm turkey with crambry sauce to codfish is enough to kill th' faith iv anny Christyan. 'Tis so; I always count th' day inded whin Hinnissy takes th' leg. All day long that man was dhrivin' away at th' burrd on th' table. He had th' first cut iv th' brist at noon an' at 8 o'clock th' pope's nose[11] fell to him. He took th' las' leg at iliven o'clock in th' night an' thin says he, 'Thanks be,' he says, 'they'se no more turkey.' 'Thanks be,' says I f'r th' turkey, 'they'se no more Hinnissy,' I says. 'Ye've lift enough iv it,' I says, 'to answer to th' thrumpet on th' last day,' I says.

"Well, Jawn, they'se wor-rse things to be thankful f'r thin havin' nothin' more to eat. D'ye know th' Hagans, down be Main sthreet? Ye do, iv coorse. Well, d'ye know that there Macchew Hagan has been out iv steady wurruk f'r near a year? A proud, black man, Hagan. A Kilkenny man, his father was a schoolmasther near where Dan'l O'Connell come fr'm, but Macchew

[11] the pope's nose—the tail piece of a turkey or chicken.

left away young an' wint to wurruk on a railroad.[12]

"I dinnaw how he come to lose his job. Faith, I niver
knew he'd lost it till las' week. Th' childher was just as
clane. Th' good woman wint to her jooties just th' same.
An' whin ye met Hagan 'twas always: 'Macchew, how
d'ye do?' 'Plaze Gawd, well, thank ye,' ''Tis a fine day,
intirely.' ''Tis so, plaze Gawd.'

"He'd niver let on, but f'r days an' days, Jawn, he
thramped th sthreets—out early, out late. Hinnissy says
he'd seen him comin' home in th' dark, staggerin like a
dhrunken man an' with his gray face down in his chist.
But whin Hinnissy said: 'Good avnin, Misther Hagan;
'tis fine weather we're havin',' he'd come back with a
smile on his white lips. 'Fine weather, plaze Gawd,'
he'd say. 'Ye'er home late?' 'Ah-h, sure,' says he, 'I like
th' walk,' he says. ''Tis gran' to be out loosenin' me ol'
bones such a night as th' like.'

"Well, Jawn, d'ye know th' man'd been downtown
walkin' fr'm house to house, carryin' coal an' poundin'
with a hose at carpets, thin thrampin' home to save th'
nickel or, more like, without enough money in his
pocket to pay ca-ar fare. He had so! But he'd have a
smile an' a proud bow f'r th' bist iv thim. Ye'd niver
know fr'm th' face iv him that he wasn't a man ar-rnin
his tin per an' without a care on his mind fr'm six in th'
avnin' to five in th' mor-rnin'.

"But th' neighbors heerd iv him not bein' well off
an' begun to talk iv keepin' him. A comity iv th' Ladies
Aid Society wint to th' house to see th' wife. She looked
thim over through th' side iv th' dure. She knew they
was comin'. 'What will ye have with me?' she says. 'We
hear ye are in disthress,' says Mrs. Cassidy, an' we've
been diligated,' she says, 'f'r to investigate ye'er case
duly,' she says, 'an raypoort thereon,' she says. 'Is that

[12] By inference, Dooley is saying that Hagan was of a slightly higher
class because his father had taught school.

all?' says th' little woman. 'That is sufficient,' says Mrs.
Cassidy—ye know her, that pompous little fat ol' wash-
erwoman that talks like an advertisement iv bakin'
powdher. 'Well, thin,' says th' little woman, 'I thank ye
kindly,' she says, an' closed th' dure on thim. Some iv
thim was f'r foorcin' their way in an' takin' an' invinthry
but they didn't do it.

"Well, las' week I was standin' in front iv Hagan's
talkin' with a Kerry man be th' name iv O'Donnell,
whin along came Hagan, r-runnin', with his hat in his
hand. Whin he seen us he stopped an' put on th' cau-
been. 'Good avnin,' says he. 'Fine night,' says I. ''Tis so,
plaze Gawd,' says he. Th' little woman met him at th'
dure. He caught her in his ar-rms. 'Peggy,' says he. 'Is it
thrue?' she says. 'Tell me, 'tis thrue, acushla.' An' he carrid her in, closin' th' dure behind him.

"Well, d'ye know what it was Jawn? They'd taken th'
black list off him an' he'd gone to wurruk. That was it.
An' to think iv a man givin' thanks to Hivin f'r bein' allowed to wurruk!"

9

While the Irish shied away from charity and relief, they
placed an extremely high value on assisting each other when
necessary. Prior to 1871 there was no municipal machinery
to provide public aid. Although 92 per cent of the population of Cook County lived within the city of Chicago, there
was no city apparatus for the distribution of funds. Instead,
these functions were left up to the county government or
private associations. The first was inadequately funded to
cope with the situation; the second, capricious and arbi-
trary.

Mr. Dooley took a dim view of the Relief and Aid Society
which was formed after the Great Fire and was run by the

city's most prominent citizens. Furthermore, the aid and relief were channeled through the Police Department, which was characterized by serious pockets of corruption and which skimmed off the top of any funds provided. As a consequence, the palliative for dire want usually had to be supplied to the poverty-stricken by the merely poor. In this column, Mr. Dooley tells the tragic tale of the Galway woman when the informal neighborhood relief system failed.

CHICAGO *EVENING POST*, December 5, 1896

"Whin th' col' spell comes along about Chris'mas time," said Mr. Hennessy, opening the stove door and lighting a small piece of paper which he conveyed to the bowl of his pipe with much dexterity, just snaring the last flicker with his first noisy inhalation, "whin th' col' weather comes on I wish thim Grogans down in th' alley'd move out. I have no peace at all with th' ol' woman. She has me r-runnin' be night an' day with a pound of tay or a flannel shirt or a this-or-that or th' other thing, an' 'tis on'y two weeks ago, whin th' weather was war-rum she tol' me Mrs. Grogan was as ongrateful as a cow an' smelled so iv gin ye cud have th' deleeryum thremens if ye sat with her f'r an hour."

"What ye shud do," said Mr. Dooley, "is to get ye'er wife to join an organized charity. Th' throuble with her is she gives to onworthy people an' in a haphazard way that tinds to make paupers. If they'se annything will make a person ongrateful an' depindent it's to give them something to eat whin they're hungry without knowin' whether they are desarvin' iv th' delicate attintion. A man, or a woman ayether, has to have what ye may call peculiar qualifications f'r to gain th' lump iv coal or th' pound iv steak that an organized charity gives out. He must be honest an' sober an' industhrious.

He must have a frind in th' organization. He must have arned th' right to beg his bread be th' sweat iv his brow. He must be able to comport himsilf like a gintleman in fair society an' play a good hand at whist. He must have a marridge license over th' pianny an' a goold edged Bible on th' marble topped table. A pauper that wud disbelieve there was a God afther thrampin' th' sthreets in search iv food an' calmin' an onreasonable stomach with th' east wind is no object iv charity. What he needs is th' attintion iv a polisman. I've often won-dhered why a man that was fit to dhraw a ton iv slate coal an' a gob iv liver fr'm th' relief an' aid.society didn't apply f'r a cabinet position or a place in a bank. He'd be sthrong f'r ayether.

"I mind wanst there was a woman lived down near Main sthreet be th' name iv Clancy. Mother Clancy th' kids called her. She come fr'm away off to th' wist, a Galway woman fr'm bechune mountain an' sea. Ye know what they ar-re when they're black, an' she was worse an' blacker. She was tall an' thin, with a face white th' way a corpse is white, an' she had wan child, a lame la-ad that used to play be himsilf in th' sthreet, th' lawn bein' limited. I niver heerd tell iv her havin' a hus-band, poor thing, an' what she'd need wan f'r, but to dhrag out her misery f'r her in th' gray year sivinty-foor, I cuddent say. She talked to hersilf in Gaelic whin she walked an' 'twas Gaelic she an' th' kid used whin they wint out together.[13] Th' kids thought she was a witch an' broke th' windows iv her house an' ivry wan was afraid iv her but th' little priest. He shook his head

[13] Speaking Gaelic was looked down upon by some Irish as being backward and countrified; it would have made Mother Clancy even less respectable and acceptable in view of the fact she had no husband. By the time this column was written, the Gaelic revival in Ireland had begun.

whin she was mintioned an' wint to see her wanst in a
while an' come away with a troubled face.

"Sivinty-four was a hard winter fr th' r-road. Th'
mills was shut down an' ye cud've stood half th' population iv some iv th' precints on their heads an' got
nothin' but five days' notices[14] out iv thim. Th' nights
came cold, an' bechune relievin' th' sick an' giv'n ex-
tremunction to th' dyin' an' comfortin' th' widows an'
orphans th' little priest was sore pressed frim week's
end to week's end. They was smallpox in wan part iv th'
wa-ard an' diptheria in another, an' bechune th' two
there was starvation an' cold an' not enough blankets
on th' bed.

"Th' Galway woman was th' las' to complain. How
she iver stud it as long as she did I lave fr others to say.
Annyhow, whin she come down to Halsted sthreet to
make application fr help to the Society fr th' Relief iv
th' Desarvin' Poor she looked tin feet tall an' all white
cheek bones an' burnin' black eyes. It took her a long
time to make up her mind to go in, but she done it an'
stepped up to where th' real estate man Dougherty,
cheerman iv th' comity, was standin' with his back to
th' stove an' his hands undher his coat tails. They was
those that said Dougherty was a big-hear-rted man an'
give freely to th' poor, but I'd rather take rough-on-
rats[15] fr'm you, Hinnissy, thin sponge cake fr'm him or
th' likes iv him. He looked at her, finished a discoorse
on th' folly iv givin' to persons with a bad moral character an' thin turned suddenly an' said: 'What can we do
fr ye?' She told him in her own way. 'Well, me good
woman,' says he, 'ye'll undherstand that the comity is
much besieged be th' imporchunities iv th' poor,' he
says, 'an' we're obliged to limit our alms to thim that
desarves thim,' he says. 'We can't do anything fr ye on

14 five days' notices—eviction notices.
15 rough-on-rats—rat poison.

ye'er own say-so, but we'll sind a man to invistigate
ye'er case, an',' he says, 'if th' raypoort on ye'er moral
character is satisfacthry,' he says, 'we'll attind to ye.'

"I dinnaw what it was, but th' matther popped out iv
Dougherty's head an' nayether that day nor th' nex' nor
th' nex' afther that was annything done f'r th' Galway
woman. I'll say this f'r Dougherty, that whin th' thing
come back to his mind again he put on his coat an' hurried over to Main sthreet. They was a wagon in th'
sthreet, but Dougherty took no notice iv it. He walked
up an' rapped on th' dure, an' th' little priest stepped
out, th' breast iv his overcoat bulgin'. 'Why, father,' he
says, 'ar-re ye here? I just come f'r to see—' 'Peace,' said
th' little priest, closin' th' dure behind him an' takin'
Dougherty be th' ar-rm. 'We were both late.' But 'twas
not till they got to th' foot iv th' stairs that Dougherty
noticed that th' wagon come fr'm th' county undertaker,
an' that 'twas th' chalice made th' little priest's coat to
bulge."

10

Reformers responded to the plight of the poor immigrants in
the city with the construction of settlement houses modeled
after London's Toynbee Hall. In one of the first American
experiments, Jane Addams (1860–1935) opened Chicago's
Hull House in 1889 and started on a path that was to lead to
a Nobel Peace Prize in 1931. Mr. Dooley was strangely mute
on Jane Addams, mentioning her only a few times and usually taking a very gentle poke at the cultural pursuits at Hull
House. Dunne knew her, of course, and they had many
friends in common. Perhaps he felt that Hull House was still
too tender a bud to withstand satire.

No one ever built a settlement house in Bridgeport. Its
citizens would have been insulted by any such effort. We

have just seen an example of the failure of the homely welfare system there, but in this column we find some of its
successes. Mr. Dooley gets off one of his best lines, "I know
th' wur-ruk iv relief is goin' on, but what th' la-ads need is
th' relief iv wur-ruk." Hennessy shares his tea with the
Schwartzes and leaves his coal out to be stolen by the
Dugans. And that good man, Father Kelly, organizes a campaign to keep the godless Clancy family fed and employed,
even though they are not parishioners.

CHICAGO *EVENING POST*, January 30, 1897

"I suppose I'm a har-rd hear-rted man," Mr. Dooley
began.

"Pooh!" said Mr. Hennessy. "Ye'er as soft as a
babby."

"I suppose," Mr. Dooley repeated sternly, "I'm a
har-rd hear-rted man. A man don't come to be six an'
fifty years iv age—"

"How manny?" Mr. Hennessy demanded.

"Five an' sixty years iv age, I said, without some iv
th' mushy sides iv his nature becomin' pethrified. But f'r
th' life iv me I can't stay in this here place an' see
what's goin' on around me without wishin' I had me
two arrums up th' elbows in th' Bank iv England an' th'
stren'th in me shoulders to hurl th' coin as far as a Tipperary man cud peg a rock at a polisman.

"Yis, I know th' wur-ruk iv relief is goin' on, but
what th' la-ads need is th' relief iv wur-ruk. I'm not
much iv a believer in wur-ruk personally, but that's because I was raised a pet. Annyhow, it's ruinin' th'
temper iv th' human race. But manny a man doesn't
know anny betther thin to think he's servin' Gawd best
be poundin' slag fr'm daybreak to sunset an' thin goin'
home too tired to stand or set or lay down. We've ham-

mered it into their heads that there's some connection
between a pickax an' a dish iv ham an' eggs, an' bedad
they can't be made to believe that wan ain't th' fruit iv
th' other. Givin' thim food don't seem to be anny use,
much less dhress suits that won't fit anny man in th'
polis station. I niver see th' fam'lies iv th' polis department so well dhressed as they've been f'r a week.

"I've no kick comin' again th' r-rich man that thrust
their hands down in their pockets an' dhraw out f'r th'
poor. They're all right. Thank heaven f'r weather cold
enough so that th' steam pipes won't heat their bed-
rooms an' a hot-wather bag won't make a carredge war-
rum enough f'r comfort. 'Tis on'y thin they think iv th'
poor. Wan iv thim says to himsilf: 'Lord, if me hooks
are frost-bitten in these sealskin gloves what must th'
poor divvles feel that have nothin' on their hands but
dirt an' chaps?' An' he throws a thousand into th' pot at
th' city hall an' has his name put in th' paper an' gets
Donovan to print his picture an' wondhers whin th'
Lord'll sind f'r him in a motorcycle iv fire. But barrin'
me joy at separatin' annywan that r-runs a gashouse or
a sthreetcar line fr'm his overcharges, I have no rel-
ligious feelin' about that man. Does he give to th' poor?
Faith, he does not. He gives to himsilf—to th' magnate
with th' frost-bitten hands an' th' cold legs. If that sort
iv givin' to th' poor is lindin' to th' Lord, some day whin
stocks go down an' th' loan 'll be called an' th' Commercial Club 'll hold a gold morgedge on paradise.[16] It will
so. To think that a man can square himsilf with his conscience be givin' wan thousan' dollars to a polisman an'
tellin him to disthribute it! Why don't they get th' poor
up in a cage in Lincoln Park an' hand thim food on th'
ind iv a window pole, if they're afraid they'll bite.

[16] Commercial Club—an association of top Chicago businessmen organized in the late 1870s to do good works and to engage in civic activity (as long as this did not interfere with corporate profits).

"Afther all, 'tis th' poor that keeps th' poor. They ain't wan sthrugglin' fam'ly in this war-rd that ain't carryin' three others on its back. A pound iv tay in ye'er house means a hot cup f'r thim poor Schwartzs' an' ye'er encouragin' petty larceny be lavin' ye'er soft coal out—I seen ye do it, ye miserable man—so that the Dugan boy cud steal it because ye don't speak to their father. Th' man Carey down th' sthreet that nobody likes, him bein' a natoryous infdel, 'd be dead if it wasn't f'r th' poor iv th' parish. He was set down f'r relief out iv th' mayor's fund. He was short coal an' wood, bread an' meeat, dhrink an' th' grace iv Gawd an' some wan put in an application f'r him. That afthernoon a pathrol wagon dhrew up in front iv his dure an' th' whole neighborhood wint over expectin' him to be arrested f'r blasphemyous language. Th' polisman fooled around in a pile iv stuff an' brought out a parcel. It contained a sprinklin' pot, a pair iv corsets, a bar iv soap, an' ax an' a hammick. Clancy wept tears iv joy. 'But, gintlemin,' he says, 'ye've forgot th' pepper an' salt.' 'What d'ye want pepper an' salt f'r?' says th' polisman. 'How th' 'ell can I make a salad out iv this hammick without pepper an' salt?' says Clancy.

"Father Kelly heerd iv th' case that night. He's wan iv th' poor iv th' parish; th' saint got an appetite f'r thruffles at college an' has been satisfyin' it on oatmeal stirabout iver since. He'd saved up tin dollars f'r to buy th' 'Life iv St. Jerome,' but whin he heerd iv Clancy he gives a sign an' says he, 'Martin,' he says, 'Jerome 'll have to wait,' he says, an' we wint down th' sthreet an' rough an' tumbled ivery coal dealer, butcher, grocer an' baker —most iv thim broke thimsilves—till we had a wagonload iv stuff. We dumped it at Clancy's an' th' pagan came out an' wanted Father Kelly f'r to set on th' coal while he proved that th' Bible was nawthin' more nor less thin a book of anecdotes an' that if historical tis-

timony was believed Queen Victorya'd be pope in
Rome today. I was f'r feedin' him a piece iv coal, but th'
good man says: 'What talk have ye? Go an' starve no
more,' an' come away with a grin on his face. He be-
haved most crazy all th' way up, runnin' behind his
parishoners an' hollerin' in their ears or makin' snow
balls an' throwin' thim at th' sthreetcar dhrivers whin
they touched their hats to thim. Near Ashland avnoo
we met Keough. Ye know him. He passes th' plate at th'
church. I niver cud. It's more thin me religion 'll stand
to put th' conthribution box under th' nose iv a man I
didn't like. But Keough does it an' he's rich. 'Keough,'
says th' good man, 'I want ye to put that crazy Galway
man, Clancy, to wurruk,' he says. 'But he's a heathen,'
says Keough. 'So he is,' says th' good man. 'He don't go
to his jootie,' says Keough. 'I wouldn't lave him,' says th'
good man. 'But there me jooty ends. I have no juris-
diction in anny other parish,' he says. 'Much less is it
me privilege f'r to visit tormint upon th' sinful,' he says.
'Clancy is a wicked man, a miserable sinner an' a vile
pagan, but he'll be a long time dead,' he says. 'I'll sind
him to ye tomorrah, an' if ye've listened to me attin-
tively f'r th' last tin years,' he says, 'ye ought to have
theological argymint enough to shake his onbelief,' he
says. 'Meanwhile,' he says, 'I'll race anny man to th'
corner,' an' he won be tin yards.

"He's a good man, that little priest."

"Man?" said Mr. Hennessy, "he's a saint!"

"Mebbe so," said Mr. Dooley, "but ye'd betther not
let him hear ye say so."

11

Another lucky stroke for the Irish arriving in the United
States was the fact that simultaneous with their great migra-

tion was the elimination of property qualifications as a requirement for voting or holding office. In Chicago, as elsewhere, the Irish quickly moved in on the nascent political machine where they could use the patronage system to provide jobs for their fellows and influence the lives of all Chicagoans.

Bridges, for example, were very important in the life of Chicago. The Chicago River meandered through the city and whoever controlled the several spans across it controlled the traffic of the immediate neighborhood as well. The politics and ethnic background of the man on the red bridge in Bridgeport was a constant topic of concern and conversation on Archey Road. The placement of a man of Polish extraction on the bridge by a Democratic mayor was tantamount to blasphemy. Even though the ward was no longer as Irish in composition as it once had been, the Irish still expected to govern it and gain the best jobs for the sons of St. Patrick. After all, they were the first ethnic group to recognize the influence they could wield through political action in an urban environment. As one Irishman warned another who wanted to move to the country:

> *I tell ye not to leave the city,*
> *Because you know 't'wud be a pity,*
> *To see men digging farms and doating,*
> *Who should be in the city voting.*

CHICAGO *EVENING POST*, May 15, 1897

"Change an' decay is all around I see," said Mr. Dooley sadly.

"What's that?" demanded his friend.

"They have got a Polacker on th' r-red bridge," said Mr. Dooley.

"A what?" gasped Mr. Hennessy.

"A Polacker," repeated Mr. Dooley. "A Polacker be th' name iv Kozminski. Th' boys was down there las' night practisin' on him fr'm th' coalyard."

"Dear, oh dear," said Mr. Hennessy, "an' is this what Lawrence McGann an' young Carther have done fr us? A Polacker on th' r-red bridge! 'Tis but a step fr'm that to a Swede loot at Deerin' sthreet an' a Bohemian aldherman. I niver though I'd live to see th' day."

In Archey Road the command of the "red bridge" is a matter of infinite concern. There are aldermen and members of the legislature in Archer road, clerks of the courts and deputy sheriffs, but their duties do not affect the daily life of the road. Whereas the commander of the bridge is a person of much consideration, for every citizen sees him day by day; it is part of his routine to chat loftily with the wayfarer, and the children help him to turn the bridge.

"'Tis all part iv what I tol' ye th' other day iv th' decay iv this ward," said Mr. Dooley. "We'll always be riprisinted in the council an' th' legislachure be people iv our own kind, fr if ye put wan Irishman among twinty thousand Polackers, Bohemians, Rooshins, Germans an' Boolgahrians he'll be th' leader iv thim all. I wanst knew a man be th' name iv O'Donnell that was prisidint iv th Zwiasek Nonowdowney Polacki, an' that's the Polacker National Society. But th' foreign ilimints have to get some recognition nowadays. They're too sthrong to be left out, on'y I wish th' Whole Thing had begun somewhere's but on th' bridge. It seems a shame to repose that sacred thrust in th' hands iv a man that no wan in th' creek can swear at an' be answered dacintly."

"They've been some fine men on that bridge in its day," said Mr. Hennessy.

"There has so," said Mr. Dooley. "D'ye ray-mimber

Dorsey th' Reaper—him that used to stand be th' hour leanin' over th' rail watchin' f'r th' remains iv Germans that had missed a thrain an' drownded thimsilves to come along. He was a fine man. Thin there was little Clancy. D'ye mind th' time whin th' lads fr'm th' mills was r-runnin' down th' road with th' little boy sojers iv th' First Rigimint chasin' thim. Whin th' last iv th' la-ads got acrost Clancy tur-rned th' bridge. 'In th' name iv th' State iv Illinye,' says th' colonel, 'I command ye to turn close that bridge,' he says. 'Wait till I light me pipe,' says Clancy. 'Close th' bridge, foolish man,' says th' colonel. 'Dam thim matches,' says Clancy, 'they won't stay lit,' he says. 'If ye don't close th' bridge,' says th' colonel, 'I'll fire,' he says. 'Sure, colonel,' says Clancy, 'ye wudden't deprive a poor wurrkin' man iv th' right to his pipeful iv baccy,' he says. ' 'Tis against th' articles iv war,' he says. 'Dam thim matches.' Th' colonel ordhered th' little boy sojers to point their guns at th' man on th' bridge. 'Colonel, oh colonel,' says Clancy. 'What is it,' says th' colonel. 'Ye'er vest is open in front, showin' ye'er shirt, naughty man,' he says. 'There's ladies on th' other side iv th' bridge an' I'd blush to have thim see ye in such a condition,' he says. Ye shud've seen th' colo-nel; he reared an' swore an' told Clancy he'd have his life. But Clancy wint on blowin' out matches till he sees th' last iv th' la-ads disappear in th' distance. Thin he wint to wurruk on his lever like a man with th' rheuma-tism, an' whin th' colonel come up he saluted him. 'I've a mind to put ye in irons,' says th' colonel. 'Faith, that's th' reward iv virtue,' says Clancy. 'I thought ye'd make me at least a loot f'r savin' ye fr'm an indacint exhibi-tion iv ye'ersilf,' he says. 'Gowan now, or I'll tur-r-n th' bridge on ye.'

"He was a great man, was Clancy," continued Mr. Dooley. "But a greater wan was me Uncle Mike, that

was on th' bridge some twenty years ago. He had a life-
long grudge again' a man be th' name iv Doherty, th'
master iv th' scow Wolfe Tone, an' 'twas in ordher to
even up th' score with him that he took th' job, for he
was be no means partial to wurruk, me Uncle Mike.
Doherty knowed he was on th' bridge an' done his best
to keep away, but wan day he had to run his stanch
boat up th' creek an' come whistlin' to th' bridge. Me
Uncle Mike seen him comin' an' give no sign fr half an
hour. Thin he crawled out iv his little gazebo, with his
pipe in his mouth, an' says he: 'What ahoy?' he says.
'Th' scow "Wolfe Tone," says Doherty, black as coal.
'Whither away?' says me Uncle Mike. 'Niver mind
whither away,' says Doherty. 'But open that there
bridge or I'll come ashore an' grind ye to powdher,' says
he. 'So ye say,' said me Uncle Mike, throwin' a chunk iv
coal at him. 'So ye say,' he says, 'but ye can't go through,
niverth'less. This here pellucid sthream,' he says (he
was a man iv fine language), 'was niver intinded to be
sailed be th' likes iv ye,' he says. 'I'm here to lave th'
navies iv th' wurruld go by,' he says. 'An' I have special
ordhers fr'm th' mayor that if an old sthreet car with th'
wheels off comes swimmin' along undher command iv
a mullet-headed Mayo man I'm to close it fr th' day.'
An' with that, he put on his coat, locked up th' pole an'
wint home. All that day th' creek was jammed with
scows an' tugs an' iron ore boats, an' no wan cud find
me Uncle Mike. Th' captains come aboard th' Wolfe
Tone an' cursed Doherty, th' superintindint iv th' rollin'
mills pleaded with him an' th' polis sarched fr me Uncle
Mike. They found him as dhrunk as a king down th'
road. He finally consinted to tur-rn th' bridge if Doherty
would stand on th' top iv his cabin an' say three times,
'Hurrah fr Mike Dooley, th' king iv Connock.' Doherty,
bein' a good natured soul at bottom, done it, me Uncle

Mike swung th' bridge an' with such a tootin' iv whistles as I niver heered, all th' fleet went through.

"Me Uncle Mike was fired th' next day. An' now they have a Polacker in his place. Dear, oh dear."

VI

Mr. Dooley on National Politics

Dunne's first dialect column, in December 1892, dealt with the national political situation, but while Dooley continued as a chronicler of these events, the early columns were more concerned with local doings.

Until 1895 the *Evening Post*, along with its morning sister paper the *Times-Herald* (the *Times* and the *Herald* were merged that year), were the most distinguished Democratic journals in the Middle West. However, in that year the owner, James W. Scott, died, and both papers were acquired by Herman Kohlsaat. Kohlsaat was a Chicago businessman, the owner of a number of bakeries and restaurants. A McKinley supporter, he was both politically and socially ambitious, and when his staff tried to make a case for retaining the *Post*'s Democratic slant, Kohlsaat replied, "This paper is going to be strictly independent, except that it will be for protection, for William McKinley, and for anything he wants." Thus, except for local political affairs where Kohlsaat and the staff were in agreement, Dunne lost the editorial page as a vehicle for his liberal/independent opinions. As a natural result, he increasingly used the Dooley columns as his outlet.

Further, in 1896 Dunne covered both national presidential conventions. All of these factors combined to increase Dooley's interest in the broader political picture and the number of columns dealing with this topic. Going national, however, did not mean that Dooley neglected

Archey Road. On the contrary, these events were discussed in terms of their impact on life in Bridgeport.

"I see," said Mr. Hennessy, "that th' Dimmycrats have gr-reat confidence."

"They have," said Mr. Dooley. "Th' Dimmycrats have gr-reat confidence, th' Raypublicans ar-re sure, th' Populists are hopeful, th' Prohybitionists look f'r a landslide or a flood, or whativer you may call a Prohybition victhry, an' th' Socylists think this may be their year. That's what makes pollytics th' gr-reat game an' th' on'y wan to dhrive dull care away. It's a game iv hope, iv jolly-ye'er-neighbor, a confidence game. If ye get a bad hand at poker, ye lay it down. But if ye get a bad hand at pollytics ye bet ye'er pair iv deuces as blithe as an Englishman who has jus' larned th' game out iv th' spoortin' columns iv th' *Lindon Times*. If ye don't win fair ye may win foul. If ye don't win ye may tie an' get th' money in th' confusion."

2

Mr. Dooley had a long-standing dislike of President Grover Cleveland, whom he usually referred to as "Big Steve." The "Big" was for his size; he weighed over three hundred pounds when he became President; and the "Steve" was for Stephen, the first name that Cleveland dropped when he reached adulthood.

Cleveland (1837–1908) was one of the most poorly prepared men to achieve the presidency. Reared in upstate New York, the son of an impoverished minister, he clerked at a Buffalo law firm until he could pass the bar. He was not a cultivated or intellectually curious man and spent most of his spare time drinking beer and eating wurst in the city's German taverns—activities which contributed to his embon-

point, but not to his knowledge. He did yeoman work for
the Democratic Party in the German wards, and in 1870 he
was elected sheriff of Erie County.

Nothing in his performance in this office indicated a capacity for higher public responsibility. The job was usually
given as a reward for political services rendered and was a
profitable one because of the fees involved. Cleveland won a
reputation as an honest incumbent, mostly because he did
little but fish, leaving the conduct of the office to a fortunately able assistant. After one two-year term, he returned
to his law practice.

Buffalo, like many other cities of the time, was run by a
corrupt ring of bosses. In 1881 a group of "clean" politicians decided it was time for a change. After several attempts to find a blue ribbon candidate for mayor, they
turned to Cleveland. His platform did not talk of reform; instead, he promised to run the city as any business should be
run, and his subsequent campaigns were all based on the
same theory. He won a resounding victory.

The city council was still composed of the same corrupt
band, and Cleveland won quick fame for vetoing most of
their self-serving proposals.

In 1882 one branch of the state Democratic Party wanted
to run an unbossed candidate for governor. Their minds naturally turned to Cleveland. It was not a draft, however;
Cleveland and his supporters worked hard and successfully
to win the nomination. Once again he ran on a platform of
things he was against. Once again he was elected. And once
again he vetoed the favorite bills of the bosses, this time taking on New York City's Tammany Hall.

Almost immediately Cleveland became a possibility for
the Democratic presidential nomination in 1884. Party
leaders felt the nation was ready for reform, and although
Cleveland scarcely ever mentioned the word, because he
had gone against the bosses, he seemed the logical choice.
When the popular Democratic leader Samuel Tilden, sev-

enty-four years old and feeling every minute of it, endorsed Cleveland, his nomination was inevitable. After a hard-fought campaign against the Republican, James G. Blaine, a campaign which reached a new low when it was revealed that Cleveland had fathered an illegitimate child, he won a narrow victory.

Cleveland arrived in Washington in 1885 with almost no knowledge or understanding of the problems that plagued the nation. He had won acclaim for what he was against; nobody, including Cleveland, knew what he was for. He had no program, leaving it to Congress to make policy, and took a very limited view of the role of the President.

After a lackluster four years, he was defeated for a second term by Benjamin Harrison and retreated to New York City to lick his wounds and make some money as a corporation lawyer. In 1892 Cleveland made a comeback, beating Harrison for the presidency in one of the dullest campaigns in history.

At the time this column was written, Cleveland was having trouble getting his bills through the Senate, particularly with regard to coinage and the tariff. Dooley advised him to use the tactics one would adopt in Bridgeport—or any other part of Chicago, for that matter—the withholding of patronage jobs and preferments in dealing with recalcitrant congressmen.

CHICAGO *EVENING POST*, October 21, 1893

POINTS FOR GROVER

MARTIN DOOLEY OFFERS SOME SUGGESTIONS
TO THE PRESIDENT

HOW THE SENATE CAN BE BEATEN

AN INTERESTING NARRATIVE OF THE ENCOUNTER OF
WILLIAM O'BRIEN, ALDERMAN, WITH THE CLAN GOOGIN

"D'ye know, Jawn," said Mr. Martin Dooley when

Mr. McKenna came in Thursday night. "D'ye know what I'd do if I was Cleveland?"

"No, faith," responded Mr. McKenna facetiously. "Turn down the damper?" this being a current phrase along the Archey road for robbing a cash drawer.

"No, sir," replied Mr. Dooley, haughtily. "I'd not. An' if ye're referrin' with ye'er scand'lous tongue to that little episode iv me an' Mike Hanrahan's game cock ye'll be after movin' out this minyit to Brighton Par-rk, where ye can bandy ye'er rough jokes with th' hoboes iv ye'er own set."

Mr. McKenna made no reply to this pointed rebuke beyond whistling a bar of "The Bowery." And Mr. Dooley resumed: "No, sir. If I was Big Steve I'd call me hackman an' I'd say: 'Dhrive me over to th' sinit.' An' whin I got there I'd cock me hat over me ear an' I'd walk in among thim an' I'd say, 'Now, here, mind ye, what is it ye la-ads wants? Ar-re ye lukin' f'r trouble with me? Is it a fight ye're after? Because if it is, they'll be nare a wan iv ye has a man on a bridge or on th' polis force nex' week.' Thim sintimints, Jawn, 'd end all this divilmint that's goin' on in th' sinit. Mind ye, now, I don't know who have th' right iv it. It's darn little I cares whether th' roly-boly that comes across that bar is in gold or silver, or cotton battin' so long as th' Eyetalian man with th' basket'll take it f'r limons an' nutmegs. But 'tis plain as th' nose on ye'er face, Jawn, that there's somebody runnin' th' game wrong.

"Now, mind ye, old Hahrson niver done it that way. I mind whin th' old grocer was in before. He wanted a ga-arbage creamery put up wist iv th' bridge an' Bill O'Brien, that was alderman in thim days, says 'No,' says he. 'We'll have no garbage creamery up here,' says he. 'I'm lukin' out f'r th' inthrests iv me constitooents,' he says, 'an' me constitooents,' he says, 'demands,' he says, 'a dump where th' goats can get a dairy lunch,' he says.

A witty lad, that O'Brien. I seen him break a man's jaw at a dance wanst be way iv a joke. 'What time is it?' says th' la-ad. 'It's just struck wan,' says O'Brien, givin' him a punch that was near to knockin' his head off.

"Well, th' main guy laughed at th' joke an' th' next night th' creamery was kilt in th' council. Th' day afther that Googin's big kid, Malachi, was fired fr'm th' rid bridge. Oh, thin there was blood flowin' in Haley's slough. Googin wint down to see th' old geezer: 'Me throw down wan iv ye'er boys—wan iv th' family iv me ol' frind Googin.' 'Tommy,' he says to th' clerk. 'What,' says th' clerk. 'Who thrun young Googin off th' rid bridge?' 'Well,' says th' clerk. 'To tell ye th' truth,' he says, 'Bill O'Brien came in today an' he says, "I want a new man f'r th' rid bridge." "What's th' matter with Googin," I says. "Googin," he says, "Googin's no good," he says. "We're tired iv those big omadhons fr'm Mayo," he says. "Throw him off my charge," says he, "I've got a young English la-ad that's worth tin Googins together." "That's an outrage," says th' Whole Thing. "Put Mr. Googin's boy back," he says. "An' whin O'Brien comes around with his friend fr'm London," he says, "call th' polis."'

"Well, sir, ye shud've seen Googin. Ye know him, Jawn. He come out here with tears in his eyes, swearin' vingince. He was a strong man, that Googin. He had eight la-ads, all iv thim vote-getters. Four iv thim worked in th' rollin' mills an' wan was conductor iv a sthreetca-ar. Th' oldest la-ad was married to Mary Haley, an' her father was foreman up in a packin' house an' voted two hundherd Dutch. Thin Mrs. Googin, she that was O'Donnell, was related to th' Dorseys an' th' Coughlins an' Tim Coughlin's youngest son was prisidint iv th' young men's sodality. Ye know th' Dorseys. They were th' best men that ever captained th' gas-house precint, an' they had a pull like a bridge horse.

Wan iv th' Dorsey girls was married to th' liftnant at Deering Sthreet an' another was sparkin' th' paymaster at th' ca-ar ba-arns.

"They was all fr'm th' war part iv Mayo, an' whin Googin come home an' rayported what Mr. Main Guy told him 'twas like whin they used to spread th' fight over beyant. First they formed th' Dennis Googin Anti-O'Brien Club an' then they formed th' County May-o Phalanx, which was christened be Coughlin's kid, and they had eight hundherd mimbers before Sundah. They put up a Dutchman named Schwartzmeister that kep' a beer cellar down be Halsted sthreet fr alderman an' wint up in a body to burn O'Brien's bar-rn. Whin Billy heard iv it he was pahrlyzed. He wint down to see th' Whole Thing. 'Well,' says th' ol' man, 'ar-re ye in favor iv th' creamery?' 'I am that,' says Bill. 'An' ye don't care fr th' dumps?' 'I wouldn't give a dam,' says Bill, 'if thim goats kape Fridah th' year round,' he says, 'if ye'll on'y haul th' Googins off.'

"So Bill he voted fr th' creamery an' th' Googin's turn'd down Schwartzmeister. Th' Dutchman didn't settle fr th' uniforms he got fr th' Mayo phalanx and th' shuriff closed him up, an' th' last I see iv him he was drivin' a pop wagon.

"No that there is pollytics, Jawn, mind ye, an' if ye meet Lawler I wish ye'd tell him th' next time Big Steve comes to see him he'd give him a wurrud iv advice how to land th' sinit. He's a smart man, Cleveland is, but he wuddent know whether to take th' elevated train or a freightca-ar to get to Finucane's Hall."

3

When running for his first term in 1884, Cleveland said he did not want to "overload the ticket with Irish." However, eventually he had to face reality—and the Irish-run urban political machines. Over the years he had made many Irish enemies especially in Chicago by not keeping his campaign promises and by not using the patronage system to reward voter loyalty. And he made these enemies at the ward and precinct level, where the Irishmen felt their greatest loyalty. Although local bosses were frequently corrupt, they were often, at the same time, heroes to their constituents. The Irish saw politics as just another sort of business endeavor, and they saw nothing wrong with a member of the profession making some money at it. The most important thing about them was that they took care of their own.

Cleveland, on the other hand, did not take care of his own. His antipathy towards the Irish was curious, since his staunchest supporters back in Buffalo had been Irishmen who opposed the violation of power by some officeholders. As governor of New York, Cleveland fought the Irish-dominated Tammany Hall in New York City. In particular, he vetoed a bill that would have lowered fares on the rapid transit system in New York City, thus benefiting the lower-income, working-class Irish.

Irish Democrats began to feel that the party was taking them for granted, and some Irish nationalists felt the party had not done enough for Irish freedom. In Chicago, the loyalty of the Irish community to the Democratic Party proved stronger than the dislike for Cleveland, but he carried places like Bridgeport by less and less each time he ran.

Even though he returned to Washington after the election of 1892, his popularity was on the wane. The conditions which generated the depression of 1893 had been building since the early 1880s, but Cleveland was blamed for them. He did not view business and individual economic recovery as concerns of the national government. He was a staunch supporter of the gold standard and seemed to favor eastern banking interests. His failure to discharge his political debts

and his "sell-out to Wall Street" cost the Chicago Democrats
the local elections in 1893 and the national Democrats the
off-year election of 1894.

CHICAGO *EVENING POST*, November 11, 1893

'TWAS JOYCE DID IT

MR. DOOLEY EXPLAINS THE REPUBLICAN
VICTORY OF TUESDAY

MR. CLEVELAND'S BAD BLUNDER

HE REFUSED TO SEND MR. JOYCE, OF THE
SIXTH WARD, TO THE COURT OF ST. JAMES

"Jawn," said Mr. Martin Dooley when Mr. McKenna
came in, "was you elected, I dinnow?"

"Elected to what?" asked Mr. McKenna.

"Dam'd if I know," said Mr. Dooley. "Crowner or
sinator or something."

"Naw," said Mr. McKenna.

"Then, begar," said Mr. Dooley, sagely, "ye'er th'
on'y raypublican this side iv Boolgahria that wasn't. Everything's raypublican this year. I'wa an' New Jarsey
an' th' State iv New York an' Omaha an', begor, they
was tin votes agin th' governmint in th' Finucane's Hall
precinct. There was, there was. 'Twould iv niver happened in th' ol' days, Jawn, avick. Whin I was a young
man before I wint into business for mesilf, it's little
figure thim tin votes 'd cut in th' rayturns. I mind th'
time when we r-rolled up twinty-sivin hundherd dimocratic votes in this wan precinct an' th' on'y wan's that
voted was th' judges iv election an' th' captains. I was a
captain, thin, Jawn, an' a man iv great influence. 'Twas
me got th' bridge f'r Doolan's boy Dinny, an' he dis-
graced me be swingin' it against th' mast iv th' Lizzie B.
Law for an' because th' man at th' wheel was a Swede.
Divvil th' liss.

"'Tis diff'rent now, an' what else could ye expect,

when they've r-run up agin' this crazy law fr'm Austhra-
lia? Faith, they tell me that th' dogs don't bark an' th'
flowers don't smell an' they cellybrate Christmas on th'
Foorth iv July in that haythen counthry an' how in 'ell
ar-re they goin' to get things straight with th' like iv an'
Austhralian system? 'Tis no wonder they've got a raypublican aldherman over be th' sivinth wa-ard an' th'
biggest Swede that iver come out iv Switzerland counts
as much as a man iv th' right sort. Be that as it may,
d'ye know who beat th' dimocrats?"

"Silver beat them," said Mr. McKenna. "Silver and
the tariff."[1]

"In ye'er deye," said Mr. Dooley. "Silver or goold or
dimons had nawthin' to do with it, no more, Jawn, than
you have to do with namin' th' pope in Rome, th' Lord
f'rgive me. No, nor th' tariff nayether. Will ye kape it to
ye'erself if I tell ye? Ye will? Thin, 'twas Willum Joyce
done it.

"I knowed he was up to some mischief whin I seen
him ridin' down th' road a-horseback th' day Hahrson
was burrid. He looked grim, an' I says to mesilf: 'Look
out there, boys,' says I. Well, sir, th' next day in come
ol' man Doherty with his ca-an an' says he: 'Dooley,
there's throuble in th' air.' 'Glory be to Gawd,' says I, 'is
that so; who's dead?' 'Nobody,' says he. 'But there's
thim that'd as soon be dead as alive afther Tuesdah
week.' 'Dear, oh dear,' says I, 'who's that?' 'Cleveland,'
says he. 'Poor man,' says I, 'an' what has he been doin'?'
I says. 'I thought things were aisy with him.' 'Aisy they
are,' says Doherty. 'They'll not be so aisy whin Willum
Joyce is through with him.' An' thin he outs with it. He
says, says he, that whin Cleveland was runnin' before

---

[1] The free coinage of silver was, of course, a major issue throughout
the 1890s. Irish-Americans in general favored a high tariff to keep
out low-priced British goods. Cleveland tried repeatedly to reduce
the tariff, and this did not endear him to the Irish.

he comes to Joyce an' says he: 'Bill,' he says, 'are ye wid
me?' 'I dinnaw,' says Joyce. 'I'm about half promised to
Bin. I might put it up f'r ye.' 'That won't do,' says
Steve. Then he thought for a moment an' says he:
'How'd ye like to be minister to England?' 'Oh, I dinnaw,' says Joyce. 'Chicago's a pretty cheerin' place.'
'Well,' says Cleveland, 'if ye give me th' sixth,' he says,
'ye can go to England,' he says. 'Look at th' chanst,' he
says. 'Ye'll be th' whole thing there. Ye can go an come
as ye like,' he says. 'An' Bill, ye know,' he says, 'what a
can iv dinnymite 'll do to a safe,' he says, 'av'n if th'
queen—' 'Hush,' says Willum, 'I've got ye.'

"Well, sir, there's no man fr'm Halsted sthreet to
Brighton Park that's half as pop'lar as Willum Joyce an'
ev'ry man an' kid in th' ward was out hollerin' f'r Cleveland because he was Willum Joyce's frind. An' Cleveland was ilicted. Th' rollin' mill precint give him th'
divvle's own majority. Whin big Steve was ilicted th'
wa-ard wint crazy. Th' whole dimocratic club raysolved
to go to England with him n' 'twas arranged that th'
Hibernian rifles should accompany him in disguise. Ol'
Donlan wint over to see him with tears in his eyes. 'Mr.
Joyce,' says he, 'I'm an ol' man,' he says, 'but I'll go
steerage,' he says, 'an' I'll make no throuble,' he says,
'but I want to get just wan crack at Balfour before I
die,' he says.

"Well, sir, Cleveland thrun him down, Jawn. Joyce
niver wint to see him, but he heard last week that an ol'
gazaboy from Delaware had got th' job. He didn't have
much time to get an organization together, but he did
what he could. An' there ye ar-re."

"But," said Mr. McKenna incredulously, "Cleveland
wasn't running."

"Jawn, ye know no more about politics than a goat
knows about th' multiplication table," said Mr. Dooley.
"Cleveland was with Larry Boyle."

Michael "Hinky Dink" Kenna and John "Little Jawnny" Powers put their best foot forward at a meeting of the Democratic Party of Cook County. While Mr. Dooley deplored their corrupt ways, he understood the environment that had spawned the "gray wolves" and realized they filled some of the needs of Chicagoans which otherwise went unmet. (Courtesy, Chicago Historical Society)

Chicago bound? Irish immigrants landed at Ellis Island in search of a better life. As Mr. Dooley recalled his own arrival, "...I got a glorious raycip- tion...th' stars and sthripes whispered a welcome in th' breeze an' a shovel was thrust into me hand an' I was pushed into a sthreet escyvatin' as though I'd been born here...I soon found that a long swing of the pick made me as good as another man, an' it didn't require a gr-reat intellect or sometimes any at all to vote th' dimmycratic ticket, an' before I was here a month I felt enough like a native-born American to burn a witch." (Courtesy, Chicago Public Library)

Women in the 1890s were limited to those sports that were considered ladylike—and not too vigorous. Jumping rope and playing tennis were permissible, but bicycling was downright daring when it first became popular. (Courtesy, Chicago Public Library)

The White Stockings baseball team of Chicago (1876) later became the Cubs. Pictured are A. G. Spalding, manager (who will become better known as a sporting-goods maker), with, clockwise, Ross Barnes, Oscar Bielaski, John Paul Peters, Paul Hines, Calvin McVey, James White, Frederick Andrus, Robert Addy, Adrian Anson, and John W. Glenn. (Courtesy, Chicago Historical Society)

above:
The Irish first came to Chicago and to Bridgeport in large numbers to work on the canals and for a while such jobs were nearly a purely Irish preserve. But by August 1896 payday on the drainage canal shows an ethnically balanced construction crew. (Courtesy, Metropolitan Sanitary District of Greater Chicago)

below:
After losing the presidential election of 1896, William Jennings Bryan (1860–1925) resolved to keep his name before the public in hopes of making a comeback. In 1898, during the Spanish-American War, he visited with General Fitzhugh Lee (right) in Cuba. Bryan was nominated for President again in 1900 and 1908, but was soundly beaten each time. (Courtesy, Chicago Historical Society)

Elizabeth Cady Stanton (1815–1902), leader of the National Woman Suffrage Association, addressed a Chicago audience during the 1890s. Her announcement of the planned publication of a women's Bible alarmed Mr. Dooley, who worried that its main object would be to provide an alibi for Eve. (Courtesy, Chicago Historical Society)

George Mortimer Pullman (1831–97) literally helped to raise the level of the city and designed the first successful railroad sleeping car. He put up a model company town, naming it after himself, for his employees so they would be near their jobs. Like everything he did, the town turned a tidy profit. In May 1894 Pullman reduced wages, but not rents or food prices at the company store. The result was the Pullman strike. When Pullman died, he was so unpopular he was buried secretly at night for fear his grave might be desecrated. This picture was taken in the 1860s shortly after Pullman, like so many of the young able-bodied leaders of business in Chicago, managed to avoid the draft for the Civil War, not even bothering to purchase a substitute, which was permissible then. (Courtesy, Chicago Historical Society)

Sanitary District trustees and contractors paused during the ceremony in 1900 celebrating the turning of water into the new Sanitary & Ship Canal, thus reversing the Chicago River. The trustees opened the new canal as quietly as possible for fear that the city of St. Louis, down the Mississippi, would get out an injunction to halt their engineering feat because it did not want Chicago's sewage floating down the Mississippi. (Courtesy, Metropolitan Sanitary District of Greater Chicago)

HARPER'S WEEKLY

JOURNAL OF CIVILIZATION

VOL. XXXVIII.—No. 1961.
Copyright, 1894, by Harper & Brothers.
All Rights Reserved.

NEW YORK, SATURDAY, JULY 21, 1894

TEN CENTS A COPY.
FOUR DOLLARS A YEAR.

THE VANGUARD OF ANARCHY.

As the American Railway Union flexed its muscles during the Pullman strike, spasms of fear racked the country. Eugene V. Debs (1855–1926), the union leader (wearing the paper crown), was widely portrayed as a dangerous radical, hell-bent on the violent overthrow of American institutions. He was to be jailed on several occasions for his activities. (Courtesy, Chicago Historical Society)

Charles Tyson Yerkes (1837–1905), as corrupt as he was handsome, controlled the traction system, bought legislators by the dozens, paid for favorable laws. In a futile attempt to improve his public image he donated funds for the Yerkes telescope and observatory to the University of Chicago in 1892. His behavior had been too outrageous for the other titans of Chicago business, and they prevailed upon him to sell them his interests in 1899 and get out of town. He was, like so many other Chicago figures of the 1890s, larger than life. In fact, Theodore Dreiser required a trilogy to tell the thinly veiled story of Yerkes' life. (Courtesy, Chicago Historical Society)

4

"Th' life iv a candydate is th' happiest there is. If I
want annythin' pleasant said about me I have to say it
mesilf. There's a hundherd thousan' freemen ready to
say it to a candydate an' say it sthrong. They ask
nawthin' in rayturn that will require a civil service examination. He starts in with a pretty good opinyon iv
himsilf, based on what his mother said iv him as a baby,
but be th' time he's heerd th' first speech iv congrat-
ulations he begins to think he had a cold an' indiff'rent
parent. Ninety per cint iv th' people who come to see
him tell him he's th' mos' pop'lar thing that iver was, an'
will carry th' counthry like a tidal wave. He don't let th'
others in . . . Childher an' dogs ar-re named afther
him, pretty women an' some iv th' other kind thry to
kiss him, an' th' newspapers publish pitchers iv him as
he sets in his lib-ry, with his brow wrinkled in thought
iv how fine a man he is."

—Mr. Dooley

If Dooley's observation about the nature of a candidate's
life is accurate, there were plenty of happy men in the
United States during the presidential campaign of 1896.

When the first gavel fell in St. Louis the Republican nomination had been all wrapped up for William McKinley by
his mentor, Marcus Alonzo Hanna, well before the GOP
delegates convened. Although the Republicans had hoped
to take an ambiguous stand on the coinage question, the increasing polarization of southern and western Democrats
around the silver issue drove the Republicans to adopt an
uncompromising position on gold money.

The Democrats met in Chicago a few weeks after the Republicans. The writing was on the wall when the Cleveland (gold Democrat) candidate for temporary chairman was beaten by Senator John W. Daniel of Virginia, a well-known silverite. The platform called for the free coinage of silver.

The leading candidate for the presidential nomination was Congressman Richard P. Bland of Missouri. He was aptly named; his candidacy did not capture the imagination of the delegates. Far more popular was Illinois' John Peter Altgeld, but as a naturalized citizen he was prevented from running by constitutional provision. William Jennings Bryan, the convention's ultimate choice, was only thirty-six years old, but had already served two terms in Congress from Nebraska and was well known for his oratorical skill. He delivered a ringing call to action to the convention—the famous "cross-of-gold" speech, which he had been rehearsing before lesser audiences for months—and there was no stopping him.

A rump group of gold Democrats abstained from voting, and they had their own candidate, Senator John M. Palmer of Illinois, to rally round.

Although not technically a Populist, Bryan espoused many of the Populist causes, and some of these found their way into the Democratic platform. Thus, when the Populist Party got together, they had little choice but to accept Bryan as their man too.

The campaign was rough and hysterical. The silver issue was vastly overemphasized, and Republicans and conservative Democrats grew panicky at the thought of having a dangerous man like Bryan in the White House. And while Bryan's excellent presence and his attempt to run a "people's" campaign gave him an initial edge, the Republicans had the money and the smooth organizational know-how of Mark Hanna.

When all the votes were in, McKinley beat Bryan in the

popular vote by 7 million to 6.5 million, and in the electoral
college by 271 to 176.

Tom Johnson, mayor of Cleveland, described the election
as "the first great protest of the American people against
monopoly—the first great struggle of the masses in our country against the privileged classes. It was not free silver that
frightened the plutocrat leaders. What they feared, then,
what they fear now, is free men."

So the Democratic campaign of 1896 had a long-lasting
effect on both parties. The assimilation of the Populists and
their platform into the Democratic Party gave the older
party a newer, fresher outlook and a toehold in the reform
movement. And the all-but-ignored platform would be remembered and its best points adopted as their own by both
major parties.

5

Theodore Roosevelt once said of Mark Hanna, "He has ad-
vertised McKinley as if he were a patent medicine." Hanna
was a prosperous man-about-Cleveland who dabbled in politics until he met McKinley. Then he saw himself as an
American Warwick, a President-maker.

They were in some ways a political "odd couple." Hanna
was quick-witted, fast off the mark, fun-loving, openhanded
with friends, a superb fund raiser. McKinley was above all
things dignified, prudent, politically adept, gracious, and
frequently broke. Both men were of Scotch-Irish descent,
but as Hanna commented to friends when describing their
differences, McKinley got the Scotch and he got the Irish.

Hanna began sneaking up on the Republican old guard in
1895 when he took a house in Georgia and invited the
McKinleys down to meet a select group of southern folks—
all of whom happened to control delegate votes. By the time

a stop-McKinley favorite son effort was mounted in the
South, it was too late. Besides the votes he'd picked up in
the South, Hanna had snatched the favorite sons' states
right out from under them. Even before the St. Louis convention of 1896, it was clear that McKinley would be the
nominee.

The only fight was to be over the platform plank on bimet-
allism. Most of McKinley's support came from the West
and the South, where feeling ran high for silver. In addition,
as a congressman, McKinley had been favorable to silver.
But Hanna wanted the support of the eastern bloc, the
"goldbugs." Working with a small group of trusted ad-
visers, Hanna crafted a moderate gold plank and then persuaded McKinley to accept it. Next, Hanna carried on a
careful charade, arguing manfully at first against Henry
Cabot Lodge, the leader of the gold forces, then gradually
giving way to popular demand.

Senator Henry M. Teller of Colorado proposed a prosilver
stance on the floor of the convention and he and his fellow
silver men attacked McKinley for what they felt was his
treachery. When Teller's motion was tabled, this man, who
had been one of the original members of the Republican
Party some forty years before, tearfully led a small group of
delegates from the hall to the vocal disapprobation of the
crowd. Hanna joined in the jeers, firmly convinced he had
carried the day and that the money issue would quickly fade
away. For once, Hanna's intuition was wrong. Smiling
faintly upon the proceedings from his seat in the press box
was former Congressman William Jennings Bryan.

Meanwhile, back in Canton, Ohio, his home town, McKinley awaited the verdict. The Associated Press had run a telephone wire from St. Louis to Canton so that McKinley
could hear the nominating speeches and the vote over the
telephone, while all hell broke loose as the word spread
through the streets of Canton.

CHICAGO *EVENING POST*, June 27, 1896

"Home again," said Mr. Dooley, greeting Mr. McKenna at the door. "How did ye enjoy havin' th' man Hanna back a dhray down onto ye?"

"You ought to have been there," said Mr. McKenna, who had wielded a mace at one of the doors at the St. Louis convention.

"Niver ye mind me," said Mr. Dooley. "I was at home feelin' comfortable an' dhrinkin' out iv a sthraw while ye was carryin' a thrunk f'r th' diligation fr'm th' Western Resarve.[2] Jawn, a raypublican is a poor-sperited thing annyhow. Barrin' a few good sthrong ar-rm la-ads like Hogan an' ye'ersilf—an' ye'er dimmycrats if ye on'y knowed it—I niver see a raypublican that had it in him to poke a fellow citizen in th' eye f'r th' sake iv his convictions. D'ye suppose this poor ol' gray haired an' decrepit man Teller'd be allowed to get up an' r-roast a dimmycratic convintion? Not in wan hundherd thousand years. Befure the first tear had thrickled down his aged cheeks some wan'd 've took him be th' whiskers an' done th' joynt swing with him. Faith, they know their company. Whin Hannigan organized his bolt fr'm th' Willum J. O'Broyns he come up to th' dure in Finucane's Hall. 'Lave me in,' he says. 'What d'ye want to go in f'r, foolish man alive?' says th' polisman. 'I've come to th' partin' iv th' ways,' says Hannigan. 'F'r five an' twenty years I've held office undher dimmy-cratic administhrations,' he says, 'but now I hold none no more,' he says. 'I'm goin' in f'r to take me lave iv that gr-rand ol' party,' he says, weepin' copyously. 'Well, thin,' said th' polisman, he says, 'ye'd betther go tover to

[2] Western Resarve—Western Reserve University, located in Cleve-land, Ohio—in other words, McKinley supporters.

Mitchigan City,' he says, 'an' withdraw be long distance
telephone,' he says. 'I just see th' comity on cradintials
decidin' wan iv ye'er contests with a bed slat,' he says.

"They'll be no Mark Hanna at th' convintion here,
an' they'll be no weepin' an' singin' songs. Ne'er a wan.
A dimmycrat in a con-vintion can't sing. If he did a
fellow dimmycrat 'd hand him wan. He doesn't care
who makes th' songs iv a nation so long as he makes th'
throuble. I suppose th' con-vintion 'll be opened with
prayer. That's th' rule, Jawn. They open ivrything nowadays with prayer, fr'm a session iv congress to a chilled
steel safe. Afther which th' good man 'll do well to go
home an' read about what follows in th' paper. It'll be
no place fr ministers iv th' gospel or women an' childher. Some wan 'd get up an' propose to give a vote iv
thanks to Big Steve. Whin they have lynched him th'
convintion 'll settle down to th' irregular ordher iv business. They'll be no comitys meetin' out iv dures to fix
things up an' read th' programme off like a composition
paper in a public school. Our frind Altgeld 'll move that
all goold bugs be run into th' sthreet. They'll be a fight
there, fr some iv th' lads fr'm New York 'll cover over
with a thing or two in their pockets. But they'll be done
—an' our own good boys 'll be on top. They'll pass a
platform hot enough to cook eggs: Raysolved, that we,
th' dimmycratic party, are in favor iv th' free coinage iv
silver, gool, paper, hair, mortar, Swiss cheese, overalls
or canned goods at a ratio of sixteen to wan, or anny ol'
ratio. Raysolved, that we pass up th' tariff. Raysolved,
that Grover Cleveland is a monkey face, an' if he was
out here we wudden't do a thing to him but roll him
fr'm th' Coliseem to th' North Branch. All in favor 'll
say 'Aye.' To 'ell with th' noes. Th' ayes have it.

"That'll be a convintion fr ye. Th' Lord sind that
they'll be a quorum left alive whin they nominate a
Prisidint. I understand arrangements are bein' made to

sind th' New York diligation home on ice. It'll go hard
with some iv thim Wall sthreet joods. They were all
right with us whin we were winning, but whin we're
losin' we want to be alone."

"Well," said Mr. McKenna with the judicial air
which only an Irish republican can assume, "You're losing this year, all right enough. I'm sorry for the democratic party. I belonged to it once."

"Save ye'er tears, Jawn," said Mr. Dooley with a
trace of anger. "Look out that it don't happen to you as
it did to Dempsey the tailor afther his boxin' match
with little Mike Foy. Dempsey cud box an' he wint
around Mike Foy like a cooper round a bar'l, whalin'
him on wan side an' th' other till th' little man had no
more wind in him thin a dale boord and was spotted
like a leopard. Fin'lly Dempsey gave him wan in th' jaw
an' flured him. Thin he took off his gloves an' wint over
to cheer him up. 'I'm sorry I done ye, Mike,' he says,
bindin' over his fallen foe. Th' fallen foe sat up suddenly an' butted him in th' stomach an' thin danced a
schottische on him be way iv divarsion, an' 'twas a
week befure Dempsey got out iv a sick bed."

6

Now it was the Democrats' turn to gather in Chicago, site
of so many exciting presidential conventions before and
since.

William Jennings Bryan arrived in Chicago as part of a
contested Nebraska delegation. He had been forced out of
Congress by President Cleveland, who considered him a
gadfly and whom Bryan made irate with his support of silver and the income tax. A true son of the Middle Border,
Bryan was most influenced by his membership in the Democratic Party and his strong Baptist faith.

When the Nebraska silver delegates were seated, they chose Bryan to represent them on the Resolutions Committee which hammered out a remarkable document. It gave the Democratic answer to the money question right off—free coinage of silver and gold at a ratio of sixteen to one. Since this was the hot emotional issue, not much attention was given to the rest of it, but the rest was perhaps even more important. It called for tighter regulation of the trusts, an income tax, increasing the scope of the Interstate Commerce Commission, an end to the abuse of the injunction in labor disputes, and a prohibition against federal meddling in local problems, particularly industrial disturbances. It talked about the common people in a way they could understand.

Once the platform had been read, Bryan rose to speak in its behalf. Despite the frightful heat and humidity of a particularly torrid Chicago summer, he quickly captured his audience; the atmosphere was electric. He finished his peroration with the now familiar words, "You shall not press down upon the brow of labor this crown of thorns; you shall not crucify mankind upon a cross of gold." And then the crowd went wild. The delegates stampeded to his support. Nothing could stop his nomination as President.

Also behind the Democrats were the silver Republicans and the Populists, but not all the latter went along willingly with Bryan. Despite Cleveland's widespread unpopularity, the Populist leaders had believed the Democrats would never repudiate him by rejecting as his successors the party satraps from the East. But the Democrats pulled the rug out from under them with Bryan and the platform. What to do? There was considerable Populist division, expressed by one leader who said, "Let the old rotten Democrat machine with its camp followers, gold bugs, place hunters, straddle bugs, humbugs, demagogues, etc. go to the devil." There was resentment against Bryan personally as well. As Ignatius Donnelly, who was one of the principal intelligences

behind the Populist movement, snorted, "We put him to
school, and he wound up by stealing the schoolbooks."

Rationality prevailed at the Populist convention at first,
when they nominated Bryan, but they also expressed independence by refusing to accept the Democratic nominee for
Vice President, Arthur Sewell of Maine. Instead, they gave
Bryan one of their own, Thomas E. Watson of Georgia, a
former congressman, who remarked that "the Democratic
idea of fusion is that we play Jonah while they play the
whale." In this way, the Populists displayed their un-
willingness to be swallowed up.

CHICAGO *EVENING POST*, September 26, 1896

"Well, Jawn," said Mr. Dooley, "this campaign is
enough to make a man hang his head in shame f'r th' in-
tilligince iv th' human race an' to wondher whither th'
gazabo Father Kelly done up so bed in th' Easther ser-
mon—what's his name? Darwin?—wasn't right whin he
advanced th' theery that th' human race is discinded
fr'm apes. If Gawd made us out iv monkeys, be hivins
we'er goin' back an' makin' monkeys iv oursilves.

"Here's this young kid Bryan comes along to a convintion an' no man thinks anny more iv him thin if he
was a song-an'-dance artist, but he takes th' nomination
away fr'm a lot iv dimmycrats that have th' tobacco
juice iv centuries on their shirt fronts. Thin he goes out
into th' counthry with a dollar in his hand an' he holds
it up befure th' people an' says he: 'This buck is worth
53 cints to anny man that it's paid to, but I'll make it
worth wan dollar to anny man that pays it out.' An' a
lot iv people believes him, though not so manny as
believed him a month ago be eight or tin millions. An'
folks goes to hear him an' he makes three hundherd
speeches a minyit, an' la-ads that wudden't be worth 8

cints if dollars were marked down to five go hollerin'
through th' streets: 'Huroo f'r Bill Bryan, th' frind iv th'
people.' They're crazy, plumb daffy, Jawnny. In this
whole City iv Chicago there ain't wan hundherd silver
men that cuddent give post-graduate insthructions to
th' inmates iv th' booby hatch out at Dunning. Not wan
hundherd.

"An' that's on'y wan side iv it. Take th' other. I wint
downtown last week to pay me dog tax, an' I see th'
sthreets full iv flags. 'What's up?' says I to a polisman.
'Ain't th' Foorth iv July over yet?' 'Thim's sound money
flags,' says th' polisman—O'Connor be name; him that
marrid Julia Casey, th' daughter iv th' blacksmith in the
Black road. 'Th' flags is put out be pathriotic Americans
to show their feelin' again' th' spirit,' he says, 'that's
abroad in th' land,' he says. 'A spirit,' he says, 'iv discon-
tin',' he says, 'an' arnychy,' he says. An' I looked up at
th' flag over me head an' 'twas stretched fr'm th' window iv Julius Eckstein, loan an' morgedge broker, to th'
window iv M. Einstein, dealer in bonds an' stocks.

"What's th' counthry comin' to? Here's Bryan beaten
so bad that he won't be much better thin foorth in this
wa-ard. I med a bet iv a two dollar hat with Hinnissy
yestherday that he wouldn't have more votes than ol'
Scattering that r-runs f'r office iv'ry year an' always gets
th' worst iv it. Th' returns 'll be about like this: McKinley, first, Livering (th' soft dhrink man), second; Scattering, third, and Bryan, foorth. But that don't stop people fr'm killin' thimsilves f'r fear he'll be ilicted. Why
there was me ol' frind th' Rhine wine man, that ought to
be happy an' continted with his Hoohenheimer an' his
Myetzelbirk, goes an' shuts th' dure an' tur-rns on th'
gas so he won't have to r-read th' rayturns. 'Tis a sign iv
th' nuttiness iv th' campaign that a man should thry to
blow himself out with hard times. I'll bet if he wasn't
broke whin he lay down, he'll be broke herafter—dead

broke, ye might say. A man that thinks to utilize th' gas company to pipe him to th' other wurruld needn't ixpict no silver knobs on his coffin.

"An' so it goes, all th' counthry as crazy as a re-form aldherman. I don't mind th' rah-rah lads at Yale. What can ye ixpict fr'm a thribe iv young chimpanzees whin th' paternal apes is hangin' fr'm th' threes be their tails an' callin' upon hivin not to cut th' bough. If they weren't daffy whin they wint to th' meetin' they'd have gone off their heads listenin' to Bryan talk. He's a queer man, that same Boy Orator iv th' Hat.[3] He says, says he: 'I am prepared to die fr me principals.' 'So are we,' says th' bughouse people. 'Thin,' says he, 'if that's th' case ye'd betther die first,' he says. An' he proceeds to talk thim to death. He goes further thin Gin'ral Sickles. Gin'ral Sickles wanst lost a leg fr his counthry at Gettysburg. Th' pop'lar theery that he lost it shakin' dice or walkin' in his sleep is wrong. He lost it fr this counthry. But what's wan leg to Sickles? He has legs to bur-rn. Ivry campaign finds him out on th' stump, shakin' off legs be th' thousand.[4] 'What'll ye give fr savin' th' counthry?' says th' cheerman. 'I'll give tin dollars,' says wan man. 'I'll give five,' says another. 'I have no money,' says Sickles, 'but I'll give a leg.' Where does he store that onlimited supply iv detachable shins that he trots out ivry time a constable's to be ilicted? An' often he disthributes his soupbones as souveneers iv th' performance he always has a kick comin' again something or somebody.

"Wan man comes in here an' wants me to have this put in th' caddychism: 'Who med this country possible?

[3] Boy Orator iv th' Hat—Bryan was known as the "Boy Orator of the Platte."

[4] Gin'ral Sickles—Union General Daniel Sickles (1825–1914) lost his leg in the Civil War, and took himself out on the campaign stump, removing his artificial leg at the slightest provocation.

Bill Bryan. Who put down th' rebellion? Bill Bryan.
Who put out th' Chicago fire? Bill Bryan. Who stands
between th' people an' tyrants? Bill Bryan. Who is th'
gr-reatest orator that iver opened his face? Bill Bryan,
sixteen-to-wan.' Another wan comes in an' says: 'Who
saved this counthry in siventeen-sivinty-six? George
Wash'nton. Who saved it in eighteen-sixty? Abraham
Lincoln. An' who saved it in eighteen-ninety-six? Heidelbach, Ickleheimer an' Company.[5] I don't know who
I'll vote f'r, Jawn. I don't want to vote f'r a play actor
that wears a waiter's necktie an' has to stop thinkin' ivry
time he talks. An' I don't see how I can vote f'r Palmer.[6]
I wasn't reegisthered befure th' war iv eighteen-
twelve."

"Vote for McKinley," said Mr. McKenna, Irish republican.

"Mebbe I will, an' mebbe I won't. I'm not sure I
know anny pollin'-place where I'm crazy enough to get
in without a challenge. Where do th' people fr'm th' ditintion hospital vote?"

7

For a while it seemed certain Bryan would carry the
country before him as dramatically as he had the Democratic convention. His magnetic personality and eloquence

[5] Heidelbach, Ickleheimer an' Company—a reference to the banking
and bonding firms of New York which supported the gold standard
(and Cleveland) by purchasing gold bonds from the government at
a lower price than would be possible on the open market; in return
for being given this preferential treatment, they bought gold from
Europe to shore up the American dollar.

[6] Palmer—Senator John M. Palmer of Illinois had had a long and
checkered career. He was, at turns, a Democrat, a Free Soiler, a Republican, a liberal Republican. In 1896 he was again a Democrat, but
he gave it one more twist and became the presidential nominee of
the gold Democrats.

were attractive not only to restive Democrats and disappointed Republicans, but to those who probably did not consider themselves members of any party.

For the first time since the slavery dilemma, the nation was presented with a moral question, a cry for social justice. The common people he so loved to talk about were enraptured with Bryan. There were plenty of crackpots and radicals, but there were many more farmers and laborers behind him.

There were practical reasons, too, for the outpouring of support. Times had been rough, very rough; the depressions and panics were coming closer and closer together. Wearied by the struggle, many Americans welcomed the notion of increasing the money supply.

So, for a while in the hot summer of 1896 it was a love feast. If the election had been held within the first month or so after the Democratic convention, Bryan probably would have won.

However, by the time McKenna and Hennessy were making their prognostications in Mr. Dooley's establishment, the tide had begun to turn, and Dunne sensed it. On this and on so many other occasions, his Dooley work demonstrated that he was an uncommonly sensitive observer of his times.

While they were spared the pontifications of television commentators and the deciding of elections by network computers, *fin de siècle* American voters had to put up with polling and interpretation of results by a bunch of embryonic psephologists. In these days when pollsters are viewed with as much solemnity as Druids casting the runes, it is well to read Mr. Dooley's wonderful nonsense on the subject.

CHICAGO *EVENING POST*, October 3, 1896

"Well, Jawnny," said Mr. Dooley, leaning over the bar and beaming upon his friend, "How's th' liliction goin', I dinnaw?"

"Why," said Mr. McKenna, "it's a pipe for Mack and Hobo.[7] They'll win easy."

"How's that?" demanded Mr. Hennessy, who had been dozing in the corner and wagging his foot to avoid Mr. Dooley's censorious remarks. "How's that? Ye mane Bryan."

"I mean McKinley."

"Why, Jawn, ye don't know what ye'er talkin' about. Bryan'll carry th' solid south, Utah, Weemoning, Nevada, Eedawho, South an' North Dakota, Kansas, Nebraska, Mitchigan, Illinye, Wisconsin, Injeeany, Ohio, Pinnsylvania, an' th' County Mayo," he added triumphantly.

"Well," said Mr. Dooley, "that ought to be enough to ilict him aldherman lave alone Prisidint. What's th' use iv him r-runnin' at all, at all? Why don't they say: 'Here, Bill, 'tis no good wearin' out ye'er lungs. Ye'll need thim whin ye go to Washington to holler "Stop thief."' Why in hivin's name don't they make it unanimous?"

"They took a vote down in Donahue's pop facthry las' week," said Mr. Hennessy, "an' it give eighteen thousan' six hundherd an' tin fr Bryan an' two fr McKinley. Th' two was co-erced."

"Who coerced thim?" asked Mr. Dooley.

"Rothscheeld," said Mr. Hennessy promptly.

"But how d'ye account fr th' vote in Dorgan's plumber's shop?" Mr. Dooley demanded.

---

[7] Mack and Hobo—William McKinley and his running mate, Garret A. Hobart of New Jersey.

"How was that?" asked Mr. Hennessy.

"Sixty-three thousan' eight hundherd an' ilivin f'r McKinley, sixty-eight f'r Erastus H. Scattering an' wan f'r Bryan."

"Coerced," said Mr. Hennessy. "But what ar-re ye talkin' about? They'se on'y two in th' shop—Dorgan an' th' helper."

"What diff'rence does that make?" asked the philosopher. "That's the beauty about iliction statistics—they're not burdened with annything like facts. All a man wants is a nice room in th' back iv a Chinese laundhry an' a lung full iv hop an' he can make a monkey out iv th' la-ad that wrote th' arithmetic. He sees majorities grinnin' through th' transom an' roostin' on th' top iv th' bed an' crawlin' up his leg. Here's wan man says Texas will go raypublican, an' th' on'y states Bryan has sure is Mississippi, Arkansaw an' Hell. Here's another claims Bryan'll carry New Hampshire an' upper Canada, an' that Bill McKinley won't get wan vote in Canton but his own, an' he wont get that if he hears Bryan make wan speech. Th' dimmycratic comity figures out that th' ilictor colledge'll have 358 dimmycratic votes sure an' that th' rest iv th' campaign 'll be devoted to rallyin' th' others. Th' raypublican comity claims that McKinley'll have all but eight votes an that those'll be given to Palmer, th' oldest livin' white man iver born out iv captivity. I hope I'll live to see Palmer ilicted Prisidint. No, come to think iv it, I don't. Afther a man gets to be eight or nine hundherd years iv age he's on'y a burdhen to his fam'ly. I'd be too decripit f'r to go to th' inaguration.

"But that's nayther here nor there. What I was talkin' about was th' political statistics. Whin a man gets so he sees funny things in green and red runnin' round th' room, whin he tells people he's sorry he iver sold Lincoln Park to th' city because now he has nowhere to

spind th' eighteen million dollars a minyit income he
derives fr'm his stock in th' Alley L Road, just befure a
wagon fr'm th' ditintion hospital backs up at his dure
an' a polisman comes in an' grabs him, he's ripe fr a job
at headquarters summing up th' raysults iv sthraw
votes. 'A poll iv Lyman J. Gage was taken yistherdah. It
was conducted on th' Austhralyan system an' it was
sthrictly private. It showed $16,000,000 fr McKinley
an' none fr Bryan.' 'Thursdah Governor Altgeld took a
secret ballot iv himself. It showed him almost solid fr
Altgeld an' Bryan.' 'Mr. Grizzly Adams made a secret
canvass iv th' Hip Lung establishmint Saturdah. It will
be raymimbered that th' employees iv this place was
coerced into wearin' McKinley buttons an' had jined th'
Long Dhraw McKinley an' Hobart Club. Mr. Adams
found on'y three men who would vote fr th' frind iv
thrusts. Th' other sivinty-three millions was fr Bryan
an' Sewall.[8] Thin he woke up.'

"An' so it goes. A man come dashin' hein here yistherdah an', says he, 'D'ye know Murphy?' 'Murphy,'
says I, 'Murphy? It sthrikes me th' name is familiar?
What does he do?' 'I mane th' Murphy that dhrives th'
sthreetca-ar.' 'Tubby sure,' says I, 'an' what of him? Has
he been chased?' 'No,' says he, 'but he's goin' to vote fr
McKinley. He's been a dimmycrat all his life.' 'Well,'
says I, 'ye don't tell me.' 'But,' says he, 'isn't it gloryous?
It shows that th' workin' min is fr Mack solid.' 'It does
not,' says I. 'It shows two things, wan iv thim bein' that
Im Jay Murphy tells ye that'he's goin' to vote fr McKinley an' th' other that ye'er a tearin' big lunatic. Since

[8] Sewall—Arthur Sewell (1835–1900), a well-to-do banker and ship-
builder from Maine, who was Bryan's Democratic running mate. The
Populists, who also nominated Bryan for president, refused to swallow
Sewell. Instead, they named Thomas E. Watson (1856–1922) of
Georgia, a former member of Congress elected on the Populist ticket.
Having two vice presidential running mates was an historic first for
a presidential nominee.

whin was a Prisidint iv th' United States ilicted be Mike
Murphy? Since whin did th' gloryous principles iv this
here governmint iv ours rest on th' decision iv th' imployees iv a pie facthry? Is th' campaign over because
somebody with a banjo in his ear has been around
larnin' how th' lads at th' ribbon counters 'r goin' to
mark their ballots? I want to tell ye, me frind, that no
sthraw vote, no, nor enough iv thim to make a stack, is
goin' to tell how this thing will ind. Th' illiction'll not be
decided that way. Th' American people will name their
Prisidint in their own way, an' I may take a crack at it
mesilf."

"An' who ar-re ye goin' to vote f'r?" demanded Mr.
Hennessy.

"That's my business," said Mr. Dooley.

"Anarchist!" roared Mr. McKenna.

"Co-erced!" hissed Mr. Hennessy.

And Mr. Dooley swore because the seltzer wouldn't
fizz before they reached the door.

8

Initially big business and the interests that supported it
were scared stiff of the public response to Bryan, but gradually they recovered enough to reach where it counted—to
their wallets. Despite the fact that McKinley was an unknown commodity on Wall Street, Hanna raised the largest
war chest ever seen in the United States—$3.5 million. It
does not seem like much today, but in those happy times it
was a huge amount. There were no restrictions on corporate
giving, and banks, trusts, corporations, and insurance companies were systematically assessed their share to save the
country from the anarchy that Bryan would bring.

While Bryan was not without financial resources himself,
having most of the silver magnates of the West behind him,

he was not nearly as solvent as McKinley and probably never had much more than $650,000 to spend on his campaign.

Most of the McKinley money was raised in the East and spent in the West, for everything west or south of Pennsylvania was looked on as questionable.

Not satisfied with merely providing the money for McKinley, established interests resorted to more elemental methods to coerce votes for him as well. If Bryan should win, workers were told, don't bother to report for work the next day. Orders were placed with manufacturers and merchants, with the proviso that they be canceled should McKinley lose. Farmers were told by the insurance companies which had granted their loans that their mortgages would be carried at a lower rate of interest if McKinley were to become President.

No place was this activity more intense than in Chicago. McKinley's regional headquarters were there under the direction of young Charlie Dawes, who would be Vice President himself one day. Millions and millions of pamphlets in many languages left the Chicago post office. A speakers' bureau of 1,400 chatty McKinley men were made available to carry the Republican gospel to the West. No propaganda effort was overlooked.

The twenty-fifth anniversary of the Chicago Fire fell on October 7, 1896, in the midst of the campaign. The city's business interests wanted to celebrate the event with a parade demonstrating the role of sound money (the gold standard) in Chicago's rise from the ashes. The city administration, which was Democratic, took a dim view of this plan and refused to declare the day a holiday. The sound-money boys closed the Stock Exchange and staged an unofficial celebration highlighted by a parade lasting five hours and featuring such business luminaries as Marshall Field and Harlow N. Higinbotham, followed by the Carson Pirie Scott & Co. Sound Money Club. As they passed the Chicago telephone building, the gold-bedecked marchers cheered into a loudspeaker which carried their salute by telephone wire to McKinley, safe on his front porch in Canton, Ohio.

That same evening the Democrats held a silver metal parade, but it was pale indeed in comparison with the Republican turnout.

CHICAGO *EVENING POST*, October 10, 1896

Mr. Hennessy, wearing a silver-painted stovepipe hat and a silver cape and carrying a torch, came in looking much the worse for wear. The hat was dented, the cape was torn and there were marks on Mr. Hennessy's face.

"Where ye been?" asked Mr. Dooley.

"Ma-archin'," said Mr. Hennessy.

"Be th' looks iv ye, ye might have been th' line iv ma-arch f'r th' p'rade. Who's been doin' things to ye?"

"I had a currency debate with a man be th' name iv Joyce, a towny iv mine, in th' Audjiotoreem Hotel," said Mr. Hennessy. "Whin we got as far as th' price iv wheat in th' year iv th' big wind we pushed each other. Give me a high glass iv beer. I'm as dhry as a gravel road."

"Well," said Mr. Dooley, pushing over the glass, "ye'er an ol' man, an' as th' good book says, an ol' fool is th' worst yet. So I'll not thry to con-vince ye iv th' error iv ye'er ways. But why anny citizen that has things in his head shud dhress himself up like a sandwich-man, put a torch on his shoulder an' toddle over this blessed town with his poor round feet is more than I can come at with all me intelligence.

"I agree with ye perfectly, Hinnissy, that this here is a crisis in our histhry. On wan hand is arrayed th' shylocks an' th' pathrites, an' on th' other side th' pathrites an' th' arnychists. Th' constitution must be upheld, th' gover'mint must be maintained, th' down-throdden farmer an' workin'man must get their rights. But do ye think, man alive, that ye'er goin' to do this be poorin' lard ile frim ye'er torch down ye'er spine or thrippin' over sthreetcar tracks like a dhray-horse thryin' to play circus? Is th' constitution any safer to-night because ye have to have ye'er leg amputated to get ye'er boot off or because Joyce has made ye'er face look like th' back durestop iv a German resthrant?

"Jawnny Mack took me down in th' afthernoon f'r to see th' monsthrous p'rade iv th' goold min. It was a gloryous spectacle. Th' sthreets were crowded with gool' bugs an' women an' polismin an' ambulances. Th' procission was miles an' miles long. Labor an' capital marched side be side, or annyhow labor was in th' usual place, afther th' capitalists. It was a noble sight f'r to see th' employer iv workin' min marchin' ahead iv his band iv sturdy fellers that to rest thimsilves afther th' layboryous occupations iv th' week was restin' undher banners that dhrilled a hole in their stomachs or car-ryin' two-be-four joists to show their allegiance to th' naytional honor. A man that has to shovel coke into a dhray or shove lumber out iv th' hole iv a barge or ele-vate his profission be carryin' a hod iv mort to th' thop iv a laddher doesn't march with th' grace iv an an-telope, be a blamed sight. To march well a man's feet have to be mates, an' if he has two left feet both runnin' sideways he ought to have interference boots to keep him fr'm settin' fire to his knees. Whin a man walks as if he expected to lave a log stuck in th' sthreet behind him he has th' gall proper f'r half-past six o'clock in th' avenin' befure payday. But 'tis not th' prance iv an American citizen makin' a gloryous spectacle iv himself.

"They were coerced," said Mr. Hennessy gloomily.

"Don't ye believe it," replied the philosopher. "It niver requires coercion to get a man to make a monkey

iv himsilf in a prisidintial campaign. He does it as aisily
as ye dhrink ye'er liquor, an' that's too aisy. Don't ye
believe thim lads with lumber ya-ards on their necks an'
bar'ls on their feet was coerced. There wasn't wan iv
thim that wudden't give his week's wages for a chanst
to show how many times he cud thrip over a manhole
in a mile. No more coerced than ye are whin ye r-run
downtown an' make an ape iv ye'ersilf. I see ye marchin'
away fr'm Finucane's with th' Willum J. O'Briens.
Th' man nex' to ye had a banner declarin' that he was no
slave. 'Twas th' la-ad Johnson. He was r-right. He is no
slave an' he won't be wan as long as people have
washin' to give to his wife. Th' man I see ye takin' a
dhrink with had a banner that said if th' mines was
opened th' mills would be opened too. He meant be
that that if money was plenty enough for him to get
some without wur-rukin' he'd open a ginmill. An' ye
ma-arched afther Willum J. O'Brien, didn't ye? Well,
he's a good lad. If I didn't think so I wudden't say it until I got me strenth back or cud buy a gun. But did
Willum J. O'Brien march? Not Willie. He was on horseback."

"Well," said Mr. Hennessy, "annyhow I proved me
hathred iv capital."

"So ye did," said Mr. Dooley. "So ye did. An' capital
this afthernoon showed its hatred iv ye. Ye ought to
match blisters to see which hates th' worst. Capital is at
home now with his game in a tub iv hot wather, an'
whin he comes down tomorrah to oppriss labor an'
square his protisted notes, he'll have to go on all fours.
As fr you, Hinnissy, if 'twill aise ye anny, ye can hang
fr a few minyits fr'm th' gas fixtures. Did th' gool' dimmycrats have a p'rade?"

"No," said Mr. Hennessy, "but they rayviewed th'
day procission fr'm th' Pammer House. Both iv thim
was on th' stand."

9

Republicans and conservative Democrats alike grew alarmed at the thought of having a dangerous "red" like Bryan in the White House, so that they willingly paid the assessments leveled on them by Mark Hanna. There were no mass media and no television or radio spots to buy; no jets to charter for cross-country stops; no armies of young canvassers to feed and house. Instead, Hanna spent his $3.5 million on an educational campaign accomplished through millions of pamphlets, hundreds of paid lecturers, and thousands of signboards mounted along roads proclaiming McKinley to be "The Advance Agent of Prosperity."

Back home in Canton, Ohio, McKinley conducted a "front porch" campaign. He ventured forth only to make two nonpolitical talks. While a respectable public speaker, McKinley was no match for Bryan and he knew it. So he stayed home, while the Republican National Committee worked feverishly to drum up crowds to travel there to visit him. The railroads were anxious to co-operate and set up a package deal with an especially low excursion rate. Surrounded by uniformed, mounted members of the Canton troop, the visitors would parade from the depot to the candidate's home, where he would regally receive their petitions, say a few words, and then shake hands with all present.

Nothing was spontaneous. The leaders of the various groups were required to submit a copy of their remarks for approval in advance, and McKinley's graceful little responses were prepared. It was a successful gimmick; by the end of September, as many as 20,000 to 30,000 were calling in one day. McKinley maintained his calmness and cordiality in the face of these invasions, which destroyed his yard, weakened the foundation of his porch, and disturbed his peace.

In contrast, Bryan campaigned around the country like a whirlwind. By the time November rolled around he had traveled more than eighteen thousand miles, made five hundred speeches, and been seen by five million people. He had to. Even the usually Democratic press in the great urban centers had deserted him, although in some cities this was offset when the Protestant clergy upheld the points of his cross-of-gold speech from their pulpits.

CHICAGO *EVENING POST*, October 17, 1896

"Ye mar-rk my wurrud," said Mr. Hennessy, "whin Bryan comes to Chicago it'll be diff'rent."

"I sup-pose so, I sup-pose so," replied Mr. Dooley. "What is th' young man goin' to do?"

"He's goin' to set fire to th' town," Mr. Hennessy said. "He's goin' to bur-rn it up. He'll make a thrall iv iloquincy fr'm Mud Lake to Cal'vary Symmetry,[9] an' whin he laves off McKinley won't have votes enough to sthring around his neck.

"Well, maybe so," said Mr. Dooley, "an' maybe not. Ye see, Hinnissy, there's two ways iv lookin' at it. I mind whin Vallandingham,[10] him that was a cop-

[9] Mud Lake to Cal'vary Symmetry—from one end of the city to the other. Mud Lake was Lake Calumet in South Chicago and Calvary Cemetery was at the northern border of the city.

[10] Vallandingham—Clement L. Vallandigham (1820–71), an Ohio congressman who opposed President Lincoln and the Civil War involvement of the North, was banished to the Confederacy in 1863. In August 1864, when the Democratic presidential convention convened in Chicago, the war had dragged on for three years and was going badly for the North. Antiwar sentiment was high and it seemed that Lincoln, a Republican, could be beaten. Vallandigham, a popular hero with the Peace Democrats, or "Copperheads," had returned North in June 1864 and was warmly welcomed when he arrived at the Sherman House hotel in Chicago in August. Afraid that the crowds might erupt into antigovernment violence, Police Commissioner "Long John" Wentworth challenged Vallandigham to a debate. (Wentworth, a

perhead durin' th' war, come to Chicago. As long as he was in Ohio he was a gr-reat man, an' us la-ads that looked f'r to see th' south whale th' divvil out iv th' north an' was iv a conthrary sthreak annyhow we r-read his speeches an' looked up to him as th' saviour iv his counthry, an' th' on'y thrue frind iv th' consitution. Well, he come up to Chicago an' they held a meetin' f'r him in fr'ront iv th' courthouse, an' he got up on a bar'l an' wint on to tell us what was r-right an' what was wrong. He'd no more thin got war-rmed up to his wur-ruk whin a big man standin' near th' bar'l knocked th' top iv it in an' th' orator an' statesman fell through. Thin they rowled him. Now, I was an admirer iv Val-landingham, but f'r th' life iv me niver aftherward cud I come to regard him with riv-rance. No wan can be th' savior iv his counthry afther he has been rowled in a bar'l. If he'd been th' pope iv Rome in th' same position 'twud have made a Jew man iv me an' I'd be votin' f'r Pammer an' Buckner this very minyit.

"Bryan was a big man hollerin' at th' crowd a block away on th' Coliseem stage an' he's a big man still in Chicago whin he's in Grand Rapids, but how big'll he be whin he climbs up in th' loft over Billy O'Toole's saloon an' talks cheek be jowl with th' gang? I've seen manny a great statesman in me lifetime, but I niver see wan that cud walk through th' yards fr'm th' exchange to Carey's saloon without smellin' like a Canalpoort avenue ca-ar on a wet day. Be hivens, George Washington cuddent do it, an' bechune you an' me, Hinnissy, I'd hate to vote f'r a man that carrid around with him th'

former congressman and mayor of Chicago, had been a Democrat until 1859, when he joined the Union Republicans; he was an ardent supporter of Lincoln.) The debate was held before the public on the courthouse steps, and Wentworth emerged as the victor by a wide margin. After that, Vallandigham was no longer a threat to internal security.

bill iv fare that ye find in th' atmosphere iv me frind
Jawn Brinnock's rindrin' house.

"Shakespere says in wan iv his plays that no man is a
hero to his bootblack. Nine tenths iv th' American people don't have an idee that th' Prisidint is rale flesh an'
blood. They vote f'r a statue. Jawnny Mack here is goin'
to vote f'r a lithograph iv McKinley that he has hangin'
in his front window. Now suppose ye was to dhrop in to
Cudney's saloon f'r a dhrink an' he was to see a man
atin' cole slaw with a pair iv tongs, an' Cudney was to
say: 'Here, Jawn, I want ye to shake hands with me
frind McKinley. He's wan iv th' right sort an' he's a candidate f'r Prisidint. Take wan iv his ca-ards an' be
good to him among ye'er people.' Would Jawnny vote
f'r him? Not in wan thousand years. Th' on'y raison he's
with MicKinley is he don't know him. Th' more people
sees a candidate f'r Prisidint, th' less votes he gets. If I
was Bryan's manager I'd keep him in a chilled-steel safe
an' have him talk in a phonography. Th' lad Hanna has
th' right idee. He makes his inthry stay at home an' on'y
those that have carfare or passes can get a squint at
him. Th' rest iv th' counthry can't tell whin he's
dhropped part iv his breakfast on his coat front or
whether he's gettin' bald on th' back iv his head.

"I bet ye Tom Gahan got up th' pro-gram f'r Bryan in
Chicago. Gahan is a frind iv mine. I knowed him whin
he was a polisman at th' ya-ards. If he was managin' th'
campaign iv George Washinton 'twud be all th' same
with him. He believes in mixin'. Wan night he'd have
George playin' sivin-up f'r th' dhrinks at Mike Dwyers,
th' nex' he'd have him dancin' in th' prize waltz at
Finucane's hall. I'd give th' sight iv wan eye to see th'
father iv his counthry umpirin' a pie-eatin' match under
th' supervision iv Tim Gahan, or ladin' th' gran' march
at th' county dimocracy ball or handin' round his cards

at a wake. 'Vote f'r George Washinton f'r Prisidint an'
Pete McGinnis f'r riprisintative in th' legislachure.'

"Th' experimint 'll be worth watchin', Hinnissy. I
suppose Bryan'll go to all th' christenins an' church fairs
befure Tom gets through with him. We'll see him rollin'
tinpins down at Turner Hall an' dhroppin' in f'r a game
iv pool at Aldherman Martin's. Maybe ye cude get him
to r-run here, Hinnissy. I've always been a dimmycrat
an' Ill threat him kindly an' hang his lithograph in th'
front window an' push him away fr'm his change. I
haven't seen a candidate since Tim Ryan r-run f'r
congress an' he passed a lead dollar on me that I was six
months gettin' off."

"Niver mind," said Mr. Hennessy, "he'll burn up th'
town."

"I hope so," said Mr. Dooley. "I'd like to see it
burned up wanst so we cud all begin fresh, like th'
Stock Exchange, without payin' what we owe an' without gettin' into th' constables' hands f'r th' same. I've
heerd that th' on'y thing anny mimber iv th' Stock Exchange has put up is an American flag f'r sound money
an' prosperity."

10

As if the 1896 campaign against the Republicans was not
bumptious enough, Bryan had trouble on his own left and
right. The gold Democrats who bolted the convention held a
conference of their own in Indianapolis in September. Delegates from forty-one states and three territories attended
and nominated Senator John M. Palmer of Illinois for President and General Simon Bolivar Buckner of Kentucky for
Vice President on the National Democratic ticket. Their
platform was mercifully brief, as platforms go, expressing
support for the gold standard and praising Cleveland. Most

of the conservative Democrats in the East endorsed the ticket, but not David B. Hill, the New York party boss. "I am still a Democrat," he said, "very still." Palmer and Buckner formed a "truth squad" to follow Bryan and point out his heresies, but they found it very hard to keep up with him.

On the left, despite the fusion of the People's Populist Party with the Democrats, making them the Popocratic Party (or the "Poopocrats," as Mr. Dooley dubbed them), there were some hard-liners who could not accept Bryan. Also, the Populist nomination of Tom Watson as an alternative vice president in twenty-six states led to bitterness. In addition, Bryan had been endorsed by the National Silver Party and by most of the silver Republicans, all of whom wanted to maintain their independence, so that the state and congressional tickets were nightmares of confusion.

Further, attempts were made to defame Bryan by placing him in a triumvirate of liberal infamy with Altgeld, who pardoned the anarchists convicted of the Haymarket bombing, and with Eugene Debs, who had helped to lead the unsuccessful Pullman strike of 1894.[11]

In an attempt to inflame the populace against Bryan, Teddy Roosevelt, a Republican police commissioner in New York City, likened these three brave men to "the leaders of the Terror of France in mental and moral attitude" and averred that he expected to meet them and their adherents literally "sword to sword on the field of battle." For him, as well as for Mr. Dooley's friend Dempsey, the campaign of 1896 was war.

CHICAGO *EVENING POST*, October 31, 1896

"Well," said Mr. McKenna, "I'll be glad whin 'tis over."

[11] For detail regarding the Pullman strike, see Chapter VIII.

"An' so will I," said Mr. Hennessy. "It's been a gr-reat strain on me, Jawn, f'r to keep fr'm handin' ye wan in th' heat iv debate."

"They won't be manny that differ with ye two on that pint," said Mr. Dooley. "Th' only man in th' United States that'll be loth to give up th' campaign is that grand ol' jack iv clubs, th' Hon. Jawn Im Pammer. It's spoort f'r him, leapin' around th' counthry dodgin' couplin' pins an' bleatin' to th' populace, an' they won't be annything f'r him an' Patsy Boliver Buckner to do afther Choosdah but croshayin'. I hear Casey's boy say th' Academy iv Science was preparin' to make a collec-tion iv th' voters f'r th' belly-straight ticket. If they can get enough iv thim it'll be very inthrestin' an' instruc-tive to th' young.

"But th' rest iv us, Jawn, 'll be glad whin th' crool war is over. I wint down to th' Polish school hall las' Wins'dah f'r to see th' young kid Bryan. There was a gr-reat crowd iv th' sons iv Kosioosko an' Poolaski there, and I addhressed wan iv thim, a man be th' name iv Dimpsey, an' says I: 'Noble Pole,' says I, 'what are ye doin' here?' 'I come,' he says, 'to get a pike at th' frind iv liberty an' champeen iv th' opprissed,' he says, 'an' to raygister me hathred iv th' plutocrats,' he says. 'I tell ye what,' says he, 'this is no ordin'ry iliction,' he says, 'this is war.' 'Wirra,' says I, 'an' that's sad,' an' I wint away because I found a frind iv liberty thryin' to lift th' clock out iv me vest pocket. I sthrayed up th' r-road an' into Davey Shannahan's headquarthers, where they was a man with r-red whiskers, hollerin' at th' Irish raypubli-can club. 'Fellow citizens,' says this hobo, 'we are in th' mi'st of no common crisis,' he says. 'Th' platform iv th' poopocratic party is nothin' less but an attack on th' foundations iv gover'mint,' he says. 'You an' me,' he says, 'must stand shoulder to shoulder again' th' foorces iv arnchy an' corruption,' he says. 'Hang out th' flag an' raysolve that if anny man lays sacreeligious hands upon

that holy banner,' he says, 'ye'll kick a lung out iv him,'
he says. 'F'r,' says he, 'this is war.'

"Jawn, I wint home with a weary heart. I seen wan
war in th' papers an' I don't want to see another. I mind
when they pinched Judge Morris f'r thryin' to let th'
rebels out iv Camp Douglas an' we formed th' home
gua-ard f'r th' protection iv our wives an' fam'lies. Oh, it
was turrible to see us dhrillin' in Finucane's Hall or
with our muskets again th' wall playin' sivin-up f'r th'
dhrinks! I niver want to see another, Jawn. But whin I
come to think it over I cuddent f'r th' life iv me make
out anny diff'rence bechune this campaign an' others
befure it. There's th' same amount iv dhrunk min in th'
sthreets, th' same little kids marchin' around with
torches, th' same Bill Mason rollin' fr'm wan wigwam to
th' other. Gin'ral Sickles has always shed his legs durin'
a presidential campaign; th' integrity iv th' gover'mint
has always been threated be domestic foes; th' ol' flag
has always been waved on high be la-ads that was
lookin' f'r a place on th' polis foorce an' min that cuddent be got to go downstairs to fix th' furnace afther
da-ark has always declared th' starry banner iv freedom
—paper, calico or silk.

"While I was thinkin' in this way in comes Dimpsey,
an' with him th' r-red-headed man fr'm Shannahan's.
'Well,' says I, 'd'ye still think its war?' 'I do,' says Dimpsey. 'So do I,' says th' other. 'Well,' says I, 'ye may relieve ye'er poor tired minds,' I says. 'Although,' I says,
'it's possible that Gin'ral Sickles has had a leg blowed off
be a bad egg,' I says, 'they niver was a war yet whin th'
combatants,' I says, 'fought with th' product iv th' female chicken,' I says. 'It may look like war now,' I says.
'An' it may look like war nex' Choosdah night, but
Winsdah mornin',' I says, 'it'll on'y be th' fag end iv th'
common dhrunk that it is,' I says, 'an' ye'll wondher
where ye got that bad taste in ye'er mouth an' why
ye'er voice sounds like a man planin' a pine knot an'

who hit ye, just as ye done befure,' I says. 'Th'
wurruld'll go on just th' same. Th' starry banners iv freedom'll be tore down, th' stock exchange will shuffle up
th' ca-ards an' begin playin' fr markers, an' men'll carry
th' immortal hod up th' laddher an' there'll not be wan
r-red brick or wan pound iv mort shy fr all that th'
counthry's been saved an' th' gover'mint at Wash'n'ton
still lives.'"

"Faith, I believe ye'er right," said Mr. Hennessy,
nursing his foot, which had been run over by the barrow of a fellow anarchist that morning.

11

On November 3, 1896, it was all over. McKinley had won by
700,000 votes. Fusion had been a failure, for Bryan did not
equal the combined Democratic and Populist showing of
1892. He lost the East, the Middle West, the border states,
California, and Oregon. Whether the voters had fallen prey
to fear and threats or whether the industrial workers he had
courted rejected him for other reasons, he lost the cities outside of the South and the silver areas of the West. The
agrarian vote was not as strong as expected: some observers
think this was due to an unusually big wheat crop which
was sold at a high price abroad.

It was obvious that Bryan had made some tactical mis-
takes and miscalculations. He underestimated the spread of
urbanization and industrialization in the West, the basic
conservatism of the farm states, and the number of gold
Democrats who would swallow their gorge, reject their
own candidate, John M. Palmer, and vote Republican. He
had let his campaign appeals grow increasingly more strident and he had emphasized the silver question to the detri-
ment of the other issues delineated in the platform. Although Bryan would run again and again for President, and
although the Populist Party would field candidates in three

more presidential elections, the heart went out of both in 1896.

As for President Cleveland, by the end of his second term he was a broken, haunted man. Like other Presidents whose leadership was to turn sour, he escaped the White House whenever he could, spending most of his time at his own private homes. He was ill-served by his appointees, and his second-term cabinet was definitely second rate. After he allowed Richard Olney, the Attorney General, to persuade him to intervene in the Pullman strike, he lost the last vestiges of his popularity, except in the business community. On leaving the White House in March 1897, he retired to Princeton, New Jersey, and while he gradually rehabilitated himself to some extent, his judgment did not improve, as evidenced by the fact that he allowed himself to be named an officer of a large insurance company at a time when it was being investigated by the federal government for misuse of the funds entrusted to it.

CHICAGO *EVENING POST*, March 4, 1897

"Well, at last there's a raypublican prisidint," said Mr. Dooley.

"Yes, thanks be to goodness," said Mr. Hennessy. "Now we can ilict a dimmycrat mayor. Since th' big lad has been in they'se been no more chanst f'r wan iv us thin f'r a bottle iv wood alcohol in a Swede lodgin' house."

"Thrue f'r ye," said Mr. Dooley. "They even have a raypublican on th' r-red bridge. Th' poor man is in a bad way. He don't dare to come down fr'm his perch. He sleeps in th' little house where he wurruks an' they hand him his food on a clothes-pole. A select comity iv th' Sixth Ward Altgeld an' B. O'Brien Marchin' Club has been waitin' f'r him to come down since a week befure iliction, whin he hung a picture iv McKinley on th' arch iv th' bridge.

"We get sthronger in Chicago whin we get weaker in
Washn'n'ton. Th' throuble with Cleveland was he's so
big an' sthrong an' hearty that they wasn't anny room f'r
anybody else at th' trough. He had both front paws in,
an' th' best you an' me got was watchin' an' admirin' his
satisfaction. Now he's out iv th' way, I don't mind sayin'
that I'd like a chanst at office mesilf. Mayor? Not me.
'Tis too common. They're wan hundred candydates f'r
mayor, includin' me modest an' injanyous friend Wash
Hesing. I wudden't f'r th' life iv me destroy th' curl iv
Wash's whiskers be projictin' me candydacy into th'
field. But if me frind Alfred Safety Trude wins out I'm
sthrong f'r chief iv polis. I'd made as good a wan as
Banock. What does a man in th' hay business know
about polis wurruk? A good observant liquor dealer
ought to undherstand th' theery an' practice iv th' polis
foorce betther thin a desk sergeant.

"But it must have been lonesome f'r Willie Bryan in
Wash'n'ton. There he was, th' poor little lad, settin'
down in front iv th' gran'stand rayportin' th' proceedin's
f'r his paper, makin' dinky little markers in his notebook
an' expectin' ivry minyit to be chased off th' grounds.
He had to show his star to get through th' lines. I
wondher if he'll stick to th' business. If he does he
ought to lave Wash'n'ton an' come out here f'r th'
spring campaign. I can see him now at wan iv Wash's
meetin's writin' it all out. 'Th' meetin' was large an'
enthusyastic. Just as Mister Hesing come on th' stage a
man in th' back iv th' hall hurled a decrepit egg at him,
but his aim was bad an' th' fruit sthruck our rayporther
on th' neck.' Chicago's th' place f'r Rayporther Bryan,
an' he ought to do well here if he sticks to business,
keeps his pencils well-sharpened an' gets acquainted
with th' Bath House."

The sketch did not appeal to Mr. Hennessy, who
muttered his anger. "I was on'y jokin'," said Mr. Doo-

ley. "Willie will niver make a good rayporther. He just isn't pop'lar enough an' he don't see th' pictheresque side iv things. What did he write about in Wash'n'ton? About a yard an' a half consarnin' th' financial question an' other issues as dead as Moses. Now th' rale rayporthers saw th' news iv th' day. They knew 'twas inthrestin' that McKinley sh'd kiss his wife an' his mother. This shows we're goin' to have a conservative administhration. If he had kissed some wan else's wife or mother they'd ixpict a radical departure fr'm th' policy iv the raypublican party. Very few presidents has iver done th' like. George Wash'n'ton caused much surprise whin he turned fr'm takin' th' oath iv office an' lammed his wife with th' good book. Thomas Jefferson asked th' band to play him a waltz an' give his aged mother a whirl aroun' th' stage. Andhrew Jackson didn't have no rilitives prisint, but whin he was swore in he handed th' chief justice a kick an' winked at th' wife an' mother iv th' secrety iv state. So it wint through th' list.

"As fr Cleveland, he seems to have kissed his wife too. I suppose that was th' foorce iv Mack's example. But it was a wondherful thing to see an' a wondherful thing to read about. Ivrybody ixpicted him to ask his wife if she had dinner ready, or maybe tell her she had a smudge on her nose. But instid iv that this gr-reat man, with his mind full iv ducks, surrounded be th' wit an' janyous an' foorth class posthmasthers iv a powerful nation, leaned lovin'ly over an' kissed his spouse. An' all th' rayporthers wept but Willie. He was bent over his copy paper writin' again an' again: 'Sixteen-to-wan, sixteen-to-wan. William J. Bryan. William Jay Bryan.'"

"Well, I'm glad th' big lad is gone," said Mr. Hennessy. "Not that he was so bad, but he made it har-rd fr us in th' sixth wa-ard."

"No," said Mr. Dooley. "Cleveland was not a bad Prisidint—fr Cleveland."

VII

Mr. Dooley on Molly Donahue and the New Woman

"Women's rights? What does a woman want iv rights whin she has priv'leges? Rights is th' last thing we get in this wurruld. They're th' nex' things to wrongs. They're wrongs tur-rned inside out."

—Mr. Dooley

Although Finley Peter Dunne was a liberal on most social issues (later in life he liked to look back on his Chicago days as belonging to his radical period), he shared the wide-spread opinion of most men of his time that the women's rights movement was a comic one. "Sufferjests," Mr. Dooley called them, and he predicted that not until there was a "political column in Butthrick's Pattherns will ye iver be able f'r to musther a corp'ral's guard iv women at th' polls." The feminists and their activities provided him with an ample target for his satiric darts.

"Th' new woman," says Molly, "'ll be free fr'm th' opprision iv man," she says. "She'll wurruk out her own way, without help or hinderance," she says. "She'll wear what clothes she wants," she says, "an' she'll be no man's slave," she says. "They'll be no such thing as givin' a girl in marredge to a clown an' makin' her dipindant on his whims," she says. "Th' women'll earn their own livin'," she says; "an' mebbe," she says, "th' men'll stay at home an' dredge in th' house wurruk," she says.

Molly Donahue, herself an example of new womanhood, was one of the early characters in the Dooley columns. Molly was the convent-schooled, piano-playing, French-speaking, china-painting, bicycle-riding, vaudeville-giving, upwardly mobile, feminist, and otherwise indomitable daughter of Malachi and Honoria Donahue. As assistant foreman of the rolling mills, Malachi Donahue was a man of stature in Bridgeport. Honoria Donahue, who supported Molly's efforts not only to keep up with the Hogans but to surpass them, presided over a large family that was typical of Bridgeport at that time. In addition to Molly, it included the boys—Sarsfield, Darcey, Matthew, Mile, Pat, and Tim—the girls—Molly, Theresa, and Aggie—and the nameless, genderless baby.

Molly and her exploits were immediately popular—so much so that when Dunne attracted national attention, the *Ladies' Home Journal* asked him to write a monthly Molly Donahue column for them. After completing four episodes, Dunne became unhappy with the series and decided to discontinue it. As Elmer Ellis, his biographer, points out, it was not, as Dunne felt, inferior work; it was just different. However, it is to the *Journal* series that we owe a deeper insight into Mr. Dooley (and the best physical description of him) as well as into day-to-day domestic life on Archey Road.

Despite Dunne's flippant treatment of the woman question, the issue was a burning one toward the end of the nineteenth century. Along with rapid industrialization, the urbanization of America had a profound effect upon the nation's social life in general and gave impetus to the continuation of the women's rights movement.

The vocational opportunities that unfolded for women in the urban environment did much to promote their struggle for equal rights, including the right to vote. Chicago women saw feminine breakthroughs in almost every field, and a

lucky minority of women on the work force went into professional and clerical jobs.

For example, Chicago women had penetrated the male
cordon surrounding the practice of medicine. There were
more than two hundred female physicians and surgeons in
the city by 1893, some of whom also were admitted to membership in the hitherto sexually segregated American Medi-
cal Association.

Since 1888 women had been legally able to serve on the
Chicago Board of Education. Likewise, they were eligible to
vote in school elections. A large number of educated women
were attracted to the teaching profession—but men received
four times as much pay for doing the same job.

Women journalists found jobs on every newspaper. They
were welcomed to membership in the Illinois Press Association, and they formed their own Illinois Woman's Press Association.

Increasingly women were attracted to the field of the law.
A Chicago woman was the first female admitted to practice
in the federal court system, in 1877, although the second
woman, also a Chicagoan, was not granted admission until
1890. Both the *Chicago Legal News* and the *Chicago Law
Times* had female editors. Further, in 1872 an active woman
lawyer succeeded in shepherding through to passage a law
providing that sex could not be used as an excuse to preclude
women from holding any position, except with the military. Of course, it was honored more in the breach than the
observance.

"Ladies" groups agitated for a wider range of opportunities for women and for the protection of the women and
children who had to work. Toward this end, temperance,
suffrage, and religious groups established the Illinois
Woman's Alliance in 1888. The Chicago Woman's Club, primarily devoted to cultural and social pursuits, also played a
lobbying role in social service and political activities in the
city. Prominent women gave so much of their time to a

number of crusades that a contemporary male visitor to Chicago was moved to comment,

"I do not believe that in any older American city we shall find fashionable women so anxious to be considered patrons of art and of learning, or so forward in works of public improvement and governmental reform as well as of charity . . ."

Epitomizing this spirit were Bertha Palmer, leader of Chicago society as well as a feminist leader, and Jane Addams, the reform-conscious founder of Hull House.

Despite these very real advances, however, the majority of Chicago women found their niche in the familiar fields of housewifery and motherhood. Some also worked outside the home; the luckiest of these could place their children in the few day-care centers scattered about the city.

According to the census of 1890, approximately 88,100 women in the United States held down jobs outside the home or did piecework in their own unhealthy tenements. Of this number approximately 41 per cent were domestics or servants. Next came workers in manufacturing and factory jobs, particularly in the clothing industry. Three times as many women as men found employment in the sweatshops, where they labored under the most dismaying circumstances.

As a result, social reformers demanded legislation against employers who exploited their female and child help. And women increasingly organized themselves into unions to bargain collectively for better hours and working conditions as well as for higher pay. Chicago women joined the Knights of Labor in sizable numbers beginning in September 1881, which was the first time that the order permitted women members. Chicago Local 1789 was the second formed by women in the United States. A leader of the Chicago labor movement was Mrs. George Rodgers, who was the first woman to be made a master workman of a district assembly in the Knights of Labor. She also was the first woman to be asked to serve as general treasurer by the Knights of Labor national convention in 1886. She turned down the job because of her other responsibilities—which included twelve children.

For women in Chicago there was the type of discrimination that has persisted to this day—male teachers in the public school system were paid much more than females with equivalent jobs—mixed with some rather bizarre signs of equality—there were at least two bucket shops, questionable brokerage houses, which catered to women only and which also provided facilities for gambling.

Although they had traveled a long way, Chicago women in the 1890s still had far to go.

2

"An' so it is with women. They haven't th' right to vote, but they have th' priv'lege iv conthrollin' th man ye ilict. They haven't th' right to make laws, but they have th' priv'lege iv breakin' thim, which is betther. They haven't th' right iv a fair thrile be a jury iv their peers; but they have th' priv'lege iv an' unfair thrile be a jury iv their admirin' infeeryors. If I could fly, d'ye think I'd want to walk?"

When discussing women and the vote, Mr. Dooley frequently averred that it was the woman behind the man who determined which way the ballot was cast and in making their choice, that women were guided most by the appearance of the candidate. For example, in 1893 there were two principal candidates running to fill the unexpired term of the assassinated mayor, Carter H. Harrison, Sr. One was the bald George Bell Swift and the other the relatively hirsute

John Patrick Hopkins. The hairier Hopkins won. However, in 1895 Swift was elected Chicago's thirtieth mayor over the tonsorially more resplendent Democrat, Frank B. Wenter. The failure of his theory passed unremarked by Dooley. As for Dunne himself, at least later in life he favored votes for women. Margaret Abbott Dunne, his wife, was an active suffragist, who raised money, helped organize support, and marched in parades.

CHICAGO *EVENING POST*, December 9, 1893

BEHIND THE THRONE

MR. DOOLEY DESCANTS ON WOMEN'S INFLUENCE IN POLITICS

WHY HOPKINS WILL BE ELECTED

THE MEN MAY VOTE, BUT THEIR WIVES AND SWEETHEARTS TELL THEM HOW, EVEN IN BRIDGEPORT

"Well, Jawn," said Mr. Dooley, "who's goin' to be elected?"

"Swift," said Mr. McKenna, who is a republican.

"Ye'er a liar," said Mr. Dooley, who is a democrat. "Swift has no more chanst iv bein' mayor than Father Dorney has iv bein' elected gran' master iv th' or-angemen—Gawd f'rgive me f'r sayin' it. Niver mind, McKinna. Don't tell me, by gar; I know. Ye can't beat that there Hopkins no more than ye cud bate a polis-man playin' forthy-fives. He have th' ca-ards up his sleeve, he have, he have.

"F'r why, says ye? Listen to me, Jawn, ye poor, deluded gom, that's been in politics since ye got out iv short clothes an' knows no more about it than ye know about th' catechism, an' ye know dam little iv that beyant 'Why did he make me?' Listen to me, avick, an' I'll give ye a pointher or two. Did ye niver know I was in politics wanst? I was that. I was captain in me precinct

whin we carrid it f'r O'Broyn be more votes than they
was men, women, childhern an' goats in th' whole sixth
wa-ard. I was in politics thin, captain iv me precint, an'
they was no man in Bridgeport wist iv Finucane's that
cud throw me down. Sare a wan. I shtud like Willim
Joyce an' Bill O'Broyn an' Stuckart rolled in wan, f'r I
was as gr-reat a han' at visitin' round an' quotin' th'
pothry iv little Mike Scanlan as Joyce, an' I could whale
hell out iv anny man fr'm Haley's to th' bridge, an' I
shtud like a king among th' Dutch. I cud ate a manger
full iv cole slaw. I was a pollytician wanst, though I've
braced up an' rayformed since, Jawn, an' I'll tell ye no
lie, th' man that gets th' women with him can shtay at
home an' write his message. He can that.

"Now, Jawn, mind ye, women don't vote, but women
r-runs thim that does vote, as Brady said at th' raffle. It
don't make no diff'rence what th' man is. He takes his
ordhers fr'm th' captain at home in wan way or th'
other, an' though he may be as big as a grain elevator
an' whin it comes to an argyment about gettin' to th'
coal though he may be able to give her th' shovel an'
win out, he does what she wants done, divvle th' liss.
An' a woman, if she had th' brains iv Daniel O'Connell,
still she'd be a woman all th' same an' f'r th' best lukin'
guy in th' race. A man says to himself: 'What's th'
qualifications iv th' candydate? Will he clane th'
shtreets, will he lower taxes, will he put me brother on
th' polis force?' he says. He asks himself thim quistions.
But with a woman, 'tis diff'rent. Says she: 'Ain't he a
nice-lukin' man?' says she. ''Tis a shame to bate such a
nice-lukin' man,' she says. 'Mike,' she says, 'ye'er goin'
to vote f'r Hopkins,' she says. 'No,' says he, 'I was
thinkin' iv votin' f'r Swift,' he says. 'What?' says she. 'F'r
that little baldheaded duck?' says his wife. 'Why, Mike,
f'r shame,' says she. 'Why,' she says, 'he ain't got no
hair,' says she. Ye can bank, Jawn, that a woman 'll
niver like a baldheaded man. Whether 'tis because iv

th' old sayin' that a man loses his hair f'r his sins or whether 'tis because whin a man is bald no woman has anny hold upon him, 'tis not f'r me to say. Now a man can stand off thim little dodgers they sends around before election day. He can stand thim off. An' he can take a long chance with a frind who grabs him be th' buttonhole in the sthreet, f'r he can call a copper if he wants to get away. But how th' 'ell is a man goin' to dodge an argyment that he gets in th' mornin' an' night an' at meal times, whin he's sober an' whin he has his rollers upon him? There's no escape unliss he'll ate his meals on th' front stoop an' sleep in th' ba-arn. None at all, Jawn.

"I seen it wur-ruk whin Tom Sinnott was a candidate f'r something or another. Donovan had him bate blind in th' sixth whin Sinnott came up to a party. They hadn't seen Donovan, but some wan had it around that he came fr'm Connock an' was a dashin' boy, but whin Sinnott appeared 'twas all off with me brave Harry. Sinnott wint to all th' balls an' christenin's fr'm wan ind iv th' wa-ard to th' other, makin' luv to th' daughters iv th' precint com-mitymen. Dam near all iv thim accipted him too, at that, f'r th' rollin' mills was shut down. Well, sir, they say whin he'd propose to a girl he'd say: 'Molly,' he'd say, 'don't say nothin' about this till afther th' 'lection,' he'd say. 'Thin we'll announce it,' he'd say, 'is ye'er father a sthrong democrat.' 'Th' sthrongest that iver lived.' 'Thin he wouldn't vote th' raypublican ticket?' 'I sh'd say not.' 'Thin give him these here pasters,' he'd say. 'Maybe ye cud get him to use thim,' he'd say. 'Here's some f'r his friends. Will ye rassle through th' nex' waltz with me, Julia.' Well, sir, whin it come election day Donovan wasn't in it. They say Sinnott lived in his cellar f'r a month, an' it cost him th' first year's salary squarin' breach iv promise suits.

"An' there ye are, Jawn."

3

Although Irish women were for the most part relegated to traditional roles, there is historical evidence that in early Celtic times it was women who led the Irish tribes. Gradually their position of leadership was eroded, probably because of the need for chieftains who were accomplished in the martial arts required to fend off the many invaders. Some belief in female superiority persisted, however; for example, in Ulster in fairly recent times, the left arm of a female child was withheld at baptism to preserve its pagan strength.

But most Irish women lived on the hardscrabble farms, for the industrial revolution had pretty much passed Ireland by, except in the North, where there was employment available in the tenement factories. Before the Great Famine, the Irish married early and had many children; after the famine, in order to practice the only form of birth control sanctioned by the Church, they married late or often not at all, since so many men had died or emigrated. For many women, this meant a life as a spinster aunt or sister, stuck away in a dark corner or up in the loft, working for one's keep, drying up early, and aging young. The lucky ones left the country.

By the 1890s a good many of these immigrant women had married and carved out a place for themselves in communities like Bridgeport. They wanted a better life for their own daughters than work as a domestic or factory laborer. They brought these girls up to be plucky, like Molly Donahue, but they also wanted them to be genteel and to emulate their supposed betters in elevating the level of social life out on Archey Road.

CHICAGO *EVENING POST*, February 22, 1895

"They'se another scandal in th' Donahue family," said Mr. Dooley.

"What about?" asked Mr. McKenna, eagerly.

"Molly give a vowdyvill," replied Mr. Dooley.

"A what?"

"A vowdyville."

"What?"

"I tol' ye twict she give a v'riety show," said Mr. Dooley, angrily. "Now d'ye know? She's been th' leader iv society so long in th' sixt' wa-ard that she was not to be downed be th' Hogans. They give a progressive spoil-five par-rty an' she med up her mind she'd toss thim over th' gashouse—socially, I mane—be havin' a v'riety show. An' she done it. Wait till I get th' Bridgepoort Tin Thousand. Where'd I lave it? Ah! Here it is! Among those prisint was, let's see—Missers an' Misdams Fla-herty, Dorsey, Schwartzmeister, Cassidy, Pug Sheehan, Cohen iv Blue Island; Misdams O'Rourke, Daheny; Misses Donahue, Clancy, Flaherty, M. Flaherty, B. Fla-herty, J. Flaherty, C. Flaherty, K. Flaherty, O'Don-nell, Sheehan an' Missers Dorsey, Hogan—th' big slob, he come with a kag iv nails aboord—Gallagher, Shaughnessy an' Dooley. That was me, Jawn. They put me in last, but I was there first—a good head befure Fa-ther Kelly.

"Molly Donahue was beamin' an' brimmin' over with wilcome. She mit th' people at th' dure an' says she: 'Come in,' she says. 'I'm glad to see ye,' says she, taking each man iv us be th' hook. I luked around f'r Donahue an' found him settin' out before the kitchen stove with his toes turned in an' his elbows on his knees, smokin' a pipe. He ducked whin th' dure opened, but

seein' it was me he put th' pipe back in his mouth an'
says he: 'This is 'ell,' he says. 'I haven't had a shmoke
th' livelong night an' I et me supper on th' back stoop,'
he says. 'Is there manny in there?' he says. 'Tin,' says I.
'Glory be,' says he, 'an' more comin'? Ye don't mind,' he
says, 'if I loosen up me boots,' he says. 'An',' he says, tug-
gin' at th' nick iv him, 'this here collar's chokin' me be
degrees,' he says. 'I feel as though I had th' croup,' he
says. 'I'm tired out,' he says, 'but be dad, we've got to
throw th' Hogans. They wurrked f'r me father on th' ol'
sod an' I'd be th' poor stick iv a man f'r to let thim put
th' comether over Molly,' he says. 'Not,' he says, 'while
I've got a cint in me pocket,' he says.

"I lift him there, Jawn, an' wint in where Sarsfield
Dorsey was playin' on th' pianny befure th' dure ladin'
into th' settin' room. Th' settin' room was th' stage an'
th' dinin' room was f'r th' audjeence. Wan iv th' Immitt
la-ads come out an' give us a song an' dance. 'I met her,'
says th' lad, 'while sthrollin' be th' brook, an',' says he,
"'twas in th' month iv June,' he says; 'th' hivinly stars
was overhead,' he says, 'an' silver was th' moon.' Thin
he done a step I'd see him practice on th' cor-rner with
th' other lads playin' mouth organs f'r him. Miss Molly
Donahue sung a song an' Gallagher sung another. Gallagher, ye know him, he spinds most iv his days an'
nights hangin' around th' stage dure iv th' Lyceeum, an'
they say he does be intindin' f'r to be a play acthor himsilf wan iv these days. He was th' stage manager, an'
whin he'd got through tellin' us that they was on'y wan
gurl in th' wurruld f'r him, he come out on th' stage an'
says he: 'Ladies an' gintlemin,' says he, 'I have to announce that we have secured th' services iv th' distinguished soubrette Mademizelle Goolah Turee iv th'
Halsted Sthreet Opera House,' he says, 'who will kindly
oblige us with a skirt dance if me frind Mr. Hogan'll
oblige us be closin' his face,' he says. 'Ladies an' gintle-

min, let me inthrojooce Mademizelle Goolah Turee,' he
says.

"With that out thripped a heifer, Jawn, that ye niver
see th' likes of. I'll not tell ye what she had on, though I
cud without detainin' ye. She was pretty, I'll say that,
with an eye in her head that'd coax a hedge priest an'
th' rosiest cheeks I iver see out iv a book. But th' carryin's on iv her. She give me a wink that sint th' blood to
me ears an' she threw a kick at th' good man, an' I seen
him make th' sign an' turn pale an' squirm down in his
seat. What she done next I won't say. I didn't see all iv
it, f'r I was lukin' through me fingers, but jist as she
turned a back somerset Mrs. Flaherty rose up. 'Mike,'
she says. 'Don't bother me,' says Flaherty, who was
crouched down like a man startin' f'r a hundherd ya-ard
dash, with his hands clutchin' th' ar-rms iv th' chair.
'Don't ye see I'm busy.' 'Michael,' says she, 'come with
me. Childher,' she says, 'this is no place f'r us.' An' out
they wint, Flaherty lukin' back till th' dure closed on
him.

"At that moment Donahue come down th' stage,
with wan shoe on an' his collar in his hand. He had his
big hand on Mademizelle Goolah Turee's showlder an'
says he: 'Woman, lave me house,' he says. 'Go,' he says,
'an' sin no more,' he says. 'As f'r th' rist iv ye,' he says, 'if
ye think th' house iv Donahue is th' Lyceem or th' dime
museem ye've made th' mistake iv ye'er life,' he says. 'If
ye're not all out on th' sthreet within th' minyit Monseer
Terence Donahue'll give an imitation iv a poor, tired assistant night foreman at th' mills inthrojoocin' a novelty
in society be clanin' out his guests with th' leg iv a
stove.' An' we lift, all but th' good man, an' he stayed f'r
to comfort th' fam'ly."

"Have you seen Donahue since?" asked Mr. Mc-
Kenna.

"Yis," said Mr. Dooley. "He come in las' night to talk

it over. He says: 'I'm havin' more variety at th' house,'
he says. 'How's that,' says I. 'I'm runnin' things me own
way this week,' he says, 'an' th' social season's closed f'r
repairs,' he says."

4

Disregarding the admonitions of Susan B. Anthony, her fellow leader of the women's rights movement, Elizabeth Cady
Stanton announced in 1895 that she intended to publish a
woman's version of the Bible. That such a volume would be
deemed heretical by most of the religious leadership in the
United States did not deter Mrs. Stanton in the least. In the
end, though, the Lord saved Mr. Dooley from harm, because the project was never completed.

Elizabeth Cady Stanton (1815–1902) was a product of
the first vague stirrings of discontent among American
women, which can be traced back to colonial times when
women who challenged the Puritan overlords refused to be
kept in their place, and brought down on their heads the
wrath of the male establishment. By the 1820s this discontent had found some direction, and particular emphasis was
placed on the creation of educational opportunities for females. At about the same time, women were afforded the
chance to work outside the home in large numbers because
of the growing demand for teachers and the successful operation of the power-driven loom which spelled an end to
cottage industry.

In addition to working outside the home, women found
an outlet from the domestic circle in the formation of
women's groups which had as their primary purpose the
advancement of good causes and the performance of good
works. Implicit in the rise of female organizations was the
challenge to the accepted conventions in almost every as-

pect of American life. The key word during the 1820s to the 1840s was "reform"—religious, educational, political, philosophical, and social reform. The reform organizations welcomed the efforts of these women, who were beginning to recognize the benefits of group action and to enjoy playing a role in the affairs of the day. For many women, participation in one reform group led to participation in another and ultimately to support for women's rights as a way of achieving other goals.

The early feminists repeatedly drew comparisons between the plight of women and that of slaves in the United States. Many women, recognizing the similarity, joined the abolition movement, where they could put to work the talent for organization they had discovered in their church, cultural, and social activities. It was through the abolition movement that women first found the courage to speak out regularly in public. At the same time, they began to formulate a philosophy of their place in society and of the rights to which they were entitled. Although they accepted the fact that they were in an inferior position legally, they refused to acknowledge that this inferiority was innate. This search for a new awareness was often frustrating; in a letter where she discussed the reason why women put up with their second class citizenship, Elizabeth Cady Stanton, explained it as follows:

> She patiently bears all this because in her blindness she sees no way of escape. Her bondage, though it differs from that of the negro slave, frets and chafes her just the same. She too sighs and groans in her chains; and lives but in the hope of better things to come. She looks to heaven; whilst the more philosophical slave sets out for Canada.

In 1848 Mrs. Stanton issued a call to the first women's

rights convention, held in her home town of Seneca Falls, New York. The women listened to addresses by such activists as Lucretia Mott and the former slave Frederick Douglass and approved a "Declaration of Principles" patterned after the Declaration of Independence and indicting men for the oppression of women. The question of obtaining the franchise was approved by a close vote—to the consternation of some who felt this was too extreme a request for the temper of the time.

The Civil War had a catalytic effect on the expectations of American women. The conflict was accompanied by an easing of social strictures, and women found many new outlets for their freshly discovered talents. They worked tirelessly as nurses, in relief agencies, and as part of the propaganda machine in obtaining support for government policies. The awareness of their genuine contributions to the nation led them to believe that the masculine establishment would reward them by voting them the franchise. Thus, what had seemed almost seditious in 1848 became a reasonable expectation in 1865.

The National Women's Loyal League was founded during the war by Susan B. Anthony and Elizabeth Cady Stanton. Their aim was to inspire patriotism, support the Fourteenth Amendment, and see that women played an honorable role in the war effort. The first postwar women's rights convention met on a hopeful note articulated by Theodore Tilton, a publisher active in liberal causes, who said, "Are we only a handful? We are more than formed the Anti-Slavery Society . . . which grew into a force that shook the nation. Who knows but that tonight we are laying the cornerstone of an equally grand movement." Sojourner Truth, once a slave and lately a leader of the abolitionist movement, urged that women be granted the vote along with the Negro male, saying, "I want it done very quick. It can be done in a few years."

Perhaps woman suffrage could have been done then, but it was not. The extension of the Fourteenth Amendment to cover women was never a serious consideration to the Congress; a further indication that the time was not right came in 1867, when a woman suffrage referendum was soundly beaten in Kansas. As a result, feminists of a more radical persuasion "repudiated men's counsels forevermore; and solemnly vowed that there should never be another season of silence until woman had the same rights everywhere on this green earth as man."

Further indications of male treachery were seen that same year. When in 1867 women tried to have the word "male" removed from the New York State Constitution along with the word "white," Horace Greeley, the editor of the New York *Tribune*, remonstrated with them, saying that it was the Negro's moment and that the feminists should wait their turn. To this, Elizabeth Stanton replied:

> "No. No, this is the hour to press woman's claims; we have stood with the black man in the Constitution over half a century, and it is fitting now that the constitutional door is open that we should enter with him into the political kingdom of equality. Through all these years he has been the only decent compeer we have had. Enfranchise him, and we are left outside with lunatics, idiots, and criminals for another twenty years."

Another humiliating blow was in store for the women who had labored in the antislavery cause. During the course of a suffrage convention meeting in Washington, D.C., in 1869, black men were heard to say that men should always dominate women and that white women were the blacks' worst enemy. Speaking in the spring of that year, Frederick Douglass—who had supported the demand for female suffrage at Seneca Falls in 1848—said:

> "When women, because they are women, are dragged

282 MR. DOOLEY'S CHICAGO

from their homes and hung upon lamp-posts; when
their children are torn from their arms and their brains
dashed to the pavement; when they are objects of insult
and outrage at every turn; when they are in danger of
having their homes burnt down over their heads; when
their children are not allowed to enter schools; then
they will have an urgency to obtain the ballot."

The reaction was swift and furious. "I will cut off this
right arm of mine before I will ever work for or demand the
ballot for the Negro and not the woman," declared Susan B.
Anthony. Ms. Anthony, Mrs. Stanton, and their followers became implacable in their opposition to the Fourteenth
Amendment, and this led to a split among the women themselves.

CHICAGO *EVENING POST*, May 18, 1895

"Th' Lord save us fr'm harm," said Mr. Dooley. "Th'
Lord save us fr'm harm. Have ye seen what they're
goin' to do downtown? They're goin' to get up a new
Bible."

"What's that? What's that?" Mr. McKenna demanded in great excitement.

"'Tis thrue I'm tellin' ye. They're goin' to get up a
new Bible fr women. A woman's Bible, d'ye mind, with
annything in th' ol' Bible that's considered be th' female
bicycle club to be a knock fr women cut out."

"What good would that do them?" asked Mr.
McKenna, puzzled.

"What good's that do thim? Why all th' good in th'
wurruld. Donahue's heerd of it iv coorse an' he's wurruked up over it. He says they'll start out in th' be-
ginnin' an' prove an alibi fr Eve. That's goin' back a
long way, but Donahue says they lay it all to th' be-
ginnin' an' his daughter Molly says that all th' throuble

come because Adam wint around fr'm pillar to post
talkin' to polismen an' raypoorters an' tellin' thim that
she put him up to it. 'An' I'll admit that they have got
th' worst iv it in th' Bible,' he says. 'Sure,' says I, 'th'
Bible is thrue,' I says. 'Ye'll not deny that, man?' I says.
'Glory be,' says he. 'Th' Lord save us, no,' he says.
'What would ye make iv me?' he says. 'A Jew man?' he
says. 'Thin,' says I, ''tis thrue. Well thin,' I says, 'what's
to be done about it?' I says. ''Tis th' statues that keeps
women fr'm comin' into their rights,' I says. 'An' ye
wouldn't find a Bible in th' legislachoor if ye'd stand
thim on their heads,' I says. 'Ye might find ma-arked
cards, but ye'd find no Bible,' I says.

"'Tis thrue,' he says. 'Ye have that right,' he says. 'An'
I told Molly so,' he says. 'I told her if she wanted annything done she'd best go an see Billy O'Broyn, I said,
for, says I, he's all right at Springfield, an' I says, if ye
go into this thing, I says, Father Kelly'll get down on ye,
I says.' 'But,' says he, 'she wint on f'r to say that it was
th' inflooence iv th' Bible. It seems that whin her
brother Darcey asked her to go out to th' ball of th'
Young Man's Sodality, an' she refused, he ups an'
quotes th' Bible to her. "Oh, woman, in our hours iv
ease, uncertain, eye an' ha-ard to get along with in th'
house." An' she says that iverywhere women meet th'
same roast, an' she's tired iv it. So her an' th' rist iv thim
is goin to rayform it. They are that. They're goin' to
lave out annything that rayflicts on th' six. They'll attimpt to show that they was a combination again Eve iv
th' snake an' her husband, an' fr'm that come all th'
throuble. Iverybody afther that thought it was his jooty
to roast, an' th' raysult is ye may search through fr'm
ind to ind an' ye won't see wan word about woman
suffrage. Iv coorse I know nawthin' about it, f'r whin I
was a la-ad an' done me readin' th' Caddychism was
good enough f'r me. We had a Bible though. It fell on
me wanst an' was like to break me neck. But we didnt

read it. Still,' he says, 'though I'd not be th' first to say th' wurrud, it ought to be rayformed,' he says. 'But iver since it come up I've been dodgin' th' Good Man,' he says, 'an' I don't dare to go to me jooty till 'tis sittled wan way or th' other,' he says.

"That's where Donahue stands, an' I'm with him. I'd as lave as not believe Adam was to blame, though he's dead, poor soul, may he rest, per omnia, an' I'd be th' last to put in a wurrud again th' dead. I want ivry wan to have a fair show, an' if fixin' th' Bible 'll help thim to vote, thin I say fix it, may th' Lord forgive me. On'y I'll tell thim this, that I've lived in Bridgeport fr forty years backed be th' Bible an' second papers signed be Judge Kercheval an' a pull at th' polis station an' I've niver had me vote counted but th' wanst and that was whin I was captain iv me precint an' a power in th' wa-ard. That's right, Jawn."

"Are they going to have the new woman in it that I hear tell of?" Mr. McKenna asked.

"Jawn," said Mr. Dooley severely, "this aint goin' to be an almanac. It's a Bible I've been tellin' ye about."

5

The year before the final split in the women's movement and probably contributing to it, the group located in New York began publication of a weekly newspaper, *Revolution*. While its main purpose was to agitate for women's rights, it took a stand on almost every major issue of the day. The sponsor of this enterprise was George Train, who had been imprisoned by the British for his Fenian activities, whose major asset was his enthusiasm for his new cause of woman suffrage, and whose major shortcoming was the conduct of financial ventures of a questionable nature. *Revolution* was forced to stop printing for lack of funds and shortly after, the suffrage movement split into two groups: the more radical Stanton-Anthony group, based in New York, became the National Woman Suffrage Association; the more moderate Boston faction became the American Woman Suffrage Association.

The Boston group had become apprehensive over the preoccupation of *Revolution* with what they considered to be the dangerous issues of the day, such as the reform of the institution of marriage. And it is true that the assault on this mainstay of Victorian life was ill-timed. The difficulty with doing away with marriage is finding a viable alternative for it. In its search for a solution the NWSA became involved with free-love advocates, an association that was to have serious consequences for the broader question of women's rights.

Through its association with Victoria Woodhull, the Stanton-Anthony group became involved in a serious scandal. Mrs. Woodhull (1838–1927) was a brilliant but eccentric woman who, with her sister, had tried her hand at the brokerage business (where she made a killing with the help of Commodore Cornelius Vanderbilt) and at publishing her own weekly journal. Forceful and persuasive, in 1871 she lobbied Congress until it held hearings on a constitutional amendment which would have given the vote to women. By all accounts, she did extremely well in presenting her case, and flushed with success, she decided to run for President in 1872 on her own Equal Rights Party ticket. Her strong opinions did not stop at votes for women; she fell for every new social prescription, ranging from spiritualism to universal language to Marxism. More shocking still, she came out in favor of licensed prostitution and free love at a time when the American attitude toward vice was increasingly more rigid.

Mrs. Woodhull felt intensely about all her causes; when Horace Greeley announced that he was opposed to woman suffrage because of its alliance with the free-love advocates, she accused him in print of having ruined the health and happiness of his wife and of being the cause of the deaths of five of his children. She further announced that editors were "lecherous monsters" who had made "disgusting revelations of their own natures to her."

Irrepressible, she took to the stage of Steinway Hall in New York in November 1871 to proclaim her support for free love (as if anyone who was interested did not already know of it). Unprepared for the storm that broke around her head as a result, she retaliated by publishing the details of an affair between Henry Ward Beecher, a clergyman so admired that he had been called the "greatest preacher since St. Paul," and Elizabeth Tilton, the wife of Theodore Tilton, one of Beecher's parishioners. That Beecher took a more than pastoral interest in Mrs. Tilton had been well known, but considering his eminence, the papers had not printed word of it. The Chicago *Tribune* was not so sensitive, however, and broke the story. The New York papers were furious at being beaten. Tilton sued Beecher for adultery, Beecher denied the charges, was sustained by public opinion, and in 1875 was acquitted because of jury disagreement. Two years later Mrs. Woodhull and her sister left the country to take up residence in England.

Behind her, Mrs. Woodhull left the women's movement in a mess. While it is doubtful whether the Woodhull-Beecher-Tilton affair delayed suffrage to any great extent, largely because of the bad press surrounding the incident, it did signal the end of attempts to formulate an ideology to continue the development of women as equals to men once suffrage was granted.

In a relatively short time, the narrowing of objectives precipitated in this way led to a similarity of intent between the National and American Women Suffrage Associations, and only the personality clashes of the leadership kept them from a final reconciliation in 1890, when they became the National American Woman Suffrage Association.

Thus, the feminist movement in the United States, which began as a radical, exciting, and innovative crusade against a wide range of social problems involving women, sacrificed these characteristics for a more respectable and proper role.

Meanwhile, back to Molly Donahue out on Archey Road. On February 15, 1898, the American battleship *Maine* was blown up in the harbor at Havana, Cuba, which was then a Spanish possession. On April 25, 1898, the United States declared war on Spain. During the interval, American public opinion was inflamed by the press and some members of the Congress. So it was a sign of the times that instead of opposing the Spanish-American War and seeing it for the imperialistic venture it was, Dunne has Molly fall victim to the jingoes and incite her menfolk to fight.

CHICAGO *JOURNAL*, March 26, 1898

DOOLEY AND THE DONAHUE FAMILY

"I'll say this fr Molly Donahue," said Mr. Dooley. "She do have spunk. Oh, 'tis she's th' spunky wan."

"What's th' colleen been doin'?" Mr. Hennessy asked.

"Well, ye know," said Mr. Dooley, "th' ol' man Donahue, him an' me don't agree about goin' to war. He wud agree with me fr in th' twenty years I've knowed him I've made him see me side iv all argymints in me early days with th' back iv me hand an' th' toe iv me boot; since we've grown old together, with ca'm an' judeecyal argymints an' a sup iv hot whisky. But Donahue has been down talkin' with O'Connor, th' morgedge shark, that has th' office on Halsted sthreet, an' O'Connor's idea iv things is diff'rent. O'Connor believes in indimnity. If a man was to kick O'Connor—an' manny's th' time I've wanted to—all he'd have to do wud be to give him $5—three kicks fr tin, rayjooced r-rates fr clubs iv more thin twinty; ginteel business so-licited. That's O'Connor.

"Well, he's been poundin' indimnity into ol' man Donahue, an' th' ol' man's been takin' his argymints home. They had it out th' other night. Molly was thryin' to pick out 'Th' Star-Spangled Banner' on th' pianny whin th' ol' man put down his paper. 'I wisht,' he said, 'they was not so much talk iv war,' he says. 'It tires me. What we want to do is to make Spain pay f'r this thing. That's what hur-rts. Take th' coin away fr'm thim.' 'Ye don't mean that, pah-pah, do ye?' says Molly. 'I do,' says Donahue. 'I mean it thruly.' 'Wud ye not go to war f'r to save yer counthry?' she says. ''Tisn't needed,' says he. ''Twud increase th' price iv livin' an' rayjooce she-curities,' says he. 'Faith,' says young Mike, 'if it didn't affect th' price iv beer it's little ye'd mind. I'm f'r war.' 'So'm I,' says Pat Donahue. 'So'm I,' says little Malachi. 'So'm I,' says Robert Immitt Donahue. 'So'm I,' says Threesa. 'So'm I,' says Aggie. 'So'm I,' says th' babby. Mrs. Donahue was settin' by knittin' a pair iv socks. She put down th' needles an' says she, 'So'm I.' 'Well, by cripes,' says Donahue, 'you always have been since I knowed ye.'

"'Lave us form th' Donahue gyards,' says Malachi. 'All r-right,' says Molly, 'we will. Mah, ye'er th' gin'ral. Fall in there. Take th' broom an' th' shovel. Now, ar-re ye r-ready f'r war?' 'Yis,' says th' family. 'Will ye uphold th' constitution iv th' United States?' says she. 'We will,' says they. 'All except ye'er pah-pah,' says Mrs. Dona-hue. 'He's afraid shecurities will have a fit. He don't know what they ar-re,' says she. 'Mar-rch, Donahues.'

"Whin Father Kelly come up th' steps he found thim mar-rchin an counther-mar-rchin' while Mike played 'Garry Owen' on a mouth organ an' th' ol' man set humped up in a r-rockin' chair groanin' with anger. 'Glory be,' says Father Kelly, 'what's broke loose?' 'This is th' Donahue guards,' says Molly, 'an' we're goin' to war because pah-pah won't stand f'r th' fam'ly.' 'Don't be disrayspickful,' says Donahue. 'She's not,' says Mrs. Donahue. 'Or if she is she'd be disrayspickful to me if she wasn't to ye.' 'Well,' says Father Kelly, 'I think th' childher an' Mrs. Donahue is r-right,' he says. 'If th' men won't fight th' women must,' he says. ' 'Twud be a bad thing f'r th' country if th' hear-rts iv th' women weren't f'r war. 'Tis thim that must do th' sufferin', f'r they stay at home whin th' men ar-re gallyvantin' in battle, shootin' at people without bein' interfered with be th' polis,' he says. 'He'd be f'r war,' says Mrs. Donahue, 'but his head is filled with nonsense be that ol' miser iv an O'Connor,' says she. 'Lave O'Connor alone, Michael,' says Father Kelly. 'He's an oppressor iv th' poor. He puts pool checks in the conthribution box.'

" 'Well,' says Donahue, 'if ye say I ought to be f'r war I am,' he says. 'If I'm not,' he says, lookin' at his wife, 'I see I'll have no peace,' he says."

6

Despite what Dunne's own attitude toward women's rights may have been, the Molly Donahue columns which follow paint a picture of growing feminist power during a time when historians largely agree that the movement was rather more quiescent than it had been. Nonetheless, women were moving inexorably toward a more modern role and demonstrating the ability to wield power, whether it was acquiring a piano, organizing a political action group, or arranging a literary evening.

LADIES' HOME JOURNAL, December 1899

MOLLY DONAHUE,
WHO LIVES ACROSS THE STREET FROM MR. DOOLEY

By the Author of "Mr. Dooley"

Mr. Martin Dooley's progresses were rare events for Archey Road. The philosopher does not go abroad. Travel, with its hurried digestion of half-facts, blunts the edge of speculation. The man does not see the world who sees much of it. From his own philosophical porch, as from some advantageous sea outlook, Mr. Dooley surveyed the expanse of life with passionless eyes, weighed the motives of the great, mocked the aspirations of the weak, directed campaigns, vetoed legislation, passed serene judgment on all worldly affairs, uncontrolled by facts or—what perhaps comes to the same thing—controlled only by such facts as got to him by way of the newspapers. He seldom went to Archey Road; Archey Road went to him. So when the whim seized him to leave his little shop Archey Road rose to welcome him, and he, in his turn, was prepared to receive affably the homage of his neighbors.

No one could mistake Mr. Dooley this day for a commonplace or unimportant personage. He did not rise in stature above his fellows, for they, too, were tall West of Ireland men. It was the indefinable grandeur of his mind that lent distinction to his personage. Well-knit and vigorous at sixty-five, his frame seemed to be warring for exit from his decent black coat. He swung his stick lightly and trod surely on the creaking wooden planks. His hat inclined a little to one side—not at a pugnacious angle, but enough to indicate certainty and determination. It was a beautiful hat, according to the best standards of taste in Archey Road. Mr. Dooley

bought it in 1865, and '65 was a vintage year for hats.
He had guarded it tenderly, and it deserved his protection, for had it not passed triumphantly through conventions, parades, riots, defying the hand of time and
the forcible caress of the exultant Democrat on election
night? Under its broad brim danced gray eyes and
shone a ruddy face, painfully shaved jaws, a nose, big,
humped, almost Hebraic, a bristling, white mustache.
Mr. Dooley is not thin. He is a philosopher. It is the
work of the mere observer, troubled by the apparent
lack of continuity in life and the uselessness of human
effort, that robs the bones of their cushions. Herbert
Spencer is thin. Mr. Dooley and Confucius are not. But
the rounding out of the philosophical figure is not to be
confounded with the grossness of habitual inertia. Mr.
Dooley had been a great handball player in his day,
and on the infrequent occasions when he condescended
to visit the court he could still amaze the firemen, who
are past masters of this game and dominoes. He had
been a hurler of renown, and the benefits of that war-
like sport, which has done more for Ireland than coercion laws, were still manifest. He could run his hundred
yards, he could pitch a horseshoe, he "cud put his
thumb on th' counther an' lep over it at wan bound."
Admirable man!

Archey Road greeted him joyfully. He stopped at the
door of Cassidy's shoe shop, and the cobbler raised his
head from a half-sole and grinned "Good mornin'" to
him.

"Fine day, plaze Gawd!" said Mr. Dooley.

"'Tis so, plaze Gawd," said the cobbler.

"How's thricks with ye?"

"Business is pickin' up."

"It seems so. I r-read in th' papers this mornin' that

our expoort business was growin' an' we've imported wan hundherd millyons iv goold in th' las' month."

"I think th' counthry's prosp'rous," said Mr. Cassidy. "I've just got an ordher f'r a pair iv calfskin boots fr'm Misther Doheny."

"Sure," said Mr. Dooley, "that's a betther sign iv good times thin what I tol' ye about—th' goold. If Doheny can ordher new boots th' la-ads that wurruks f'r him on th' canal may git th' ol' wans." And off he went. Heads came to the windows as he passed. It was "Good-mornin' to ye, Missus Slatthry! An' is it well ye ar-re?" And, "Good-mornin', Misther Dooley! 'Tis little we see iv ye nowadays. Ar-re ye well?"

"F'r an' ol' man with wan fut in th' grave an' th' other in th' hearse, thrivin', thanks be! An' how're all th' good folks?"

"Terence does be havin' a col' on his chist. I'm worrid be his cough."

"Do ye go down, thin, to Doctor Casey at the dhrug store an' git him to give ye a bottle iv that mixture he give me las' year. 'Tis not plisant to take, but it goes at a med'cine f'r sthrong men. I was three weeks thryin' to stave off noomony iv th' lungs with th' savin's iv slate pincils that th' good doctor down be Halsted Sthreet calls aunty pyreen, an' aunty cammyoo, an' aunty this-an'-that-an'-th'-other-thin', whin with th' las' breath in me body I crawled to see Casey. He was a horseshoer wanst, an' he mixes his med'cines in an anvil. He says, says he, 'I'll fix ye in a minyet,' he says. 'I've something here that cured Mullaney's horse,' he says, 'an' 'twill make ye r-right in no time if ye have stren'th to take it.' I took wan dose iv it an' whin I come to I was cured. Anny disease that's pow-rful enough to get a hold on Terence needs to be threated like a fire in a furniture facthry. Don't waste time on thim aunty med'cines. They was intended to make a sickness a perm'nint luxury. Git Casey's mixture f'r man an' baist, put him in bed, slap a musthard plasther on him that'll keep his mind employed an' lave thim fight it out. May th' best man win. If Terence's alive in th' mornin' he'll not have stren'th to cough. If he aint do ye let me know."

He stopped at the grocer's and chatted about the price of potatoes. He lingered with Hoffmeyer, the butcher, to discuss the feud between His Imperial Majesty the Emperor of Germany and His Majesty the American Hog. He had a nod for the banker, a bow for the beggar. The motorman on the flying trolley-car shouted, "Hello," the conductor, "Good-by" to him. Truckmen disentangled their hands from the reins to wave him welcome. A Chinaman peeped out of a basement laundry and smirked, "Mollin'!" to which Mr. Dooley replied; "Hello, there, Jawn; whin did ye hear fr'm Li Hung Chang?" The policeman, even the policeman, humbly addressed him. And finally, to put the crowning touch on the glory of his parade, he had a sedate bow and smile from Sister Anastasia and Sister Mary Joseph convoying toward the church a cirrus of white wreaths and white veils. He stood with his hat off while the first communicants passed, their modest eyes on the ground, and he watched them till they turned the corner to illuminate another grimy street.

So Mr. Dooley's progress on this pleasant morning was gratifying to his piety as well as his self-esteem. It gave him a sense of power touched with a strong feeling of duty. If he had been the Czar of all the "Rooshas" he would have convoked a peace congress. As he was more practical he went across the street to the home of Malachi Donahue, the assistant foreman at the rolling-mills. Fortune had smiled on Mr. Donahue the day before. A pig of iron, kindly disposed by Providence, through the unusual agency of a Hungarian laborer, had fallen on his foot and compelled the assistant foreman to take a day off, and he was enduring it on his front stoop in the thrall of a white collar. Mr. Donahue had heard not infrequently at picnics, home rule demonstrations and other social gatherings, of the Malachi who "wore the collar of gold that he won from the proud invader." But was the pious and valiant Malachi's collar a size or two too small for his shirt of mail? Was it frayed behind? Did his daughter gather most of King Malachi's throat in the buttonhole when she forcibly adorned him of a Sunday morning?

The collar was the shadow on his hearth; it was the skeleton in his closet; it was the fly in his ointment; it was, in short, anything Irish you wish to call it. And it was the weapon of domestic discipline that converted a proud assistant foreman, sure in his decision of great problems like the dumping of slag and the switching of freight cars, into an irresolute, apologetic serf. He was properly collared this day as he sat on the top step, with his hands under his chin where they could furtively tug at the accursed band, ample Mrs. Donahue in a rocking-chair behind him, Molly Donahue sitting a step below him brushing back the wisps of dark hair that had strayed out in the ardor of the domestic battle just now drawing to a close. Collared and cornered, Mr. Dooley knew it the moment he saw the group from the corner.

The issue was a serious one upon which Mr. Donahue had opposed his small vocabulary and collared will to the conversational artillery of Mrs. Donahue and the cavalry charges of his pretty daughter. He had essayed the role of the reluctant father on the great American piano question. He had invited his own destruction, for an American girl's mind made up for a piano is invincible. In every American home this simple German device for the promotion of insomnia is regarded by an

influential part of the family as a necessity a degree or
two ahead of a cook-stove. In Archey Road it is the one
sure and visible symbol of the achievement of social
ambition. One may be "very dacint people" and not
own a piano, but one cannot be "fine people" unless
one boasts of a dark mahogany box which takes up
more than half the little parlor, and is only opened Saturday mornings when Miss O'Brien, the church organ-
ist, comes down to give Mary Ann a lesson in the
"Child of the Regiment," or on state occasions when
the said Mary Ann provokes the march from "Norma"
out of its weird interior. At other times it stands uno-
pened, gloomy and forbidding under its purple pall
with its great legs neatly encased in puckered cambric
pantaloons. It is not regarded as a medium for the expression of music so much as a landmark of progress toward wealth and culture. "The Murphys have a
pianny," runs like fire down the road, and the Murphys
have "arrived." But when the "pianny" comes out,
when the rumors of lost jobs and illness culminate in
the withdrawal of the behemoth on the shoulders of
swearing Germans, that is the day of tragedy. The Murphys are down! Hope goes out with the piano!

The Donahues had moved up steadily from the day
when Malachi came out to wheel coke in the rolling-
mills. Physical strength had told at first, afterward the
caution, steadiness and administrative ability that are
the possessions of a considerable part of the race, and
toward the drawing-in of his days the little Connaught
man passed for well-to-do according to the moderate
scale of riches in Archey Road. Musically, there had
been evolution in the family. The time had been when
Mrs. Donahue could not only tolerate but even admire
the witchings of a bagpipe plied by the elbow of a
blind piper who wandered from town to town and
neighborhood to neighborhood like his forerunners in

minstrelsy. But this was long before the advent of
Molly Donahue. The piper gave way to the more
refined but less spirited "accorjeen"; the "accorjeen"
disappeared when young Tim learned the cornet in Father Matthew's band. Tim blew himself out on the cornet with the advent of a cottage organ which no one
but Miss O'Brien could play, and now the forces of social expansion could be stayed no longer. They demanded the real thing and the piano war was on.

"Martin," said Mr. Donahue without looking up from
the cigar which he held where the ashes could fall on
his black trousers, "ye niver had a pianny, did ye?"

"Niver," said Mr. Dooley. "I wanst ownded a horn
that I used in a serrynade again' a fam'ly I didn't like.
Th' musical threat was interrupted be th' head iv th'
fam'ly, an' whin I found a horn as an insthrumint iv
definse was no good again' a hoe handle I abandoned
music. But I knowed a man wanst that put a pianny to
good use be backin' it up again' th' dure whin th'
lan'lord come f'r th' rint. Ye're not thinkin' I'm thryin' to
be Paddyrooski iv th' ward, ar-re ye, Malachi?"

Mrs. Donahue sniffed, and said: "Sure no; 'tis little
taste th' Donahues has in music. But here he is makin'
money hand over fist, an' doin' nuthin' f'r it but talkin'
hard to Polish men at th' mills, an' us at home without a
pianny, an' th' Caseys down th' sthreet, an' Misther
Casey wurrukin' f'r him, an' thim with a pianny, an'
Mrs. Casey puttin' on more airs an' tossin' her bonnet
that hard at mass 'twud put out th' altar lights, an'—"

"Oh, mah!" Molly interrupted. "It isn't that we care
for the Caseys. Pity sakes, I wouldn't give a cent if they
had a thousand pianos. But pappah is so obdewrate."

"So what?" demanded Mr. Dooley, while Mr. Donahue straightened up as if from a blow.

"So—so pig-headed, then," said Molly.

"Oh!" said Mr. Dooley in a tone of relief, and Mr.
Donahue sank back again.

"So pig-headed," Molly went on, "he can't see what's the use of having one in the house, and yet he's been letting me take music lessons for a year."

"I hadn't annything to say about it," said Mr. Dona-hue discontentedly. "But why shud we pay wan hun-dherd dollars f'r a pianny whin ye have th' cottage or-gan that I bought f'r ye on'y two years ago? I didn't want that anny more thin I wanted a doctor. But it's quiet annyhow. I don't see th' good in a pianny. I have a man wurrukin' f'r me be th' name iv Scanlan, an' befure th' year's out he'll lose his job, he's gettin' that weak fr'm his havin' wan iv thim things in his house. 'Tis th' five-finger exercise, an' th' rhoomatic scale in th' mornin' at six, an' 'tis 'I Want Ye, Me Honey, Yis I Do,' an' 'F'r She is th' Belle iv Noo York, Did-de-doo,' till midnight, an' th' man's goin' into a decline. Blasht this collar, 'tis cut-tin' th' neck off me."

"Faith, 'tis you that'd be settin' out here without enough on ye f'r dacincy if it wasn't f'r me," said Mrs. Donahue. "Whin I think iv what we go through an' him an assistant foreman! What good does it do f'r us to thry an' be ginteel? It isn't th' money he cares about, it's th' low, Donahue hatred in doin' annything to show ye're betther thin yer neighbors."

"Now, mah!" put in Molly, with a warning glance. "I know pappah wants to be nice and kind, don't you, pappah? And I'm sure he'll listen to reason. Now, I'll leave it to Mr. Dooley if any self-repecting girl in these days could stand to have an old cottage organ in the house when nice people come to see her from down-town. We'll leave it to Mr. Dooley."

It was the stroke of consummate generalship. Mr. Dooley had come to arbitrate. In a moment he was en-gaged for the forces of the piano.

"Hm'm," said Mr. Dooley, "I'm no musician, an' th' 'eight iv me enjyment is f'r to hear a German band,

consistin' iv a pickle-oo an' a bass drum, playin' 'Listen
to th' Mockin'-Bur-rd.' But, as Mary here says, whin it
comes to decidin' quistions iv etiket, I'm the boy to do
it again' th' wurruld. F'r forty year I've ladled it out be
th' pint an' quart to th' fash'nable society iv this ward,
an' Dooley's etiket f'r man an' baist is known fr'm wan
end iv th' counthry to th' other. An' I say this to ye,
Malachi, that it's not on'y th' proper an' rale thing to
have a pianny, but seein' that Tim Clancy, th' assistant
foreman on th' North Side, an' Mortimer Casey, the assistant foreman at South Chicago, both has wan, it ain't
anny sure thing that whin th' news gits out that ye're
scrapin' 'long without wan ye won't lose yer job. Get a
pianny, Malachi, an' thank Heaven they didnt ask f'r a
steam calliope."

"Oh, I s'pose 'tis no use talkin' again' this ol' blath-
erer," said Mr. Donahue, rising and knocking more
ashes on his clothes. "Ye have yer own way, no matther
what I say. Go an' buy yer pianny, an' may it—may it
choke ye!"

The light of triumph which had been shining in Mrs.
Donahue's face glowed into a smile of content.

"We have wan already," said she.

"Ye have what?" gasped Mr. Donahue.

"We have a pianny," said Mrs. Donahue. "Molly an'
I knew ye really wanted wan, so we put in yistherday
befure ye got home, an' we was savin' it f'r a surprise."

"Well, I'm—" Mr. Donahue began. Then recovering
himself he called to his friend: "Come on down th'
sthreet," and they marched away, Mr. Dooley looking
back with a grin. Down the street Mr. Donahue tore
the tyrannical collar from his neck. Relieved physically
and mentally from the thrall he struck himself on the
breast and exclaimed: "I'll be masther iv me own
house."

"Ye will so," said Mr. Dooley. "But don't say it too loud; th' fam'ly may hear ye."

So the piano was in, and the Donahues had made good their title to the refinement that ought to go with wealth. It was up and down the road that day, and Mr. Donahue heard it at every corner, and each time with a new pang.

7

LADIES' HOME JOURNAL, February 1900

MOLLY DONAHUE,
WHO LIVES ACROSS THE STREET FROM MR. DOOLEY

By the Author of "Mr. Dooley"

Politics is a more important part of the life of Archey Road than of other communities. It is the passionate amusement of the men. In other places it possesses only an ephemeral interest. Once or twice a year the flames of party enthusiasm are fanned by the newspapers, and patriotic citizens march to the polls to save their country by different routes. In the intervals they take about as much interest in the process of safeguarding the Republic as they do in the Martian primaries. It is different in Archey Road. Politics is a daily theme of conversation and speculation. It penetrates every humble home, and intimately affects the lives of all the denizens of the Road. With many families it is the means of subsistence, much gayer and more satisfactory than shoveling slag at the rolling mills. But in all cases it is regarded as a man's game, a fierce pastime, like a continuous football match, from which the gentler sex does well to abstain.

While Archey Road remained a little *imperium in im-*

perio, cut off by its own peculiar ways from the urgency of the larger world without, the thought of woman suffrage never entered the heads of the ladies of Mr. Dooley's kingdom. Mrs. Mahoney might know that Mr. Hogan's son Tim was a candidate for the high office of swinger of the red bridge, but she could not guess, nor did she care to guess, the gravely important measures that were moving to bring about the installation of Timothy in that lofty sinecure. If she had shown any curiosity she would have encountered a stone wall of impenetrable reserve on Mr. Mahoney's part. So she was content to leave the large questions involved to the care of Mr. Mahoney, and to listen to brief expositions of the game at the supper table with unfeigned indifference. Politics was Greek to her, as it is to pretty nearly all women.

But Archey Road is no longer secluded. The tentacles of the surrounding civilization, the trolley car and the newspaper, have clasped it. There happened a vigorous revival of woman suffrage in the neighboring community. Injured ladies spoke bitterly of the crime their fathers had committed in denying them the fundamental right of American citizenship, which undoubtedly is to cast an imperfect ballot for unknown persons with awkward names. Woman suffrage clubs were formed, and met to hear addresses from talented young gentlemen wearing lawn ties. A Legislature, exhausted by the labor of a long session of frank bribery, languidly passed a bill permitting women to vote for the officers of an agricultural college, and the millennium had arrived.

Molly Donahue pondered these weighty matters, and she and her mother discussed them eagerly over their sewing. A woman was just as competent as a man to rule the nation—the women ruled the men, anyway.

Wasn't Molly as capable of understanding political problems as her brother? Wasn't her mother as well qualified as her father to rule the country? Mrs. Donahue admitted that she was better qualified, but somewhat uneasily, for the subject was new to her.

The matter was first broached at a family gathering on the front porch at the crisis of a political campaign.

"I wondher," said Mrs. Donahue, "will manny women vote this time."

"What'll they be doin' votin'?" Mr. Donahue demanded.

"We've got a right to vote," said Molly.

"Ye've got a right to r-run a motor car, too," said Mr. Donahue; "but ye don't do it. We won't let ye."

"An' who's we, Mr. Donahue?" said his wife. "Shure, if I wanted to r-run a motor car I'd do it, an' no wan'd stop me. I mightn't be able to kill as manny people as yer frinds now at it, but in time I'd larn."

Mr. Donahue, undismayed by this bit of sarcasm, went on: "A woman doesn't know annything about politics, an' if she has sinse she won't thry to larn. Politics comes nath'ral to a man. I knew how to vote befure I'd been here a month, an' Timothy cud mark a ballot befure he cud r-read. But ye'd not know whether to put a cross on yer ballot or cut it on th' bias."

"I could learn," said Molly stoutly. "And I'm sure I could vote as intelligently as Tim."

"Yes, you could!" said Timothy. "If you women had a vote and there was two candidates up, and one of them was a good strong man that worked hard out here at the mills, and the other was a dude earnin' eight-fifty a week at a department store, with his hair plastered over his eyes, and a high collar, you'd vote for him. I know you!"

"Oh, is that so!" said Molly. "Well, I know this, that if women had a vote you wouldn't see all these red-

faced loafers in office. We wouldn't be marching out
with torches cheering for some man who's ruining the
homes of the country. We'd use our minds, wouldn't
we, mah?"

"We wud!" said Mrs. Donahue sternly.

Mr. Donahue had no reply at the moment. He
thought of several things to say as he climbed up to his
room. But Molly Donahue and her mother remained a
long time in the parlor discussing female suffrage, and
the outgrowth of this talk was the Archey Road
Woman's Suffrage Club. It was, as Mr. Timothy said, a
warm organization. It met at the Donahues', and Mr.
Dooley and Malachi, sitting out at the fire and fixing up
the slate that at some far-distant day was to shatter the
hope of the Hon. John Reilly to go to Congress, could
hear the Hon. John himself explaining to the assembled
ladies how they could achieve the long-sought object of
their ambitions.

"It is not," he said, "that the ballot is an essential
concomitant of citizenship that it is so highly esteemed,
but that it has been demanded by a large part of the
population—that is, the males—as essential to the
proper manifestation of their interest in the government consequent upon general usage in all parts of the
world. Ladies, when you demand a vote with sufficient
energy and assert your equal rights to a voice in the
gover'ment of this fair city and this imperyal nation,
then, and not till then, will you take your rightful place
as rulers of the country." (Applause.)

"He belaves in hollerin'," said Mr. Donahue. "He
doesn't know 'tis quiet wurruk that wins in politics."

"'Tis that!" said Mr. Dooley. "An' annyhow, wom-
en'll niver vote. In th' first place, th' men won't lave
thim do it. They have th' monnopoly now, an' they're
far fr'm foolish enough to let go iv anny iv it. Thin no
woman cares f'r politics. Down in her heart she hates

an' despises it, an' wondhers what it's all about. An' I
don't blame her. Not till they start a political column in
Butthrick's Pattherns will ye iver be able f'r to musther
a corp'ral's guard iv women at th' polls. I belave if ye
was to take th' strongest woman sufferejest in th'
counthry an' sarch her ye'd find she didn't care whether
Willum J. O'Brien was Aldherman or Congressman. Th'
on'y time th' likes iv thim knows who's President is
whin th' President gets married. He has their devotion
in his wife's name."

"Well, I dinnaw about that!" said Mr. Donahue.
"'Tis lookin' dangerous whin Mrs. Donahue begins to
think iv votin'. In times past she niver knew 'twas iliction day till she saw th' pathrol wagon go by. Listen to
Molly now in th' nex' room."

Miss Donahue was reading a thoughtful paper on
"Taxation Without Representation; or, The New Battle
of Bunker Hill." Her father listened with an expression
of repressed horror on his face to the heresies and in-
delicacies of this composition: "Weren't women as good
as men? Didn't they have the same brains, the same
eyes to see, the same ears to hear? Couldn't they watch
the course of human events with equal intelligence?
Weren't they today taking their place beside men in
every calling of life? And, above all, didn't they pay
taxes? Then why were they denied at least the same
share in the control of the government that was the
right of the Bohemians and Poles?" (Applause.)

"There's somethin' in that," whispered Mr. Dooley,
"on'y th' argymint is wake in wan p'int. Th' Bohemians
an' Poles have a r-right, 'tis thrue, but they haven't th'
necessary polis protection."

"Yes," went on Molly Donahue, "we've been meek
too long. The time has come for action, and I heard a
lady at a meeting say that this is the year to show that
we appreciate our opportunities. I'm going to vote!"

"D'ye think she manes it?" said Mr. Donahue hoarsely. "D'ye railly think she manes it?"

"She does now," said Mr. Dooley. "She's niver been through an iliction."

"If I thought she railly meant it!" Mr. Donahue said with a fierce gesture that spoke much louder than words.

He watched the proceedings of the Woman's Suffrage Club as carefully as he could through the concealment practiced by that liberty-loving organization. Molly was unceasing in her work for the cause. The house was littered with pamphlets by the many charming ladies who have spent their lives discussing this interesting question. Mr. Donahue knew the plot was thickening. Moreover, the supper-table talk of politics and politicians sometimes evoked a significant question.

"Casey is pop'lar on th' North Side," said Mr. Donahue.

"Is he the man that is running for clerk of the something or other?" asks Molly.

"F'r clerk iv th' somethin' or other!" cries Mr. Donahue with supreme sarcasm. "An' ye think ye ought to have a vote!"

"Oh, I don't care what he's running for," says the undaunted Molly. "What sort of man is he?"

"Casey is a fine man," says Mr. Donahue. "A fine, lib'ral man. Isn't that so, Tim?"

"Yes," says Timothy. "Our fellows are not very strong for him, but I guess he's all right."

"But what sort of man is he?" Molly persists. "What does he do?"

"He's an ol' settler. Been here sinse befure th' war."

"But what does he do?"

"He's in th' liquor business."

"Ah!" Molly smiles knowingly at her mother. Mrs. Donahue returns the smile, and Mr. Donahue, perceiving opposition, enters a terse defense of Mr. Casey to the effect that although he is a liquor dealer the gentleman in question is an honest man, a lifetime resident of the city and a frequent taxpayer. The rest of his virtues are comprehended in the statement that "no wan iver got th' worst iv it fr'm Casey." Mr. Donahue is reenforced in his belief that women were not created for politics by the fact that this encomium does not impress the ladies. They continue to smile, and Mr. Donahue is maddened to silence.

Election day is by far the most important festival of the year in Archey Road. Very few men work who don't have to. The newspapers speak about the contest as a battle of the ballots, but often this mild ammunition is supplemented by stout sticks and fists, and the polls take on the appearance of a real battlefield.

The preliminary affrays were over, and there was quiet in the polling place of the Sixth Precinct. Mr. Donahue as judge of election sat back in his chair puffing contentedly at a cigar and chatting with the captain of the fire engine company in whose engine house the polling booth was situated. Mr. Dooley had dropped in to overlook the count. Ten or fifteen other men lounged about the big room smoking evil cigars. The street swarmed with "workers" wearing badges to indicate the candidate for whom they were supposed to be "working."

Presently the shouting of small boys proclaimed the advent of the unusual, and to the bewilderment of watchers, challengers and voters the Archey Road Woman's Suffrage Club marched up to the engine house, led by the valiant President Molly. Courage was written on their faces. The purpose to rescue their country, according to plans and specifications laid down by the late Miss Anthony, shone in their eyes. They wore the badges of their society carefully worked in pink silk on satin, and they faced the bewildered election officials with defiance. The firemen rushed from the scene to put on their coats, and the other men in the engine house laid aside their cigars and removed their hats, all except Mr. Donahue. He sat with his eyes bulging and his mouth open.

"Ladies," said the second judge, wiping his mouth with his cuff, "what kin we do for you?"

"We have come to vote," said Molly Donahue. "Would you mind opening a window?"

The judge, the clerks, the challengers and the loungers dashed to the windows and banged them wide open.

"That's better!" said Molly. "This is a fearful smelly place. Now will you gentlemen take our ballots?"

"Where are they?" asked the smart clerk who managed all fine decisions for the officials.

"We have them all written out," said Molly, drawing a sheet of note-paper from her pocket. "In some cases where the candidates seemed equally good we have given half a vote for each."

"But ye can't vote," sputtered Mr. Donahue in a paroxysm of rage. "Ye can't vote, foolish child. I tell ye women can't vote. They—they—why, marciful Hivins, 'tis again' th' Constitootion iv th' United States."

"It is not!" said Molly. "The law allows us equal suffrage, and you must accept our ballots or be liable to punishment."

"Accept their ballots! Liable to punishment! Do ye hear that? Do ye hear that, Martin?"

"I do," said Mr. Dooley, "an' she's right. If ye don't take th' ballot she can put ye in jail, Malachi. I'd do it, too, if anny man rayfused me sacred sufferage."

"But who iver heerd iv such a thing? I've been a

judge iv iliction f'r twinty years, an' ne'er a famale has enthered this injine-house."

"It's so," said the smart clerk. "You wasn't around when the instructions was given. They can vote f'r trustees of the colledge down there somewhere in the country. Cassidy, whatcher do with them female ballots you got at the election commissioner's office?"

"I put 'em in th' driver's sate iv th' hose-cart," said Cassidy. "I didn't think we'd need 'em. I'll get 'em an' ye kin be makin' a ballot-box out if that cigar-box."

"But can't we vote the whole ticket?" Molly asked.

"No, ma'am," said the smart clerk.

"Well, I declare!" said the Archey Road Woman's Suffrage Club as one woman. "Why, we've written out every name."

"Makes no diff'rence, ladies!" explained the smart clerk. "Can't vote f'r nobody but them trustees."

"Oh, very well!" said the Archey Road Woman's Suffrage Club in a tone that boded ill for the smart clerk. And they retired to the little curtained booths, where, with the aid of a flickering candle and a dirty stump of a lead pencil, they managed after some minutes of study to indicate their choice. When they emerged Mr. Donahue sat rigid. As Mrs. Donahue prepared to cast her ballot he rose and shouted: "I challenge that vote!"

"On what ground?" asked Judge No. 2.

"On th' groun'," roared Mr. Donahue, "that th' voter is iv unsound mind. Anny woman is that votes."

Mrs. Donahue deigned no reply, but fixed her husband with a stony glare. The second judge grinned and said: "I wouldn't take no responsibility for throwing it out."

Mr. Donahue had fired the only shot in his locker and he subsided again into apoplectic silence. With due ceremony the names were enrolled, affidavits of residence presented, and the votes deposited carefully in the cigar-box. After which the Archey Road Woman's Suffrage Club marched proudly out, and as the door closed on them the elder election judge rose and cried: "Ye have th' votes, but th' jooty iv countin' thim belongs to pah-pah!"

Late that night Mr. Donahue appeared before his family with a smile of great content on his face.

"How is the election going?" asked Molly.

"It's goin' pretty well," said Mr. Donahue.

"Are our candidates elected?"

"Not with yer assistance, annyhow," said Mr. Donahue triumphantly. "I'm sorry to inform ye, fellow citizens iv th' Raypublic, that th' iliction officials, bein' me, was onable f'r to count yer votes. Ye, Molly, ar-re undher age, an' Mrs. Donahue, I regret to tell ye that ye marked yer ballot in such a mussy way that I was obliged f'r to throw it out. So I took th' liberty iv absthractin' both iv thim, th' famale vote iv th' precint bein' too small f'r to carry downtown, an' I presint thim to ye. Perhaps ye kin use thim f'r curl papers. Fellow citizens, ajool I'm goin' to bed, an' if a polisman calls f'r ye in th' night f'r vi'latin' th' iliction laws plaze thry not to wake me up."

Concluding this, the longest speech of his life, Mr. Donahue bowed low and went jauntily to his room.

8

LADIES' HOME JOURNAL, March 1900

MOLLY DONAHUE,
WHO LIVES ACROSS THE STREET FROM MR. DOOLEY

By the Author of "Mr. Dooley"

Mr. Donahue's victory in the franchise dispute was
over almost before he could celebrate it. The extreme
nobility of the enemy made it possible for her [Molly]
to desert the vanquished field and occupy a new and
dangerous position safely fortified by the world's best
literature. The world's best literature had never before
troubled the Donahues. True, they possessed a library,
as all reputable families do. It consisted principally of
the Bible and the works of William Carleton. The Bible
was quite as big as a trunk—a Douay Bible heavily
bound and gilded, which had been taken down from
the shelf only when it was required as a means of re-
cording the christenings, deaths and marriages in the
Donahue family. The latter two were few in number;
the first made a list of importance.

It had been many years since the good Book had
been disturbed from its saintly rest. Mr. Donahue had
never read it. He accepted it and reverenced it, and decided not to be familiar with it. In exposing the features
of his house to occasional strange visitors he merely
waved his hand toward the book, relying on its presence to attest his piety, and its majestic dimensions to
speak for his liberality. But William Carleton he knew
by heart. We see no lives of William Carleton; no one
celebrates his birthday; no tablet is sunk in the wall of
the little house at Dublin in which he lived well into

this generation; nor have even the cheap magazines
represented to us William Carleton at the age of six
with his teething-ring; at twelve, leaning on a cricket
bat (or hoe); at twenty, writing poetry; at forty, regretting it. Yet Carleton was and is a popular author who
could challenge even Sienkiewicz or Mrs. Holmes.[1] He
is enshrined, as the saying goes, in the hearts of his
countrymen, and nowhere else more securely than in
the bosom of Mr. Donahue. That gentleman could sit
by the hour listening to his sombre tales of Irish life and
emphasizing the points with a wagging head.

"Well, that Willie Reilly was a case! D'ye think he
railly done it?" The remark was less in doubt than in
approval. He believed in the acts of Willie Reilly quite
as much as he did in the Acts of the Apostles. "Valen-
tine M'Clutchy" and "The Emigrants of Ahadarra"
were real people to him. "Carleton is th' gr-randest
writer that iver lived," was his deliberate judgment.

But it was not long before Carleton and his Willie
Reilly were unseated from their positions in the Donahue family. Books, as Mr. Dooley has declared, are
"rooning th' constitootion an' th' lithry taste iv our fair
land." They poured into the Donahue household as the
winter wore on.

There was a book with a Latin name (about whose
meaning and pronunciation there was much dispute)
by a gentleman with a name about whose pronunciation there was no dispute, for no one pretended to

[1] William Carleton (1799–1869) was a popular Irish author of both
sad and funny tales about the life of the Irish peasantry. Henryk Sienkiewicz (1846–1916) won a Nobel prize for literature. Among his
writings was the best-selling *Quo Vadis*. Mary Jane Hawes Holmes
(1825–1907) was an American novelist who became popular after
the Civil War. She wrote thirty-nine novels which sold over two million copies.

know. "A Boogahrian," Mr. Donahue explained to his crony.

There was a humorous book whose humor Mr. Donahue could not comprehend. Indeed, the poor gentleman was greatly deficient in his understanding of that gift in spite of the absurd belief that all Irishmen have a "keen appreciation of humor." A majority of them have, or the race would have disappeared from the earth long ago. But there is a sturdy minority, represented with dignity in the Irish papers, and Mr. Donahue was of the minority.

There were the works of a handsome and gifted young American novelist whose heroes and heroines (and occasionally his villains as well) are as handsome and gifted as their sire.

How often had Molly Donahue turned from the young Englishman in riding breeches, or the young American in evening clothes, to gaze with horror at her father sitting at the stove in his shining black coat, his brown flannel shirt, his white and painful collar. She reflected that even the Hon. John Reilly was not as one of these. Perhaps Washington would be his making. She thought of him addressing the House of Representatives in (or from) riding breeches. He wore a flower in his buttonhole and carried a crop in his hand.

Other books came also. Mr. Donahue listened, murmuring dissent to Mr. Hall Caine's "Good Man Gone Wrong" series. He could not understand how the clergy could succumb to the lines of the temptress. Father Kelly didn't. The little Lutheran preacher down the street, whom Mr. Donahue saluted with the condescending good will of a man determined to make the most of a companionship soon to end—the little preacher didn't. Who then were these strange people who stumbled on their way to the sanctuary? It is regrettable to say that Mr. Donahue regarded them as being beneath pity.

But Mr. Donahue could not withstand the tide. Books, new books, lovely books, elegant books, poured in on the Donahue family. The Archey Road Literary Club rose and flourished. The Archey Road Research Club took a place beside it. The musicale became more casual, woman's suffrage was sunk, the gatherings of the Donahue family grew as literary as a meeting of an Authors' Society.

Mr. Donahue's winter nights were ruined for him. You may imagine the picture. Mr. Donahue is sitting beside the stove in a rocking chair, having surreptitiously removed his slippers. At the table are Mrs. Donahue, Miss Donahue, and Master Timothy. Mrs. Donahue, with an expression of determination, is reading "Richard Carvel"; Miss Donahue is carefully perusing "The Christian"; Master Timothy is grinning over "David Harum," skipping all of the passages that are not in David's own words.[2]

Mrs. Donahue looks up. "Pap-pah," she says, "put on yer slippers."

"What?" says Mr. Donahue, sitting up suddenly. "Oh, tubby shure. Molly!"

"Yes."

"R-read me somethin' fr'm 'Willie Reilly.'"

"Oh, ye an' yer 'Willie Reilly,'" Mrs. Donahue retorts.

[2] *Richard Carvel*, described as a Revolutionary romance, was published in 1899 and quickly became a best seller. It was written by Winston Churchill (1871–1947), born in St. Louis and a graduate of Annapolis—not to be confused with England's Winston Churchill, who used the middle initial "S" (for Spencer) so he could be readily differentiated from his American namesake. *David Harum, A Story of American Life* was a novel written by Edward Noyes Westcott (1840–98), a prominent Syracuse, New York, banker. It was published posthumously in 1898 and became extremely popular.

"What's th' matther with 'Willie Reilly?'" Mr. Donahue asks plaintively.

"Oh, but don't you see," says Molly, "that we've got
beyond that. We can't go on forever reading your old
'Willie Reilly'."

"I want ye to undherstand," says Mr. Donahue, "that
th' man that wrote that book was wan iv th' gr-randest
writers that iver was befure ye was bor-rn. The Queen
was so imprissed with his wurruks that she give him a
pinsion iv wan thousan' pounds sterlin' a year, an' he
didn't have to write another line. I'll have ye to know
that."

"Well, then, for mercy's sake, why don't you read
him yourself?" says Molly.

This is a fierce blow. Mr. Donahue can read, never
fear, but what pleasure is there that can weigh against
the pain of following your finger with your eye across
line after line of fine type? Mr. Donahue, fully realizing
that he is defeated again, sinks back into his chair.

Molly Donahue regretted the attitude of her father
toward the world's best literature, but she did not on
this account desist from her exertions to urge him along
the straight and difficult way of modern culture. She
debated books with him in a vain attempt to persuade
him of the obvious beauties of "The Man with the
Hoe," "Quo Vadis," "Richard Carvel," and other subjects of discussion in the literary world. She even went
so far as to read selections from these admirable books
to her obdurate parent. The obdurate parent was unsof-
tened. He discarded the philosophy of "The Man with
the Hoe" as worthless, when it was laboriously explained to him.

"Th' man is a walkin' dillygate," he said. "D'ye think
if I had felt that way I'd iver be assistant foreman at th'

rollin' mills? I wud not. They don't give responsible jobs to th' likes iv thim."

"But this isn't about the rolling mills," Molly explained.

"It makes no diff'rence," her father retorted. "'The Man with th' Hoe' or th' man with th' shovel, 'tis all alike. Dhrink an' idleness ar-re at th' bottom iv this pome."

It will be seen that Mr. Donahue had a conservative opinion of the industrial problem, as became a man drawing his four dollars a day and paying taxes on land. He was equally decided with respect to the other books. He measured them by the standard of "Willie Reilly" and found them to be utterly worthless.

Meanwhile, Molly Donahue marshalled her Literary Club, her Research Club, and her Culture Club. Archey Road, and more especially that part of it that belonged to the Donahue family, was dragged violently from the bog of Irish folk-tales in which it had sunk. If Molly expected recognition, if she looked in the papers for a list of "Messrs. and Mesdames" that would show that her labor for the regeneration of her uncouth city was appreciated, she never betrayed the weakness. Her flushed face and blazing eyes on the nights when the various societies met were signals of the true spirit of the zealot. She organized debates as to whether Markham or Riley were the greater poet; whether the pen were mightier than the hoe; on the esoteric meaning of "Quo Vadis" and "Gallegher"; on the literary relationship between "Ian Maclaren" and Robert Louis Stevenson. In short, Molly's "evenings" were a close reproduction of "evenings" in thousands of American homes, especially in the Western metropolis where Molly lives.

It even came to pass that the Archey Road Literary

Club engaged the services of a semi-professional poet. He was not, as Mr. Dooley said, "a journeyman pote." He hoped some day to arrive at that point of perfection where he would be paid for the principal business of American authors—to poorly read their own works for the pleasure of the public. At present his vocation was a clerkship in a law office. By night he put on his singing robes and soared. He was the first real, published author who had crossed the horizon of the cultivated classes in Archey Road. He was a tall gentleman of such robust frame that Mr. Donahue declared he "ought to be wurrukin' f'r a livin'." He was introduced by the Hon. John Reilly in a speech of perfect finish, including a high tribute to the art of poetry, and he read his verses with manly courage and an accent unknown to Mr. Donahue's circle.

The discussion that followed under the direction of Molly Donahue was solemn and intense. Miss O'Brien confessed that she liked the "heart poems" better than those that dealt with social questions. She thought the poet equally resembled Longfellow, Tennyson and Riley. Mr. Reilly took issue with her on this point. He felt that the mission of the poet was a public one. He was inspired for the purpose of ameliorating the condition of the race. If he swerved from this duty he was wantonly hurling away the tools given to him by Providence and the public schools. Mr. Reilly, while admiring the passages that reminded Miss O'Brien of Longfellow, greatly preferred those that reminded him of Lowell.

The decision was drawn, for the poet himself confessed that he admired both equally. It appeared that he sometimes came home filled with a desire to sing. At other times he was afflicted by the sufferings of mankind.

Molly Donahue moved a vote of thanks to the distinguished guest, who spent the rest of his happy evening giving autographs to the club.

Mr. Donahue did not attend the meeting. He ate a hasty supper and then repaired to the home of Mr. Dooley, where he sat on a trunk and gruffly vented his abhorrence of all forms of literature, particularly poetry. In Mr. Dooley he found, as ever, a patient and considerate listener.

"Why shud men, grown men, write pothry?" Mr. Donahue demanded, with a great show of spirit.

"Well," said Mr. Dooley, "'tis this way with thim. A pote's a man with somethin to say that he hasn't thought out. Now, ye're in a way, Malachi, a pote. Whin ye're at home bustin' to expriss yerself, an' not knowin' exactly what it is ye want to say, or how ye ought to say it if ye knew, ye have th' makin's iv a pote in ye. Ye needn't look savage. Ye'll niver be wan while ye feel sthrong about yer throubles. A pote doesn't feel railly bad. He on'y thinks he does. He's able to find wurruds to pour out his heart in, an' more thin that, he's able f'r to cut up th' wurruds into proper len'ths an' have thim fit into aich other like matched flurin'. Think iv a man sittin' down with a woild passion in his hear-rt and thryin' to measure it with a pocket-rule! 'This line is two feet too long,' he says; 'I'll have to saw it off. If I nail on a couple iv wurruds here 'twill fit nicely,' he says. 'Six an' six is twelve,' he says, 'an' two eights is sixteen,' he says. 'I'll shift this plank up a foot an' keep this wan f'r th' ind iv th' job,' he says. An' whin he's through he nails it together an' sinds it off, an' 'tis a pome. An' thin he packs up his tools in a bag an' goes home to r-rest like a thrue mimber iv th' Union. No sir, th' man that's rale mad, that's mad clear through, can't spake plainly. He splutters as ye do, avick. That's wan raison I'm again' pothry. There ar-re other raisons, but that's wan iv thim. But we've got to take iverythin' in life, th' good with th' bad. Ivery man that r-reads must r-read his peck iv pothry. Was Reilly there?"

"He was," said Mr. Donahue.

"I suppose he liked th' pothry?"

"I suppose so."

"Well," said Mr. Dooley, "'twud be a gr-reat sorrow to tear him away fr'm it an' throw him into what he calls th' crool vortex iv national politics."

Mr. Reilly would have been dismayed if he had heard what was said in the conference that followed. He never knew how near devotion to the Muses came to wrecking a brilliant career.

VIII

Mr. Dooley on the View from Archey Road

Finley Peter Dunne was a man ahead of his time; so much of what he wrote for Dooley would have qualified him for charter membership in the muckrake pack eight to ten years later. He saw through the corruption around him and especially he penetrated the protective shield that surrounded successful businessmen. As Mr. Dooley said, "whin business gets above sellin' tin pinny nails in a brown paper cornucopy, 'tis hard to tell it fr'm murther." And then he went after George Pullman, or the meatpackers, or Rockefeller.

Yet Dunne was not afraid to wax sentimental occasionally over such events as the reversal of direction of the Chicago River or the golden days of Chicago journalism. At the same time, he could make fun of such evidence of man's silly side as the romanticization of the Chicago Fire.

Although he was loath to stir from Archey Road, Mr. Dooley kept his finger on the pulse of Bridgeport, Chicago, and the nation with the aid of his imagination and the newspapers. While there was a generation gap between Dunne and Dooley, the old philosopher was sometimes given to looking backward with an eye for details that a historian might envy. Dooley's attitude toward the past was that it "always looks betther than it was. It's only pleasant because it isn't here." He dealt with the Civil War, for example, in an unemotional way.

Through Mr. Dooley, Dunne could write about any person or any subject with impunity.

2

To the tenets of Douglas we tenderly cling,
Warm hearts to the cause of our country we bring.
To the flag we are pledged—all its foes we abhor—
And we ain't for the nigger but we are for the war.
                                        —Irish poem, 1861

The Irish in Chicago were faced with a difficult choice in 1861 with the coming of the American Civil War. Without education or experience, they were forced to make a living with their hands. For this reason, they feared the competition of unskilled and semiskilled free blacks.

Further, the Irish were opposed to the new Republican Party, with its supercilious Yankee Whigs, Abolitionists, and anti-Catholic Know-Nothings. Almost to a man, the Chicago Irish had backed Stephen A. Douglas against Abraham Lincoln in the election of 1860. Douglas was their idol, and when he announced his support of the Union, saying, "No one can be a true Democrat without being a patriot," his devoted followers lined up behind him, displaying their loyalty by quickly volunteering for army duty. However, they remained staunch Democrats who frequently questioned the wisdom of continuing the conflict and eventually the freeing of slaves.

The war became a moral crusade in 1862, when circumstances dictated that Lincoln alter his position by issuing the Preliminary Emancipation Proclamation on September 22. This embittered many of the Irish pro-Union men who felt they had been double-crossed on this question. In the off-year elections of 1862 Democrats ran on platforms opposed to Lincoln and emancipation. Confederate victories brought celebrations in Bridgeport; Union triumphs were greeted with silence.

The war was not going well for the North, and by the time the presidential year 1864 arrived, it seemed that the Democrats might elect their candidate, General George B. McClellan. However, Northern victories, especially General William T. Sherman's in the battle of Atlanta on September 1, changed the political picture and Lincoln was swept into a second term on a wave of popular sentiment that was exhibited even in the heart of Bridgeport.

CHICAGO *EVENING POST*, June 2, 1894

DOOLEY AND THE WAR
THE PHILOSOPHER'S MEMORIES OF THE GREAT REBELLION
DECORATION DAY REFLECTIONS
HOW THE GREAT CONFLICT APPEARED TO THE PEACEFUL PEOPLE IN ARCHEY ROAD

"Jawn," said Mr. Dooley the other evening, "did ye see th' p'rade yesterday?"

"Yes," said Mr. McKenna.

"Was it good?"

"Fine."

"Who led th' polis?"

"Mike Brinnan, on horseback."

"Be hivins," said Mr. Dooley, "I wisht I'd been there, f'r whin I knowed Mike Brinnan he couldn't ride a thrunk without houlding on. But I've made it a rule niver to go out on Dec'ration Day. It turns th' hear-rt in me gray f'r to see th' women marchin' to Calv'ry with their veils over their heads an' thim little pots iv gyraniums in their hands. Th' sojers has thim that'll fire salutes over their graves an' la-ads to talk about him, but there's none but th' widdy f'r to break her hear-rt above th' poor soul that died afther his hands had tur-rned to leather fr'm handlin' a pick. But thin what's th' odds? Dam' th' bit iv difference it makes to a man wanst he's tucked away in Calv'ry whether he died f'r his counthry or was r-run over by a brewery wagon. Whin Gavin nails th' lid on th' grate an' sinds down to th' corner grocery f'r th' pallbearers we're all akel an' all heroes.

"Ye was a little bit iv a kid, Jawn, durin' th' war an' ye raymimber nawthin' about it. But to me th' mim'ry iv it is as fr-resh as paint. I wint through it all. I mind so well as if it happened yisterday whin Thomas Duggan came up th' road wan afthernoon an' says he: 'Barrygard,'[1] says he, 'is firin' on Sumter.' I'd niver hear-rd iv Barrygard an' says I: 'Is he,' I says; 'whin did he lose his job on th' Alton?' I says. 'Tut, tut,' says he. 'Barrygard is a ginral,' says he, 'an' Sumter's a fort,' he says, 'an' th' southern states have left th' Union. 'Ah, well,' says I. 'Let thim go,' I says. 'There's plenty left,' I says. 'Don't mind it, Tom,' I says. 'How's Maggie an' th' little wans?' But he was half crazy with th' news an' whin others come in ye scarce could hould him. 'I'm a dimocrat,' says he, 'that's voted th' ticket,' he says, 'iver since I put fut in this counthry,' he says. 'But whin anny man fires on that there flag,' he says, 'I'm a dimocrat no longer,' he says. 'I'm goin' into th' ar-rmy,' says he. 'Is there anny to go along?' he says. Dorgan, th' plumber, said he'd go an' little Kerrigan an' Doherty that wurruked in th' box factory, an' young Hinnissy afther he

[1] Barrygard—Pierre Gustave Toutant de Beauregard (1818–93) of Louisiana attended West Point and was cited for gallantry during the Mexican campaign of 1847. He was appointed superintendent of West Point in January 1861 but served only five days before he was relieved because of his Southern sympathies. Before he could be transferred to other duty he resigned from the U. S. Army and was appointed a brigadier general of the Confederate Army based in Charleston, S.C. On April 12, when the U. S. Army garrison at Fort Sumter refused his surrender demand, he ordered the bombardment of the fort, touching off the first engagement of the Civil War. He later fought at the first battle of Bull Run, Shiloh, and Petersburg. After the Civil War he refused offers to command the armies of Egypt and Romania. Instead he became the manager of the Louisiana lottery.

found out what it was, he said he'd go along, too. That
shtarted Duggan, an' befure two weeks was out he had
gone up an' down th' r-road an' enlisted fifty men, an'
they wint off with Mulligan. I raymimber Mrs. Duggan
comin' in to get a pint iv beer th' night they wint away.

"I heerd no more about th' war fr a long time, fr I
didn't read th' pa-apers in thim days, an' bedad, I wisht
I'd niver shtarted to r-read thim. There's nawthin' in
thim but hell an' horrors. But in th' coorse iv a year we
heerd tell iv what th' A-archey road lads was doin'.
Poor Duggan died iv th' fever, an' Dorgan, th' plumber,
was made a sergeant an' ye cuddent walk on th' sa-ame
side iv th' sthreet with Mrs. Dorgan. Thin wan day a
lad with a leg gone an' a face as white as a ghost's came
into me shtore. 'Do ye know me?' he says. 'No,' says I.
'I'm Larry Hinnissy,' said he, an' he tould me all th'
news iv th' war—how th' south was likin' th' divvle out
iv th' north an' how th' throuble was they didn't make
Thomas Francis Meagher[2] gin-ral iv th' ar-rmy. Hinnissy said th' whisky in th' south was bad.

"Thin me cousin Mick was dhrafted. Ye didn't know
Mick, Jawn. He was th' biggest coward an' liar outside
iv his brother that iver lived. He always swore that he
was tin years younger than me. He'd say: 'I was bor-rn
th' year Father Hogan was sint to Curlow, an' 'twas Fa-

[2] Thomas Francis Meagher (1823–67) was born of a wealthy
Waterford, Ireland, family. He served for a time in Parliament and
was a founder of the Irish Confederation. After delivering a hot-
tempered speech in Dublin he was arrested for sedition and sentenced
to death for high treason. The sentence was commuted to banishment
to Tasmania. He escaped in 1852 and settled in New York, where he
quickly became a leader of the Irish American movement. At the out-
break of the Civil War he quickly joined the U. S. Army and fought
at the first battle of Bull Run. The second year of the war he returned
to New York to organize the Irish Brigade, which he then commanded.
The Brigade fought bravely at the second battle of Bull Run, Antietam,
Fredericksburg, and Chancellorsville. Meagher was appointed a brigadier general in 1864 and at the end of the war he was named secretary and acting governor of the Montana Territory.

ther Hogan confirmed you. Ye must have been fifteen
year old th' night iv th' big wind, f'r I raymimber ye
carrying me out in ye'er arms f'r to see th' bonfires and
that ye stole a little goold watch me father 'd give me
f'r a present. Thin d'ye mind when me brother Dan
liked ye so bad, th' night iv th' election iv th' Sullvans,'
he says. 'I was too small to hol' his coat, I raymimber.'
Well, wan day he comes up to me with tears in his eyes
an' he says, says he, 'Martin,' he says, 'how old am I?'
'Fifty years,' I says. 'Ye'er a liar,' he says, 'but will ye
swear to it?' he says: 'I'm dhrafted.' 'Ah-ha,' says I,
'there's ye'er game is it?' I says. 'No Mick,' says I, 'I'll
swear to nawthin,' I says. 'I admit,' I says, 'ye'er only
thirty,' I says. Well, sir, ye shud've seen him. He proved
be th' year iv th' big potato rot that I was tin year
younger thin him. He showed me be letthers he'd wrote
that he must be fifty. Be addin' up th' dates he knew
ye'd thought he was here before th' flood. I made him
go down on his knees before twinty men an' declare on
his oath he was between fifty-five an' sixty. Thin I give
him th' laugh an' he had to go to Canada f'r to escape
th' dhraft.

"Th' lads that had gone out so brave an' gay come
back wan be wan an' ivrybody talked war talk. I raymimber th' battle iv Gettysburg well. 'Twas th' day I
put in new bar fixtures. Wan night there was a free
fight up an' down Archey road because Dan Dorgan
said Shur'dan³ was a betther gin-ral thin Thomas

³ Shur'dan—Union General Philip H. Sheridan (1831–88) was the
son of poor Irish immigrants, who settled in Albany, N.Y., which made
him a favorite of Irish Americans in the North. He won an appointment
to West Point and served as an officer of the cavalry on the frontier
until the beginning of the Civil War. He fought brilliantly at Perry-
ville, Chattanooga, and as a major general he commanded the cavalry of the Army of the Potomac in 1864 and later the Union forces
in the Shenandoah Valley, where he won a decisive victory. He distinguished himself in 1865 at Five Forks and finally at Appomattox.
At the end of the war he became the military governor of the 5th

Francis Meagher. Thim was th' only two afther Mulligan[4] was kilt that th' Archey road cared for. Nearly all
th' Mayo men was f'r Shur'dan. Well, sir, thin th' first
thing we knowed th' war was over. Father Kelly comes
in wan day an' says he: 'Praise be to Gawd,' he says,
"'tis inded.' 'Th' war?' says I. 'Yis,' says he. 'Well,' I says,
'I'm glad iv it,' I says, an', Jawn, I was that."

3

By 1864 disillusionment with the Civil War was widespread
in the North. Although many of them were in their twenties
and thirties, the leaders of Chicago commerce managed to
avoid the draft and stayed home counting the money that
rolled in. As for the meat packers, they not only did not
serve in the army, but they made the Union soldiers' lives
miserable by providing tainted meat to the Quartermaster
Corps. While it was possible to buy a substitute to take their
place in the draft, most businessmen did not even bother to
do that.

The young men who had marched off to war as if they
were on their way to a picnic soon learned the horrors of
civil conflict. Casualties were high.

District (Louisiana and Texas) under the Reconstruction Acts and in
1867 commander of the Division of Missouri, which was headquartered
in Chicago. In 1884 he succeeded General Sherman as commanding
general of the U. S. Army and, shortly before his death, was promoted
to general.

[4] Mulligan—James Mulligan was commander of the Irish Brigade
of Illinois, a regiment of volunteers organized shortly after the Civil
War began. Their first engagement was fought in September 1861 at
Lexington, Missouri, where they were left without reinforcements or
supplies and were forced to surrender. Mulligan was held prisoner
until he was exchanged by the Confederates for one of their own. After
his release he returned to Chicago to muster a new unit, and he fought
as their leader until he was killed in battle at Winchester, Virginia, in
September 1864. His last words were, "Lay me down and save the
flag."

While the businessmen piled up obscene profits by pur-
veying frequently faulty goods to the government, other entrepreneurs whose activities more obviously qualified as illegal and immoral were making a killing too. The few honest
men who remained on the much-reduced police force were
powerless to combat the raging crime wave.

Another factor which contributed to the unease of the citizenry was the location at Thirty-Fifth and Cottage Grove,
just east of Bridgeport, of Camp Douglas, an internment
camp for Confederate prisoners, about 10 per cent of whom
were Irish. Although at the beginning the public accepted
the camp, with many Chicagoans paying regular visits there,
as the war dragged on its population grew rapidly, while at
the same time more and more of its soldier guards were
shipped off to the front. The ratio of guards to prisoners
grew ever smaller.

The Peace Democrats, or Copperheads, decided to hold
their 1864 convention in Chicago. After the meeting opened,
an informer approached the commander at Camp Douglas
and told him of a plot to free the prisoners during the convention. The rebels would then presumably lay waste to
Chicago before escaping. Reinforcements were sent in to the
camp and the leaders of the plot, knowing they were betrayed, scuttled their plans.

Just before the November election another alleged plot
was revealed by which the Copperheads planned to add to
their numbers by liberating the men at the camp. Several
men were arrested and tried in the first Chicago conspiracy
trial. Three unfortunates were convicted. It is not clear
whether this conspiracy actually existed, but the constant
fear of such cabals probably led the authorities to keep antiwar activity to a minimum.

CHICAGO *JOURNAL*, March 12, 1898

DOOLEY'S COMMENTS ON COPPERHEADS

"Where was I durin' th' las' war?" said Mr. Dooley,
in response to a slightly sarcastic question from Mr.
Hennessy. "Where was I durin' th' las' war? I was here,
right here. Whin th' shot was flyin' thickest an' th'
smoke iv battle hung acrost th' sky I was at me post iv
jooty, dalin' out encouragement at two f'r a quarter to
th' pathriotic people that stayed at home with me. 'Tis
be no manes th' lightest part iv war f'r to stay at home,
an' if it hadn't been that me whole fam'ly was down at
th' front stealin' hens an' bein' potted be bushwhackers,
an' they was no wan be mesilf to maintain th' honor iv
th' name iv Dooley at th' prim'ries, I'd've shouldered a
musket, put a little foolish hat on me head, an' gone off
f'r to slay th' inimies iv me counthry, an' lay th' foundations iv lung troubles an' a pinsion.

"That is, I wud as I look back at it now. 'Tis th' wars
iv th' past that we are bravest in, an' annyhow I was a
bit iv a copperhead. I'd heerd so much iv Stephen A.
Douglas[5] in th' Market hall that I cud argy with ye on

[5] Stephen A. Douglas (1813–61), Illinois' "Little Giant," was born
in Vermont. His father, a doctor, died only months after his birth and
the family was left in dire straits. As a result, Douglas apprenticed
himself to a cabinetmaker when he was fifteen. In 1833 he moved
West to Illinois to seek a new life, finding it first as a school teacher
and then as a lawyer. His political rise was meteoric even when compared with other young men of ambition of the time. Short (just five
feet), cerebral, and dynamic in personality, he became state's attorney in two years, was elected to the legislature the same year, and
the year after that was appointed U. S. Registrar of Deeds in Springfield. After his defeat in 1837 in a congressional race he was appointed,
in 1841, to the state supreme court, but resigned after two years to
try for Congress again. This time he made it; he stayed in the House,
where he was chairman of the Committee on Territories, until 1847,
when he was elected to the Senate. He quickly became head of that

th' constitutional r-right f'r to go off an' make a dam nuisance iv himsilf. I was a copperhead, if ye plaze, but I got over it, thank Gawd, an' become a military strat-eejan. I cud lay out a battle with a piece iv chalk on th' back iv a dure that'd make Napoleon Boneypart, th' gr-reat impror iv th' Frinch, look like th' prisidint iv a peace society. An' so I spint thim dark days, which was no darker thin anny others, but full iv good times, with bands playin' an' people goin' to th' theayter an' young men gettin marrid an' arnin' five a day at th' blacksmith business—I spint thim dark days makin' war with a chunk iv chalk an' havin' rayqueem masses said f'r th' repose iv th' souls iv me cousins an' uncles who were down south with Mulligan havin' th' time iv their lives.

"Th' copperheads durin' th' war were not bad people, Hinnissy. Bein' a copperhead was a matther iv principle to thim. A man that's wrong on principle I can stand. Iv coorse th' best thing to do with him is to kill him, but ye can't help rayspictin' him aven whin ye're batin' him over th' head. But a copperhead that's a copperhead just because he's a poor, sick soul an' because they'se as much as wan twinty-five in it f'r him, an' because if he stands f'r his counthry some wan is li'ble to get his busi-ness away fr'm him, th' on'y thing to do with that kind iv copperhead is to have ye'er sister go over an' pull his

body's Committee on Territories. Slavery was the burning question before the committee, and Douglas developed the doctrine of popular or squatter sovereignty, under which each territory would decide for itself whether to admit or exclude slavery. He was considered as presidential timber in both 1852 and 1856. In his Senate re-election campaign in 1858 he engaged in a famous series of debates with Abra-ham Lincoln which helped propel both men into the presidential race of 1860. Nominated by the northern wing of the divided Democratic Party in that year, Douglas fought what was to be his last political battle with his accustomed brilliance, but he went down to defeat with 29 per cent of the popular vote. After Lincoln's election Douglas of-fered him his hand and his help, traveling throughout the country in behalf of the Union. Overtired by his exertions, he contracted typhoid fever and died in June 1861, much mourned.

hair. It won't do to shoot th' poor thing. He'd close up on a bullet wound. Lave him to th' women. They'll take care iv him.

"A man may fight f'r fun, an' that's th' best way iv fightin', an' he may fight f'r money, an' that's th' nex' best way. But th' man who r-runs away f'r money is a fool as well as a cow'rd, f'r he niver gets th' money. 'Tis like Willum J. O'Brien an' th' Pollacky he got to sell out Casey whin Casey, poor man, thought to go to th' council. 'What d'ye want?' says Willum J. O'Brien. 'I want th' money f'r dumpin' Casey,' says th' Pollacky. 'Me frind,' said Willum J. O'Brien, 'if ye'd dumped Casey just because ye was a mane divvle an' had threachery in ye'er heart,' he says, 'I'd rayspict ye,' he says. 'I mightn't like ye,' he says, 'but I'd give ye a piece iv money f'r to keep r-right with ye,' he says. 'But,' he says, 'no wan is undher obligations f'r to hand anny har-rd-arned coin to a fool that throws a frind f'r th' price an' hasn't since enough to get th' price in advance,' he says. 'Casey,' says Willum J. O'Brien in a loud tone, 'here's th' man that thrun ye,' he says. 'He's come f'r his money,' he says. 'I give him to ye an' ye can keep th' change,' he says. An' whin Casey got through with th' Pollacky th' on'y thing he needed money f'r was to pay his fun'ral expinses."

"Willum J. was r-right," said Mr. Hennessy.

"Willum J. O'Brien," said Mr. Dooley, "in matthers iv etiket is always r-right."

4

The summer of 1871 was one of the hottest and the driest in memory. In Chicago the dried leaves began to fall in mid-summer, and the slightest activity would stir up clouds of dust. The flimsy wooden construction of most Chicago buildings were all too susceptible to the slightest spark; during the first week of October increasingly weary firemen responded to at least forty alarms; from Saturday, October 7, to Sunday, October 8, they fought a blaze that caused almost $1 million damage on the city's West Side. The exhausted firefighters had barely returned to their station house when another alarm summoned them to a new conflagration.

Just around nine o'clock Sunday evening a fire broke out in a small barn behind the residence of Patrick O'Leary on DeKoven Street on the near West Side. Whether the flames were started by Mrs. O'Leary's cow kicking over a lantern (as legend has it) or by a drifter taking shelter there (as the O'Learys had it) is not known. A local fire company arrived on the scene after a fairly short period. The wind was strong and the fire spread swiftly. The overworked firemen needed help, but for a long while none came. Although an alarm had been turned in, the fireman who stood watch in the city courthouse tower spotted the flames but erred in judging their location. The wrong alarm was sent out twice, and the bewildered men from the Little Giant fire company struggled on alone.

Chicago's population in 1871 was 300,000. There were just two hundred firemen for the whole city, only seventeen fire engines, and 48,000 feet of hose, at least one third of which was useless. The odds were not good.

Carried along by a fast, angry southwest wind, the flames leapt and danced their way through the near West Side, through part of the sporting district, past the downtown business section. Philip Sheridan, the general most beloved by the Irish whose military headquarters were in Chicago, wanted to save their South Side homes by the judicious use of explosives. North Side residents thought themselves safe—until air-borne burning brands jumped the river and sent them fleeing for their lives. Those who were lucky made it through the stampede of men, women, children, and animals to the lake, where they stood neck deep in the increas-

ingly warmer water, with damp cloths over their noses and
mouths to prevent their lungs from being seared.

Back in the burning streets the looters began their depre-
dations even in the face of the threat of a terrible death.
Many of them never made it to safety with their booty, but
others made the most of the opportunity.

Around midnight, a worried Mayor Roswell B. Mason tel-
egraphed pleas for more fire-fighting equipment to nearby
cities. Soon the waterworks Chicagoans were so proud of
went, and water had to be pumped directly from the river
onto the flames.

Just outside the fire zone, in Bridgeport and places as far
as Indiana and Michigan, people sat up late to watch the
hot, unnatural glow in the sky as the flames devoured the
city.

CHICAGO *EVENING POST*, October 14, 1893

THE DAY OF THE FIRE

MR. MARTIN DOOLEY'S REMINISCENCES ARE LATE
BUT BRIEF AND AS TRUE AS MOST MEMORIES

WHAT REARDON SAID TO HIM AND HE TO REARDON

NANNY DOOLEY AND THE DRIED APPLE PIE

"Well, well," said Mr. Martin Dooley to Mr.
McKenna, who had dropped in again because he was
still lonesome for Colonel McNeery, departed. "Here
we a-are again, alive an' well, thanks be to th' saints.
Was ye out be Jackson Par-rk last Mondah? Ye was.
Was I? I was not. Truth, me time f'r engagin' in little
skylarkin' games with all th' rist iv th' wurruld beside's
gawn by this long since. I avoid crowds now, Jawn, f'r
I've no daysire to have me right eye carried back to
Bloomin'ton on th' ind iv an ambrelly as a souveneer iv
th' fair. No, faith, none at all. So I set home here an'
r-read th' reminiscences iv th' fire, an' to be truthful

with ye, Jawn, there seems to be a dam sight more reminiscences than they was fire. 'Twas that way always. I mind now it used to be a sayin' thru Connock that if all th' ol' men that swore they'd kill sojers with a pike in '98 had been out fr'm undher th' bed in thim days th' Irish parlyment'd be passin' laws in London city years gawn by.

"Now, I raymimber th' fire, Jawn, like as if it was but yisterday. I fix it in me mind be th' fact that wan iv th' Dolan girls was married th' day before an' th' big dance down be Finucane's Hall happened two days aftherward. In thim days this here Archey road was not what it is today. Wist iv th' river there was nawthin' but prairie an' between th' river an' me there was nawthin' but a Dutchman that r-run a cabbage patch an' Pether Divlin's goat, Billy Divlin, that roamed th' lenth iv th' West Side an' fin'ly swum th' river an' made f'r Brighton Park. He was th' on'y swimmin' goat I iver see. Some said he had webbed feet and that he was a cross iv a swan, an' Divlin held to this whin he was in liquor, though it seemed dam'd improbable to me, f'r Billy Divlin was as ugly a goat as I iver set eyes on, an' th' perfume iv him! They may be some that likes goats, Jawn, but I pass thim up. I won't deny that they've got their advantages. They're aisy to keep, for wan thing. They'll ate annything. I niver knowed a goat to die iv indigestion but one. Nanny Dooley, they called her, an' she belonged to me brother. Whin his daughter come home fr'm school it got into her head to fuss around cookin' an' she made dhried apple pie out iv a cookbook. Me brother Mike was hot timpered fr'm workin' on th' canal all day an' he says, 'Arabella,' says he, 'I left me pick out near th' Sag,' he says, an' with that he hoisted it out iv th' window. Well, sir, th' goat was a dam game goat an' she wint at that pie an' fought it all over th' wa-ard. She'd'v et th' Columbus monumint, this

Nanny Dooley would, an' she fin'ly got a mouthful iv th'
pie. Thin she come home an' Mike heard her bleatin'
pitiful in th' backyard. He wint out an' found her lyin'
in th' corner with her paws on her stummick. She give
him wan look out iv th' corner iv her eye like a human
bein', thin rolled over an' died.

"But what th' 'ell am I doin' gassin' away about goats
an' th' like iv that whin I beggan to tell you about th'
fire. Well, sir, it blew great th' night iv th' weddin' an'
th' nex' night too, be th' same token, an' I was settin'
near th' dure iv th' shop whin ol' Mike Larney, th'
piper, him that died whistlin' th' 'Rambler fr'm Clare,'
come in, an' says he, 'They do be a big fire downtown,'
he says. 'Do they,' says I. 'An' where,' I says. 'All over
th' south side,' says he. 'Th' Lord be between us an' ha-
arm,' says I. 'Is it comin' this way, it is?' 'No, thanks be
to Gawd,' says he. 'It's travelin' north,' he says. 'That's
good,' says I, and we had a drink an' I shut up an' wint
to bed.

"Th' nex' morning young Connie Reardon come in
with a can. 'Th' fire is spread,' says he. 'Dear, oh dear,'
says I. 'Where is it now?' 'It's over in th' north side,'
says he. 'Good,' says I. 'That's where th' Dutch lives.'
'But it's burned down th' city hall.' 'Well,' I said, 'that's
bad f'r th' Cullertons but no har-rm done me.' 'An' th'
gas house,' he says. 'Well,' says I, 'I'm not goin' to have
me teeth extracted,' says I. 'An' I'll need no gas th'
night.' 'But th' wather works is gone.' 'Let it go,' says I.
'It's kilt more people than chollery.' An' he wint out
mad because I didn't hurroo.

"I was inthrested, iv coorse, in findin' out how th'
town looked after th' fire but business began to pick up
nex' week with th' drivers iv brick wagons that come
down from some kilns they opened, an' 'twas near a
year before I went over. Th' town didn't look no

diff'rent excipt that most of th' buildin's was new. An' them's me reminiscences iv th' fire, Jawn."

"'Tis a quare thing to cilly-brate—a fire. They'll be gettin' up a holiday f'r th' chollery or th' smallpox in this wild town one iv these days."

5

Sometime Tuesday morning, October 10, the Great Fire died out, and a welcome rain began to fall. Destroyed was a two-thousand-acre tract bounded by the west side of the South Branch of the Chicago River, Lake Michigan on the east, and Fullerton Avenue on the north. Two hundred fifty bodies were found; the toll was probably much higher, and many vanished without a trace, fused by the intense heat of the inferno. About eighteen thousand homes were gone; only two dwellings had survived in the burned area—the mansion of Mahlon Ogden and the cottage of Richard Bellinger. At least ninety thousand were homeless. The value of the property destroyed was nearly $200 million.

Reconstruction began immediately—in fact it began before the fire was out. To curb the looting, five thousand temporary policemen were appointed. Because of a power struggle between the mayor and Governor John M. Palmer, martial law was declared, troops were sent in, sent out, and sent back in again.

A Relief and Aid Society was established to help the fire victims and to dispense the vast quantities of supplies being shipped from people all over the world. These heartfelt gestures were not limited to just food and clothing; Queen Victoria contributed several volumes to help re-establish the public library (which did not exist in the city until *after* the fire).

Almost all the expressions of hope for Chicago's survival were sincere, but at least one was not. St. Louis, Missouri, had long felt itself in keen competition with upstart Chicago. When he heard of the disaster, one member of a distinguished group of Hegelian philosophers located in St. Louis recalled that "we with some public display sent money for the homeless and provisions for the hungry, and even resolutions of sympathy for the unfortunate city—all of which was of right appearance; but privately everywhere could be heard without unhappy tears the pious spiritual ejaculation: 'Again the fire of heaven has fallen on Sodom and Gomorrah.'"

Chicagoans did not waste much time on self-pity. One businessman, W. D. Kerfoot, quickly posted a sign out on the street near the smoking ruin of his real estate office, which read "All gone except wife, children and energy." By mid-November fifty thousand new buildings were up, and bartenders were serving whiskey again. As early as 1872, when they laid a cornerstone recalling the "glorious resurrection" from the fire, Chicagoans began celebrating their great disaster, somewhat to the dismay of outsiders. And in Bridgeport, according to Mr. Dooley, the ill wind that spurred the flames did indeed blow some good.

CHICAGO *EVENING POST*, October 9, 1897

"Ar-re ye goin' to attind th' cillybration iv th' fire?" asked Mr. Hennessy.

"Th' cillybration iv th' fire!" Mr. Dooley replied. "An' why shud I cillybrate th' fire? An' why shud annywan? D'ye hear iv people cillybratin' th' famine iv forty-eight or th' panic iv sivinty-three or th' firin' on Fort Sumter? We've had manny other misfortunes an' they're not cillybrated. Why don't we have a band out an' illuminated sthreet ca-ars f'r to commimorate th' day that Yerkuss come to Chicago? An' there's cholera. What's th' matther with cholera? Why don't we have an ipidimic

day, with floats showin' distinguished citizens in con-
vulsions an' a procission iv hearses? That'ud be a pretty
sight. Some time I expect to see Tanner's inaug'ration
cillybrated because it happened, an' th' people, or
manny iv thim, lived through it. We cud have a ripri-
sintation iv Tanner bein' pursued by a yellow fever
mickrobe an' durin' th' intertainment mimbers iv th'
legislachure 'ud pass among th' audjience pickin'
pockets.

"F'r mesilf, who was here whin it happened, though
I see little iv it, th' Chicago fire doesn't stir up anny
wild desire to get out an' mar-rch an' shoot off Roman
candles. Not much. I'm good f'r th' Foorth iv July an'
Pathrick's day, an' other naytional holidays, but I've got
to quit at th' fire. I'm not up to rejoicin' over th' misfortunes iv me fellow men. Iv coorse I know th' fire was a
good thing—Oh! a fine thing, f'r Chicago. It desthroyed
old buildin's so that new wans cud be put up. But did
ye iver think that th' ol' buildin's was homes f'r poor
people? Ye hear iv th' men who be nerve an' interprise
took advantage iv th' fire to build up fortunes. D'ye iver
think iv thim that had no nerve an' interprise afther th'
fire to begin new again? Poor souls."

"Was you here during th' fire?" asked young Mr.
Aloysius Hogan, who had come in to drink a small bottle of pop and listen to the conversation of the elders.

"I said I was," retorted Mr. Dooley. "I was here,
right here. I niver moved. I stayed right on th' old
homestead an' heerd about th' fire fr'm men who came
in to tell about it. I've heerd about it manny times
since. Out this way we didn't pay much attintion to it.
Me nex'-dure neighbor was a man be th' name iv
Clancy, an' I cud just see th' smoke iv his chimbly on a
clear day. But down be Halsted sthreet, where they was
as manny as four houses in a block, th' excitement was

turrible. People moved their furniture out on th' sthreet an' poored wather on th' roof. Bimeby they sint a man over th' creek to see how th' fire was goin' on. He come back at night. 'It's all right,' he says. 'Th' fire has swpt across DeKoven sthreet an' is now movin' north, desthroyin' th' intire business district an' th' whole North side,' he says. 'Saved,' cried Malachi Geohegan, that ownded a house about as big as a chicken coop, with nawthin' in it but wan bed, a stove an' a table. 'Is th' courthouse gone?' says a German named Schmidt. 'It is,' says th' messenger. 'An' th' jail,' he says. 'Thank hivin,' said Schmidt. They was a warrant out f'r him f'r keepin' a saloon without a license, an' he wud've been arristed if anny policeman cud be found to put a fut in Bridgepoort in thim days. It's all changed now. They'se nawthin' else here but polismin.

"So ivery wan rayturned to his home an' thought no more iv it till th' papers come out. They was about as big as a porous plasther, an' they looked like wan afther usin'. Thin we seen what a divvle iv a misfortune we'd been through. Afther a while people we knowed come over an' lived on us till th' winter. Thin we heerd that money was poorin' in an' they wint over to get relieved. Be th' same token, this relieved us too. They got things to eat an' clothes to wear an' manny other conthributions. Wan iv thim that 'd lived with me sint me a hammick an' a pair iv boot trees that he got fr'm th' comity. Those iv thim that wanted a house to wear around got wan. They were more useful as watch char-rms or pocket pieces thin to live in, but a lot iv th' people iv our race took thim over to Goose Island, an' be patchin' thim up with what lumber they could find lyin' around loose made a comfortable mansion. Ye can see thim in th' twenty-third wa-ard to this day if ye can find thim. I knowed a man be th' name iv Murphy—a clan man— that kept buildin' around th' relief house until now he has a mansion four stories high. I wint over to see him las' year. 'Where's th' little house ye got fr'm th' relief comity afther th' fire?' I says. 'It's th' back stoop on th' third flure,' he says.

"But that's nayther here nor there. What I started out to say was I'll have no cillybration iv th' fire. I don't care if we did get a new jail. Th' ol' wan was good enough f'r me."

6

When George Pullman built his model factory town on Lake Calumet outside Chicago in 1880, his experiment received a warm welcome from the public. The community became a major attraction, with visitors numbering in the thousands, ranging from the merely curious to government officials who came to study and to learn. The town's environment was expected to produce a more stable, dependable, and ambitious working man.

The depression of 1893 came late to the town of Pullman because of the increased demand for Pullman cars generated by the World's Columbian Exposition which was held in Chicago that year. However, by June of 1893 George Pullman said he saw signs of approaching "Jacksonian hard times." Accordingly, Pullman decided that the way to weather the economic storm was to continue production while reducing costs. To Pullman, the best way to cut costs was to cut salaries. Between the summer of 1893 and May 1894 when the strike began, wages were slashed by an average of 25 per cent, with some workers receiving pay cuts of up to 70 per cent.

Although the strike was primarily attributed to these wage cuts, there were other factors which convinced the workers of the need for drastic action. Among these were paternalism, refusal to allow workers to own their homes, high rent, water and gas charges, and tyrannical behavior on the part of foremen.

The company refused to discuss any of these problems, while aggravating the already sensitive situation by the continuation of such hated on-the-job activities as blacklisting, favoritism, nepotism, and firings without cause. In the spring of 1894 the workers decided that their only recourse was to organize by joining Eugene V. Debs's American Railway Union (ARU). Unable to reach a negotiated settlement and faced with the threat of a lockout, the local union walked out in late June. Following continued refusals of company representatives to submit to arbitration, sympathetic strikes spread across the country, tying up railroad traffic. The ARU declared a nationwide boycott in late June.

Declaring that the strike was interfering with the federal mail, U. S. Attorney General Richard Olney obtained, on July 2, a federal injunction restraining ARU officials from continuing the strike. They went on with it anyway. Then, after spontaneous demonstrations at railroad yards around the city turned violent, federal troops were dispatched to Chicago by President Grover Cleveland. This action was taken over the heads of both Governor John Altgeld and Mayor John Hopkins. Although all three were members of the Democratic Party, Governor Altgeld did not share Cleveland's enthusiasm for big business, and the President's action was regarded by some as retaliation for Altgeld's unpopular but liberal pardon of the men convicted for inciting the Haymarket riot in 1886.

On July 7, 1894, Debs was arrested, and on July 10 officers of the ARU were indicted for violating the injunction. In a last ditch effort to save face for the union, Eugene Debs requested the assistance of Samuel Gompers, the national labor leader, in delivering a message that the union would settle the strike if the company would agree to reinstate the strikers without prejudice. Gompers refused to intervene, but Mayor Hopkins agreed to be the go-between. Convinced that the need for negotiation was past, the association which represented the railroads declined the offer. The strike was broken and the Pullman works reopened on August 2; none of the strikers was re-employed by the company. During the course of the strike the workers suffered great hardships, and many of them had drifted away to other places and other jobs. George Pullman was eventually forced to loosen his grip over the town when the courts ruled that his corporation could not legally own Pullman and control passed to the City of Chicago.

Mr. Dooley's first column on the Pullman strike reflected the general reaction of the newspapers that the walkout was a "stupid blunder" because of the inequality of the contending forces. Judging from this sketch, Dunne felt both sides had blundered and that the company was making too much of the situation. As for the policy of the *Evening Post*, it was definitely antistrike, antiunion, and anti-Debs. Once again Dunne was able to use Dooley as a vehicle for expressing his real sentiments, which had to be disguised on the editorial page.

Members of the American Railway Union refused to handle any trains hauling Pullman cars; this led to shortages of some goods, none of which were vital, except possibly to the comfort of the wealthy, and Mr. Dooley chose to point this out ironically by bemoaning his lack of lemons and ice.

The general managers association saw the Pullman boycott as their big chance to crush the union once and for all. Federal judges had consistently ruled that such union activities as strikes and boycotts were criminal conspiracies or constituted restraint of trade. Soon Pullman cars were appearing on trains that had never hauled them before—especially mail trains. Next, the managers hired 100,000 men to act as strikebreakers and guards. Almost to a man these were desperate characters. In Chicago they were recruited from the Levee, one of the toughest, worst parts of town. To gain even more control, the managers association arranged to have one of their lawyers appointed U. S. Assistant Attorney General for Chicago. The nomination was rushed through, and this man's first act was to seek an injunction which would pave the way for federal troops to be sent in. All of this was accomplished with the wholehearted connivance of Attorney General Olney, who had also been a railroad lawyer until he was elevated to the Cabinet by Cleveland.

Calmer heads called upon Pullman to treat with the union. Leading Chicago citizens such as Mayor Hopkins, financier Lyman Gage, social arbiter Bertha Palmer, social worker Jane Addams—all urged peaceful settlement. Even Mark Hanna, who was surely not prounion, was incensed. "That damn fool Pullman! Any man who won't meet employees half way in these times is an ass!" he trumpeted.

As soon as the scabs and soldiers hit town, there was violence; that the strikers were behind it appears doubtful. Eugene Debs was clapped into jail, and when Clarence Darrow, his lawyer, tried to make bail for his client, so many obstacles were thrown in his way that it was impossible. The whole situation was fraught with unconstitutional behavior on the part of federal government officials.

During the trial, Darrow tried to put Pullman on the stand, but the industrialist managed to elude the subpoena by slipping away to his luxurious vacation estate. The criminal conspiracy charge was dropped but Debs did get a six month sentence for contempt—a charge that is not tried before a jury.

CHICAGO *EVENING POST*, July 7, 1894

DOOLEY'S VIEW OF IT

THE PHILOSOPHER COMMENTS ON THE PRESENT CRISIS

WANTS LEMONS AND LIBERTY

THE CONSTITUTION AND MR. PULLMAN AS VIEWED
FROM AN ARCHEY ROAD STANDPOINT

"Th' counthry," said Mr. Dooley, "do be goin' to
wrack an' roon. I have nayether limons n'r ice in th'
house. Th' laws is defied an' th' constitootion is vilated.
Th' rights iv citizens is thrampled upon an' ye can get
nayether ice n'r limons f'r love 'r money. Ordher out th'
sojers, says I, an' tache th' miscreents what th' 'ell. For
why did George Wash'n'ton an' Andhrew Jackson and
Jeremiah Houlihan fight an' die if a band iv thraitors
can come along an' wrinch from an American citizen
his limons an' his ice! Am I right! Am I right, Jawn! Am
I right! Am I right! I am.

"This ain't no sthrike. A sthrike is where th' la-ads
lave off wurruk an' bate Germans an' thin go back to
wurruk f'r rajooced wages an' thank hivin f'r it. This
here is a rivolution again constitooted authority. I seen
it in th' pa-aper an' by gar it must be thrue. I niver
r-read th' constitootion an I niver seen anny wan that
r-read it, but it must be all right, for an' because 'twas
made wan hundherd years ago or more be min that is
now dead an' in their graves. God rest their sowls, especially Jawn Carroll iv Carrollton, that was a grandfa-
ather iv Carroll, th' stove docther.[6] He was, he was.

[6] Carroll, th' stove docther—The Carroll family of Maryland was one
of the most distinguished Irish Catholic families in America. Charles
Carroll of Carrollton played a prominent role during the Revolutionary
period and was one of the signers of the Declaration of Independence.
A cousin, Daniel Carroll, was a signatory of the Articles of Confederation in 1781.

Carroll said so. Could thim pathriots do wrong? Did they know what was best f'r us afther fightin' f'r our liberties? I should smoke a ham.

"Th' constitootion, Jawn, provides f'r Pullman. I don't know th' ma-an, but I wint in wan iv his ca-ars to th' convintion at Peeory with th' lith'ry club, an' I must say th' convayniences is nice. All ye have to do is lave ye'er shoes on th' flure an' ye git some wan's else's in th' mor-rnin'. Thin ye crawl into th' side iv th' ca-ar an' whin ye'er removin' ye'er pa-ants a dhrunk man fr'm th' eighth wa-ard comes an' climbs on ye'er back f'r to get into th' hole above ye. 'Tis nice an' quite, an' th' smill iv it is not ba-ad. Ye have some excitement findin' ye'er shirt in th' mornin', but 'tis all a matther iv sport.

"This here Pullman makes th' sleepin' ca-ars an' th' constitution looks afther Pullman. He have a good time iv it. He don't need to look afther himsilf. He have limons an' ice to give to his neighbors if he wanted to. He owns towns an' min. He makes princes iv th' rile blood iv Boolgahria[7] go round to th' kitchen dure. He is stiffer than wan iv his own towels. Whin he has throuble ivry wan on earth excipt thim that rides in smokin' ca-ars whin they rides at all r-runs to fight f'r him. He calls out George Wash'n'ton an' Abraham Lincoln an' Gin'ral Miles an' Mike Brinnan an' ivry human bein' that rayquires limons an' ice an' thin he puts on his hat an' lams away. 'Gintlemin,' says he, 'I must be off,' he says. 'Go an' kill each other,' he says. 'Fight it out,' he says. 'Defind th' constitution,' he says. 'Me own is not of th' best,' he says, 'an' I think I'll help it be spindin' th'

---

[7] Boolgahria—Pullman had been granted an honorary title by the King of Italy. Mr. Dooley tended to class all non-Irish foreigners as Bulgarians.

summer,' he says, 'piously,' he says, 'on th' shores iv th'
Atlantic ocean.'[8]

"That's Pullman. He slips out as aisely as a ba-ar iv
his own soap. An' th' whole wurruld turns in an' shoots
an' stabs an' throws couplin' pins an' sojers ma-arch out
an' Gin'ral Miles looks up th' sthreet f'r some wan to
show that he can kill min too. Ye take Abraham Lincoln, but give me Pullman."

Mr. Dooley paused for a while after this deliverance.
Then he said: "Jawn, are ye goin' home?"

"Yes," said Mr. McKenna.

"Then dhrop off at Willum Joyce's," said Mr. Dooley,
"an' get th' constitootion an' (whisper) look at th' sic-
tion about sleepin' ca-ars an' see if it don't say something about limons an' ice too."

7

The strike began in an almost holiday atmosphere; picnics,
ball games, and dances were organized to occupy the strikers' unaccustomed leisure time. However, the feeling that
they were on a lark was dispelled by the company's announcement that its stores would no longer grant credit.
What little savings the workers might have had went
quickly, and the American Railway Union was too young
(one year) to have a treasury adequate to support its
members. It was soon easy to see the effect of the strike on
the model town, for instead of being scattered throughout
the city, the unemployed were all located in a small geo-
graphic area in and around the company town of Pullman.
Real starvation and dire want rapidly became apparent, and
these circumstances were not eased by the end of the boycott because of the company's refusal to rehire the strikers.

[8] During the heat of the battle, Pullman departed the city on one
of his railroad cars for his vacation retreat.

The situation was desperate, and Dunne abandoned his usual approach to attack George Pullman savagely. The response to this column was immediate. According to Elmer Ellis:

> When the typesetter ran off his proof of this piece he passed it out in the composing room and later when Dunne stepped into the room for a moment the typesetters started to drum their sticks on their cases and then broke into the more customary applause of handclapping. It was painfully embarrassing because it was so unusual yet so natural, and Dunne remembered it as one of the great thrills of his life.

Pullman was delighted that the strike and the strikers were broken, and he refused to even countenance requests that he contribute to a relief fund to benefit the most pathetic victims, the starving women and children. A congressional investigating committee was appointed to look into the conditions surrounding the strike. It found that dividends for the depression year of 1894 had risen by just about the same amount that Pullman had cut wages. And $25 million of undistributed earnings were being carried on the company books. Rents were at least 25 per cent higher than the same quarters would command nearby; Pullman purchased gas and water from Chicago and then resold both at enormous profits; very few people could afford the $3.00 annual charge to use the library Pullman was so proud of; and the few who had the money to frequent his hotel did not dare to be seen there. Pullman even charged a high rental for the church; after all, as he pointed out, it was not there for religious purposes, but rather "for the artistic effect of the scene."

George Pullman became one of the most hated men in America. When he died three years later funeral services were held furtively in his Prairie Avenue mansion and his

body was removed under the cover of darkness to Graceland
Cemetery. There a pit had been excavated as large as a
room, lined with eighteen inches of reinforced steel and con-
crete. The casket was lined with lead, wrapped in tar paper,
and covered with asphalt, and then the grave was filled in
with concrete-topped steel rails. It was said that all these
precautions were taken to safeguard the grave from desecra-
tion by angry former employees. But Ambrose Bierce is reported to have observed that, "It is clear the family in their
bereavement was making sure the son of a bitch wasn't
going to get up and come back."

CHICAGO *EVENING POST*, August 25, 1894

WHAT DOES HE CARE?

DOOLEY DISCOURSES AGAIN ON HIS FRIEND
MR. PULLMAN

DOCTRINE OF "WHAT TH' 'ELL"

ARCHEY ROAD PHILOSOPHER REVIEWS HIS AMIABLE
FELLOW TOWNSMAN'S PECULIAR QUALITIES

"Jawn," said Mr. Dooley, "I said it wanst an' I sa-ay
it again, I'd liefer be George M. Pullman thin anny man
this side iv Michigan City. I would so. Not, Jawn, d'ye
mind that I invy him his job iv r-runnin' all th' push-
cart lodgin'-houses iv th' counthry or in dayvilopin' th'
whiskers iv a goat without displayin' anny other iv th'
good qualities iv th' craythur or in savin' his tax list fr'm
th' assissor with th' intintion iv layin' it befure a mathri-
monyal agency. Sare a bit does I care f'r thim honors.
But, Jawn, th' la-ad that can go his way with his nose in
th' air an' pay no attintion to th' sufferin' iv women an'
childher—dear, oh, dear, but this life must be as happy
as th' da-ay is long.

"It seems to me, Jawn, that half th' throuble we have
in this vale iv tears, as Dohenny calls Bridgepoort, is

seein' th' sufferin' iv women an' little childhren. Th'
men can take care iv thimsilves, says I. If they can't
wurruk let thim go on th' polis foorce, an' if they can't
go on th' polis foorce let thim follow th' advice big
Pether Hinnissy give th' Dutchman. 'I dinnaw vat to do,'
sa-ays th' Dutchman. 'I have no money an' I can get no
wurruk.' 'Foolish man,' says Hinnissy. 'D'ye know what
th' good book says? To those that has nawthin' something will be given,' he says; 'an' those that has a lot,' he
says, 'some wan'll come along with a piece iv lead pipe,'
he says, 'in a stockin',' he says, 'an' take away what they
got,' he says. 'D'ye see that big man over there?' he
says, pointin' to Dorgan, th' rale estateman. 'Go over an'
take him be th' neck an' make him give up.' Well, sir,
th' German, bein' like all iv th' ra-ace but Hesing, was a
foolish la-ad, an' what does he do but follow th' joker's
advice. Sare Dorgan give him a kick in th' stummick,
an' whin he got out iv th' hospital he wint to th' Bride-
well, an', by dad, I'm thinkin' he was betther off there
than most poor divvles out iv it, f'r they get three meals
a da-ay, av'n if there ain't no toothbrushes in th' cells.

"But as I said, Jawn, 'tis not th' min, ye mind; 'tis th'
women an' childhren. Glory be to Gawd, I can scarce
go out f'r a wa-alk f'r pity at seein' th' little wans settin'
on th' stoops an' th' women with thim lines in th' fa-ace
that I seen but wanst befure, in our parish over beyant,
with th' potatoes that was all kilt be th' frost an' th' oats
rotted with th' dhrivin rain. Go into wan iv th' side
sthreets about supper time an' see thim, Jawn—thim
women sittin' at th' windies with th' babies at their
breasts an' waitin' f'r th' ol' man to come home. Thin
watch thim as he comes up th' sthreet, with his hat over
his eyes an' th' shoulders iv thim bint like a hoop an'
dhraggin' his feet as if he carried ball an' chain. Musha,
but 'tis a sound to dhrive ye'er heart cold whin a
woman sobs an' th' young wans cries, an' both because

there's no bread in th' house. Betther off thim that lies in Gavin's crates out in Calv'ry, with th' grass over thim an' th' stars lookin' down on thim, quite at last. An' betther f'r us that sees an' hears an' can do nawthin' but give a crust now an' thin. I seen Tim Dorsey's little woman carryin' a loaf iv bread an' a ham to th' Polack's this noon. Dorsey have been out iv wurruk f'r six months, but he made a sthrike carryin' th' hod yistherday an' th' good woman pinched out some vittles f'r th' Polacks."

Mr. Dooley swabbed th' bar in a melancholy manner and turned again with the remark: "But what's it all to Pullman. Whin Gawd quarried his heart a happy man was made. He cares no more f'r thim little matthers in life an' death than I do f'r O'Connor's tab. 'Th' women an' childhren is dyin' iv hunger,' they sa-ays. 'They've done no wrong,' they sa-ays. 'Will ye not put out ye'er hand to help thim?' they sa-ays. 'Ah, what th' 'ell,' sa-ays George. 'What th' 'ell,' he sa-ays. 'James,' he sa-ays, 'a bottle iv champagne an' a piece iv crambree pie. What th' 'ell, what th' 'ell, what th' 'ell.'"

"I heard two died yesterday," said Mr. McKenna. "Two women."

"Poor things, poor things. But," said Mr. Dooley, once more swabbing the bar, "what th' 'ell."

8

During the legislative session of 1895, the Illinois General Assembly passed a bill making it mandatory for all schools whether public or private to fly the American flag. Refusal to comply was punishable by fine. Denouncing this law as meddling of the state with the Church, the German Lutherans stated that while all of their forty parochial schools flew the flag as a matter of love, they would not do so as a matter of law. Mr. Dooley quickly gave them credit for being yet another political lobbying group to be considered when it was ticket-making time.

CHICAGO *EVENING POST*, August 17, 1895

"Jawn," said Mr. Dooley, "they's no holdin' down th' Lutheryans. They've broke out again."

"What have they been doing?" asked Mr. McKenna. "There's three families of thim in my ward."

"I hear they've put up a roar about histin' th' flag over their school-houses. Ye see, th' ligis-lachure whin it met passed a law finin' annywan that ownded a school-house tin bucks fr not histin' a flag on th' roof. They was great pathriots in th' ligis-lachure. I think Billy O'Broyn must iv been th' inthrojoocer iv th' bill, fr he's a bigger pathriot thin George Washin'ton was. I see him wanst hit a man with a monkey wrinch fr thryin' to haul down th' flag fr'm Finucane's Hall, where they was holdin' a convintion. Wash'ton never done that much. 'Twas wan iv Wall's la-ads fr'm th' fifth he hit, an' undher th' protiction iv th' flag they wint ahead an' nommynated a rale ol' American ticket, O'Malley fr assissor, Ole Johnson fr supervisor, Schwartzmeister fr collector an' Piacek fr town clerk— he's th' wan that runs th' buildin' association over be Laurel sthreet. Ne'er a wan iv thim but his folks had come over on th' Mayflower or some other iv th' Cunard boats.

"Jawn, I'd be a pathriot mesilf if th' neighborhood wasn't so poor. Hinnissy was tellin' me some Frinch woman over in th' Noter Dam parish, where we used to go whin Father Kelly was takin' up th' Easther collic-tion, she says that whin a man has got so that ivry polis-man knows him, an' whin they have handbills out fr

him an' whin they've showed him f'r inspection at th'
Cinthral station, he becomes a pathriot. I used to live
next dure to a man that covered his house with th' stars
an' sthripes on th' Foorth iv July an' had thim over th'
chairs iv his pa-arlor f'r tidies. He used to play 'Hail Co-
lumbia' on a mouth organ, an' I used to put me coat in
th' safe at night.

"Did ye iver see a man that wanted to free Ireland
th' day afther to-morrah that didn't run f'r aldherman
soon or late? Most iv th' great pathriotic orators iv th'
da-ay is railroad lawyers. That's a fact, I'm tellin' ye.
Most iv th' rale pathriots wurruks f'r th' railroads too—
thrampin' th' thracks. Th' ligislachure 'd 've passed a
law finin' a man f'r not wearin' th' stars an' sthripes f'r
pants. Most iv th' mimbers 'd like to wear thim f'r th'
sake iv havin' th' sthripes runnin' th' right way, an' th'
stars to take th' curse off.

"But thim comes in th' Lutheryans. I niver heerd tell
iv thim till three or four years ago. We'd had th' Scan-
dinavyan vote, an' th' Polack vote, an' th' Bohemian
vote, an' th' Boolgahryan vote to take care iv an' I'd
lived in th' wa-ard f'r twenty-six years an' niver heerd of
th' Lutheryans. But wan day Willum Joyce come into
me place f'r to consult me about th' ticket, f'r I was captain iv me precint wanst, an' I've not lost me drag with
th' la-ads. 'We've got to do something f'r th' Lutheryans,' says he. 'F'r why?' says I. 'If ye go out to satisfy
ivry ma-archin' club,' I says, 'that comes up over night,'
I says, 'ye'll ilict no wan,' I says. ''Tis not a ma-archin'
club,' says he, ''tis a church,' says he, 'an' they all stand
together,' he says, 'an' whin wan votes wan way they all
vote that way,' he says. 'Well,' says I, 'that may be ye'er
idee iv a church, Willum,' I says, f'r though he was th'
comity man I knowed him whin he was a kid; 'but, by
dad, it'll need no new license f'r to organize as a ma-
archin' club,' I says.

"Well, Jawn, 'twas thin I larned how little I knowed iv politics, though I'd been precint captain in me day an' cud get out more votes an' have thim counted than anny wan bechune th' bridge an' th' powder maga-zeens. Th' iliction come off an' th' Lutheryan vote was too big fr th' boxes. Ivry man on th' road become a Lutheryan. Some iv th' la-ads was in here wan night an' says Sorenson, th' big Swede that lives down below Deerin' sthreet, he says: 'Who's this here Luther, anny-how?' he says. 'He may be a good fellow, but no wan has seen th' color iv his money,' he says. 'I don't know annything about that,' says Gallagher, 'but he's a gr-reat organ-izer,' he says.

"Well, 'tis th' Lutheryans that are roarin' again puttin' flags on th' schoolhouses. Th' legislachure that stole ivrything in sight fr'm th' money iv poor Hawkins to th' inkwells in their desks wants to make thim pathriots enough not to care whin they're robbed, an' th' Lu-theryans are afightin' it because it ain't th' German flag. An'—"

"Well, what is it?" Mr. McKenna asked briskly.

"I was on'y wondhrin," said Mr. Dooley, "if there ain't some money left in th' gooldbrick game."

9

One day in the later summer of 1895 some workmen from Chicago's water department were excavating at Forty-second and Loomis streets. In the course of their work, they discovered several unmetered pipes that tapped into the main line. This prompted a series of sensational disclosures about illegal sewer pipelines.

Made curious by their findings, the workmen followed the pipes to their final destination—to the stockyards plants of several prominent meat packers. A search of the city files revealed no record of the pipes and also that some of the water maps for the area had been stolen by some miscreant for unknown purposes. Upon further investigation it was found that in addition to this wholesale water robbery, the packers had virtually exhausted the water supply to the township of Lake on Chicago's South Side. In one instance, an illegal pipe diverted water from a neighborhood fire hydrant to a packing plant. As one of the daily newspapers put it, while the packers had water to burn, the taxpayers did not have a drop.

While stealing a large share of the water they needed for their operations, the packers also paid below-average rates for the water that came through legal pipes, all of this at an enormous loss to the city. Beneficiaries of the illegal rates and pipes included Swift & Company, Armour & Company, and Morris & Company.

At first the packers tried to get by without making any statement, and next they refused to do so because of the inflamed state of public opinion. Finally they issued a declaration claiming that the pipes were old, disused ones (contrary to evidence found in city files and by city inspectors) and that they laid the pipes to help out the city. For those who did not swallow either of these explanations, they pleaded that their sin was a matter of omission rather than commission.

CHICAGO *EVENING POST*, September 7, 1895

"Jawn," said Mr. Dooley, "why sh'd anny wan want to steal wather?"

"I give it up," replied Mr. McKenna.

"It seems sthrange, doesn't it," Mr. Dooley went on. "They ought to be enough to go 'round. I'll bet ye tin no wan in Archey road 'll iver be cha-arged with what Hinnissy calls this hanyous offinse.

"I suppose 'tis because they wasn't annything else they cud take. They's wan man in th' lot that'd steal even wather. Th' pa-apers say 'tis exthordinary that ladin' citizens sh'd hook th' dhrink, but I know a thing or two about this ladin' citizen. I heerd it fr'm Schwartzmeister whin him an' me was frinds, befure he put in th' pool table. This here wan came over fr'm Germany[9] a long time ago befure th' fire. Well, he was a smart la-ad, an' he done well dhrivin' cattle an' sellin' thim, an' he changed his name an' wint into th' packin' business.

"Whin he wint away fr'm Germany he lift behind a brother, an' niver heerd tell iv him f'r twenty-five or thirty years. Th' man lived though, f'r all iv that, a quite, dacint ol' lad. He had a little holdin' an' a cow an' a pig an' th' use iv th' neighbor's horse, an' he'd have gone peaceful an' continted to his grave but f'r wan thing. He was sick an' he heerd how well th' other was doin' an' he wrote to him. Th' rich wan answered, told him to come over an' that he'd look out f'r him. An' he sint him a steerage ticket.

"Th' ol' man's name was Max. Well ivery wan all over th' parish heerd iv Max's luck an' they wint to see him off on th' thrain an' to cheer him. Th' las' wurruds he said befure he wint was to his wife. 'I'm goin',' he says, 'far away,' he says. 'Aber,' he says, 'avick, I'll come back whin I've got settled an' bring ye an' th' kids over,' he says.

"Jawn, it ain't nice in th' steerage iv an imigrant ship. I know. It smells an' it's hot be night an' cold be day. But Max he bore up an' thought iv th' good brother, d'ye mind, waitin' f'r him with a carredge an' four horses. He got to Chicago in th' smokin'-ca-ar. They

[9] This here wan came over fr'm Germany—probably a reference to Nelson Morris, of Morris & Company, who was a German immigrant.

was no wan at th' deepo to meet him. 'They must be some mistake,' he says to himself, he says. 'I'll go up to his house,' he says. He got a German polisman to tell him where th' brother lived an' trudged up there with his kit on his back. Th' servant tol' him to raypoort at th' office th' nix' day. An' whin he raypoorted what job d'ye think they give him, Jawn? They put him in th' shovel gang at th' salt house.

"Ye niver wurruked in a salt house? Did ye iver mow away clover hay in a counthry barn iv a hot afthernoon? Did ye iver tind a blast in July? Well, nayther iv thim is as near to wurrukin' in a salt house as holy wather is to hell.

"Fr'm sivin o'clock in th' mornin' till six at night this here Max shoveled away. All th' wather that's been stolen fr'm th' city be his brother wudden't kill th' thirst that lay like fever on his lips nor aise his poor, tired ol' back. But there was th' wife an' childher at home an' he pegged away, makin' no kick an' lettin' on to no man who he was.

"Salt shovelin' ain't crochayin', Jawn, an' it ain't tindin' a cow, be a dam sight. An' Max wint fr'm bad to worse till he cud bare raise his shovel, he was that weak. Th' foreman cursed him an' th' other min crowded him till wan day th' boss wint to his brother an' says he: 'That there man Max ye sint me is no good,' he says. 'What's th' matther iv him?' says th' millionaire. 'He's not sthrong enough,' says th' boss. 'Thin fire him,' says th' brother. An' th' nix' mornin' whin Max come around with his dinner pail on his arrum th' boss says: 'Ye can go up an' get ye'er time. We've no further use fr ye.'

"Max stayed around town fr a week. Thin he put what money he'd saved into a steerage ticket an' wint away. He niver set eyes but wanst on th' rich wan. An'

he's back there in Germany now. Th' county is takin'
care iv him."

"Maybe," said Mr. McKenna, "that accounts for one
man stealing water."

"Yis," said Mr. Dooley, "but it'd take more thin an
eight-inch tap to wash away that sin."

10

Although Chicago was ever a city of unique characters, Wilbur Fisk Storey was a *rara avis*. Originally from Vermont,
Storey was a fearless man of strong personality and excep-
tional good looks who became another Chicago success story
—for a while. When he reached his forties, he decided to become a publisher and acquired the Chicago *Times* from
Cyrus McCormick in 1861. It would be his duty, he said, "to
print the news and raise hell."

Storey was a Democrat, devoted to Stephen A. Douglas
before Douglas' death and to his principles afterwards. This
made him and his paper popular with Chicago's Irish population, who also adored Douglas. As the Civil War
progressed, Storey became impatient with some of the
excesses of the national government, especially censorship
and the suspension of individual freedoms, and he expressed
himself freely in the pages of the *Times*. Eventually this got
to be too much for the commanding general of the relevant
military district. Ambrose E. Burnside was one of the many
military disasters President Lincoln had to contend with,
and after a number of abject failures, he was dispatched
well behind the front lines where it was felt he could do no
harm (although eventually he was given further field com-
mands and was only disposed of for good when he botched
the Battle of the Crater in 1864). This proved to be another
military miscalculation. In 1863, Burnside ordered the suppression of the *Times* for printing true stories that the fed-

eral government, without due process, had imprisoned citizens who objected to the war and had ordered executions of soldiers for military offenses. Word of this quickly spread, and an angry crowd of Storey supporters took to the streets, threatening that if the suppression order was carried out, they would not allow the *Tribune*, the local house organ of the Republican Party, to publish either. Joseph Medill, the *Tribune*'s publisher, chose a hired gun named Charles Jennison to organize what amounted to a small private army to protect his property until United States forces might be called out.

Alarmed members of the establishment of both parties met and sent a communiqué to Washington, urging Lincoln to countermand the order to suppress the *Times*. While they waited for word from him, the more articulate of them went before the restive crowd. Finally, a United States district judge ordered the army to take no action, saying, "I personally have contended and shall always contend for the right of free discussion and the right of commenting under the law and under the Constitution upon the acts of officers of the government." So Storey continued his colorful and expensive coverage of the war, admonishing his war correspondents to "telegraph fully all the news you can get, and when there is no news, send rumors." As for Burnside, he achieved a degree of lasting fame when a certain kind of tonsorial adornment originally worn by him was named the "sideburn."

Storey did not mellow with age. In 1869 he editorialized "Bawds at the Opera House! Where's the Police?" The object of his wrath was Lydia Thompson, the leading lady of Chicago's first burlesque show which featured her "British Blondes," who appeared partly in the buff and partly covered by flesh-colored tights on stage at the Opera House, which was owned by Uranus Crosby, one of Storey's dearest foes. It was not that naked or nearly naked ladies had not appeared for the delectation of Chicagoans before; the Civil

War period brought some particularly outrageous and per-
verted sex shows. But it was the first time such a review appeared at a supposedly respectable house. The same day the
attack appeared, Miss Thompson lay in wait for Storey as he
took his daily constitutional down Wabash Avenue. As he
hove into view, the lady pulled out a whip and lunged at the
newsman, landing only a single blow before he had her by
the throat, while Mrs. Storey, a doughty lady, rendered the
actress insensible by bashing her over the head with a purse
containing a Bible and a prayerbook bound partly in metal.
At the same time, Storey dealt as harshly as he could with
company manager and the company flack who were along to
enjoy the fun.

When the case came to court, the judge, who had been on
the receiving end of Storey's editorial treatment himself,
found the defendants guilty but suspended even their fines,
and Lydia exited to the cheers of the crowd, which promptly
turned out in droves to see her and her fellow *artistes.*

Prompt as he was to denounce it in others, Storey was not
above a little hanky-panky himself. He became enamored of
the former wife of a convict and divorced his first wife to
marry her in 1870. He indulged her in everything and even
fostered her social climbing by making it known that receiving the second Mrs. Storey would mean favorable coverage
in the pages of his paper. When she died, in 1873, he accused the attending physician of malpractice. That worthy,
pressed beyond endurance, went to the *Tribune,* which
printed his revelation that the lady had actually died of
"licentious living." Storey lashed back, this time at the editor of the *Tribune,* accusing him of having a social disease
not usually mentioned in the pages of a family newspaper.

Gradually, Storey lost his grip on reality, claiming to be
receiving instructions from an Indian squaw. The paper was
taken away from him, he was declared insane, and he died
in 1884, quite mad. Chicago journalism was never quite the
same.

CHICAGO *EVENING POST*, June 26, 1897

"I don't think," said Mr. Dooley, "that th' pa-apers is as good now as they used to be whin I was a young man."

"I don't see much diff'rence in thim," said Mr. Hennessy. "Except they're all full iv pitchers iv th' prisidint an' secrity iv th' Milwaukee Avnoo Fife an' Dhrum E-lite Society. They give ye th' same advice to vote th' mugwump ticket between ilictions an' th' straight ticket at ilictions, an' how th' business in pig iron is slowly but surely pickin' up, an' how to make las' year's dhress look like next year's be addin' a few jet beads an' an accorjeen pleat. They're as bad now as they iver were an' I've quit readin' thim."

"Ah, but sure," said Mr. Dooley, "ye don't raymimber th' ol' days. Ye don't raymimber Storey's *Times*. That was th' paper f'r ye. What th' divvle did ol' man Storey care f'r th' thrade in pig iron? 'Twas no more in him thin th' thrade in poolchecks. He set up in his office with his whiskers thrailin' in an ink pot an' wrote venomious attacks on th' characters iv th' leaders iv high society an' good-natured jests about his esteemed contimprary havin' had to leave Ohio because he stold a cukstove. He didn't have no use f'r prominint citizens except be way iv heavin' scandal at thim. He knowed what th' people wanted. They wanted crime, an' he give it to thim. If they wasn't a hangin' on th' front page some little lad iv a rayporther'd lose his job. They was murdher an' arson till ye cudden't rest, robbery an' burglary f'r page afther page, with anny quantity iv scandal f'r th' woman's page an' a fair assortmint iv larceny an' assault an' batthry f'r th' little wans. 'Twas a paper no wan took into his house—f'r th' other mimbers iv th' fam'ly—but 'twas a well r-run paper, so it was.

"Ye can hardly find anny crimes nowadays. To look at th' pa-apers ye'd think they was not wan bit iv rale spoortin' blood left in th' people iv this city. Instead iv it I have to pay to know that Mrs. Dofunny iv Englewood has induced her husband to stay away fr'm home while she gives a function—an' what a function is I dinnaw—an' among thim that'll be prisint, if they can get their laundhry out, 'll be Messers an' Mesdames Whatd'ye-Call-Thim an' Messers an' Mesdames This-an'-That an' Miss-What-D'ye-Call-Her-Now, an' so on. What do I care about thim? Now, if Misther Dofunny had come home with a load on an' found his wife r-runnin' up bills f'r tea an' broke up the function with his dinner pail it'd be worth readin' about. But none iv th' papers'd say annything about it, now that Storey's gone. Why, mind ye, las' week th' Willum J. O'Brien Lithry an' Marchin' Club give a dance, an' befure it got through th' chairman iv th' flure comity fell out with th' German man that led th' band an' ivery wan in th' place took a wallup at some wan else with a wind instrument. I looked f'r it in th' paper th' nex' day. All they had was: 'Th' Willum J. O'Brien Lithry an' Marchin' Club, includin' th' mos' prominent mimbers iv society in th' sixth ward, give a function at Finucane's Hall las' night. O'Rafferty sarved an' music was furnished be Weinstein's orchesthry. Among those prisint was so-an'-so.' Th' rayporther must've copied th' names off th' blotter at th' polis station. An' there was not wan wurrud about th' fight—not wan wurrud!

"Now, if it had been in ol' Storey's day this is th' way it'd read: 'Bill O'Brien, th' tough aldherman fr'm th' sixth ward, has a club named after him, most iv thim bein' well known to th' polis. It is a disgrace to th' decent people iv Bridgepoort. Las' night th' neighbors complained to th' polis iv th' noise an' Lift'nant Murphy

responded with a wagon load iv bluecoats. On entherin'
th' hall th' gallant officers found a free fight in progress,
wan iv th' rowdies havin' hit th' leader iv th' band, who
responded be knockin' his assailant down with a b-flat
cornet. Th' disturbers iv th' peace were taken to Deerin'
sthreet station an'll be thried befure Judge Scully in th'
mornin'.' That's th' way ol' Storey 'd give it to thim. He
didn't know much about functions, but he was blue
blazes on polis news.

"I dinnaw what's comin' over th' people. Whin I was
young if a rayporther wint rubberin' around a dance we
might give him a dhrink an' we might throw him in th'
canal. It depinded on how we felt tord him. It wasn't
rispictable in thim days to have ye'er name in th' paper.
It niver got in except whin ye was undher arrest. Now I
see har-rd wurrukin' men thrampin' down to th' newspaper offices with little items about a christenin' or a
wake an' havin' it read to thim in th' mornin' at
breakfuss befure they start to th' mills. On'y th' other
day th' Bohemian woman that r-runs th' cabbage patch
up be Main sthreet come in an' says she: 'We have a
party at th' house to-night,' she says. 'Have ye?' says I.
'What for?' I says. 'Me daughter is comin' out,' says she.
'Is she?' says I. 'That's nice iv th' mayor,' says I. 'How
long was she in f'r?' says I. An' she wint away mad.
What's worse, this here society don't stop afther death.
Here's a notice in th' paper: 'Ann Hochheimer'—she
married a German—'nee O'Toole.' Nee O'Toole! Nee
O'Toole! What does that mean? Nee nawthin'! Her
name was O'Toole befure she was marrid, f'r twinty
odd years. I knowed her well."

"Well," said Mr. Hennessy, with a sheepish smile. "I
must be goin'. We have a progressive euchre party at
my house an' I must be there to r-ring th' bell."

"Ye'd betther stay here an' play me forty-fives f'r th'
dhrinks," said Mr. Dooley with compassion.

"Now," said Mr. Hennessy, in hollow tones, "me name's in th' pa-aper an' I must riprisint."

And Mr. Dooley, the untainted one, stood alone—the solitary green spot in a desert of "society."

11

John A. Logan (1826–86) held almost every elective office in the state of Illinois, from local attorney to United States senator. In addition, he had a brilliant military career during the Civil War, rising to the rank of major general. His "spread-eagle oratory and contentious spirit" got him elected to Congress in 1858. He attended the Democratic Convention of 1860 as a delegate pledged to Stephen A. Douglas and was suspected by some of being a Southern sympathizer. He was a Democrat only until the Civil War, when he joined the Republican Party and the army. To some people he was a great hero, known as "Black Jack," one of the best of the citizen soldiers; to others, including the citizens of Bridgeport, he was "Dirty Work" Logan, so named for his questionable anti-Lincoln activities during the campaign of 1860. He returned to the House after the war, and eventually served two terms as senator from Illinois. He had the support of the Illinois delegation for President at the GOP convention of 1884, but he finished fourth, and ran instead as the vice presidential candidate with James G. Blaine. He was a favorite of the veterans, organized and served as president of the Grand Army of the Republic, and initiated the Memorial Day observances in the North in 1868. He died in 1886.

A monument dedicated to General Logan was unveiled before a crowd of cheering thousands, including Mr. Hennessy, on July 21, 1897. Augustus Saint-Gaudens (who became a close friend of Dunne) was the sculptor of the martial equestrian statue which depicted Logan in his role as the "hero of Atlanta." During this battle, in August 1864, Union troops were getting the worst of things. Logan was a corps commander and succeeded to temporary command of the Army of the Tennessee when the excellent General James B. McPherson was killed in this battle. However, General Sherman did not want a political general commanding an entire army and replaced Logan with Oliver O. Howard.

Welcomed by federal troops, government officials, cannons, and a hail of bullets, the statue remained an obscure attraction in Chicago's lake-front Grant Park until the Democratic National Convention of 1968, when it became a rallying point for rioting demonstrators.

CHICAGO *EVENING POST*, July 24, 1897

Mr. Hennessy appeared at Mr. Dooley's establishment Thursday night looking greatly discomposed. He was flushed and dirty and tired. As he buried his nose in a tall glass of beer, from which his friend had considerately removed the "collar" by a dexterous wave of the finger, he conveyed the information that he had been in Mitchigan avnoo joining in the Logan ceremonial. Whereupon Mr. Dooley lectured him on the beauties of the quiet life.

"Iv coorse," he said, "that's where ye'd be."

"It was gr-rand," said Mr. Hennessy. "They was anny quantity iv sojers fr'm th' reg-lar ar-rmy an' th' gov'nor, an' such a crowd as ye niver see th' like iv. I was near cr-rushed to death."

"Sure," said Mr. Dooley. "An' it's a gr-rand pity ye wasn't. F'r th' likes iv you there's no enjoyment this side iv bein' kilt. Why don't ye go out an' have ye'erself run over be a steam rowler an' have an 'ell iv a time. I wud if I was you.

"Hinnissy, ye'er an' ol' fool. Ye wurruk hard over at
th' mills. I see ye off at half-past six in th' mornin' an'
whin ye come home ye'er so tired ye walk as though ye
had a horse hitched to each leg. Ye get a holiday an'
how d'ye enjoy it? Ye'er off downtown with th' sun
cukkin' th' back iv ye'er head like a mustard plasther. Ye
go where th' crowd is thickest an' ye stand f'r hours
where Bohemian women can spill head cheese sand-
wiches on ye'er good clothes an' polismin shove ye
fr'm pillar to post an' pickpockets steal ye'er watch—f'r
what? To see a lot iv Swede farmhands, that've gone
into th' ar-rmy because they're afraid to wurruk puttin'
in hay, march by in wrong time, bumpin their muskets
into each other, or to plaze ye'er eyes with a squint at
John Tanner lookin' like th' man that owns a liv'ry stable an' has just won a tournament pitchin' hor-rse shoes.
There might be some use in wantin' to see Yerkuss. I'd
go round th' corner to look at him mesilf an' pray
heavens he wudden't take such a likin' to me that he'd
want to steal me. But I'd as lave go downtown to see
wan iv Yerkuss' bridge horses marchin' up th' sthreet as
to see John Tanner. He don't stand a divvle iv a lot
higher with Yerkuss thin th' bridge horse even if he
does live at th' Audiotoroom instead iv havin' a stall
with th' other crathers in th' Halsted sthreet bar-rn.

"An' ye didn't know Logan. I did, an' divvle a hair iv
his head did I like whin he was alive. I seen him an'
heerd him talk in a tent wanst down be Main sthreet
an' th' things he said about th' dimmycrats, Hinnissy,
was enough to make ye want to put a can iv dinnymite
under his statue an' let it go at that. Th' kindest wurrud
he had was chicken thief. I followed his carredge f'r a
mile to get a shy at him with a piece iv har-rd coal.
Sure, half th' people who wint to see him in brass wud'v
hanged him in life—an' been burned in 'ell be th' other
half. That was because he was a fighter. A man that's a
fighter, an' a good fighter, needs inimies, an' it's al-

ways a question with thim whether he has more frinds
or inimies. He wakes up in th' mornin' an' finds th' bal-
ance is in favor iv his frinds an' he says, says he: 'I'll go
out an' make a few inimies,' or he sees he's long on
inimies an' he goes out and does a few iv thim up.

"I knowed Logan, I tell ye, an' though I'd've nailed
him with a chunk iv anthracite twinty years ago, I'd put
a wreath on his grave today. It on'y takes a little while
to smooth out th' charackter iv a man that fought long
an' hit har-rd. But not f'r Logan nor f'r Charles Stewart
Parn'll would I thrust mesilf to that crowd downtown.
I've been here mesilf man an' boy 40 years, an' 'tis 20 iv
thim since I seen th' lake. I've been in State street four
or five times in all these years. I've been to th' Audio-
torium twict an' wanst I wint by th' Masonic temple on
me way to get a car comin' fr'm th' city hall. What for
should I lave quiet an' peace to dodge cable cars an'
have me pocket picked? If there's annything goin' on I
see it in th' pa-apers an' it reads betther than it looks.
To me th' Logan monymint is a hundherd miles high
an' made iv goold. That's because I niver seed it. If I'd
gone with you it'd be no higher thin an Injun cigar sign
and built iv ol' melted down dog tags an' ol' joolry. Th'
crowd was magnificent to read about; if I'd seen it it
wud've been just a million sweatin', badly dhressed
people, squallin' babies, faintin' womin an' a bad smell."

12

The term "muckraker" was coined by Theodore Roosevelt in
a speech he gave in 1906. He likened the reform journalists
so popular then to the "man with the muckrake" in John
Bunyan's *Pilgrim's Progress* of 1678, saying,

Now it is very necessary that we should not flinch from
seeing what is vile and debasing. There is filth on the

floor, and it must be scraped up with the muckrake . . .
But the man who never does anything else . . . speed-
ily becomes, not a help to society, not an incitement to
good, but one of the most potent forces of evil.

While the term was new, there was certainly nothing new
about investigative reporting. What had changed was people's attitudes. Previously editors had preferred to present
the amassers of great wealth as American heroes, men of
vision and nobility and thrift. Those who could not pull
themselves up did not deserve to survive, let alone complain. Gradually, after the Civil War, a few editors began to
publish stories that demythologized the tycoons, revealing
these men as the ruthless manipulators of the unregulated
economic system that they were. People began to wonder if
what Balzac said was not true—that in back of every great
fortune there was a great crime.

Dunne anticipated the muckrake movement by several
years, and though he knew all the prominent muckrakers
and worked with some of them, he was never a full-fledged
member, nor did he want to be. Nonetheless, a goodly number of his columns were directed at the same targets, and
were just as effective, if not more so, as the muckrakers'
most strident attacks.

In the 1870s and 1880s people who paid attention to
business trends noticed that a pattern had been developing
so that while the output of an industry increased dramatically, the ownership/management within that same industry
became concentrated just as rapidly. What was evolving
was a considerable number of near monopolies striving for
over-all control of some area of manufacture, and this was
frequently accompanied by obtaining exclusive patent
rights. It was the opinion of the average American, when he
became aware of this situation, that these budding monopolies with their unethical methods stood in opposition to the
American democratic ideal.

Widespread antagonism to the great industrial trusts is usually dated from March 1881, when the *Atlantic Monthly* published an article by Henry Demarest Lloyd entitled "The Story of a Great Monopoly," attacking the Standard Oil Company. Soon there was public agreement that something should be done to break the trusts, but no one knew just what. The Constitution had no applicable provision, except the right to control interstate commerce. Individual states first relied upon the common-law doctrine of conspiracy in restraint of trade, and toward the end of the 1880s a number of states passed antitrust laws on this basis. In 1890 Congress passed the Sherman Antitrust Act (named for Senator John Sherman of Ohio, a colleague said, with perfect congressional logic, because "Sherman had nothing to do with framing it whatever"). It was not to be enforced vigorously, however, until 1902, during Theodore Roosevelt's tenure in the White House.

Once again ahead of his time, Mr. Dooley took on the "thrusts" and their most odious exponent, John D. Rockefeller of Standard Oil, in 1899. Dooley displayed a keen grasp of economics. When John D. talks about his three partners—the state of New Jersey, the railroads, and the Deity, John D. also tells how he shares the wealth with them —the fees to the first, the freight to the second, and to the honor of the third he had raised a great college. That great college was in Chicago.

Stephen A. Douglas had founded the first University of Chicago with Baptist support in 1856, but after a series of financial reverses it was shut down in 1886. A graduate of that University of Chicago, Thomas Goodspeed, who was on the staff at the Baptist theological seminary of south suburban Morgan Park, contacted Rockefeller, whose staunch Baptist faith had convinced him that God had chosen him to be wealthy. After some extensive lobbying by local coreligionists, Rockefeller agreed to donate $600,000 for the purpose of erecting a new

university if local Baptist churches would meet it with another $400,000. Eventually this was accomplished, and Mar-
shall Field was persuaded to contribute a ten-acre tract just
outside the site chosen for the World's Columbian Exposition.

The uncompleted school was opened in October 1892 by
its thirty-six-year-old president, William Rainey Harper.
Harper was an Ohio boy who fitted the approved Chicago
mold for aggressiveness and energy. He was a hustler, but
he was an academic hustler. He was later to be limned by
one-time Chicago faculty member and economist Thorstein
Veblen as a "captain of education" as evil as the captains of
industry Veblen despised. Veblen had a grudge against
Harper; when Veblen's wife left him over his attentions to
other women, there was a scandal and the university trustees told Harper he must get rid of Veblen. Untroubled by
any consideration of academic freedom, Harper did as he
was bid and went off to teach Sunday school. Veblen was
not your conventional college professor and led a slightly
offbeat life. In his book *The Theory of the Leisure Class*,
written while he was in Chicago, Veblen coined another
phrase that has stayed in the language—"conspicuous consumption," which meant that the rich spent so much time
getting money and spending and showing it off solely in
order to display their power.

Rockefeller was pretty thoroughly despised across the
United States, but he usually was sure of a warm reception
on the new campus in Hyde Park, on Chicago's South Side.
In 1896 he appeared at the first convocation, where happy
students greeted him, chanting:

> *John D. Rockefeller, wonderful man is he—*
> *Gives all his spare change to the U. of C.*

Rockefeller responded with enthusiasm, and over the next
twenty years his contributions to this "best investment" he
said he had ever made was around $50 million.

CHICAGO *JOURNAL*, February 4, 1899

MEDITATIONS OF MARTIN DOOLEY
ON THE SUBJECT OF TRUSTS

"Well, well," said Mr. Hennessy, "I wondher whin this here formin' iv thrusts 'll stop. I've been an al-ternate to five aldhermanic convintions whin they was denouced, but they're sthronger thin iver, an' are sthranglin' th' liberties iv our counthry, be hivins, day be day. What th' divvle ar-re they, annyhow?"

"A thrust," said Mr. Dooley, "is an illegal combination to rayjooce prices. 'Tis to prevint foolish people fr'm spindin' too much money. A lot iv raypublicans is in th' same business, an' says wan iv thim, 'Behold,' he says, 'th' suff'rin' iv th' poor,' he says, 'they're overcharged,' he says, 'be cormorants in human form,' he says, 'fr to desthroy th' rapacious crathers,' he says, 'that ar-re gr-rindin' th' faces off th' poor,' he says, 'lave th' poor come ar-round an' poke their noses into a first-class imery wheel, instead iv bein' polished be little two-f'r-a-cint grin'stones all over th' counthry,' he says. 'We'll be abused,' he says, 'an' popylists an' arnychists 'll denounce us as inimies iv civilization,' he says, 'but in our holy wurruk we must ixpict such threatment,' he says. 'Look at me,' he says. 'Be desthroyin' competition, I, with th' help iv th' good Lord, an' th' railroads, an' th' state iv New Jarsey, have rayjooced th' price iv ile so a poor man can have an explosion today f'r three cints, that, whin I was a boy, he cudden't buy f'r anny money,' he says. 'I'm a benefathur iv me kind,' he says. 'An' if they're not manny iv me kind,' he says, ''tis no fault iv mine,' he says. 'I've helped th' poor. I've give dividends to th' three pardners I mintioned. Wan iv thim gets its fees,' he says, 'th' other gets its freight,' he says, 'an' to th' third,' he says, 'have I put up a colledge,'

he says, 'for to prove that a Baptist,' he says, 'can mix
up with th' ile business an' not go broke,' he says. 'Still
I'm not appreciated be me counthry,' he says. 'They call
me an octopus,' he says, 'an' a plutocrat,' he says. 'But,'
he says, 'I parsavers in th' good wurruk,' he says. 'Lave
us niver mind th' assaults iv th' ungodly,' he says, 'but
in th' inthrists iv th' poor desthroy th' hellish competition that is grajully,' he says, 'roonin' th' widow an' th'
orphan with high-priced prunes,' he says. An' so th'
Prune thrust is for-rmed.

"F'r mesilf, Hinnissy, I can't make out whether a
thrust is a good thing or a bad thing. McKenna says 'tis
a good thing because it rayjooces th' price. Schwartzmeister that belongs in th' Arbeiter Bowlin' club says
'tis th' natheral way iverything is goin'. Ye think 'tis
sthranglin' our fair land an' so does th' whole Willum J.
O'Brien Lithry an' Mar-rchin' club. But to me it looks
like jus' th' diff'rence between a man bein' robbed be
wan sthrong ar-rm man at a time an' bein' sarched be
twinty. A la-ad at th' mills gets his month's pay an' goes
down to Halsted sthreet an' has a tub iv beer an' some
wan lifts his watch. On his way home a pickpocket gets
his pin; thin a strong ar-rm boy at Deerin' sthreet holds
up f'r his money. At his doorstep two or three young an'
inexperyenced robbers throw him down an' take th'
shoes off his feet. Now, if twas a thrust, if these here
competin' merchants was to unite an' meet th' la-ad at
th' start, they cud sthrip him clane as a bone an' lave
nawthin' f'r th' loathesome an' disunited competitors up
th' sthreet. They'd be sthrong enough to do business in
spite iv th' polis, they'd have no throuble in bein' incor-
poryated in New Jarsey, where th' green goods comes
from, an' they cud prove to anny intilligent man that
'tis betther to be skinned early an' be th' latest methods
thin to thrust th' job to a lot iv rough' an tumbles, with-

out capital, an' not havin' th' inthrests iv th' counthry at stake."

"An' what ar-re th' poor la-ads up to th' sthreet goin' to do?" asked Mr. Hennessy, whose democratic sympathies were instantly aroused by the misfortunes of the crushed footpads.

"They're goin' to wurruk f'r th' Burglers thrust," said Mr. Dooley. "Each iv thim that's a good mechanic'll be given a piece iv lead pipe an' a woolen sock, an' tol' to go out an' increase th' comfort iv th' poor an' th' sthreet cars'll give thim rayjooced rates to thravel fr'm wan dark alley to another, an' th' council 'll pass an' ardhnance prohibiting anny way fr'm importin' sandbags an' jimmies into th' city. Afther a while a man can be robbed as aisily in his own house as in an alley. That's what th' thrust will do, it will so."

"I hears," said Mr. Hennessy, "that they're for-rmin' a Whisky thrust."

"Whisky thrust?" said Mr. Dooley, "has roo'ned manny a man. But I don't believe it. Ye can't rayjooce th' price iv whisky. 'Tis fixed be th' laws iv nature. Even me frind Jawn D. Rockyfeller, that they say is into it, can't make two cases iv deleeryum threemens, as Hogan says, grow where wan grew befure. But if he thries it, look out f'r a Thirst thrust. I think, be th' way ye're lookin' at that bar, ye'd be allotted a majority iv th' stock."

13

Chicago's serious problems with the pollution of the water supply started at almost the same time the city was incorporated, in 1833. The Chicago River was filthy and it, as well as the street sewers, emptied into Lake Michigan, which was the city's source of drinking water. In order to obtain a fresh supply, the city fathers tunneled out past the pollution point. As Chicago grew, however, the tunnels had to be extended farther and farther. This was at best a temporary expedient; and about fifty out of every thousand people in town fell victim to water-borne diseases every year. As a result, in 1856 the city began building the first "integrated" sewerage system in the United States; in fact, it was the only one in the world outside of Hamburg, Germany, to consolidate both storm and sanitary drains. Because almost all of the downtown area of Chicago had been low and marshy land, the sewers were built at ground level. The buildings were then jacked up and earth packed beneath them to assure drainage. For a long time, streets, sidewalks, and buildings were at all different levels, and a simple walk through the city meant going up and down many times. The Tremont House, a six-story luxury hotel, was lifted up by the then-young George Pullman, who employed 1,200 men to turn the jackscrews so gently that not a single guest was disturbed nor a single pane of glass broken.

The new system worked for a while. The sewers still emptied into the Lake, however, so more tunnels for obtaining drinking water were dug—some say as many as sixty-four—before another method was found. During the Civil War, the effluent from the rendering and meat-packing houses, which were working overtime to supply the troops, could be tasted in the drinking water. At a cost of $3 million, the Illinois & Michigan Canal, which began at about Ashland Avenue and the South Fork of the South Branch of the Chicago River and ran down to the Illinois at Utica, was deepened so as to reverse the flow of the Chicago River away from the lake. This was effective until land developers weakened the system by cutting another drainage ditch so that the system had to be supplemented with giant pumps. It was a risky operation, but in Chicago business was business, and money talked.

Then in August of 1885, a real downpour, a "frog

strangler," fell. It was too much of a burden for the over-worked pumps. The storm emptied the sewers, streets, and river right back into the lake again. Deaths from cholera and typhoid shot up. But Chicagoans had just rebuilt their city after the fire and they were not about to be stopped by a small matter like death-dealing pollution.

A "sanitary district" was created to develop a new plan. This was to dig a new channel from the Chicago River to the Des Plaines River at Lockport, a distance of twenty-eight miles, and most of it solid rock. It was just the kind of intrepid venture that Chicagoans loved then and still love now. In order to reverse the flow of the Chicago River for all time, more earth would be moved than when the Panama Canal was dug. If put together, the excavated soil and rock would be sufficient to build twenty-five pyramids the size of the Great Pyramid of Cheops. Construction began in 1892 and was completed in 1900 at a cost of $71 million. Plenty of this was paid out in the form of graft. Taxpayers grew angry, but in their own perverse way they were proud too, and excursions and picnics to visit the digs were a common form of family entertainment. The citizens of St. Louis, who always had hated Chicago, took a dim view of Chicago's project to dispatch its wastes down stream to them and threatened injunctions.

The trustees of the sanitary commission decided to defeat the opposition with a *fait accompli,* so they decided to turn the water on with as little fanfare as possible. They slipped away to Lockport where, as they awaited the governor's approval, a jokester employed by a local newspaper read from a document that sounded ominously like an injunction. Just as the trustees were about to go into nervous fits, the prankster broke into merry laughter, revealing the hoax. The "O.K." came through from Springfield, the water began to run backwards from the Lake—and St. Louis filed its injunction. Too late. Chicago had beaten them again.

In the city's Loop, people ran to the bridges to watch the Chicago River, which "had become a synonym for liquid hideousness," turn blue. It was expected at the time that the river water would become so pure that boys would be fishing in it and castles would rise along its shores. However, these predictions never came true because the swift growth of business and industry along the river bank continued the pollution at an alarming level.

Today, the Metropolitan Sanitary District, with all due Chicago modesty, congratulates itself for the feat of reversing the flow of the river with the slogan "the eighth wonder of the modern world."

CHICAGO *JOURNAL*, January 13, 1900

MR. DOOLEY'S FAREWELL TO THE CHICAGO RIVER

"Th' Chicago r-river risin' in Benton Harbor an' imtyin' into th' Mayor iv St. Looey!" exclaimed Mr. Dooley. "What d'ye think iv that?"

"I don't believe it," said Mr. Hennessy.

"'Tis thrue, though," Mr. Dooley went on. "Whin Tommy Gahan got through shovelin' mud out iv th' dhrainage canal with th' help iv ye'er rilitives on th' dhredge, th' river that'd been coorsin' placidly through its banks an' soap facthries an' carryin' th' cast-off diseases iv Halsted sthreet to th' proud but timp'rate people iv th' Lake Shore dhrive was backed up in th' shafts. It's runnin' th' other way now, Hinnissy, an' befure manny months they won't be a smell iv it lift.

"It don't seem right f'r to threat it that way. It's been a good frind iv Chicago an' what good's th' lake? Th' Illinye Cinthral owns it an' sare a wave iv it do I iver see but what comes through a hose. They're turnin' th' river out an' puttin' th' lake in, an' nex' summer they'll be a mugwump vote in this precint that niver knew

wan befure. They're deliverin' th' good ol' river over to
Saint Looey an' 'twill be th' makin' iv th' town.

"Man an' boy, I've lived beside th' Chicago river f'r
forty year, Hinnissy, an' if they ain't anny wan else to
stand up f'r it, thin here am I. It niver done naught f'r
me but good. Manny's th' time I've set on th' bridge
smokin' me pipe an' watchin' th' lights iv th' tugs dancin'
in it like stars, an' me knowin' all th' captains, be
hivins, fr'm th' boss iv th' O. B. Green, with th' fine
whistle that sounded like a good keen at a Connock-
man's fun'ral, to th' little Mary Ann Gray that had a
snow-plow attachment on th' prow f'r to get into th' slip
over be th' r-red bridge. I had thim all be name, an'
fr'm thim I larned th' news iv th' Boheemyan settlemint
down th' crick, where I was not on visitin' terms, fr'm
an illiction where we had to use couplin' pins to pre-
sarve th' peace. Thim lads will niver sail in anny thin
river iv dhrinkin' wather. They wudden't know how to
control their tugs. They'd go so fast they cudden't take
th' curves at th' lumber yards.

"'Twas th' prettiest river f'r to look at that ye'll iver
see. Ye niver was annything iv a pote, Hinnissy, but if ye
cud get down on th' Miller dock some night whin ye an'
th' likes iv ye was makin' fireworks in th' blast, an' see
th' flames blazin' on th' wather an' th' lights dancin',
green at th' sausage facthry, blue at th' soap facthry,
yellow at th' tannery, ye'd not thrade it f'r annything
but th' Liffey, that's thinner but more powerfuller. D'ye
mind whin it was on fire? That was a gran' sight. It
burned like a pitcher frame facthry. Chief Swenie come
down with thruck nine an' chemical fourteen an' a lot
more iv th' best, but thry as he wud, he cudden't put it
out. He was deprissed be th' sthruggle an' me Uncle
Mike wint up, that was a gr-reat joker, an' says he:
'Chief,' he says, 'they'se on'y wan way ye can put out
that fire.' 'How's that?' says th' chief. 'Tur-rn th' river

upside down,' says me Uncle Mike. Well, sir, ye'd have thought th' chief 'd die laughin', he was that pleased. He told me aftherward me Uncle Mike was a case.

"But ye cudden't burn up th' river. It was as good as ever afther th' fire, on'y a little smoky in its smell. Gran' ol' river! Onhealthy, says ye? Onhealthy? Th' river was niver onhealthy. 'Twas th' lake. Th' river wint sthrollin' out visitin' its friends, an', though I niver liked th' comp'ny it kept on thim sprees, I'll say that it always come back—lookin' a little pale, 'tis thrue, but it always come back. An' th' lake helped itself to what th' river had on it an' handed it to sthrangers an' joods with poor digestions. Onhealthy! Did ye iver see a healthier lot iv childher, or more iv thim, than lives along th' river? If ye think 'twas onhealthy, go up some day an' thry a roll with Willum J. O'Brien. He's been here near as long as I have. Or luk at me! No, sir, ye might jus' as well say I'm onhealthy if I wint down f'r a visit with Schwartzmeister with a package iv rough-on-rats in me pocket, an' he was to steal it from me an' give it to his customers. Th' Chicago river niver was intinded as a dhrink. It didn't go ar-round advertisin' itself as a saisonable beverage! It ain't moxie, an' it ain't sasparilly, an' it aint ice crame soda wather. It had other business more suited to it, an' 'twas consistent in ivery way.

"Now that it's goin' out I'll niver go to th' bridge again. Niver. I feel as though I'd lost an ol' frind an' a sthrong wan. It wasn't so much that I see it ivery day, but I always knew it was there. Night an' day me frind was there."

"Ah, go on," said Mr. Hennessy. "What diff'rence does it make wan way or th' other?"

"Ye have no pothry," said Mr. Dooley. "Well, here's to it annyhow, an' hopin' that it'll have a good time in Saint Looey. Be hivins, th' ol' la-ad will keep thim awake down there. He will that."

Afterword

Dooley's national popularity has amazed and puzzled many, including his creator.

Why, indeed, should the views of a Bridgeport barkeep interest and amuse so many who were neither Irish, nor Chicagoans, nor Democrats, nor immigrants? Without diminishing in any way Dunne's personal talents and gifts, which were splendid indeed, the answer lies to some extent in the urban history of the period.

Much of the modern city as it is known today, its advantages as well as its problems, originated at the turn of the century: the great population growth of major cities, including the role of immigration; the change in appearance of the cities due to building projects, erection of landmarks, and the like; the development of cultural pursuits—the founding of operas, ballets, orchestras, and museums; technological advances, such as the automobile, electrified street lighting, the telephone system, roads, bridges, and tunnels.

Uplifting as these achievements may be, the seamier aspects of city life, many of which still disfigure our cities today, were also taking shape: crime and corruption; political chicanery made possible by manipulation of ethnic, immigrant blocs; labor activity and its violence; radical agitation.

Chicago's place in this rapidly urbanizing landscape was unique. Its desolation by fire coupled with a semifrontier audacity released an almost frantic burst of energy. So eager

were the Chicagoans to rebuild that they did not even pause
to enact zoning codes that would prevent the reconstruction
of inflammable wooden buildings, despite the fact that they
were literally standing in the ashes of their city.

The determination to revive Chicago brooked no interference. Results were what counted, and Chicagoans of the
period had no time to waste on niceties of method or unfortunate side effects. And if this opened wide the way to the
exploiter, the criminal, the corrupt, the boodler, it was an
inevitable price of progress.

Chicago, in truth, was every growing American city. This
is not to say that it was a paradigm; on the contrary, each
city had its own peculiar development and destiny. But the
problems and solutions, successes and failures, inspirations
and disasters that occurred or would occur in other cities as
they pursued their individual fate all were concentrated and
magnified in Chicago. If other cities boasted commercial enterprise, Chicago was the player with the nation's railroads.
If other cities had political agitation, Chicago had Haymarket. If other cities had labor troubles, Chicago had Pullman.
If other cities had corrupt politicians, Chicago had raised
graft to a high art.

At the center of this ferment was Mr. Dooley, keeping a
skeptical and humorous eye on the view from his Bridgeport
saloon. And behind Dooley was Finley Peter Dunne, both
creator and creature, firmly fixed in the urban environment
and influenced by it. More than a quintessential Chicagoan,
Dooley was a quintessential urbanite, who drew his exam-
ples, anecdotes, and knowledge from city surroundings.
Whether the issue was silver coinage or the Spanish-
American War, Dooley, the city dweller, could apply the
mental tools of Archey Road and find that other urbanites
would get the message, irrespective of issue, dialect, or lo-
cale.

Dooley had a comment on every significant phase of
urban life and thereby struck a responsive note with new-

landed urbanites everywhere. But the Dooley columns also imparted the flavor of life in the city. Mr. Dooley's Chicago was a fast-paced and exciting place to live. Something was always going on, a world's fair, a speech, a strike, or a political movement. Moreover, the columns were liberally dashed with subtle qualities of the urban lifestyle, for instance, the necessity for coexistence among ethnic groups. Most of the immigrants in Chicago and in other cities had come from rural areas of the Old Country. In America's cities they were thrown together cheek by jowl. They clustered in ethnic neighborhoods, but at some point, usually a very definable line, the neighborhood ended and some sort of co-operation or truce had to begin. Dooley could relate with pride, in one column, how he evened a score with "the Polacker swinging the red bridge," by rolling a beer keg at the man and breaking his leg. Yet, in another column on the Pullman strike, he would tell how Irish workers lucky enough to have a little money in the house during the strike contributed food to their Polish working-class brethren who were not so fortunate. Such small beginnings, growing out of the "same boat" situation that ethnic urbanites found themselves in, formed an important early underpinning of the broad ethnic coalitions that play such a large role in modern city politics.

Dooley's awareness of the ethnic and rural heritages in the city may have, paradoxically, assured his acceptance by America's new urbanites. Many were neophytes at city life and still clung to the traditions of the rural folk. One of those traditions, which has attained the status of myth, is the cracker-barrel philosopher—the wise, unsophisticated commentator who punctures the overblown with humor, exposes evil with irony, but never loses his tolerance for human weakness. Dooley was in this great line. Had Dunne offered his thoughts on his own, in his own speech, they probably would have generated no more than a mild interest in the views of a newsman from an energetic, but on the whole rather vulgar, city. Dooley, however, bridged the gap between rural and urban, homespun and sophisticated. Dunne's significant contribution was to have made Dooley a cracker-barrel philosopher with a crucial difference; his cracker barrel was not at the general store, but at city hall.

It would be mistaken for us to consider Dooley only a humorist or an advance man for the muckrakers. He was more, but assessing his influence is not something that can be done objectively by reference to numbers, reforms, legislation, or monuments. His monuments exist, but they are of a different order.

What Dooley said was remembered and often repeated by the high and the low, his observations became bon mots, his insights a standard of awareness. How deep and long such influences may run perhaps can be judged by an incident that occurred in Chicago not long before the writing of this book. Chicago Mayor Richard J. Daley was engaged in a dispute with Illinois Governor Daniel Walker, the details of which are not relevant here. Governor Walker endorsed anti-Daley candidates in Chicago aldermanic elections, but Daley called forth his precinct legions and they delivered the mayor's vote with a vengeance. Asked to comment on the soundness of the thrashing received by the Walker-backed candidates, Daley responded with a quote from Mr. Dooley that "politics ain't bean bag."

This, more than fifty years after the publication of the last Dooley column! How much more influence on other men Dooley exerted during the flower of his popularity can only be estimated, but that influence went deeper than the mere parroting of what Dooley said. Those who adopt another man's language also adopt, however thinly or fleetingly, his frame of mind. Obviously, not everyone who quoted Dooley or imitated him was a Dooley himself, but it cannot be denied that through the accumulation of points well taken, issues refined to a memorable epigram, and social commentary vivified by example, Dooley educated the attitudes of many. He exemplified and raised urban consciousness; he helped countless thousands of his readers find or keep their bearings during a period of uprooting social change; he expressed what many felt but all could not say; he was among the first and best transmitters of American urban culture.

Selected Bibliography

BIBLIOGRAPHIC NOTE

For those who would like to know more about Finley Peter Dunne, there are two splendid books available. It is well that Elmer Ellis' *Mr. Dooley's America: A Life of Finley Peter Dunne* is a thorough, scholarly work, because through a series of deaths and mishaps, almost all of Dunne's letters, manuscripts, and papers have been lost, and many of the people to whom Ellis had access are now dead. Philip Dunne's delightful affectionate recollections of his father, together with Peter Dunne's reminiscences, make reading *Mr. Dooley Remembers* a most pleasurable experience.

For those who would like to know more about Mr. Dooley, Dunne published seven volumes of Dooley's collected wisdom over the years of his own life. Since his death, there have been a number of collections of the collections, five of which are listed in this bibliography.

All the columns appearing in *Mr. Dooley's Chicago* were taken directly from the appropriate newspaper, and with the exception of a mere handful have never been reprinted before.

BOOKS

Addams, Jane. *Twenty Years at Hull House*. New York: The Macmillan Company, 1910.
Ade, George. *The America of George Ade*. Edited, with an introduction, by Jean Shepherd. New York: Putnam, 1960.

——. *Fables in Slang and More Fables in Slang.* New York: Dover Publications, 1960.

Andreas, Alfred T. *History of Chicago.* 3 volumes. Chicago: A. T. Andreas, 1884–86.

Baedecker, Karl, ed. *The United States with an Excursion into Mexico: A Handbook for Travelers.* New York: Charles Scribner's Sons, 1893.

Barnard, Harry. *Eagle Forgotten: The Life of John Peter Altgeld.* Indianapolis: Bobbs-Merrill, 1938.

Blair, Walter. *Horse Sense in American Humor.* New York: Russell & Russell, 1942.

——. *Native American Humor.* San Francisco: Chandler Publishing Company, 1960.

Blanc, Marie Therese. *The Condition of Woman in the United States: A Traveller's Notes.* Boston: Roberts Brothers, 1895.

Brown, Thomas N. *Irish-American Nationalism, 1870–1890.* Philadelphia: J. B. Lippincott Company, 1966.

Buder, Stanley. *Pullman: An Experiment in Industrial Order and Community Planning, 1880–1930.* New York: Oxford University Press, 1967.

Burchard, John, and Albert Bush-Brown. *The Architecture of America: A Social and Cultural History.* Boston: Little, Brown & Company, 1961.

Byrne, Stephen. *Irish Emigration to the U.S.: What It Has Been and What It Is.* New York: Catholic Publication Society, 1873.

Chatfield-Taylor, Hobart C. *Chicago.* Boston and New York: Houghton Mifflin Company, 1917.

Condit, Carl W. *The Chicago School of Architecture: A History of Commercial and Public Building in the Chicago Area, 1875–1925.* Chicago: University of Chicago Press, 1964.

——. *The Rise of the Skyscraper.* Chicago: University of Chicago Press, 1952.

Cromie, Robert. *The Great Chicago Fire.* New York: McGraw-Hill, 1958.

David, Henry. *History of the Haymarket Affair: A Study in the*

American Social-Revolutionary and Labor Movements. New York: Russell & Russell, 1936.

Davis, Allen F., and Mary Lynn McCree, eds. *Eighty Years at Hull-House.* Chicago: Quadrangle Books, 1969.

Dedmon, Emmett. *Fabulous Chicago.* New York: Random House, 1953.

Dennis, Charles H. *Eugene Field's Creative Years.* New York: Doubleday, Page & Company, 1924.

Dowd, Douglas. *Thorstein Veblen.* New York: Washington Square Press, 1964.

Dreiser, Theodore. *A Book About Myself.* New York: Boni & Liveright, 1922.

Dunne, Finley Peter. *Dissertations by Mr. Dooley.* London and New York: Harper & Brothers, 1906.

——. *Mr. Dooley at His Best.* Edited by Elmer Ellis. New York: Charles Scribner's Sons, 1938.

——. *Mr. Dooley in the Hearts of His Countrymen.* Boston: Small, Maynard & Company, 1899.

——. *Mr. Dooley in Peace and in War.* Boston: Small, Maynard & Company, 1899.

——. *Mr. Dooley, Now and Forever.* Selected, with commentary and introduction, by Louis Filler. Stanford: Academic Reprints, 1954.

——. *Mr. Dooley on Ivrything and Ivrybody.* Selected and with an introduction by Robert Hutchinson. New York: Dover Publications, 1963.

——. *Mr. Dooley on Making a Will and Other Necessary Evils.* New York: Charles Scribner's Sons, 1920.

——. *Mr. Dooley on the Choice of the Law.* Compiled and arranged by Edward J. Bander. Charlottesville: Michie Company, 1963.

——. *Mr. Dooley's Opinions.* New York and London: Harper & Brothers, 1906.

——. *Mr. Dooley's Philosophy.* New York: R. H. Russell, 1900.

——. *Mr. Dooley Remembers: The Informal Memoirs of Finley*

Peter Dunne. Edited, with an introduction and commentary, by Philip Dunne. Boston: Little, Brown & Company, 1963.

————. *Mr. Dooley Says*. London and New York: Harper & Brothers, 1910.

————. *Observations by Mr. Dooley*. New York: R. H. Russell, 1902.

————. *The World of Mr. Dooley*. Edited, with an introduction, by Louis Filler. New York: Collier Books, 1962.

Ellis, Elmer. *Mr. Dooley's America: A Life of Finley Peter Dunne*. New York: A. A. Knopf, 1941.

Farr, Finis. *Chicago: A Personal History of America's Most American City*. New Rochelle: Arlington House, 1973.

Field, Eugene. *Sharps and Flats*. Collated by Slason Thompson. New York: Charles Scribner's Sons, 1900.

Fleming, Thomas J. *The Golden Door: The Story of American Immigration*. New York: Grosset & Dunlap, 1970.

Flexner, Eleanor. *Century of Struggle: The Woman's Rights Movement in the United States*. New York: Atheneum, 1968.

Friedman, Milton, and Anna Jacobson Schwartz. *A Monetary History of the United States*. Princeton: Princeton University Press, 1963.

Furnas, J. C. *The Americans: A Social History of the United States, 1587–1914*. New York: G. P. Putnam's Sons, 1969.

Gale, Edwin O. *Reminiscences of Early Chicago and Vicinity*. Chicago: Fleming H. Revell Company, 1902.

Ginger, Ray. *Altgeld's America: The Lincoln Ideal vs. Changing Realities*. Chicago: Quadrangle Books, 1965.

————. *The Bending Cross: A Biography of Eugene Victor Debs*. New Brunswick: Rutgers University Press, 1949.

Handlin, Oscar. *Race and Nationality in American Life*. Garden City, N.Y.: Doubleday Anchor Books, 1957.

————. *The Uprooted*. New York: Grosset & Dunlap, 1951.

Harrison, Carter Henry. *Growing Up with Chicago*. Chicago: R. F. Seymour, 1944.

————. *Stormy Years: the Autobiography of Carter H. Harrison, Five Times Mayor of Chicago*. Indianapolis: Bobbs-Merrill, 1935.

Hofstadter, Richard. *The Age of Reform from Bryan to FDR*. New York: Vintage Books, 1960.

Hutchinson, Edward P. *Immigrants and Their Children, 1850–1950*. New York: John Wiley, 1956.

Johnson, Claudius Osborne. *Carter Henry Harrison I, Political Leader*. Chicago: University of Chicago Press, 1928.

Kirkland, Joseph. *The Story of Chicago*. 3 volumes. Chicago: Dibble Publishing Company, 1892–1894.

Kogan, Herman, and Lloyd Wendt. *Chicago: A Pictorial History*. New York: E. P. Dutton, 1958.

——. *Lords of the Levee: The Story of Bathhouse John and Hinky Dink*. Indianapolis: Bobbs-Merrill, 1943.

Leech, Margaret. *In the Days of McKinley*. New York: Harper & Brothers, 1959.

Lewis, Lloyd, and Henry Justin Smith. *Chicago: The History of Its Reputation*. New York: Harcourt, Brace & Company, 1929.

——. *Oscar Wilde Discovers America (1882)*. New York: Harcourt, Brace & Company, 1936.

Lindsey, Almont. *The Pullman Strike: The Story of a Unique Experiment and of a Great Labor Upheaval*. Chicago: University of Chicago Press, 1964.

McKenna, John J. *Stories by the Original "Jawn" McKenna from "Archy" Road of the Sun Worshippers Club of McKinley Park in Their Political Tales and Reminiscenses*. Chicago: J. F. Higgins, 1918.

McPhaul, John J. *Deadlines & Monkeyshines: The Fabled World of Chicago Journalism*. Englewood Cliffs, N.J.: Prentice-Hall, 1962.

Masters, Edgar Lee. *The Tale of Chicago*. New York: G. P. Putnam's Sons, 1933.

Monroe, Harriet. *A Poet's Life: Seventy Years in a Changing World*. New York: Macmillan, 1938.

Mott, Frank L. *American Journalism: A History of Newspapers in the United States through 250 Years, 1690–1940*. New York: The Macmillan Company, 1947.

———. *A History of American Magazines, 1885–1905.* Cambridge, Mass.: Harvard University Press, 1957.

O'Broin, Leon. *Fenian Fever: An Anglo-American Dilemma.* New York: New York University Press, 1971.

O'Neill, William L. *Everyone Was Brave: The Rise and Fall of Feminism in America.* Chicago: Quadrangle Books, 1969.

———. *The Woman Movement: Feminism in the United States and England.* New York: Barnes and Noble, 1969.

Palmer, Vivien M. *Social Backgrounds of Chicago's Local Communities.* Chicago: Local Communities Research Committee, University of Chicago, 1930.

Parker, Gail Thain, ed. *The Oven Birds: American Women on Womanhood, 1820–1920.* Garden City, N.Y.: Anchor Books/Doubleday & Company, 1972.

Pierce, Bessie Louise. *A History of Chicago.* 3 volumes. New York: Alfred A. Knopf, 1937–57.

———. *As Others See Chicago: Impressions of Visitors, 1673–1933.* Chicago: University of Chicago Press, 1933.

Pringle, Henry F. *Theodore Roosevelt.* New York: Harcourt, Brace, 1931.

Reminiscences of Chicago During the Civil War. Chicago: Lakeside Press, 1914.

Rourke, Constance. *American Humor: A Study of the National Character.* Garden City, N.Y.: Doubleday & Company, 1931.

Russell, Charles E. *The American Orchestra and Theodore Thomas.* Garden City, N.Y.: Doubleday, Page & Company, 1927.

Shackleton, Robert. *The Book of Chicago.* Philadelphia: Penn Publishing Company, 1920.

Shannon, William V. *The American Irish.* New York: The Macmillan Company, 1966.

Smith, Henry Justin. *Chicago's Great Century, 1833–1933.* Chicago: Consolidated Publishers, 1933.

Smith, Page. *Daughters of the Promised Land: Women in American History.* Boston: Little, Brown & Company, 1970.

Stead, William T. *If Christ Came to Chicago: A Plea for the Union of All Who Love in the Service of All Who Suffer.* Chicago: Laird & Lee, 1894.

Steevens, George Warrington. *The Land of the Dollar.* New York: Dodd, Mead & Company, 1897.

Tandy, Jeannette. *Crackerbox Philosophers in American Humor and Satire.* Port Washington, N.Y.: Kennikat Press, 1925.

Tugwell, Rexford Guy. *Grover Cleveland.* New York: The Macmillan Company, 1968.

Twain, Mark. *The Autobiography of Mark Twain.* As arranged and edited, with an introduction and notes, by Charles Neider. New York: Harper & Brothers, 1959.

Unrivaled Chicago: Containing Historical Narrative of the Great City's Development, and Descriptions of Points of Interest . . . Chicago and New York: Rand, McNally & Company, 1896.

Ward, Martindale C. *A Trip to Chicago: What I Saw, What I Heard, What I Thought.* Glasgow: A. Malcolm and Company, 1895.

Wharton, Edith. *A Backward Glance.* New York: Appleton-Century Company, 1934.

Whitlock, Brand. *The Letters and Journal of Brand Whitlock.* Chosen, with a biographical introduction, by Allan Nevins; introduction by Newton D. Baker. New York and London: Appleton-Century Company, 1936.

——. *Forty Years of It.* With an introduction by Louis Filler. Cleveland: Press of Case Western Reserve University, 1970.

Williams, Kenny J. *In the City of Men: Another Story of Chicago.* Nashville: Townsend Press, 1974.

Wittke, Carl. *The Irish in America.* Baton Rouge: Louisiana State University Press, 1956.

Woodham-Smith, Cecil. *The Great Hunger, Ireland 1845–1849.* New York: Harper & Row, 1962.

Ziff, Larzer. *The American 1890's: Life and Times of a Lost Generation.* New York: Viking Press, 1966.

PERIODICALS

American Magazine
Atlantic Monthly
The Bookman
Century
Collier's
Cosmopolitan
Harper's Weekly
Ladies' Home Journal
Literary Digest
McClure's Magazine
North American Review
Spectator

NEWSPAPERS

Chicago *Daily Journal*
Chicago *Daily News*
Chicago *Daily Tribune*
Chicago *Evening Post*
Chicago *Inter-Ocean*
Chicago *Times*
Chicago *Times-Herald*
New York *Morning Telegraph*

Index

394

Barbara C. Schaaf was born, reared, and educated in Chicago, receiving her B.A. in American history from Roosevelt University and her M.B.A. from the University of Chicago. She has been active in politics since she was sixteen and has attended every Democratic National Convention since 1956. In 1960 she served as Executive Secretary for the National Committee of Business and Professional Men for Kennedy/Johnson in Chicago and in 1968 as Financial Secretary for the Robert Kennedy Campaign Committee in Illinois. Since then, she has been legislative assistant to Anthony Scariano of the Illinois House of Representatives, research assistant in American history and urban affairs at the University of Chicago, Executive Assistant to Eleanor McGovern, and Director of Public Relations for the Chicago Dwellings Association. It is through her experience in politics and Chicago history that Barbara Schaaf became fascinated by Martin Dooley and wrote *Mr. Dooley's Chicago,* her first book.